Labour Law in Poland

Labour Law in Poland

Second Edition

Zbigniew Hajn
Leszek Mitrus

This book was originally published as a monograph in the International Encyclopaedia of Laws/Labour Law and Industrial Relations.

Founding Editor: Roger Blanpain
General Editor: Frank Hendrickx
Volume Editor: Frank Hendrickx

Wolters Kluwer

Published by:
Kluwer Law International B.V.
PO Box 316
2400 AH Alphen aan den Rijn
The Netherlands
E-mail: international-sales@wolterskluwer.com
Website: lrus.wolterskluwer.com

Sold and distributed in North, Central and South America by:
Wolters Kluwer Legal & Regulatory U.S.
7201 McKinney Circle
Frederick, MD 21704
United States of America
Email: customer.service@wolterskluwer.com

Sold and distributed in all other countries by:
Air Business Subscriptions
Rockwood House
Haywards Heath
West Sussex
RH16 3DH
United Kingdom
Email: international-customerservice@wolterskluwer.com

Printed on acid-free paper

ISBN 978-94-035-0761-3

e-Book: ISBN 978-94-035-0762-0
web-PDF: ISBN 978-94-035-0763-7

Printed in the United Kingdom.

The Authors

Zbigniew Hajn is a professor of Labour Law at the University of Lodz (Poland).

He was born in 1955 in Lublin, graduating in Law from Lodz University in 1978 and passing the judge exam in 1980. He became a Doctor of Law in 1986 and received his Habilitation in 1999, becoming a professor at Lodz University in 2001 and attaining full professorship in 2016. Since 2003 he had been a judge of the Supreme Court of the Republic of Poland. He was in active service until November 2016, now he is a 'judgè in rest'.

From 2002 to 2006 he was a member of the Labour Law Codification Commission established by the Prime Minister for the new codification of individual labour law and collective labour law. He has also been a Member of Legislative Council (2006).

He is the author of over 130 publications on labour law and industrial relations. Among these are books on the legal position of an employer, legal position of employer organizations, collective labour law system etc. He is also the editor and co-author of books on employee's representation at the workplace, free movement of workers within EU, legal problems of workplace democracy, commentary to the labour code and others.

From 1996 to 2009 he was the deputy editor-in-chief of the periodical *Studia Prawno-Europejskie* (Studies on European Law). At present he is a member of the scientific councils of the periodicals *Europejski Przegląd Sądowy* (European Court Review) and *Monitor Prawa Pracy* (Labour Law Monitor) as well as a member of editorial committee of the *Państwo i Prawo* (State and Law) monthly.

Leszek Mitrus is a professor of Labour Law at the Jagiellonian University in Kraków (Poland). Born in 1970 in Kraków, he graduated in law from Jagiellonian University in 1994 and passed the judge exam in 1996. He became a Doctor of Law in 2001 and received his Habilitation in 2007, becoming a professor at Jagiellonian University in 2014.

He is the author of about 120 publications on Polish, European, and international labour law and social security law. Among these publications are books on free movement of workers, EU directives on employment contract and influence of European labour law on Polish legal system, as well as termination with notice of an employment contract due to reasons concerning an employee. He is also the co-author of commentaries to the Treaty on the Functioning of the European Union, the Charter of Fundamental Rights of the European Union and the Polish Labour Code.

He is a national expert of the European Labour Law Network and a member of the editorial board of monthly – *Monitor Prawa Pracy* (Labour Law Monitor) and a corresponding board member of quarterly – *European Labour Law Journal*. From September 2016 to March 2018 he has been a member of the Commission for Codification of Labour Law.

Table of Contents

The Authors 3

List of Abbreviations 21

Introduction 23

Chapter 1. General Background
L. Mitrus 23

§1. Geography, Location, Size and Boundaries 23

§2. The Political System 23

§3. Vital Statistics 25

Chapter 2. Historical Background 27

§1. Until World War II
Z. Hajn 27

§2. The Communist Period
L. Mitrus 31
I. Introductory Remarks 31
II. The Period Before the Codification of Labour Law 32
III. The Period After the Codification of Labour Law 34

§3. The Democracy Period
L. Mitrus 35

Chapter 3. Notion of Labour Law
Z. Hajn 41

§1. Labour Law 41

§2. Distinctions and Relationships Between Labour Law and Other Branches of Law 41

Chapter 4. Role of Government Institutions in the Shaping and Administration of Labour and Industrial Relations Policy
L. Mitrus 44

§1. Degree of Government Intervention 44

§2. Incomes Policy 45

§3. Competences of Ministries in Labour and Industrial Relations Policy 46

§4. SLI 47

Chapter 5. Sources of Labour Law 49

§1. Introductory Remarks 49

§2. The Constitution 49
I. The Role of the Constitution as a Source of Labour Law 49
II. The Constitution and Fundamental Rights 50
A. The Constitution as a Source of Fundamental Rights 50
B. The Principle of Proportionality 51

§3. Ordinary Legislation 51

§4. Autonomous Sources of Labour Law 52
I. General Remarks 52
II. CLAs and Other Collective Agreements 54
A. CLAs 54
B. Other Collective Agreements 54
C. The Role of General Agreements 55
III. Internal Workplace Regulations 56
IV. Statutes of Employers 56

§5. The Role of Court Decisions 56

§6. The Role of Customs and Other Extralegal Norms 56

§7. The Character of Labour Law Norms 57

§8. Relationships Between Different Sources of National Labour Law 58

§9. International Law 59

§10. EU Law 60

Chapter 6. Fundamental Principles of Labour Law
L. Mitrus 62

§1. General Remarks 62

§2. Constitutional Principles 62

§3. Principles of Individual Labour Law 63
I. Right to Choose an Occupation 63
II. Respect for Employees' Dignity and Other Personal Rights 64
III. Equality of Employees and Prohibition of Discrimination 65
IV. Right to Fair Remuneration 65
V. Right to Rest 66
VI. Health and Safety at Work 66
VII. Social and Welfare Employee Needs 66
VIII. Improvement of Employee Qualifications 66
IX. Protection of Minimum Level of Employee Rights 67

§4. Principles of Collective Labour Law 67
I. Social Partners' Dialogue 67
II. Right of Association 68
III. Right to Bargain 68
IV. Right to Organize Workers' Strikes or Other Forms of Protest 68
V. Employee Participation 69

Chapter 7. Equal Treatment and Protection Against Discrimination in Employment
L. Mitrus 70

§1. Introductory Remarks 70

§2. Scope of the Principle of Equal Treatment 71

§3. Forms of Discrimination 75

§4. Criteria Covered by the Prohibition of Discrimination 76

§5. Permitted Differentiation of the Situation of Employees 78

§6. Protection Against Discrimination 79

Part I. Individual Labour Law 83

Table of Contents

Chapter 1. Individual Employment Relationship
Z. Hajn 83

§1. Characteristics of the Individual Employment Relationship 83
I. Basis of the Employment Relationship; Freedom of Establishing and Determining the Content of the Employment Relationship 83
II. Characteristic Features of the Employment Relation 84
III. Employment Relation and Civil Law Contracts for Performance of Services 84

§2. The Employee 86

§3. The Employer 86
I. The Notion 86
II. Representation of the Employer in Labour Law Matters 87

§4. Work Establishment 88
I. Notion 88
II. Work Establishment and Employer 88
III. A Part of Work Establishment 89

§5. Transfer of Work Establishment or a Part of it to Another Employer 89
I. Legal Regulation 89
II. Notion and Effects 90
III. Safeguarding Employee Rights 92
IV. Transferee Liability for Debts 92
V. The Right of the Employee to Terminate the Employment Relationship 92
VI. The Duty of the Transferor and Transferee to Provide Information to Employees 93

Chapter 2. Conclusion of the Employment Contract
Z. Hajn 94

§1. The Beginning, the Form and the Language of the Employment Contract 94
I. The Beginning of the Employment Contract 94
II. The Form 94
III. The Language 94

§2. Content of the Employment Contract and Information Related to the Employment Relationship 95
I. Content of the Employment Contract 95
II. The Duty of the Employer to Provide Information Related to the Employment Relationship 95

III. The Duty of the Employee to Provide Information Related to the Employment Relationship 96

§3. Types of Employment Contract 97
I. Introductory Remarks 97
II. The Contract for an Indefinite Period 97
III. The Contract for a Definite Period 98
IV. The Contract for a Trial Period 100

Chapter 3. Rights and Duties of the Parties to the Employment Relationship
L. Mitrus 101

§1. Introductory Remarks 101

§2. Duties of the Employee 102
I. Duty to Perform Work Conscientiously and Carefully 102
II. Duty to Follow Employer's Instructions 102
III. Duties to Observe the Order at the Establishment 103
IV. Duty to Observe Health and Safety Regulations 104
V. Duty to Care for the Interest of the Work Establishment 104
VI. Duty to Respect Confidentiality 105
VII. Duty to Respect the Principles of Social Coexistence 105

§3. Duties of the Employer 106
I. Duty to Provide the Employee with Work 106
II. Information Duties 107
A. Information on the Content of the Employment Relationship 107
B. Making Employees Familiar with the Scope of Their Duties 107
C. Other Information Duties 107
III. Duty to Organize the Work Process 107
IV. Duty to Counteract Discrimination 108
V. Duty to Ensure Safe and Healthy Working Conditions 108
VI. Duty to Pay Remuneration Timely and Correctly 109
VII. Duty to Facilitate the Improvement of Professional Qualifications 109
VIII. Duty to Create Favourable Conditions for Employees Starting Work 110
IX. Duty to Satisfy the Social Needs of Employees 110
X. Duty to Apply Objective Criteria when Evaluating Employees 111
XI. Duty to Keep Documentation in Matters Connected with the Employment Relationship 111
XII. Duty to Influence the Rules of Social Coexistence 111
XIII. Duty to Counteract Mobbing 112
A. Definition of Mobbing 112
B. Liability for Mobbing 113
XIV. Duty to Issue a Work Certificate 115
XV. Other Duties 115

Chapter 4. Working Time

Z. Hajn 116

§1. Legal Notion of Working Time 116

§2. Length of Working Time 117
I. Basic Working Time 117
II. Length of Weekly Joint Working Time 117
III. Reduced Working Time 117
IV. Extended Working Time 118

§3. Rest Periods 118
I. Daily and Weekly Rest Periods 118
II. Break from Work 118

§4. Organization of Working Time 119
I. Systems and Schedules of Working Time 119
II. Establishing Systems and Schedules of Working Time 120

§5. Overtime Work and Other Activities Beyond Normal Working Hours 121
I. Overtime Work 121
II. Other Activities Beyond Normal Working Hours 122
A. Introductory Remarks 122
B. Duty Shifts 122
C. Business Trips 123
D. Training Courses 123

§6. Night Work 123

§7. Work on Sundays, Public Holidays and Saturdays 124

§8. Working Time of the Management Staff 125

§9. Annual Vacation Leave 126
I. The Right to Annual Leave 126
II. The Length of Annual Leave 126
III. Rules for Granting Annual Leave 126
IV. Leave on Request 127
V. Remuneration for the Time of Leave 127

§10. Special Leave and Exemptions from Work 127
I. Introduction 127
II. Unpaid Leave 127
III. Educational Leave and Exemptions from Work 128
IV. Occasional Exemptions from Work 128
V. Sick Leave and Other Justified Absences from Work 128

VI. Other Leave and Exemptions 129

Chapter 5. Remuneration and Other Payments
Z. Hajn 130

§1. Notion of Remuneration 130

§2. The Amount of Remuneration 130

§3. Fixing the Remuneration for Work 132

§4. Components of Remuneration 133

§5. Protection of Remuneration for Work 133

§6. Other Payments 135

Chapter 6. Termination and Change of Employment Contract
Z. Hajn 136

§1. Ways of Termination 136
I. General Characteristics 136
II. The Form and Content of the Declaration Concerning Termination 136
III. Dissolution of Employment Contract by Mutual Consent 137
IV. Dissolution of Employment Contract with Notice 137
V. Termination of a Contract of Employment Without Notice 138
A. Termination Without Notice by the Employer 138
B. Termination Without Notice by the Employee 139
VI. Termination Without Notice but upon Prior Notification 139
VII. Expiration of an Employment Contract 140

§2. Protection of an Employee Against Dismissal 140
I. General Remarks 140
II. General Protection Against Dismissal 141
A. Grounds for the Notice to Terminate a Contract of Employment 141
B. Justification of Contract of Employment Termination Without Notice 142
C. Trade Union Control of the Justification of Contract of Employment Termination 143
III. Special Protection Against Termination of Employment Relationships 143
A. Special Protection Against a Notice to Terminate 143
B. Special Protection Against Termination of an Employment Contract Without Notice 144

§3. Legal Sanctions for Defective Termination of an Employment Relationship 145

I. Sanctions for Defective Termination of a Contract of Employment by Consent of the Parties 145
II. Employee Claims in Case of Wrongful Termination of a Contract of Employment with Notice 145
III. Employee Claims in Case of Wrongful Termination of a Contract of Employment Without Notice 147
IV. Employee Claims in Case of Wrongful Expiration of an Employment Relationship 148
V. Legal Effects of Termination of a Contract of Employment Without Notice by the Employee 148

§4. Change of the Terms of the Employment Contract 148
I. Ways of Change 148
II. Notice to Change the Existing Terms of Work and Pay 149
III. Unilateral Change of the Content of a Contract of Employment 149
IV. Change of the Content of a Contract of Employment by Mutual Consent 150

§5. Dismissals for Reasons Not Related to Workers (Collective Redundancies) 150
I. Introductory Remarks 150
II. Collective Redundancies 151
A. The Concept of Collective Redundancy 151
B. Procedure for Collective Redundancy 152
C. Limitations of Employee Protection Against Termination of the Employment Relationship under the ETA 153
III. Individual Termination 154
A. Conditions of the ETA Application to Individual Termination of the Employment Relationship 154
B. Limitation of Protection Against Dismissal 154
IV. Special Rules for Dismissals in the Event of Employer Bankruptcy and Liquidation 154
V. Benefits to Employees Made Redundant for Reasons Not Attributable to Employees 155

§6. Employer's Duties Related to the End of the Employment Relationship 155

Chapter 7. Atypical Employment Contracts
Z. Hajn 157

§1. Introductory Remarks 157

§2. Part-Time Work 157
I. Equal Treatment 157
II. Limitation of the Number of Working Hours Permitted above the Agreed Duration of Working Time 158

III. Work-Sharing 158

§3. Temporary Work 159
I. Introductory Remarks 159
II. Legal Model of Temporary Work 159
III. Rights and Duties of the Parties 160
IV. Temporary Work Based on a Civil Law Contract 161

§4. Telework 161
I. Regulatory Framework 161
II. Legal Notion and Main Principles of Legal Regulation of Telework 162
III. Rights and Duties of the Parties 163

§5. Putting an Employee at the Disposal of Another Employer 163

Chapter 8. Protection of Special Groups of Employees
Z. Hajn 164

§1. Women; Workers Taking Care of Children 164
I. Introductory Remarks 164
II. Protection Against Hazardous or Onerous Work 164
III. Leave of Absence 165
A. Right to a Break for Breastfeeding a Child 165
B. Time off for Medical Examinations 166
C. Other Instances of Family-related Leave of Absence 166
IV. Leave Related to Birth and the Raising of a Child 166
A. Types of Leave 166
B. Maternity Leave 167
C. Parental Leave and Child-Raising Leave 167
D. Paternity Leave 168
V. Guarantees of a Secure Use of Parental Rights 168
VI. Equal Treatment 169

§2. Young Workers 170
I. The Approach to the Legal Regulation of the Work of Young Employees 170
II. Notion of Young Persons 170
III. Employment of the Juvenile 170
A. Limitations of Employment of the Juvenile 170
B. The Basis for Employment of the Juvenile 171
C. Employment Contract for Vocational Training 171
D. Regular Contract of Employment 172
IV. Employment of Children 172

§3. Disabled Workers 173
I. Legal Framework 173

II. Rights of Disabled Employees 174

§4. Posted Workers
L. Mitrus 175

Chapter 9. Liability of Parties to the Contract of Employment 179
Z. Hajn 179

§1. Employee Liability 179
I. Types of Liability 179
II. Liability for Breach of Order of Work 179
A. Introductory Remarks 179
B. Penalties 180
C. The Procedure of Penalty Administration 180
D. The Right of Appeal to Court 180
III. Financial Liability of Employees 181
A. Introductory Remarks 181
B. Special Rules on Employee Liability 181
C. Aggravated Liability 182
D. Employee Liability for Damage Caused to a Third Party 183

§2. Employer Liability 183
I. Liability for Damage 183
A. General Rule 183
B. Liability for Damages Caused to the Employee by Tort 183
C. Liability for the Employee's Personal Effects 184
D. Liability for a Loss Following from an Accident at Work or Occupational Disease 184
II. Liability for Offences and Petty Offences Against Employee Rights 184

Chapter 10. Employment Relationships Based on Appointment, Election, Nomination or a Cooperative Contract of Employment
L. Mitrus 186

§1. Introductory Remarks 186

§2. An Appointment 186

§3. An Election 187

§4. A Nomination 188

§5. A Cooperative Employment Contract 189

Chapter 11. Covenants of Non-competition
L. Mitrus 191

§1. Introductory Remarks 191

§2. Prohibition of Competition During an Employment Contract 191

§3. Prohibition of Competition after the Expiry of an Employment Contract 193

§4. Other Provisions on Prohibition of Competition 195

Chapter 12. Inventions of Employees
L. Mitrus 196

§1. Introductory Remarks 196

§2. Employee Work 196

§3. Transfer of Economic Rights to the Employer 197

§4. Special Regulations 199

Chapter 13. Limitation of Claims under the Employment Relationship 201

Chapter 14. Settlement of Individual Labour Disputes
Z. Hajn 204

§1. Introduction 204

§2. Settlement of Labour Disputes Before the Labour Court 205
I. Jurisdiction of Labour Courts 205
II. Characteristics and Organization of Labour Courts 205
III. Parties to the Proceedings Before Labour Courts 207
IV. Proceedings Before the Labour Court 207
V. Costs 210

§3. Settlement of Disputes under Workplace Procedures 210
I. Workplace Conciliation Proceedings 210
II. Workplace Complaint Procedures 211

§4. Other Methods of Resolving Labour Cases 211
I. Introduction 211
II. Judicial Conciliation Scheme 212
III. Mediation 212

IV. Arbitration Court 212

§5. Resolution of Labour Law Disputes under Administrative Court Proceedings 213

Chapter 15. The Organization of the Labour Market and Combating Unemployment
L. Mitrus 214

§1. Introductory Remarks 214

§2. Objective Scope of the Employment Promotion Act 215

§3. Subjective Scope of the Employment Promotion Act 216
I. Introductory Remarks 216
II. Unemployed Person 216
III. A Person Seeking a Job 218

§4. Active Methods of Combating Unemployment 219

§5. Public and Private Employment Agency Service 221

§6. Unemployment Benefit 223

Chapter 16. Employment of Foreigners
L. Mitrus 224

§1. Introductory Remarks 224

§2. 'Foreigner' Status in the Light of the Employment Regulations 225

§3. Foreigners Taking Up Work Without a Work Permit 226

§4. Foreigners Taking Up Work after Obtaining a Permit 228

§5. Consequences of Illegally Entrusting Work to a Foreigner 231

Part II. Collective Labour Law
Z. Hajn 235

Chapter 1. The Concept and Foundations of Collective Labour Law 235

§1. The Concept of Collective Labour Law 235

§2. Trade Union Freedoms 236
I. Legal Framework 236
II. Individual Rights 237
III. Collective Rights 238

§3. Social Partners' Dialogue 238
I. Constitutional Meaning 238
II. Tripartite Dialogue 240
A. Social Dialogue Council 240
B. *Voivodeship* (Province) Social Dialogue Councils 242
C. Other Tripartite and Multipartite Bodies 243

Chapter 2. Trade Unions and Employer Organizations; Ad Hoc Employee Representatives 244

§1. Legal Basis and Status of Trade Unions and Employer's Organizations 244

§2. Trade Unions 245
I. Notion 245
A. Introduction 245
B. Membership Composition 245
C. Special Tasks 246
D. Trade Union Self-Governance and Autonomy 247
E. Voluntary Membership 247
F. Internal Democracy 248
G. Formalized Organizational Structure and Durability 248
II. Description and Structures 249
A. General Remarks 249
B. Nationwide Intersectoral Union Organizations 249
C. Supra-Establishment Regional and Sector-Based Organizations 251
D. Workplace Union Organizations 251
E. Membership 252
III. Establishment, Dissolution and Transformations of Trade Unions 253
A. Establishment 253
B. Dissolution 254
C. Transformations 254
IV. Representation of Employees 255
A. Individual Cases 255
B. Collective Cases 256
V. Representativeness 257
VI. Statutory Competences 258
A. Introduction 258
B. Participation in Law-Making 258
C. Impact on Public Opinion 259
D. Participation in Control of Working Conditions 260
E. The Right to Information 260

F. Protection of Trade Union Representatives 261
G. Trade Union Facilities 262

§3. Employers' Organizations 264
I. Notion 264
II. Description and Structures 264
III. Establishment, Dissolution and Transformations 266
IV. Representation of Employers 267
V. Representativeness 267
VI. Statutory Competences 268

§4. Employee Representatives Appointed Ad Hoc 268

§5. Structure of Interest Representation and the System of Collective Labour Relations 269

Chapter 3. Collective Bargaining 271

§1. General 271
I. Legal Framework 271
II. Existing System of Collective Bargaining; Levels of Negotiation 271

§2. CLAs 274
I. Legal Notion 274
II. Personal (*Ratione Personae)* Scope of Application 274
III. Parties 275
A. Employers' Side 275
B. Unions' Side 275
IV. Conclusion of CLA and Its Entry into Force 276
A. Conclusion of a CLA 276
B. Entry into Force 276
C. Agreement on Application of Another CLA 277
V. Extended Application of a CLA 277
VI. Contents of a CLA 278
VII. Amendments to a CLA 280
VIII. Suspension of Application of a CLA 280
IX. Termination of a CLA; Completion of a CLA Application 280
A. Termination 280
B. Completion of a CLA Application 280

§3. Other Nominate Normative Collective Accords 281
I. General Remarks 281
II. Types of Nominate Normative Accords 282
III. Issues of Difference 283

Chapter 4. Collective Disputes; Strikes and Other Legal Industrial Actions 285

§1. Notion of Collective Dispute 285
I. Statutory Regulation 285
II. Representation of the Parties 286
III. Notifying the Dispute 287
IV. Social Peace Clause 288

§2. Legal Conflicts (Interpretation of the Content of Collective Agreements) 288

§3. Settlement of Collective Disputes by Means of Statutory Procedures 289
I. Introduction 289
II. Negotiations 289
III. Mediation 290
IV. Arbitration 290
V. Goodwill Mission 291

§4. Agreed Procedures 292

§5. Strike 292
I. The Right to Strike 292
II. Legal Definition 294
III. Illegal Strike 295
IV. Procedural Requirements 296
V. Limitations of the Right to Strike 297
VI. Protection of Employers' Interests 298
VII. Legal Situation of Participants, Organizers and Persons Leading the Strike 298

§6. Protest Actions Other than Strikes 300

§7. Lockout 301

§8. Completion of a Collective Dispute 302
I. Ways of Completion of a Collective Dispute 302
II. Agreement Ending a Collective Dispute 302
III. The Arbitration Award 303

Chapter 5. Participation of Employees in Workplace Management 304

§1. Legal Basis 304

§2. Scope of Participation 306

§3. Employee Representation in Management of National Work Establishments 307
I. Introductory Remarks 307
II. Work Establishment Trade Union Organization 307
III. Employee Councils 309
A. General Remarks 309
B. Election and Powers of Members of the Employee Council 309
C. Rules of Council Operation 310
D. Powers of the Employee Council in the Field of Information and Consultation 310
1. Types of Power 310
2. Information 310
3. Opining 311
4. Consultation 311
E. Confidential Information 311
F. Sanctions for Violation of Duties 312
IV. Employee Representatives Sitting on Company Bodies 312
V. Social Labour Inspection 313
VI. Information and Consultation on Matters of Occupational Safety and Health 314
A. Concept of Protection of Employee Life and Health 314
B. Information on Matters of OSH 314
C. Consultation on OSH Matters 315
D. OSH Committee 315

§4. Employee Representation in Management of Union-scale Undertakings 316
I. Introductory Remarks 316
II. European Works Councils 317
A. Scope of Application of the Act 317
B. Determining the Way of Exercising the Right to Information and Consultation 317
C. Standard Rules 318
D. Confidential Information 319
E. Protection of and Facilitation for Employee Representatives 319
III. Employee Participation in Management of European Company and European Cooperative Society as well as a Company Emerged as a Result of Cross-border Mergers of Companies 319
IV. Employee Share Ownership 320

Selected Bibliography 321

Index 325

List of Abbreviations

CC	Civil Code 1964 (Act of 23 April 1964; consolidated text: *Journal of Laws* 2017, item 459, as amended)
CDSA	Collective Disputes Settlement Act 1991 (Act of 23 May 1991; Consolidated text: *Journal of Laws* 2018, item 399)
CLA	Collective Labour Agreement
CPC	Civil Procedure Code 1964 (Act of 17 November 1964; consolidated text: *Journal of Laws* 2018, item 155, as amended)
EOA	Employers' Organization Act 1991 (Act of 23 May 1991; Consolidated text: *Journal of Laws* 2015, item 2029)
EPA	Employment Promotion Act 2004 (Act of 20 April 2004; consolidated text: *Journal of Laws* 2017, item 1065, as amended)
ETA	Employment Termination Act 2003 (Act of 13 March 2003; consolidated text: *Journal of Laws* 2016, item 1974)
EU	European Union
LC	Labour Code
PLN	Polish zloties
OSH	Occupational Health and Safety
SDCA	Social Dialogue Council Act 2015 (Act of 24 July 2015; Journal of Laws of 2015, item 1240)
SLI	State Labour Inspection
TUA	Trade Union Act of 1991 (Act of 23 May 1991; consolidated text: *Journal of Laws* 2015, item 1881)

List of Abbreviations

Introduction

Chapter 1. General Background

L. Mitrus

§1. Geography, Location, Size and Boundaries

1. The Republic of Poland (Polish: *Rzeczpospolita Polska*) is a Central European country. It borders Germany, the Czech Republic, Slovakia, Ukraine, Belarus and Lithuania, and also Russia (Kaliningrad Oblast). Poland lies in the eastern part of the European Union (EU) and its borders are, at the same time, the EU's external borders. The area of Poland is 312,679 km^2, and the population is 38.5 million. Poland is divided into sixteen *voivodeships* (provinces). The smaller administrative units are known as *powiat* (often referred to in English as counties) and *gmina* (communes or municipalities).

§2. The Political System

2. Among the political foundations introduced by the Constitution of the Republic of Poland of 2 April 1997 (Journal of Laws of 1997, No. 78, item 483, as amended)[1] the following principles deserve highlighting: the sovereignty of the people, the sovereignty and independence of the state, the democratic state of law, political pluralism, the separation of powers, the social market economy, and also the inherent human dignity which determines the system of rights and freedoms of an individual. The Constitution expressly states that the Republic of Poland shall be the common good of all its citizens (Article 1). It is worth adding that Poland is a member of international organizations and European structures. On 26 November 1991 Poland acceded to the Council of Europe, and since 1 May 2004 it has been a member of the EU. Poland also belongs among the founding countries of the International Labour Organization and the United Nations.

3. According to Article 10 item 1 of the Constitution, the system of government of the Republic of Poland shall be based on the separation of and balance between

1. The Constitution of the Republic of Poland, Sejm Publishing Office, Warsaw 1997, pp. 3 et seq.

the legislative, executive and judicial powers. According to Article 10 item 2, legislative power shall be vested in the Sejm and the Senate, executive power shall be vested in the President of the Republic of Poland and the Council of Ministers and the judicial power shall be vested in courts and tribunals. Thus, the legislative power is exercised by the Sejm (the lower chamber) and the Senate (the higher chamber). The Sejm is comprised of 460 Members of Parliament (MPs) whereas the Senate is comprised of 100 senators. MPs and senators are elected through elections that are universal, equal, direct, proportional and anonymous. Their term of office is four years.

4. Executive powers are vested in the President and the government (Council of Ministers). The President is the head of state. He is elected in a universal election for a five-year term and can be elected only twice. The President is the highest representative of the state, ensures that the Constitution is obeyed, and upholds the sovereignty and safety of the state and the inviolability and indivisibility of its territory. The Council of Ministers is composed of the Prime Minister (premier), deputy prime ministers and ministers. The Council of Ministers is responsible for internal and foreign policy. Its authority includes all the state policy issues that are not reserved for other state organs or local governments. The government, the Prime Minister and ministers may issue orders for executing Acts of Parliament, only on the basis of a statutory authorization. However, this is permissible only under Acts and for their execution.

5. Judicial power lies in the hands of the courts and tribunals. Under Article 175 of the Constitution, the administration of justice in the Republic of Poland shall be implemented by the Supreme Court, the common courts, administrative courts and military courts. The court system is made up of courts of general jurisdiction: district, regional and appellate courts, and specific courts: military and administrative. Employment courts are separate organizational units of district courts whereas employment and social insurance courts are separate organizational units of regional and appellate courts. Article 183 of the Constitution provides that the Supreme Court shall exercise supervision over common and military courts regarding judgments (Article 183). Competent for labour law litigation are the Labour Law, Social Security and Public Affairs Chambers of the Supreme Court.

6. Furthermore, under Article 188 of the Constitution, the Constitutional Tribunal shall adjudicate regarding the following matters: the conformity of statutes and international agreements to the Constitution; the conformity of a statute to ratified international agreements whose ratification required prior consent granted by statute; the conformity of legal provisions issued by central state organs to the Constitution, ratified international agreements and statutes; the conformity to the Constitution of the purposes or activities of political parties; complaints concerning constitutional infringements.

§3. Vital Statistics

7. According to the information provided by the Central Statistical Office,[2] in December 2016 the population of Poland reached 38,432,000 persons; in the third quarter of 2017, 15,293,000 persons were economically active. The structure of the economically active population is as follows: 58% in the service sector; 31.6% in the industrial sector; the remaining 10.5% active in the agriculture sector. The employment rate of the population aged 15 years and above reached 56.7% (59.3% for males and 44.6% for females).[3] The structure of employed persons by employment status in 2017 was as follows: There were 1,640,400 employed persons. In this category there were 2,935,000 self-employed persons and 13,081,000 employees. There were 14,608,000 full-time employed persons and 1,228,000 part-time employed persons. Estimated by working contract, 9,741,000 employees had a permanent job while 3,340,000 had a temporary job.[4] Thus, in Poland the proportion of those with a fixed-term employment contract is relatively high and reaches approximately 25.5% (in comparison to 27.9% in 2015 and 26.8% in 2016).

With regard to demography, in the years 2006–2012 a positive birth rate was registered. The highest rate was registered in 2008. It amounted to 35,100. However, in the last two years there has been a negative natural increase. In 2013 it reached minus 17,700, while in 2014 it reached minus 1,300. Thus, the decrease in population amounted to minus 0.1% in 2013 and minus 0.03% in 2014. It can be expected that this tendency will continue in the future.[5] However, in 2017 the number of delivered children amounted to 403,000, i.e., more than 20,000 in comparison to 2016.

8. According to the data provided by the Ministry of Labour, in February 2018 the number of registered unemployed persons reached 1,126,700. The registered unemployment rate amounted to 6.8% among which 54.1% were women.[6] In general, the level of unemployment shows a decreasing tendency. At the same time, there is a differentiation of unemployment level in specific categories. It should be emphasized that in the fourth quarter of 2017, the unemployment rate among young people reached 14.8%.

9. The statutory minimum remuneration in Poland 2018 amounts to PLN 2,100 *brutto* (approximately EUR 510) per month. It refers to work performed in the framework of an employment relationship. In the recent years, there has been a small, but continuous, rise in the statutory minimum remuneration: It amounted to PLN 1,850 in 2016 and PLN 2,000 in 2017. Moreover, since 2017 there has been a minimum wage for certain categories of civil law contractors. In 2018 it amounts

---

2. *Demographic Yearbook of Poland 2017* (Warsaw, Central Statistical Office, October 2017), p. 30.
3. http://rynekpracy.org/x/902899, last accessed 25.08.2018.
4. Rynek pracy w Polsce 2017, https://www.mpips.gov.pl/analizy-i-raporty/raporty-sprawozdania/rynek-pracy/sytuacja-na-rynku-pracy/rynek-pracy-w-polsce-w-2017-roku/, last accessed 25.082018.
5. *Demographic yearbook of Poland 2015* (Warsaw, Central Statistical Office, October 2015), p. 30.
6. http://stat.gov.pl/obszary-tematyczne/rynek-pracy/bezrobocie-rejestrowane/stopa-bezrobocia-rejestrowanego-w-latach-1990-2018,4,1.html; accessed on 25.08 2018.

to PLN 13.70 per hour (around EUR 3). In February 2018 the average monthly remuneration amounted to PLN 4,599.72 (approximately EUR 1,000).[7]

10. According to the data provided by the Central Statistical Office, those belonging to trade unions constitute a proportion of 5% of the population of Poland (taking adults into account) and 11% of employed persons. Workplace trade union organizations are most common in medium enterprises, i.e., entities that employ between 50 and 249 persons. Trade unions existed in 55% of such enterprises. Then, trade unions existed in 31% of undertakings that employ more than 250 people. With regard to undertakings that employ fewer than 50 persons, trade unions existed in 14% of such entities. On average, there were more workplace trade unions in the public sector (62%) than in the private sector (38%).[8] Thus, in Poland the ratio of unionized employees is relatively low.

7. http://stat.gov.pl/obszary-tematyczne/rynek-pracy/pracujacy-zatrudnieni-wynagrodzenia-koszty-pracy/przecietne-zatrudnienie-i-wynagrodzenie-w-sektorze-przedsiebiorstw-w-lutym-2018-roku,3,75.html, last visited 25.08. 2018.

8. *Notka informacyjna, Związki zawodowe w Polsce w 2014 roku* (Warszaw, Główny Urząd Statystyczny, 13 Jul. 2015).

Chapter 2. Historical Background

§1. Until World War II

Z. Hajn

11. The origins of Poland's labour law coincide with the regaining of its independence after 123 years of partitions between its neighbouring empires (Russia, Prussia/Germany and Austria). Before that time the territory of Poland was governed by the legislation of invading states. Notwithstanding this, the time of the partitions was not without influence on employment relationships after independence was regained. First of all, it was during the partitions that industrialization, quickly developing in the latter half of the nineteenth century, took place. This led to a rapid growth in the number of workers employed in the factory system, especially in the textile, metallurgy, mining and shipbuilding industries. Meanwhile, Polish political parties were formed and their social programmes were of capital importance for the further development of labour legislation. Active in the field were, *inter alia*, socialist parties inspired by the Marxist ideology. These included the Polish Socialist Party, combining class warfare with the struggle for the independence of Poland, and the Social Democratic Party of the Kingdom of Poland and Lithuania, which held the idea of a struggle for national independence obsolete. Polish trade unions were also created, some of them having national/Christian characters (e.g., *Zjednoczenie Zawodowe Polskie* – Polish Union of Occupations) and others being national/liberal organizations (so-called *Polskie Związki Zawodowe* – Polish Trade Unions). There also existed working class trade unions led by the socialist parties, which – after 1916 – were united in the *Komisja Centralna Związków Zawodowych* (Central Committee of Trade Unions). In addition, Polish employers' organizations came into being, of which organizations the most important was *Związek Przemysłowców Królestwa Polskiego* (Union of Polish Industrialists of the Kingdom of Poland) operating in the territories remaining under Russian rule.

12. After the re-establishment of independence, the government of the newly emerged Polish state was faced with the problem of a variety of legal systems operating in its territory. Whatever differences existed between them, their common feature was the poor development of labour law legislation. The regulations hardly met the expectations of the working classes, raised by the end of the war, the regained independence and victorious revolution taking place in the nearby Russia. It was those factors, together with the formation of the International Labour Organization, the growing emancipation of labour law as part of the legal system and the need for legal, social and economic integration of the state that pushed forward the idea of developing the labour law from scratch. The process of creation of the new labour law lasted almost throughout the entire interwar period, leading to the gradual replacement of Russian, German and Austrian legislation, as existing in the territories earlier occupied by the alien powers, by Polish legislation covering the whole country.

13. The years immediately following the regaining of independence were of particular importance for the shape taken by the new labour law. The period was marked by heavy conflicts with the country's neighbours over its frontiers and the very existence of Polish statehood. It was also at that time that a grinding war took place between Poland and Russia, the latter attempting to transfer the Bolshevik revolution to the West. Considering the situation and the initially existing revolutionary tension, manifested by the operation of the councils of workers' delegates, the first government of Poland, dominated by socialists, enacted a number of laws very favourable to workers. The actions satisfied the working classes and helped calm their mood. The new legislation concerned, in particular, the matters of working time,[9] trade unions,[10] settlement of collective disputes in agriculture,[11] state labour inspection (SLI),[12] mandatory sickness insurance[13] and unemployment insurance[14] and, later on, also holiday leave[15] as well as the protection of young people and women at work.[16] The Constitution of Poland, adopted in 1921, recognized labour as the foundation of the wealth of the Republic and declared that it would remain under the particular protection of the state. It also proclaimed the protection of juvenile workers and women and the right of association of both workers and employers. The standards of employee rights, as adopted in the above provisions, were high. Not only did they comply with the effective international rules but in many instances surpassed them. Among other things, they set the weekly working time at the level of forty-six hours, granted high overtime payments, made holiday leave a widely applied statutory scheme, set the minimum threshold for employment of the juvenile at 15 years of age and introduced mandatory leave from work for pregnant employees. A very liberal decree on trade unions secured a full freedom of association and found trade unions to be the representatives of all employees, for both those being trade union members and the non-unionized. In the years that followed, new areas of employment relationships were regulated, including, in particular, practical vocational training in industry and commerce,[17] the prevention of occupational diseases[18] and occupational safety and health.[19] Pension, sickness and accident insurance schemes were consolidated and harmonized[20] and a Labour

9. Decree of 1918 on an 8-Hour Working Day, replaced in 1919 by the Act of the Working Time in Industry and Commerce.
10. Decree on Employee Trade Unions of 1919.
11. Decree of 1918.
12. Decree of 1919.
13. Decree of 1919, replaced by an Act of Parliament in 1920.
14. Decrees of 1924, 1925 and 1927.
15. Act of 1922 on Holiday Leave in Industry and Commerce.
16. Act of 1924.
17. The Industrial Law of 1927.
18. Decree of 1927.
19. Decree of 1928.
20. Social Security Act of 1933.

Fund was established in 1933 to pool and distribute resources for unemployment benefits and the financing of public works.

14. An essential factor consolidating labour law as a branch of the legal system was the adoption, in 1928, of two presidential decrees on employment contracts of blue-collar workers and on employment contracts of white-collar workers. The Acts reinforced the special nature of the contract of employment and attached particular social weight to it. From the formal point of view, they had, however, the nature of specific civil law provisions. Hence, applicable to the contract of employment were also the rules of the Code of Obligations[21] which played the role of the general part of labour law. Their practical importance for the general regulation of employee rights and obligations was, nevertheless, minimal as they concerned, in practice, the employment of domestic workers.

15. The distinctive nature of labour law was also stressed by the creation of a statutory basis for the making of autonomous sources of labour law. As regards workplace regulations, the basis for those was provided by the above-mentioned decrees on employment contracts. As opposed to them, the collective labour agreements (CLAs) which had been, for a long time, concluded *via facti*, were initially provided for by the Code of Obligations as legal acts purely contractual in nature, and then regulated by the Act of Parliament of 1937. The law, enacted after years of negotiations with employers' organizations, recognized the normative character of provisions of CLAs, extended the binding force of the latter to non-unionized workers and adopted the rule whereby the stipulations of employment contract less favourable than CLA provisions were automatically deemed void. Given the short period remaining until the outbreak of WWII the Act was not likely to exert a significant impact on the practice of concluding CLAs. A characteristic feature of the practice at that time was the domination of company-level CLAs and the significant share of CLAs concluded by non-union employee representatives.[22]

16. The main weak point of Poland's pre-war labour law was the poor observance of its provisions by the employers, criticizing what they referred to as excessive 'social burdens'. Such a situation resulted partly from insufficient legal instruments established to control the observance, and partly from the fact that the standards of the employee rights were actually incompatible with the development of the economy. The reaction to the weaknesses was twofold. First, the autonomy and effectiveness of the operation of the SLI[23] was reinforced and separate labour courts[24] and social security courts[25] were established; the move improved their efficiency and reduced the costs of asserting employee claims. Second, meeting the

21. Decree of 1933.
22. For instance, in 1933, as many as 237 out 329 collective labour agreements concluded in large and medium-sized industrial companies were those covering a single company: W. Szubert, *Układy zbiorowe pracy* (Warsaw, Państwowe Wydawnictwo Naukowe, 1960), p. 55.
23. Decree of 1927.
24. Decrees of 1928 and 1934.
25. Act of 1939.

demands of the business circles halfway, certain employee rights were limited. Pressure exerted by the circles, blaming labour law for the economic difficulties, proved successful, especially in times of the great economic crisis. In particular, in 1933 the weekly working time limit was raised to forty-eight hours, the hourly rates for overtime work were reduced and remuneration for holiday leave was reduced. Partial withdrawal from the changes took place in 1935.

17. Criticism was also expressed over the caste nature of labour law for the period in question. A characteristic feature of the law was the distinction made between white- and blue-collar workers, the former being markedly privileged. Notwithstanding this, particularly advantageous was the legal status of public servants and other state agents (who were, however, subject to administrative law, and not labour law legislation). On the other hand, farm workers were in a highly disadvantageous position, being left outside the scope of operation of the legislative regulation; their rights and duties were provided for by CLAs and judgments of out-of-court redressal bodies.

18. And yet, despite the above-mentioned weaknesses, the short (just twenty years) interwar period was of critical importance for the development of the Polish labour law system. The main areas of employment relationships were provided for, a system of labour courts and state supervision of working conditions was established, and the whole territory of the state was, to a considerable extent, covered by the new and original body of legislation. The influence of pre-war legal architecture, legislative technique and specific legal solutions can still be seen in contemporary Polish labour law.

19. It should be added that during the period in question the theoretical foundations of labour law as a separate branch of the legal system were formed. Great contributions to the case were made by practitioners developing, as early as since the 1920s, collections of labour law Acts and regulations and commentaries to labour law. The first labour law manuals were published in 1930.[26]

20. The above-described development of labour law in pre-war Poland took place under conditions of strong social tension felt, in particular, during the great crisis. Strikes became very frequent in the years 1932–1933. It was at that time that sit-down strikes emerged, just as did the so-called black strikes which were a combination of sit-down and hunger strikes. Union density did not exceed one-fifth of those employed.[27] The trade union movement was divided. Most influential was the leftist umbrella organization of *Związek Stowarzyszeń Zawodowych* (Union of Trade Associations) having close links with the Polish Socialist Party (around 60% of all union members before 1926). Another major federation was the *Zjednoczenie Zawodowe Polskie* (Polish Union of Occupations) with 31% of union

26. A. Raczyński, *Polskie prawo pracy* (Warsaw, Księgarnia F. Hoesicka, 1930); Z. Fenichel, *Zarys polskiego prawa robotniczego* (Warsaw, Gebethner i Wolff, 1930).
27. S. Grzybowski, *Pracownicze związki zawodowe. Droga rozwoju* (Kraków, 'Czytelnik' Spółdzielnia Pracy i Użytkowników, 1948), p. 49.

members before 1926, focused on economic issues. Christian trade unions related to Christian Democrats accounted for about 4% of the total community. After 1926 two new trade union federations were formed, viz. *Centralne Zrzeszenie Klasowych Związków Zawodowych* (Central Association of Class Trade Unions) and *Związek Związków Zawodowych* (Trade Union Alliance) which, using radical slogans, managed to attract a considerable proportion of trade union members (about 25%) and, thus, to cause a further split in the trade union movement. Besides trade unions, employee associations continued to operate, governed by the Act on Associations. Of certain practical importance were also informal workers' delegations, strike committees and other representations of the kind which, as lately as in the 1930s, concluded CLAs and conducted collective disputes on behalf of non-associated workers.

21. On the employer side the basic organizational form were trade associations which, after the country had regained independence, were quickly turned into nationwide organizations. Top (umbrella) organizations were also formed soon. Big industries were quickly grouped to form the *Centralny Związek Polskiego Przemysłu, Górnictwa, Handlu i Finansów* (Central Alliance of Polish Industry, Mining, Commerce and Finance) in 1919, later (as of 1932) renamed to become the *Centralny Związek Przemysłu Polskiego 'Lewiatan'* (Central Alliance of Polish Industry 'Leviathan'). The organizations of smaller employers formed the *Centralny Związek Średniego i Drobnego Przemysłu* (Central Alliance of Medium-Sized and Small Industry) in 1934.

§2. The Communist Period

L. Mitrus

I. Introductory Remarks

22. The development of the Polish labour law during the period of communism (1945–1989) passed through a number of stages, and individual legal institutions were undergoing significant modifications with the reconstruction and development of the country and with the extension of workers' and social rights. Those changes were also influenced by political events, including especially the social unrests in the years 1956, 1968, 1970, 1976, and also those from 1980–1981 which ended up with the imposition of martial law on 13 December 1981. Then, the economic crisis of the 1980s and the wave of strikes in the years 1988–1989 lead to the 'round table' negotiations and to a peaceful political transformation. Notwithstanding the above facts, a number of features common to the Polish labour law in the communist era can be identified.

23. First of all, we must note that in the previous system the regulations of labour law had strong ideological overtones. They were also related to the political and economic realities of the time. In this context, the leading role of the Communist Party (Polish United Workers' Party) should be emphasized. The party influenced all fields of life, including the questions of employment and of functioning of employees' representations. Moreover, of great significance was the planned character of the socialist economy which was centrally managed by the state and which was also the owner of the nationalized assets. The means of production had been, in large measure, nationalized and were the property of the state. The role of employers was usually performed by state institutions and the regulations of labour law were oriented mainly at regulating the labour relationships in large state enterprises. As a rule, the amount and rules of pay were established top-down at the central level.

24. In the communist era, labour law regulations were rigid, with a relatively small margin of departures from general rules, e.g., depending on a particular industry. As a rule, the state had a monopoly for establishing regulations pertaining to labour law, although a practice of concluding collective agreements for individual industries was formed with time. At the same time, a theory of 'non-conflict' in a socialist society was propagated, which led to the negation of the right to strike among other things. Until the 1980s there was virtually no development in the collective labour law. The role of trade unions was different from its present role, and its function was that of a 'transmission belt' between the ruling party and the working class. It should be noted, however, that in the communist era the state fulfilled a protective function and was involved in active social policy. In addition, there was a visible tendency to extend the scope of workers' rights by law and also to recognize their common character, i.e., to grant them to all workers. A similar situation existed with regard to protection under national social insurance, where the relevant regulations underwent far-reaching transformations. Despite numerous amendments which were enacted after 1989, a number of institutions of the present-day labour law have their roots in regulations adopted in the previous political system.

II. The Period Before the Codification of Labour Law

25. The end of World War II marked a fundamental change in political, economic and social relations. However, pre-war statutes remained, at first, in force but, of course, they were modified and adjusted to the new reality. Decrees on employment contracts of white-collar and blue-collar workers, as well as the Code of Obligations, were still in force. However, new regulations were gradually introduced. As early as 6 February 1945, a decree on the establishment of works councils[28] was issued, which introduced a new workers' representation and which acquired broad competence with regard to the functioning of firms employing workers. In the beginning, numerous collective agreements were concluded at the firm level. That practice was, however, abandoned after 1950 owing to the progressing centralization of the national economy and due to the growing disregard for market mechanisms.

---

28. *Journal of Laws* (1946), No. 8, item 36, as later amended.

26. Gradually, new statutory regulations were enacted which extended the scope of workers' rights. Often, particular institutions had already been the subject of collective agreements and the legislator had given them a common character. Changes concerned mainly maternity protection, extension of annual leave as well as the professional training and protection of junior workers. Significant progress was achieved in industrial safety. On the other hand, freedom of labour was limited. Graduates were assigned to work for a specific employer. Certain categories of specialists were not allowed to freely change their place of employment. Moreover, the Law of 19 April 1950 on protecting the socialist work discipline[29] aimed at countering missing days at work and provided for a number of penalties. For example, such a penalty could be a reduction in pay or even a jail term. In a way, work discipline became a domain of criminal law. At that time, labour law concentrated less on its protective function focusing instead on the administration of work and on providing sanctions for failure to obey regulations. This aspect of the development of Polish labour law is assessed with explicit disapproval today.

27. In 1956, the most repressive acts of the post-war labour law were repealed. Furthermore, a new decree of 18 January 1956 on the restrictions on the admissibility of termination of employment contracts and on the protection of unbroken employment record (*Journal of Laws* 1956, No. 2, item 11, as later amended) restricted the possibility of immediately terminating an employment contract and established a new institution of restoration of employee to his or her job. The extension of workers' rights continued, e.g., those relating to junior workers or industrial safety. Of great importance was the Act of 29 April 1969 on workers' annual leave.[30] The national insurance system was also gradually extended. Many acts which regulated the legal situation of certain professional groups, especially in the clerical apparatus, were also in force.

28. The new Trade Union Act of 1 July 1949[31] introduced the principle of uniformity of the trade union movement. Therefore, trade union pluralism was excluded. Gradually, trade unions were entrusted with more and more new functions, such as the execution of the tasks of the social work standards and safety inspectorate or the management of some aspects of national insurance. Trade unions were, thus, charged with numerous administrative tasks and, in addition, they were expected to encourage workers to increase work output. Under the understanding, then prevailing unions constituted a 'transmission belt' between the ruling party and the working class. Their role was, therefore, basically different from the modern one. In addition, there were transformations in the field of representation of works staff. The final form was introduced by the Act of 20 December 1958 on workers' self-management[32] which addressed the supervision and control of the operation of

---

29. *Journal of Laws* (1950), No. 20, item 168.
30. *Journal of Laws* (1969), No. 12, item 85.
31. *Journal of Laws* (1949), No. 41, item 293.
32. *Journal of Laws* (1958), No. 77, item 397.

enterprises. The self-management was supervised by trade unions. Against a background of the legal systems of other communist states the extensive regulations concerning workers' self-management were characteristic of Polish labour legislation.

III. The Period After the Codification of Labour Law

29. Starting from the 1960s, the need for codification of labour legislation was more and more often mentioned in the literature of the subject, which coincided with tendencies prevailing in other communist countries. Additionally, after 1970, the social policy of the state was intensified. Economic growth was accompanied by a further development of social rights, e.g., those pertaining to maternity protection or increase in wages. An important landmark in the development of Polish labour legislation was the passing of the Labour Code (LC) on 26 June 1974. The Code came into force on 1 January 1975. Poland was the last state of the then communist bloc that codified its labour law. The LC that was enacted then remains valid till today, although with time its shape underwent major changes. The LC has been amended more than a hundred times to adjust its regulations to the conditions of market economy and due to the need to implement EU directives.

30. The new LC was the decisive factor in the emergence of labour law from civil law. At the same time it introduced a significant qualitative change to the labour law of that time. The following are the most significant changes that should be mentioned: A uniform notion of employee was introduced, which meant a resignation from distinguishing between the categories of white-collar and blue-collar workers. The scope of the regulations of the LC included all employees on the principle of universality, with a possibility of introducing modifications in respect of specific groups of employees. Protection of employment stability was introduced by the principle that termination of a permanent contract of employment had to be justified. Examination of employee disputes was reorganized by introducing a possibility to appeal against decisions of works union committees to court. Further, employees' liability for damage done in the employer's property was regulated on new principles. These principles were more lenient than the civil law.

31. The LC is the basic source of individual labour law until today. In its original version the Code contained general regulations; it regulated the situation of the parties to the employment relationship, including the types of contracts of employment, protection of their stability, as well as the rights and duties of the parties, the disciplinary responsibility and financial liability of employees, the protection of the labour of women and juveniles, industrial safety, the examination of disputes related to labour law, and the limitation period for claims. It dealt also with the conclusion of collective agreements. In addition, the Code's subject matter was completed by numerous implementing Acts enacted as government orders. In a later period the Code became subject to multiple and far-reaching changes. In addition, a number of extra-Code Acts concerning labour law were adopted; therefore, the Code does not fulfil the condition of the universality of legal regulation.

32. The economic crisis and the social protests of the years 1980–1981 brought about significant changes in the development of Poland. The 'Solidarity' trade union came into being and, in practice, it became a mass social movement and an alternative to the ruling communist party. The opposition formulated a number of demands of political and social nature. As regards labour law, the demands concerned, first of all, the new shape of the collective labour law. As a result of the wave of strikes in 1980 post-strike agreements were made between the government party and the striking workers. Those agreements demonstrated a will to reach a compromise and they charted the directions of system changes. Further, on 25 September 1981 the new Act on the Self-Management of the Staff of a State Enterprise was passed. The process of transformation was interrupted by the introduction of martial law in Poland on 13 December 1981. This meant, among other things, suspension of civil liberties and the banning of 'Solidarity'. On 8 October 1982, a new Trade Union Act[33] was passed. As well as the principles of functioning of trade unions, it also regulated collective disputes and the right to strike.[34] In the mid-1980s, the growing economic crisis triggered aspirations for the introduction of economic reforms. They aimed at decentralizing the economy and increasing the independence of enterprises. These actions of the authorities were not successful, and growing economic problems led to a new wave of strikes. A dialogue that started between the government party and the opposition led to the start of the 'round table' talks at the beginning of 1989, and the agreements reached then enabled free elections and a peaceful change of the political system.

§3. The Democracy Period

L. Mitrus

33. The change of the political system in 1989 starting from the round table talks between 'Solidarity' and the communist government led to the emergence of quite new economic and social conditions.[35] New phenomena unknown in the communist system appeared. The change-over from a centrally controlled economy to a market economy required transformation on the part of employers. The privatization of state enterprises was often accompanied by group layoffs or bankruptcies. Unemployment, unknown in the previous system, appeared on a large scale. The earlier regulations of labour law turned out to be inapplicable to the new reality, which necessitated far-reaching changes. The necessity to adjust labour law to the new conditions of the market economy became the main driving force behind the changes that took place in labour law after 1989. From today's perspective, the literature of the subject emphasizes that from the economic point of view the transformation was a success. At the same time the authors notice the lack of adequate

33. *Journal of Laws* (1982), No. 32, item 216.
34. *See* J. Wratny, *Związki zawodowe w prawodawstwie polskim w latach 1980-1991* (Lublin, Redakcja Wydawnictw Katolickiego Uniwersytetu Lubelskiego, 1994), pp. 40 et seq.
35. *See* E. Kovacs, N. Lyutov, L. Mitrus, 'Labor law in Transition: From a Centrally Planned to Free Market Economy in Central and Eastern Europe', in: Finkin and Mundlak (eds), *Comparative Labor Law* (Cheltenham UK; Northampton, MA, USA, Edward Elgar Publishing, 2015), pp. 403 et seq.

attention to the negative social effects of the economic reforms. Moreover, from the beginning of the transformation there was no consistent vision of the development of labour law. Individual amendments often had the character of temporary changes and reactions to specific needs of the moment. As early as 1989, regulations which were most incompatible with the new realities, e.g., a prohibition on taking up additional employment without the employer's permission, was repealed. Solutions concerning transfer of a work establishment to another employer (such regulations were in force in Poland also in the interwar period), bankruptcy of the employer and also a totally new Collective Redundancies Act were adopted. Acts concerning assistance to unemployed persons and fighting unemployment were also enacted. Also, in 1989 the principle of union pluralism was reinstated.

34. After the turning point of the political system, a basic change occurred in the field of collective labour law. In the previous system there were neither 'real' social partners nor dialogue and negotiations between them. Therefore, there were no established traditions and customs in this respect and no legal regulations resulting from evolution and compromise. For these reasons, the shape of the collective labour law in Poland was, in 1991, determined by three Acts which still have a fundamental significance for industrial relations in Poland. These are the Acts on trade unions, on employers' organizations, and on the settlement of collective disputes. In other words, due to historical conditions the shape of the contemporary collective labour law in Poland is determined by a decision made by the legislator at the beginning of the transformation of the political system. Another significant change in the field of collective labour law was the complete amendment of the part of the LC dealing with collective agreements of 1994. Freedom of bargaining and the scope of collective agreements were considerably extended. From today's perspective we must say that contrary to the assumptions made then, collective agreements have not become the dominant sources of labour law. Polish labour law is still, first of all, a statutory law, and collective agreements and other group arrangements have a supplementary character. Moreover, the Tripartite Committee for Social and Economic Affairs started its activities in 1994. This was a forum for dialogue between the government party, trade unions and employers' organizations.[36]

35. An important step in the development of labour law after the political turning point was a comprehensive amendment of the LC in 1996. The catalogue of labour law principles was modified and the scope and significance of autonomous sources of labour law, including collective agreements and works rules, was increased. The chapter of the Code dealing with wages was changed to make it more flexible. Regulations aimed at preventing the abuse of civil law contracts and fixed-term contracts were also adopted. Contractual non-compete clauses were made possible. A number of regulations containing sanctions for infringement of work

36. *See also* A.M. Świątkowski, 'The Role of the State and Trade Unions During the Polish Process of Transformation', in Świątkowski (ed.), *Yearbook of Polish Labor Law and Social Policy*, Volume 8 (Krakow 1998), pp. 27 et seq., M. Seweryński, *Polish Labour Law: From Communism to Democracy* (Warsaw, Dom Wydawniczy ABC, 1999).

discipline were repealed. Without a doubt, those changes had a pro-market character. Another issue addressed was the need to restrict the role of state institutions and to increase the importance of social partners. As can be seen, the legislative tactics consisted in amending the existing LC rather than enacting a new one. It is worth adding here that the new Constitution of the Republic of Poland of 2 April 1997 introduced a concept of 'social market economy' as one of the foundations of the new political system.

36. In the first period after the transformation, adjusting the labour law to the conditions of the market economy was of a predominant importance. Gradually, the necessity to implement EU directives gained prominence. In the light of the association agreement of 1991, Poland undertook to adjust its internal legal system to EU requirements. For this reason, EU regulations became determinants for actions taken by the Polish legislator, and the process of Europeanization of the Polish legal order became an important factor in the changes in the Polish labour law. Poland was obliged to introduce a number of changes in a relatively short time. A significant number of changes had been introduced already before Poland's accession to the European Union, which took place on 1 May 2004. Now the necessity to ensure the compliance of internal legislation with EU directives is one of Poland's obligations as a Member State of the EU. Moreover, Polish labour courts apply a pro-EU interpretation of national law, which refers mainly to equal treatment in employment, restructuring of enterprises (transfer of an undertaking to another employer, bankruptcy of the employer, group layoffs) and working time. Contrary to fears expressed sometimes before Poland's accession to the EU, the application of EU law has not caused significant problems in the ruling practice of Polish courts.

37. The role of the 'European factor' in the shaping of Polish labour law gradually increased. Here, special significance is attributed to the amendment of the LC in 2003, whose basic aim was the implementation of related directives. The importance of changes caused by the Europeanization was different for individual institutions. Under the influence of EU legislation, extended regulations concerning prohibition of discrimination in employment appeared in Polish legislation (in its original version the Code regulated only the equal treatment of men and women). The chapter of the Code dealing with working time was completely changed and made more flexible. New regulations concerning posting of employees to other Member States in connection with the provision of services were introduced. New duties to inform employees were imposed on employers. Minimum annual leave was lengthened and employee rights related to parenthood were extended. Industrial safety standards were raised. The necessity to implement EU directives resulted in the emergence of new employee representations which function concurrently with trade unions. The European Works Councils Act which implemented the then Directive 94/45 was passed in 2002. Then, in 2006, the Employees Informing and Consulting Act, which implemented Directive 2002/14, was passed.

38. The effect of EU legislation on Polish labour law is many-sided and far-reaching. The literature of the subject emphasizes that the necessity to introduce EU standards changed the national labour law to a great extent by granting employees a number of new rights, and it also enforced the introduction of new employee representations which function alongside trade unions. At the same time, the authors point to a number of imperfections in the process of implementation which, not infrequently, consists in the automatic 'transposition' of directives. The implementation of directives has brought an even more pronounced vagueness to Polish labour law.[37] It should be also added that Poland is a party to the European Social Charter of the Council of Europe and that it has also ratified a considerable number of International Labour Organization conventions, e.g., in the field of the right to unionize. On the other hand, the fact that by the so-called British and Polish Protocol Poland excluded the application in its legal order of Chapter IV 'Solidarity' of the Charter of Fundamental Rights of the European Union, which deals with social rights, must be judged negatively.

39. Obviously, not all regulations of Polish labour law are the result of the implementation of EU legislation. In 2001, The Tripartite Committee Act was passed which introduced a statutory basis for its activity. A far-reaching amendment of the LC of 2002 was caused by the aspiration to make labour law more flexible, with the aim of reducing the level of unemployment. The measures, then adopted, included, among other things, a possibility to temporarily suspend the application of some labour law regulations in an enterprise; working time and the regulations concerning annual leaves were made more flexible. Also, in 2002 the Act on Minimum Remuneration for Work was passed (earlier it had been regulated by legal acts of lower level). Atypical forms of employment also became a subject of the legislator's interest. In 2003 the Employment of Temporary Workers Act was passed, and in 2007 a chapter dedicated to telecommuting was added to the LC. The range of employee rights connected with parenthood was considerably extended in recent years, and, also, regulations concerning issuing of certificates of employment were made more flexible. Poland suffered from the economic crisis less than other Member States. Nevertheless, in the 2009–2011 period there was, in force, the Act on Relieving the Effects of the Economic Crisis for Employees and Entrepreneurs (so-called anti-crisis act) (Journal of Laws 2009, No. 125, item 1035). It provided for some changes to make the application of fixed-time contract easier, extension of working time accounting periods to twelve months as well as subsidies for employers wanting to avoid layoffs for economic reasons.[38] A possibility to extend the accounting periods to twelve months was permanently introduced to the Labour code by the amendment of July 2013. This makes it easier for employers to plan the working time; nevertheless, these regulations met with strong resistance and criticism from trade unions. In October 2013, the Special Measures Addressing Protection of Jobs Act,[39] which provided for assistance to entrepreneurs facing group layoffs, was passed. This resulted, to a large extent, from the political situation in the east of Europe and a slump of exports to Russia.

---

37. *See* L. Mitrus, *Wpływ regulacji wspólnotowych na polskie prawo pracy* (Warsaw, Zakamycze, 2006), pp. 103 et seq.; W. Sanetra (ed.), *Europeizacja polskiego prawa pracy* (Warsaw, Wydawnictwo Naukowe Scholar, Instytut Pracy i Spraw Socjalnych, 2004), pp. 14 et seq.
38. *See* L. Mitrus, 'Anti-Crisis Regulations of Polish Labour Law', *European Labour Law Journal*, Vol. 1., No. 2, 2010, 269.
39. *Journal of Laws* (2013), item 1291.

40. The core of individual labour law in Poland remains the LC. Numerous changes have made this legal Act complicated and difficult to apply in practice. Many questions remain the subject of extra-Code Acts, which causes the Code to fail to meet the requirement of a comprehensive legal regulation. A proposal to recodify labour law was put forward by lawyers specializing in labour law. The committee for the codification of labour law that was active in the years 2002–2007 prepared drafts of two new codes, for individual and collective labour law. However, these drafts did not become the subject of legislative action.[40]

41. A big problem in present-day Polish labour law is the visible segmentation of the labour market. On the one hand, workers employed under open-ended contracts enjoy full protection against termination. On the other hand, the regulation concerning fixed-term contracts is very liberal and generates the possibility of abusing fixed-term employment. Poland, alongside Spain, has the largest proportion of fixed-term contracts among the EU Member States. The amendment of 25 June 2015 to the LC[41] is expected to solve this problem to a certain extent. According to the amendment, after three years a fixed-term contract will be transformed into an open-ended contract. Although the direction of changes seems to be right, the new regulations arouse many doubts.[42] Another problem is the abuse of civil-law contracts and evasion of labour law. In the 'old Member States', similar problems are created by bogus self-employments.

The shape of the collective labour law also arouses a number of doubts. The Constitutional Tribunal, in its verdict of 2 June 2015,[43] decided that the regulation of the Trade Unions Act, which grants employees the right to unionize but refuses such right to persons providing work on another basis, especially civil-law contracts, is unconstitutional. Therefore, changes in Polish labour law extending the right to unionize can be expected[44]. The subject of the new regulations is social dialogue at the national level. In June 2013 trade unions suspended their participation in the Tripartite Committee, accusing the government party of ignoring the achieved agreements and of deciding alone about vital social issues, especially those related to increasing the retirement age, making working time more flexible and the amount of the minimum wage. Since that time, social dialogue at the national level has been virtually non-existent. At the beginning of 2015 trade unions and employers' organizations presented the principles of the new Social Dialogue Council Act. The Act of 24 July 2015 on the Council of Social Dialogue and other institutions of social

40. For the texts of the drafts, *see*, *Kodeks pracy, Zbiorowy Kodeks pracy. Projekty opracowane przez Komisję Kodyfikacyjną Prawa Pracy* (Katowice, Wydawnictwo Uniwersytetu Ekonomicznego, 2010). *See also* L. Florek, 'Czterdziestolecie kodeksu pracy', *Państwo i Prawo*, 3/2015, 21.
41. *Journal of Laws* (2015), item 1220.
42. *See* J. Stelina, 'Nowa koncepcja umowy o pracę na czas określony', *Państwo i Prawo* 11/2015, 41.
43. Case K 1/13, 80/6/A/2015.
44. *see* L. Mitrus, *European Trade Unions in Age of Flexicurity and Segmented Labor Markets: The Case of Poland.* "Comparative Labor Law & Policy Journal", Volume 38, Fall 2016, pp. 59 et seq.

dialogue (SDCA) took effect on 11 September 2015. The new institution has broader competence and is based, to a larger extent, on the partnership principle, than the earlier Tripartite Committee.

42. According to the Ordinance of the Council of Ministers of 9 August 2016 on the Commission for Codification of Labour Law,[45] the committee to elaborate the new regulations in the field of labour law was created. The Commission initiated its works in September 2016. The members were appointed by representative trade unions and representative employers' organizations, as well as by the government. The task of the Commission was to elaborate the drafts of a new LC and a new Collective LC within eighteen months. In March 2018, the drafts were presented to the Minister of Family, Labour and Social Policy. At the moment it is not clear whether the drafts or their parts will constitute the subject of parliamentary legislative process.

45. Journal of Laws 2016, item 1366.

Chapter 3. Notion of Labour Law

Z. Hajn

§1. Labour Law

43. Labour law is defined as all the legal regulations governing social relations related to the work done under an employment relationship, i.e., – putting it broadly – to the gainful work done voluntarily under the direction of another person (the employer). Essential for the determination of the scope of Poland's labour law is the fact that the employment relationship is the basis for the work done both in private and public sector, the work of public servants not being excluded. Employment in the uniformed services, for instance in the armed forces, police, Prison Service, Agency of Internal Security, Intelligence Agency, Government Protection Bureau, State Fire Service and Customs Service, is not regulated by labour law provisions. The relationships are provided for by the administrative law.

44. In labour law textbooks, the branch of law in question is divided into individual and collective labour law, or – at least – the latter is regarded as part of labour law in general. The individual labour law provides for the legal status of the employee and employer as parties to the employment relationship. It includes legal relations preceding the conclusion of the employment relationship, the employment relationship itself (conclusion thereof, changes to it, its termination and content, the responsibilities of the parties, protection of employment) and the resolution of individual labour disputes. Collective labour law deals with the rights of employee groups (and employers' rights and obligations related to them) and defines the ways of protection of the collective interests of both employees and employers. This part of labour law comprises provisions on trade unions and employers' organizations, collective bargaining and collective disputes. General opinion has it that provisions on employee participation in company management also belong to collective labour law. Beyond that division, there remain regulations concerning the organizational functions of the state in the area of employment and labour protection, which determine the structure, tasks and powers of the governmental agencies in that respect. This holds particularly true as far as the implementation of state policy regarding support of employment and prevention of unemployment, the work of the handicapped persons, the employment of foreigners and state supervision of working conditions and labour law observance are concerned. The provisions in question are often referred to as the 'labour administration law'.

§2. Distinctions and Relationships Between Labour Law and Other Branches of Law

45. The closest affiliations of labour law are with social security law and civil law.

46. According to the Constitution, social security protection is not an employee's but a citizen's right (Article 67 Part 1 of the Constitution). The protection is universal in nature (i.e., it covers all citizens) and complete (i.e., it concerns any events that may compromise a person's ability to work and gain the means of subsistence). For these very reasons social security provisions constitute a separate branch of law, the object of which differs from that of labour law legislation; characteristic of the branch are also different methods of legal regulation. In a majority of cases it is still, however, the work done under an employment relationship that gives a person entitlement to social security benefits. This makes it indisputable that both branches of law remain in a close relationship with each other.

47. Social security is provided for by a number of comprehensive pieces of legislation concerning individual types of insurance. These are:

- the Act of 17 December 1998 on Pensions from the Social Insurance Fund;[46]
- the Act of 25 June 1999 on Cash Benefits under Social Insurance in the Event of Sickness and Maternity (consolidated text: *Journal of Laws* of 2017, item 1368, as amended);
- the Act of 30 October 2002 on Social Insurance for Accidents at Work and Occupational Diseases (consolidated text: *Journal of Laws* of 2015, item 1242, as amended).

Matters common for all types of insurance are dealt with by the Act of 13 October 1998 on the Social Insurance System (consolidated text: *Journal of Laws* of 2017, item 1778 as amended). The Act, proclaiming social insurance as a scheme universal in scope and based on the equality principle, protects all persons who earn their keep. It makes social insurance mandatory not only for those earning means of subsistence but also for all who have any permanent source of income (such as a scholarship, unemployment benefit or social assistance allowance).

48. Labour law is a branch separate from civil law, and the Civil Code 'does not encroach on labour law provisions' (Article XII §1 of the Act of 1964 – Provisions Implementing the Civil Code). Genetic and normative ties of labour law with civil law are, however, obvious. In particular, in cases not regulated by labour law provisions, the provisions of the Civil Code apply to the employment relationship, as appropriate, unless they are inconsistent with the principles of labour law (Article 300LC). The fundamental principles of labour law are indicated in Article 18^3 LC. The labour law principles within the meaning of Article 300 LC, however, are not those expressly indicated in the provisions mentioned there, but rather more general rules, as derived by courts of law and legal scholars from the norms of labour law. It follows from the above that the LC is only applicable to the employment relationship and only on condition that a specific case is not regulated by labour law provisions and that relevant Civil Code Articles are not inconsistent with those of labour law.

---

46. Consolidated text: *Journal of Laws* of 2018, item 1270, as amended.

It is under the above conditions that the general provisions of the Civil Code on legal transactions are, in particular, applicable, including the form of such transactions, the effects of declarations of will and their interpretation, defects in the declarations, conditions, time limits, representation, as well as provisions concerning the performance of obligations and the effects of their non-fulfilment, liability for damages etc.

In practice, in judicial rulings it is also considered admissible to apply, as appropriate, Civil Code provisions not only to employment relationships but also to other labour law relations arising from obligations strictly related to employment relations, such as preliminary employment contracts, non-competition agreements and others. Under the rule of the appropriate (and not direct) application of Civil Code provisions the judiciary also refer to the liability arising from torts related to the employment relations.[47]

47. Cf., e.g., resolution of seven judges of the Supreme Court of 30 May 1975, V PZP 3/75; the Supreme Court judgment of 11 Jun. 2003, I PK 273/02.

Chapter 4. Role of Government Institutions in the Shaping and Administration of Labour and Industrial Relations Policy

L. Mitrus

§1. Degree of Government Intervention

49. According to Article 20 of the 1997 Constitution, a social market economy based on the freedom of economic activity, private ownership, solidarity, dialogue and cooperation between social partners shall be the basis of the economic system of the Republic of Poland. Thus, the Constitution refers to the concept of 'social market economy', which constitutes the background of the economic and social system of Poland and which means the need to conduct an active social policy by state institutions. This policy includes, among other things, labour problems and industrial relations. Therefore, reducing the role of the state to the role of a 'night watchman' as proposed in the liberal doctrine and leaving social issues exclusively to the market mechanism is not acceptable. At the same time, constitutional regulations do not declare a welfare state. The social market economy assumes that free market mechanisms should be adjusted by the actions of state institutions.[48]

50. In the communist era, the state organized, basically, the whole of the social life. The centrally planned economy, by its nature, assumed a far-reaching interference in the labour market and employment relations. There were no social partners or a dialogue between them within the meaning of the standards of the International Labour Organization.[49] The role of state institutions gradually changed in the transformation period after 1989. Structural changes were taking place in the economy, privatization processes were reducing the public sector while the private sector and small and medium enterprises flourished.

51. The questions of giving a new shape to industrial relations and of the role of state institutions in this process appeared. The state was the actor that initiated the changes by enacting the relevant legal regulations. At the same time, state institutions acted as a party to the tripartite dialogue that was gradually developing. The institutionalization of that dialogue was based on the Act of 6 July 2001 on the Tripartite Commission for Social and Economic Affairs and the Provincial Commissions for Social Dialogue.[50] According to this Act the government party had a stronger position than trade unions and employees' organizations. The functioning of social dialogue can undergo changes on the basis of the Act of 24 July 2015 on the Social Dialogue Council and Other Institutions of Social Dialogue,[51] which took

48. M. Skąpski, *Funkcja ochronna prawa pracy w gospodarce rynkowej* (Kraków, Zakamycze, 2006), pp. 19 et seq.
49. Cf. Introduction, Chapter 2, §2.
50. *Journal of Laws* (2001), No. 100, item 1080 as later amended.
51. *Journal of Laws* (2015), item 1240.

effect on 11 September 2015. The goal of this Act was the reactivation of the trilateral dialogue at the national level and, also, the promotion of the dialogue at the regional level. In practice, the execution of these goals is dependent upon the will and cooperation of the bodies involved. The chairmanship of the Social Dialogue Council will be held on a rotation basis by the government party, the unions' party and the employees' party. The activities of the government party are coordinated by the minister competent for labour issues. The Social Dialogue Council enjoys a broad scope of authority, *inter alia,* on wages policy issues. It also has consulting rights in the legislative process.

52. Polish labour law is, first of all, a statutory law, while collective agreements play a secondary role in practice.[52] From this perspective, of great importance is the role of the state, which is the actor which establishes the laws determining the minimum standards of employee rights and, also, the legal framework of the social dialogue and industrial relations. The detailed character of the statutory regulations naturally limits the scope of negotiations between employers and unions. The role of the state in the domains of labour law and industrial relations is, therefore, vital and diverse. First, the state acts as the legislator establishing labour law regulations. Second, it is a participant in the tripartite dialogue with the social partners. Third, state institutions act as an employer in the public sector. The significant participation of the state in the economy is one of important factors shaping industrial relations in Poland.

§2. Incomes Policy

53. In Poland there is a minimum monthly wage applicable to all sectors of the economy. It is the subject of the Act of 10 October 2002 on the minimum wage.[53] According to Article 2 of the Act, the minimum wage is fixed every year by the social partners acting within the Social Dialogue Council (formerly: the Tripartite Commission for Social and Economic Affairs). If the government party, employers' organizations and trade unions fail to jointly fix the amount of the minimum wage for the next year, then the Council of Ministers will fix the amount by order, not later than 15 September. The amount of the minimum wage has been fixed in this way in recent years. The Ordinance of the Council of Ministers of 12 September 2017 on the Amount of the Minimum Remuneration for Work in 2018[54] determines its amount at PLN 2,100 per month (about EUR 510). These issues are presently the subject of a public debate and, in particular, the trade unions are calling for changes in the legal regulation of the minimum wage. There are plans to tie the minimum wage to the average wage in the national economy and, also, to introduce a minimum hourly rate instead of a fixed remuneration per month. Since January 2017 the minimum wage is applicable not only to employees within the meaning of

52. *See* Introduction, Chapter 5.
53. Consolidated text: *Journal of Laws* 2017, 847.
54. *Journal of Laws* 2017, item 1747.

the LC but also to certain categories of civil law contractors. The minimum wage of this category of persons is calculated on an hourly basis. In 2018 it amounts to PLN 1,370 (about EUR 3).

54. The Social Dialogue Council mentioned in the previous paragraph has, among other things, the authority to mould wages and social benefits (for more on this *see* Part II, Chapter 1, §3, II, A).

§3. Competences of Ministries in Labour and Industrial Relations Policy

55. In the field of labour law and industrial relations, the competent government institution at the central level is the Ministry of Family, Labour and Social Policy. The powers of individual ministries are specified by the Act of 4 September 1997 on the Government Administration Departments.[55] This determines the responsibilities of the government administration departments and the competence of the minister in charge of the given department (Article 1). The Minister of Family, Labour and Social Policy is a member of the Council of Ministers (the government). His competence includes three thematic areas. The department of 'Labour' is responsible for issues concerning employment, counteracting unemployment, labour relations and work conditions, wages and employee benefits, collective labour relations and collective disputes, as well as trade unions and employers' organizations (Article 21 of the Act). Moreover, the competence of the ministry includes the departments of 'Family' (Article 28a of the Act) and 'Social Security' which concerns, among other things, the coordination of national social security systems within the EU (Article 31 of the Act). The Ordinance of the Prime Minister of 13 December 2017 on the detailed scope of application of the activities of the Minister of Family, Labour and Social Policy[56] determines the competences of the Minister under discussion.

56. The Minister of Family, Labour and Social Policy does not enjoy the right of legislative initiative. This is the right of the Members of Parliament, the Senate, the President of the Republic and the Council of Ministers, and also of a group of at least 100,000 citizens having the right to vote in parliamentary elections (Article 118 of the Constitution). Both the government and the MPs may, thus, initiate a legislative process concerning labour law, and such actions can be inspired by the proposals from trade unions or employers' organizations or by a common position of the social partners. The Minister of Family, Labour and Social Policy has the right to issue secondary legislation to the LC or other Acts if a specific regulation grants him such power. For example, the minister responsible for labour issues issued an ordinance concerning the certificate of employment, the detailed principles of

55. Consolidated text *Journal of Laws* 2017, item 888.
56. *Journal of Laws* 2017, item 2329.

granting the annual leave and determining the wage for this period, the situation of junior workers, health and safety at work or the keeping of employee records. This is also of great practical significance for the functioning of enterprises and for employee issues. Furthermore, the tasks of the minister competent for labour issues can result from other regulations, e.g., Article 241^{11} §1 LC obliges the minister to keep the register of multi-plant collective agreements, whereas Article 11 of the Collective Disputes Resolution Act of 23 May 1991 concerns the obligation to prepare the list of mediators in agreement with the social partners.

§4. SLI

57. Article 24 of the Constitution provides that work shall be protected by the Republic of Poland. The state shall exercise supervision over the conditions of work. The Act of 13 April 2007 on the SLI,[57] provides a legal framework for labour inspection activities. The SLI is an authority set up in order to execute supervision and inspection of the observance of labour law provisions. It is subordinated to the Sejm (the lower chamber of Parliament). The supervision of the inspection is executed by the Labour Protection Council. The Chief Labour Inspectorate and District Labour Inspectorates constitute organizational units of the SLI. The supervision covers all employers and – with regard to health and safety and legality of employment – also entrepreneurs who are not employers but for whom natural persons carry out work, including self-employed persons, irrespective of the legal basis of performing such work.

58. The SLI enjoys a broad range of competences. The Inspection should ensure the supervision and inspection of the observance of labour law provisions, especially with regard to the regulations and rules on health and safety at work, the provisions on employment relationship, remuneration for work and other benefits connected to an employment relationship, working time, employee leaves, the rights connected to parenthood, employment of juvenile employees and disabled persons. The Inspection also exercises control over the legality of employment and other paid activities, as well as work performance by foreigners. Within the scope of competence of the SLI falls also pursuing infringements of employee rights and infringements connected with carrying out paid labour. In case of identifying an infringement a labour inspector can – depending on the case – issue a mandate or lodge a motion, with a competent court, to penalize the persons responsible for the identified irregularities. The labour inspector is also entitled to initiate legal action in cases relating to the establishment of the existence of an employment relationship. Within the duties of the SLI falls also submitting to the relevant authorities information on identified infringements of provisions concerning social security, tax law, employment of foreigners, running a temporary agency work and infringement provisions on promotion of employment and countervailing unemployment by

57. Consolidated text *Journal of Laws* 2017, item 786.

unemployed persons or an inspected entity. Moreover, the SLI should cooperate with the authorities of EU Member States responsible for supervision of working and employment conditions. It should also provide information on minimum employment conditions in the framework of posting of workers.[58]

58. D. Makowski, Inspekcja pracy jako instytucja państwowego nadzoru nad przestrzeganiem prawa pracy (Labour Inspectorate as an Institution of State Supervision over Observance of Labour Law), Wydawnictwo Uniwersytetu Łódzkiego, Łódź 2017, pp. 93 et seq.).

Chapter 5. Sources of Labour Law

§1. Introductory Remarks

59. Sources of law are legal Acts containing law provisions. They can be divided into those internal, coming from domestic public bodies and agencies, and the external ones, i.e., the provisions of the EU and international law. The order of their application, the rules of precedence and hierarchy of norms in particular, follow from the Constitution, international agreements and the LC.

60. Labour law provisions are contained, first of all, in legal Acts referred to, in the Constitution of Poland, as the sources of universally binding law, i.e., in the Constitution itself, statutes, ratified international agreements and regulations. In addition, labour law is composed of sources referred to as autonomous or specific. They are legal provisions created autonomously by social partners or exceptionally by the employer alone.

§2. The Constitution

I. The Role of the Constitution as a Source of Labour Law

61. The Constitution is the supreme law of the Republic of Poland (Article 8 part 1 of the Constitution). It also proclaims itself as the Basic Law for the state. The importance of the Constitution as a source of labour law results from two main facts. First, it establishes the fundamental principles of the political and socio-economic system of Poland as well as the guarantees of protection of basic rights essential for employment relations. These include, *inter alia*, the rules of a democratic state ruled by law, social justice, equal treatment and prohibition of discrimination, the social market economy, solidarity, dialogue and cooperation between social partners, freedom of economic activity, protection of private property, protection of personal freedom and dignity of the human being, privacy protection rules, etc. Included by the Constitution in the fundamental principles of the political and socio-economic system is also the principle of protection of labour by the Republic of Poland. A guarantee of the rule lies in the state supervision over the conditions of work and freedom of the creation and functioning of trade unions, socio-occupational organizations of farmers, societies, citizen movements, other voluntary associations and foundations.

62. Second, established by the Constitution are detailed guarantees and rights concerning employment relations. As far as individual rights are concerned, these include, in particular, the freedom to choose and to pursue any occupation and to choose one's place of work, a prohibition on employing children below 16 years of age, a minimum level of remuneration for work, safe and hygienic conditions of work, statutorily specified days free from work as well as annual paid holidays.

Apart from that, public authorities should pursue policies aiming at full, productive employment by implementing programmes to combat unemployment, including the organization of and support for occupational advice and training, as well as public works and economic intervention. As far as collective employment relations are concerned, the Constitution provides for freedom of association in trade unions and in employers' organizations, the right to collective bargaining and the right to organize workers' strikes or other forms of protest.

63. As a rule, provisions of the Constitution are directly applicable. It is, however, a rare case that a constitutional provision alone is quoted as the basis for a ruling, as the ordinary statutes providing for human rights in the labour law sphere do so in a manner much more detailed than the Constitution does. Besides, the principle of direct application of constitutional norms is not unlimited. According to Article 8(2): 'The provisions of the Constitution shall apply directly unless the Constitution provides otherwise.' For instance, Article 81 specifies a number of rights, such as the right to a minimum level of remuneration for work, to occupational advice and training, safe and hygienic conditions of work, aid to disabled persons and some others, which can be invoked only within the limits set by statutes. These rights may not, therefore, be applied directly.

II. The Constitution and Fundamental Rights

A. The Constitution as a Source of Fundamental Rights

64. The Constitution adopts the term 'freedoms and rights of persons and citizens' (Chapter II), to be understood as freedoms and rights, the source of which is constituted by 'the inherent and inalienable dignity of the person' (Article 30). The freedoms and rights have been described in scholarly writing as the rights ensuring the protection of values of particular importance for an individual as well as for the functioning of the society. They are distinguished from other rights in that they are guaranteed by the Constitution and protect the individual, mainly against the organs of public authority; they also protect values of particular importance for an individual. In the discussion about human rights, the rights and freedoms mentioned above may be treated as the equivalent of the notion of fundamental rights.

65. The Constitution makes a distinction between the freedoms and rights of the person. Most generally, whereas a 'freedom' obliges the public authorities to restrain themselves from any action that would impede or make the enjoyment of that freedom impossible, a 'right' imposes on the authorities a duty to take actions to ensure the execution of that right.

66. The rights provided for by the Constitution are called the 'constitutional rights'. Besides, the whole of the law within the constitutional meaning, i.e., the statutes, ratified international agreements, regulations and local law may be the source of fundamental rights as well. However, extra-constitutional fundamental rights *sensu stricto*, i.e., human rights regulated only by ordinary statutes (such as, for instance, the prohibition of multiple punishments for the same offence), or by a statute and an international treaty at the same time, such as the right of the worker to fair remuneration, foreseen in the LC and, among others, in the International Covenant of Economic, Social and Cultural Rights of 1966, are rare. The constitutional regulation of fundamental rights is, as a rule, supplemented by the more detailed provisions of the statutes. It should be stressed that almost all constitutional rights have been complemented by statutory law. The consequence is, as the Constitutional Tribunal has observed, that the Constitution is usually applied together with the statutes.[59]

B. The Principle of Proportionality

67. According to Article 31(3) of the Constitution: 'Any limitation upon the exercise of constitutional freedoms and rights may be imposed only by statute, and only when necessary in a democratic state for the protection of its security or public order, or to protect the natural environment, health or public morals, or the freedoms and rights of other persons. Such limitations shall not violate the essence of freedoms and rights.'

68. The above-quoted provision expresses the principle of proportionality of the state interference in the sphere of rights and freedoms of the individual. This principle is a guarantee that constitutional human rights cannot be undermined by legislative regulation. However, some of the fundamental rights, mainly social ones, are not subject to this rule. Referring to the majority of the rights, the Constitution lays down a rule that the scope and forms of their implementation shall be specified by a statute. Therefore, the legislator is free to determine the scope of the right if the latter's essence is preserved, the circumstance being subject to the Constitutional Tribunal control. Within the above-mentioned category of rights there fall, among others: the right to a minimum level of remuneration for work, the right to work not more than the set maximum permissible number hours of work, the right to safe and hygienic conditions of work, the right to days off as well as annual paid holidays, the right to social security, etc.

§3. Ordinary Legislation

69. The main source of Poland's labour statutory law is the LC – an Act of Parliament adopted in 1974, though amended many times over the decades that passed. The importance of the LC within the system of labour law sources lies primarily in the fact that the Act provides comprehensively for the labour relation, a concept being the centre of the discussed branch of law. In addition, the Code institutes the

---

59. Decision of the Constitutional Tribunal of 22 Mar. 2000, p. 12/98; *see* more in: Z. Hajn and M. Seweryński, 'Fundamental Human Rights in Polish Labour Law', in Ryland (general ed.), *An Era of Human Rights, International Legal Essays in Honour of Jo Carby-Hall* (Patrington, Barmarick Publications, 2006), pp. 311–339.

rights and duties of all employees and employers, save for the duties and obligations detailed in specific provisions (Articles 1 and 5). The Code also provides for the fundamental labour law principles (Articles 10–18[3]), determines the rules for creation and operation of specific sources of labour law, sets up the method for the extension of labour law provisions onto other contracts for performance of services (Article 303) while also determining the conditions for the application of the provisions of the Civil Code to employment relations (Article 300).

70. As mentioned above, the LC is hardly a complete piece of legislation, either in terms of its scope *ratione personae* or the matters it covers. The Code is the main source of regulations concerning employment relations in the private sector of the economy (where an overwhelming majority of the employees work now). To certain groups of employees specific laws are applicable, though, the groups including, *inter alia*, judges and public prosecutors, public servants (employed in governmental agencies of various levels), public school teachers, personnel of the public healthcare system, sailors and miners. The extent to which their employee status differs from that established by the LC is not the same. The farthest-reaching peculiarities concern public servants.

71. As regards matters covered by the LC, these include, first of all, the contract-based employment relationship (establishment and termination of the relation, rights and duties of parties to the contract of employment and types of the liability they are subject to). Besides, the Code provides for certain issues of labour dispute resolution settlement. As opposed to the Code, matters covered by specific pieces of legislation include, *inter alia*, collective redundancies, the protection of employees in the event of the insolvency of their employer, the employment of temporary workers, minimum remuneration for work, labour inspection, the promotion of employment and the institutions of the labour market. The LC does not provide, either, for collective labour relations (save for CLAs). The issues are addressed by separate laws, on trade unions, employers' organizations, the settlement of collective disputes, works' councils, European works councils and other matters. As regards labour law court disputes, the Code of Civil Law Proceedings is fundamental in that respect.

72. As mentioned above, the LC does not provide for matters where, considering the nature of the employment relationship as an obligation, it is sufficient to refer to the appropriate application of the Civil Code rules, due to the fact the Civil Code is a subsidiary source of labour law.

§4. Autonomous Sources of Labour Law

I. General Remarks

73. The autonomous sources of labour law, frequently referred to also as specific labour law sources, include CLAs and other collective agreements, workplace regulations and statutes of employers. According to the LC, stipulations of legal acts of those type constitute labour law to the extent to which they determine the rights and obligations of the parties to an employment relationship and are based on the statute (Article 9 §1 LC). Incorporation of the provision into the LC, made by an Act of 26 February 1996 on Amendments to the LC, resolved a long-standing dispute on the legal nature of the Acts, leading to the recognition of their normative character, as stressed, in particular, by the adherents to the concept of a so-called 'local labour law'.[60] This means that not all stipulations of the above-indicated Acts are labour law provisions but only those that set forth the rights and duties of the parties to the employment relation.

74. The autonomous labour law sources are not the 'sources of universally binding law' within the meaning given to the term by the Constitution. Nevertheless, the impact they exert is similar to that of legal Acts enacted by the state authorities. In particular, they shape the content of employment relations automatically and directly just as the articles of a piece of legislation do. Their violation may directly constitute the cause for an action or a cassation appeal as if it were a violation of a substantive universally binding law.[61] The *ignorantia iuris nocet* rule is, however, not applicable to them. Consequently, an employee should not bear the consequences of his/her ignorance of a CLA or workplace regulations if the employer did not make it possible to the person in question to get himself/herself familiar with their content. Similarly, a judge is not expected to be acquainted, ex officio, with the content of the Act, on the *iura novit curia* principle.[62]

75. The specificity of the autonomous labour law provisions consists also in the fact that they can be suspended, in whole or in part, where the employer is facing financial difficulties. In practice, this concerns CLAs and pay rules. The suspension may not last longer than three years. A CLA may be suspended by means of an agreement concluded by the employer with the trade union organization being a

60. *See*, J. Jończyk (ed.), *Lokalne prawo pracy* (Wrocław, Wydawnictwo Uniwersytetu Wrocławskiego, 1976), passim.
61. The Supreme Court sentence of 29 May 1998, I PKN 138/98; the Constitutional Tribunal sentence of 10 Jun. 2003, SK 37/02.
62. In the grounds of its judgment of 5 May 2009 I PK 6/2009 the Supreme Court stated that: 'Crucial for the recognition of a certain agreement (or other act) as one containing provisions of labour law within the meaning of Article 9 § 1 of the Labour Code is whether the act meets the criteria indicated in the said provision, i.e. whether it is based on the statute and determines the rights and responsibilities of parties to the employment relation. It is that very assessment that allows to determine if the act from which the party derives its claims is one of normative nature (contains labour law provisions constituting the substantive law) or is just an act of contractual character (determining mutual obligations of parties thereto); in other words – if the claims of the party are based on substantive law. The assessment can only be made by court of law. And the court is, in fact, obliged to make it, since it is on the assessment that a legal qualification is provided, regarding the legal relation or right being the subject matter of the dispute; it is also on the assessment that the legal basis for the settlement is ascertained. Considering, however, the characteristics of the acts in question, the fact that they are not published in particular, as a result of which the fact of their existence is often only known to the parties who made them (possibly also to the entity having made the regulations), the judge is not obliged, ex officio, to know the content of the acts on the *iura novit curia* principle.'

party to the CLA.[63] Suspension of the pay rules is achieved through an agreement between the employer and the company trade union organization or, absent such an organization, with a representation of the employees appointed in the mode adopted at a specific work establishment. The text of the agreement on the suspension of provisions other than a CLA is submitted by the employer to the relevant labour inspector (Article 9^1 LC).

II. CLAs and Other Collective Agreements

A. *CLAs*

76. According to Article 9 §1 LC a collective agreement is a source of law only in its normative part containing the provisions which shape the content of contracts of employment. Such provisions concern remuneration for work, working hours, holidays and work leave, health and safety at work, job security and other things. As opposed to them, provisions defining the obligations of parties to the agreement have no such character. Provisions constituting what is termed as the 'third part of a collective labour agreement', in which the parties can regulate other matters, are not reckoned towards the provisions of labour law, either. In practice, the part contains obligations of the employer towards the staff of an establishment in social matters. An agreement, or, strictly speaking, its normative part, comes into force upon its entry into the register (for more *see* Part II, Chapter 3, §2).

B. *Other Collective Agreements*

77. Collective accords, other than CLAs, are also negotiated and concluded. They are sources of labour law, provided that they are based on a statute and regulate the rights and duties of the parties to the employment relationship. These accords are called 'nominate normative collective agreements'. They include, *inter alia*, agreements related to the CLAs, like agreements on the implementation of a CLA to other parties, agreements on rules for collective redundancies, agreements concerning employees' rights in the event of a transfer of the undertaking, crisis-driven agreements etc. (*see* Part II Chapter 3, §3).

78. Collective agreements not based on a statue are defined as 'innominate collective agreements'. These are not sources of law but merely sources of obligations for the parties to them.[64] The attempts to qualify particular collective accords, like the agreements ending a collective dispute or numerous agreements connected with privatization or restructuring of enterprises (so-called social agreements) to one of the groups is controversial. In general, courts tend to qualify the agreements into the category of nominate ones. Such an attitude prompts the replacement of CLAs

63. Article 241(27) LC. In its judgment of 24 Oct. 2006, SK 41/05, the Constitutional Tribunal stated that Art. $241(27)^7$ §3 LC conformed to the Constitution.
64. For example, a judgment of the Supreme Court of 2000, I PKN 541/99.

with the – less formalized – other accords which, however, do not provide the employees with the same guarantees as CLAs.

C. The Role of General Agreements

79. General agreements are a special type of collective accords concluded by the most representative social partners on socio-economic (sometimes also political) issues of key importance for the country. In its judgment of 6 May 1997 (U 2/96) the Constitutional Tribunal described one of the agreements, a so-called Pact on State-Owned Enterprise, as a political agreement with indirect legal effects. A similar opinion on the nature of general agreements prevails in scholarly writing.[65] In Poland, the agreements are usually concluded with the participation of the government, more seldom between the social partners alone. A characteristic feature of the accords is the obligation of the state (government) to take up specific actions, most frequently to make amendments to the existing law or to enact new provisions. Amendments to the law in force are also the main objective of general bilateral (autonomous) accords in which the parties focus on the development of a joint position towards the government.

80. Poland's first general agreements were the historical accords signed in Szczecin, Gdańsk and Jastrzębie in 1980, which sanctioned the emergence of the free trade union movement. They were bilateral, trade union–government accords. As opposed to them, the Pact on State-Owned Enterprise in the Process of Transformation of 22 February 1993 was tripartite in nature. The Pact outlined the assumptions for the legal Acts that provided the basis for the transition of Poland's economy from a centrally planned to a market system. In particular, the Pact dealt with the process and instruments of privatization, financial restructuring of companies and banks and social issues. The accord in question authorized the enactment of specific pieces of legislation concerning the financial restructuring of business entities and banks, protection of employee claims in case of the employer's insolvency, company welfare fund, amendments to the LC regarding CLAs and issues of occupational safety and health. The Pact also called into being the Tri-partite Committee for Social and Economic Issues, to which body the supervision over its implementation was entrusted. Further on, other general agreements initiating changes to the existing law were concluded, an example being the tripartite Pact on Social Guarantees for Citizens of 14 July 1995, by way of which instrument directions and most essential means of implementation of state social policy were agreed on, regarding housing assistance, combating unemployment, the organization and financing of scientific research, family benefits and social assistance pensions, guaranteed minimum income, social security and acquisition of entitlements to benefits under the scheme, healthcare system reform, etc. The Pact on Anti-Crisis Measures of 13 March 2009 was a bilateral agreement signed by the organizations of employees and employers represented in the Social Dialogue Council. The accord was an

65. *See*, for instance, L. Garlicki, 'Refleksje nad charakterem Porozumienia Gdańskiego', *Państwo i Prawo*, vol. 1 (1981), 3.

autonomous agreement, yet the partners assumed in it their expectations about the legislative initiatives that it would be accepted by the government, following the arrangements made in the Pact.

III. Internal Workplace Regulations

81. Terms of remuneration and other terms and conditions of work may also be decided in internal workplace regulations. The most important are work rules and pay regulations. The pay regulations determine the terms of remuneration for work and other work-related benefits (Article 77^2 LC). The workplace regulations define the organization and order of the process of work and the related rights and duties of an employer and of employees (Articles 104–104^3 LC). These regulations are obligatory at workplaces with at least fifty employees unless a collective agreement comprises questions covering the subject matter of such acts. Yet, an employer who employs at least twenty and fewer than fifty employees has to introduce the regulations at the request of the trade union operating within the given establishment.

IV. Statutes of Employers

82. The statute, as an Act providing for the organization, tasks, scope and mode of operation of the entity being an employer, is a source of labour law only insofar as it contains stipulations concerning the content of employment relations of its personnel. In practice, it is the members of the governing bodies of the entity that are covered by the statute. Certain statutes, however, (the observation holding true as far as the statutes of higher education institutes and worker cooperatives are concerned in particular) provide for employee rights and responsibilities to a wider extent. This does not pertain to the statutes granted by Acts of universally binding law.[66]

§5. The Role of Court Decisions

83. The case law is not a source of law in Poland. However, judgments of common courts (the judgments of the Supreme Court in particular) play a crucial role in the interpretation of labour law.

§6. The Role of Customs and Other Extralegal Norms

84. A custom, meaning a practice that is permanent and well established in a certain community, is not a source of law in Poland. Customs play an important role in employment relations, however. They determine, *inter alia*, the scope and mode

66. *See also* the Constitutional Tribunal sentence of 10 Jun. 2003, SK 37/02, in which the Tribunal stated that Art. 9 §1 LC, inasmuch as it concerns statutes of entities, conforms with the Constitution.

of performance of the obligations of the parties of employment relations, since the contract of employment procures not only the effects expressly indicated in it but also those that follow from the law, the rules of social coexistence and the established customs (Article 56 CC), and obligations of both employees and employers should be performed by them in accordance with, among others, the established customs (Article 354 CC). Also the LC makes references to company (work establishment) customs (practices) (e.g., Articles 9^1 §2, 29 §3, 77^2 §6, 94^1, 94^2, 163 §2, 237^{13a}). For those very reasons it should be assumed that, as the Supreme Court has put it, the scope of employee responsibilities is determined by rules of law, stipulations of the contract of employment and – as regards the specific shape of the duties – the customs adopted at the work establishment.[67]

85. An essential role in the application of the individual labour law provisions is also played by the so-called rules of social coexistence and the rules of social and economic objectives of law. They are general clauses setting the limits for the execution of rights. The former makes reference to moral standards adopted in the society, the latter to the purpose which the law intends to serve. An action violating the principles in question is considered to be a violation of law. As such, it is not considered as an exercise of rights, nor does it enjoy protection. In practice, it is the rules of social coexistence that are of special importance. According to the judiciary, the assessment of an employee's or employer's behaviour for compliance with the rules depends on the circumstances of a specific case, and the court of law should indicate a specific rule (moral standard) to which it refers.

§7. The Character of Labour Law Norms

86. Unlike in civil law where the relatively binding norms (*ius dispositivum*) prevail, an overwhelming majority of labour law norms providing for employee rights and responsibilities stemming from employment relationships are partly imperative norms. Parties to the employment relationship may deviate from such norms only in favour of the employee. Any deviations to the detriment of the employee are void by virtue of law and are replaced by respective legal provisions (Article 18 §§1 and 2 LC). As a result, minimum standards of employee interests are set out in labour law, and these interests must not be prejudiced in the contract of employment. In this way the employee is protected against pressure from the

67. The Supreme Court sentence of 23 Oct. 2003, I PK 425/02. In another of its sentences the Supreme Court stated that 'as a rule, no significant degree of fault (Article 52 § 1 item 1 LC) can be attributed to the employee that violates provisions of work rules on the leaving of the work-stand during working hours and the granting of the holiday leave, if the employee's behaviour conforms with the custom accepted by the employer' (judgement of 26 Jun. 1998, I PKN 211/98). In the sentence of 27 Apr. 2007 (I PZP 18/97) the Supreme Court observed that if – at a specific work establishment – it was customary for the employer to take care for the employee's clothing, failure to meet the duty was a violation of an obligation following from the contract of employment. *See also* K. Jaśkowski, 'Funkcje zwyczaju w prawie pracy', in *Gdańskie Studia Prawnicze*, *supra*., pp. 127 et seq.

employer as the more powerful party to the employment relationship. This particular feature of labour law is referred to as the 'principle of employee's privilege'.[68] It is applicable, however, only to the rights and duties under the employment relation.[69] The appraisal that a specific stipulation of the contract of employment is more favourable to the employee has to be unbiased and should be based on the findings made *ex ante*, i.e., not at the termination of the employment relationship but before it has been concluded.[70] Deviations from the principle of employee's privilege are allowed by law exceptionally. For instance, Article 151 §4 LC allows, at work establishments not covered by a CLA or workplace regulations, the raising of the annual limit of overtime over by 150 hours by means of a contract of employment.[71]

§8. Relationships Between Different Sources of National Labour Law

87. The point of departure for determining the hierarchy of labour law provisions is the observation that it is the Constitution that occupies the top position in the hierarchy. Situated below are, successively, Acts of Parliament and secondary legislation implementing the latter, multi-company CLAs and accords, company CLAs and accords, workplace regulations and employer statutes. In principle, provisions of the acts form a hierarchical whole in which the subordinate legislative provisions have to conform with higher-rank Acts.

88. This principle of hierarchy of the sources of law is, as far as labour law is concerned, modified by the principle of the most favourable provision. Expressed by the principle is a special feature of labour law which boils down to the establishment of special rules for resolution of the conflicts of labour law provisions situated at various levels of the legal act hierarchy. According to the principle, provisions of CLAs and other collective accords, workplace regulations and employer statutes may not be less favourable to employees than provisions of the Acts of Parliament and other universally binding provisions of law are (Article 9 §2 LC). Provisions of a multi-company CLA must not, in turn, be less favourable to employees than the provisions of the company CLA covering them, while workplace regulations and statutes may not contain provisions less favourable to the employees than the rules contained in CLAs and other collective accords (Article 241^{26} §1, Article 9 §3 LC). As a result, provisions of the autonomous labour law

68. *See* Z. Góral, 'Zasada uprzywilejowania pracownika', in Baran (ed.), *Zarys systemu prawa pracy. Tom I. Część ogólna prawa pracy* (Warsaw, Wolters Kluwer business, 2010), pp. 663 et seq.
69. Considering that, the Supreme Court ruled, for instance (in its sentence of 10 Sep. 2004, I PK 592/03), that Art. 18 §2 LC is not applicable to the non-competition agreement after termination of the employment relation, even though the agreement is concluded during the relation.
70. The Supreme Court resolution of 9 November, 1994 I PZP 46/94.
71. In its ruling of 24 Feb. 2004, K 54/02, the Constitutional Tribunal ascertained conformity of the provision with the Constitution. In the opinion of the Tribunal, the principle of employee's privilege is not a constitutional one, the legislator being entitled to provide for exclusions and deviations from it.

Acts which are more favourable to employees take precedence over the less favourable provisions of the Acts ranking above them. It should be stressed that the principle is applicable solely to the provisions concerning employee rights and responsibilities following from the employment relation. It does not apply to provisions not concerning the latter.

§9. International Law

89. Ratified international agreements after their promulgation in the *Journal of Laws* of the Republic of Poland (*Dziennik Ustaw*) are sources of universally binding law in Poland. The Constitution adopts the principle of direct application of such agreements. A ratified international agreement constitutes part of the domestic legal order and is applied directly, unless its application depends on the enactment of a statute. In case of a conflict with statutory law the treaty ratified with a prior consent expressed by a statute prevails over statutory law, though not over the Constitution (Article 87 in conjunction with Article 91 paragraphs 1 and 2 of the Constitution). The court, thus, may base its judgment directly on such a treaty. There are many examples of the direct application of international treaties by the courts.[72]

90. As far as non-ratified agreements are concerned, the general rule of the Constitution serving as guidance on the issue reads: 'The Republic of Poland shall respect international law binding upon it' (Article 9). Agreements like this are not sources of law. Nevertheless, the opinion held among the judiciary is that courts of law are obliged to interpret Polish law in a way securing, to the greatest extent possible, its conformity with the content of the non-ratified international agreement binding on Poland.[73]

91. International agreements, ILO conventions in particular, are of special importance for the collective labour law, which – in its very essence – deals with issues of fundamental human rights. In that respect the Constitution provides that 'The scope of freedom of association in trade unions and in employers' organizations may only be subject to such statutory limitations as are permissible in accordance with international agreements to which the Republic of Poland is a party' (Article 59 paragraph 4 of the Constitution). This means that statutory limitations of the trade union freedom conform with the international agreements concerning the freedoms only if they do not go beyond the scope of the admissible limitations of trade union freedoms in the international agreement allowing to impose the limitations to the smallest extent.

---

72. *See*, A. Wyrozumska, *Umowy międzynarodowe. Teoria i praktyka* (Warsaw, Wydawnictwo Prawo i Praktyka Gospodarcza, 2006), pp. 560 et seq.
73. *See*, e.g., the Supreme Court sentence of 29 Nov. 2005, II PK 100/05 concerning the salary of an employee working for a Polish employer in Germany, claimed under a non-ratified agreement between Poland and Germany.

92. In addition to the conventions, covenants and charters of international organizations ratified by Poland (ILO, United Nations and the Council of Europe in particular), sources of labour law also include bilateral agreements concerning mostly the employment of Polish citizens abroad and foreigners in Poland.

§10. EU Law

93. The existence of EU legal provisions concerning employment relations and their application in Poland does not give rise to any problems that would need a discussion (for a difference of the situation in other Member States, if any). The influence of the EU law on the development of Polish labour law since the beginning of the 1990s has already been discussed (*see* Introduction, Chapter 2 §3).

94. Some attention should be paid to the issue of the relationship between Poland's and EU labour law provisions. As regards the primary law, having the nature of international agreements, it is the rules governing the relation of Polish national law to the international agreements ratified by the consent expressed in a statute contained in Article 91 parts 1 and 2 of the Constitution that are applicable. Applicable to the secondary law is Article 91 part 3 of the Constitution, providing that: 'If an agreement, ratified by the Republic of Poland, establishing an international organization so provides, the laws established by it shall be applied directly and have precedence in the event of a conflict with statutes.' The provision does not, however, concern the relation between the EU law and the Constitution. In the opinion of the Constitutional Tribunal it is, thus, not possible to recognize the superiority of a Community legal norm over norms of the Constitution in case of a conflict between them.

95. It seems, however, that – given the essential concurrence between the fundamental rights and freedoms lying at the foundation of both the Constitution and the EU law in the broadly termed sphere of labour relations – emergence of the above-presented conflict of norms in the sphere is highly unlikely.

96. It should be emphasized, however, that due to the Protocol on the Application of the Charter of the Fundamental Rights of the EU to Poland and to the United Kingdom (UK), Poland is not bound by Chapter IV 'Solidarity' of the EU Charter of Fundamental Rights. Article 1(1) of the above-mentioned protocol provides that the Charter does not extend the ability of the Court of Justice of the European Union, or any court or tribunal of Poland or of the UK, to find that the laws, regulations or administrative provisions, practices or actions of Poland or of the UK are inconsistent with the fundamental rights, freedoms and principles that it reaffirms. Article 1(2) states that the Title IV of the Charter, which contains economic and social rights, does not create *justiciable* rights, unless Poland and the UK have provided for such rights in its national law. Thus, Poland used the opt-out clause as far as social rights enshrined in the EU Charter are concerned.[74]

74. *See*, e.g., C. Barnard, 'The 'Opt-Out' for the UK and Poland from the Charter of Fundamental Rights: Triumph of Rhetoric over Reality?', in Griller, Ziller (ed.), *The Lisbon Treaty. EU Constitutionalism without a Constitutional Treaty?* (Vienna, New York, Springer, 2008), pp. 262 et seq.

Chapter 6. Fundamental Principles of Labour Law

L. Mitrus

§1. General Remarks

97. In the Polish doctrine, the problem of labour law principles is of major importance. First, the provisions that were in force before the codification of labour law, as well as the LC enacted in 1974, allow applying the provisions of civil law to an employment relationship, provided that they are 'not contrary to the principles of labour law' (Article 300 LC). Thus, principles of labour law constitute a major factor that determines the admissibility of the Civil Code application to an individual employment relationship. Second, the LC contains Chapter II 'Fundamental principles of labour law' (Articles 10–18^{3a} LC). The principles expressly introduced in the above-mentioned relate both to individual and collective labour law. Moreover, they are further expanded in other statutory regulations (*see* below, §3). It is worth mentioning that the other codes, like, e.g., the Civil Code or the Penal Code, do not contain their own lists of major principles that would emphasize the specific features of particular branches of law.

98. It is commonly accepted that the list of labour law principles, as indicated in the LC, is not exhaustive. In fact, several further principles have been elaborated by the doctrine and judiciary. In this context we can mention the personal work performance by an employee, the stability of an employment contract concluded for an indefinite period or limited financial liability of an employee for damages caused to an employer. Thus, in the course of time, the principles of labour law have gained much more importance than just the original issue of civil law application to an employment relationship. Currently, they should be regarded as sui generis general meta-norms that determine the scope and the shape of labour law. In practice, particular labour law principles have different status. They can serve as guidelines for the legislator while enacting new regulations or constitute interpretative guidelines for the judiciary. At the same time, some of the principles of labour law can be directly enforceable. The latter situation relates, e.g., to employer's duty to respect personal rights of an employee or a prohibition of discrimination in employment.[75]

§2. Constitutional Principles

99. In Poland, labour law and social policy enjoy strong constitutional protection. The Constitution of the Republic of Poland of 2 April 1997 directly relates to several social issues. Article 20 introduces the notion of a 'social market economy' (*see* Introduction, Chapter 4 §1). Moreover, Article 24 provides that 'work shall be protected by the Republic of Poland'. Therefore, we can argue that not only

75. *See also* Z. Góral, Principles of Labour Law (in:), K.W. Baran (ed), Outline of Polish Labour Law System, Wolters Kluwer, Warszawa 2016, pp. 45 et seq.

'employees' in the meaning of the LC, but all 'workers' (civil law contractors included) enjoy the constitutional protection.[76] The Constitutional Tribunal in the recent judgment of 2 June 2015,[77] declared the unconstitutionality of those provisions of the Trade Unions Acts that confine the right to unionize only to employees in the meaning of Article 2 LC (with some minor exceptions) (*see also* §2 of Chapter 2, Part II).

100. There are further constitutional principles that relate directly to labour law. Article 59 concerns the freedom of association, the right to bargain as well as the right to organize strikes or others form of protest. Article 65 emphasizes the right to choose and pursue an occupation, statutory minimum remuneration and the duty of public authorities to carry out policies aiming at full, productive employment. Article 66 concerns safe and hygienic conditions of work and the right to days free form work and annual holidays.

§3. Principles of Individual Labour Law

I. Right to Choose an Occupation

101. Article 65 item 1 of the Constitution provides that everyone enjoys the freedom to choose and to pursue his/her occupation and to choose his/her place of work. Exceptions shall be specified by statute. According to Article 65 item 2 of the Constitution, an obligation to work can be imposed only by statute. Article 65 item 5 of the Constitution states that public authorities shall pursue policies aiming at full, productive employment by implementing programmes to combat unemployment, including the organization of and support for occupational advice and training as well as public works and economic interventions.[78] Polish law does not use *expressis verbis* the notion 'the right to work'.[79] By contrast, it focuses on the freedom to work and to choose an occupation. Certainly, the above-mentioned provisions do not constitute a ground for an enforceable claim to be employed. The state is obliged to carry out an active social policy in order to provide assistance for those seeking work.

102. The right under discussion is also subject to statutory regulations. Under Article 10 §1 LC, everyone has the right to freely chosen work. No one, except in situations stipulated by a statute, can be prevented from exercising their profession.

76. A. Sobczyk, *Prawo pracy w świetle Konstytucji RP. Tom I. Teoria publicznego i prywatnego indywidualnego prawa pracy* (Warsaw, C.H. Beck, 2013), pp. 37 et seq.
77. K 1/13, 80/6/A/2015.
78. In the recent literature for an extensive analysis of this matter, *see* A. Sobczyk, *Wolność pracy i władza* (Warsaw, Wolters Kluwer Business, 2015), pp. 151 et seq.
79. Z. Góral, *O kodeksowym katalogu zasad indywidualnego prawa pracy* (Warsaw, Wolters Kluwer Business, 2011), p. 64 et seq.; A. Krzywoń, Konstytucyjna ochrona pracy i praw pracowniczych (Constitutional protection of labour and employee rights, Wolters Kluwer, Warszawa 2017, pp. 337 et seq.

According to Article 10 §2 and §3 LC, the state determines the minimum remuneration for work and pursues a policy aimed at full productive employment. In addition, under Article 11 LC concluding an employment relationship and determining conditions of work and employment, regardless of the legal basis of this relationship, requires a unanimous statement of intent from both parties. Although it is not expressly regulated, in principle forced labour is prohibited.

103. Article 65 item 3 of the Constitution states that the permanent employment of children under 16 years of age shall be prohibited. The types and nature of admissible employments shall be specified by statute. Employment of young persons is subject to Section Nine of the LC (Articles 190–206). Minor employees (16–18 years of age) enjoy special status, *inter alia* they are obliged to undergo vocational training and other forms of education; they also enjoy particular protection with regard to health and safety. In addition, under Article 304^5 LC work or other paid job can be carried out by a child under the age of 16 only for an institution conducting a cultural, artistic, sporting or advertising activity. In such a case, prior consent of a representative or custodian of the child is required alongside the permission of relevant labour inspector. Any other child labour is prohibited. The above-mentioned regulations implement the Council Directive 94/33/EC of 22 June 1994 on the protection of young people at work.[80]

II. Respect for Employees' Dignity and Other Personal Rights

104. Under Article 11^1 LC, an employer is obliged to respect the dignity and other personal employee rights. Article 23 of the Civil Code indicates several personal rights, namely health, liberty, dignity, freedom of conscience, family name or pseudonym, image, privacy of correspondence, inviolability of home and scientific, artistic, inventive or rationalizing achievements. According to Article 24 CC, a person whose personal rights are endangered by the action of another may seek to redress such an action unless it is not unlawful. In the case of an infringement it is possible to require the wrongdoer to remove the results of the infringement, in particular, to make an appropriate declaration in an appropriate form. Where the infringement causes pecuniary loss, the injured person can demand compensation.

105. Thus, respect for employees' dignity is one of the employer's basic duties. For example, discrimination, harassment and mobbing would constitute a breach of the principle under discussion. An employer is also obliged to respect employee's privacy, which is particularly important due to technological development and the various methods of control exercised by an employer.[81] For example, in the opinion of the Supreme Court the employer can exercise his/her/their competences that stem from employee subordination, especially with regard to the control and supervision

80. *Official Journal* L 216, 20/08/1994 P. 0012 – 0020.

81. *See also*, M. Wujczyk, *Prawo pracownika do ochrony prywatności* (Warsaw, Wolters Kluwer Business, 2012), pp. 85 et seq.

of work performance by employees. However, while exercising his/her/their managerial competences, the employer should refrain from actions that might violate employee dignity.[82]

III. Equality of Employees and Prohibition of Discrimination

106. Under Article 11^2 LC, employees have equal rights in respect of the same performance of the same duties; this principle applies, in particular, to the equal treatment of men and women in employment. Article 11^3 LC provides that any discrimination in employment, direct or indirect, in particular in respect of gender, age, disability, race, religion, nationality, political views, trade union membership, ethnic origin, creed, sexual orientation or in respect of the conditions of employment for a definite or an indefinite period of time or full- or part-time, is prohibited. Further provisions are the subject of Chapter IIa LC 'Equal treatment in employment' – Articles 18^{3a} –18^{3e} (*see* Chapter 7 of the Introduction). According to Article 18 §3 LC the provisions of employment contracts and other acts on the basis of which an employment relationship is established and which violate the principle of equal treatment in employment are null and void. The relevant provisions of labour law shall apply instead. When there are no such provisions, the relevant provisions of a non-discriminatory character shall apply instead.

IV. Right to Fair Remuneration

107. Article 65 item 4 of the Constitution provides that a minimum remuneration for work or the manner of setting its level shall be specified by statute. The conditions for exercising this right are subject to provisions of labour law and state policy on remuneration, in particular by determining the minimum remuneration for work. The Act of 10 October 2002 establishes the minimum remuneration for work.[83]

108. Moreover, under Article 13 LC, an employee has the right to fair remuneration for work. There are no statutory criteria to determine the level of fair remuneration. Poland has not ratified Article 4 of the European Social Charter that relates to just remuneration. The provision under discussion applies to employees only; it does not cover civil law contractors. Article 13 LC does not constitute the ground for an enforceable claim to demand raise of salary, except for the situation of raising the salary to the amount of minimum remuneration. It is commonly accepted that 'minimum remuneration' and 'fair remuneration' are not interchangeable notions. In other words, minimum remuneration does not have to be regarded as fair remuneration.

---

82. The Supreme Court judgment of 22 Apr. 2015, II PK 166/14.
83. Consolidated text *Journal of Laws* 2018, item 373 introduces a statutory minimum wage in Poland. It is updated each year by the Council of Social Dialogue or the Government; *see* Introduction, Chapter 4, §2.

V. Right to Rest

109. According Article 66 item 2 of the Constitution, an employee shall have the right to statutorily specified days free from work as well as annual paid holidays; the maximum permissible hours of work shall be specified by statute. Thus, the state is obliged to enact statutory regulations that concern the above-mentioned issues. In addition, Article 14 LC states that an employee has the right to rest, guaranteed under provisions on working time, days free from work and holiday leave. Working time is subject to section 6 of the LC (Articles 128–151^{12}) and holiday leave is regulated by section 7 of the LC (Articles 152–173).[84] Certainly, the social partners enjoy competences to make collective arrangements on working time and additional holiday leave.

VI. Health and Safety at Work

110. Under Article 66 item 1 of the Constitution everyone shall have the right to safe and hygienic conditions of work. The methods of introducing this right and obligations of an employer should be specified by a statute. According to Article 15 LC, an employer is obliged to ensure healthy and safe working conditions for his/her/their employees. The specific provisions are provided by section 10 of the LC (Articles 207–237^{15}) and subordinate regulations. The duty refers not only to employees but also other persons carrying work (Article 304–304^{1}LC).

VII. Social and Welfare Employee Needs

111. Article 16 LC provides that an employer, according to existing circumstances and conditions, should satisfy welfare, social and cultural needs of employees. Thus, duties of an employer are not only limited to paying remuneration but also to carry out additional activities with the goal to satisfy, through the means available, certain employee needs. This provision does not constitute the ground for an enforceable claim. However, the Act of 4 March 1994 of companies' social benefits fund[85] provides the legal framework for a duty to create a social fund at the work establishment (*see* Part I, Chapter 3, point IX in §3).

VIII. Improvement of Employee Qualifications

112. According to Article 17 LC, an employer is obliged to help employees to improve their professional qualification. This provision does not constitute the basis of an enforceable claim. For example, an employee may not demand from his/her

---

84. *See* A. Bigaj, *Prawo do urlopu wypoczynkowego* (Warsaw, Wolters Kluwer Business, 2015), pp. 42 et seq.
85. Consolidated text *Journal of Laws* 2018, item 1316.

employer to organize a particular training. In addition, Articles 102–103[6] LC regulate professional qualifications of employees. The LC expressly introduces the possibility that an employee may acquire and implement knowledge and skills, subject to the employer's initiative or consent. The contract between parties can provide certain benefits for such employees, e.g., training leave or time free from work (*see* Chapter 3, §3 point VIII).

IX. Protection of Minimum Level of Employee Rights

113. In principle, an employee is a weaker party to an employment relationship. Therefore, labour law aims at protecting employee's rights. In Poland, this rule has been expressed in Article 18 LC. According to Article 18 §1 LC, provisions of employment contracts and other acts on the basis of which an employment relationship is established (i.e., an appointment, an election, a nomination or a cooperative employment contract) may not be less advantageous to an employee than the provisions of labour law. Under Article 18 §2 LC, any provisions of an employment contract or acts defined in §1 are null and void and the relevant provisions of labour law shall apply instead (*see* above Chapter 5, §7).

114. Article 18 LC does not constitute interpretative guidelines that any doubts should be resolved in favour of an employee. The basic idea of this principle is just to establish the minimum level of employee rights. Social partners or parties to an employment relationship are free to improve employee situation, e.g., by extending the scope of statutory rights or granting additional benefits. At the same time, it is not permitted to worsen employment conditions.[86] We can say that Article 18 LC introduces the very basic idea of labour law and should be regarded as the most important labour law principle. Very few provisions of labour law are mandatory and do not allow any deviations from statutory regulations (*see also* §7 in Chapter 5 of the Introduction).

§4. Principles of Collective Labour Law

I. Social Partners' Dialogue

115. Article 20 of the Constitution refers to the social market economy. The Supreme Law expressly provides that one of the basic pillars of this concept is the dialogue and cooperation of social partners. Currently, the tripartite dialogue is subject to the Act of 24 July 2015 on the Social Dialogue Council.[87] This body enjoys a broad range of competences with regard to labour law and social policy issues (*see* §3 of Part II, Chapter 1).

86. *See* L. Mitrus, 'The Relationship Between Statutory Law, Collective Agreement and Employment Contract. The Case of Poland', in György (ed.), *Recent Developments in Labour Law* (Budapest, Akadémiai Kiadó, 2013), pp. 63 et seq.
87. *Journal of Laws* (2015), item 1240.

II. Right of Association

116. Several principles of collective labour law enjoy constitutional status. The right of association is subject to Article 59 item 1 and Article 59 item 4 of the Constitution. Poland has ratified ILO Conventions No. 87 and No. 98 on freedom of association, as well as the European Conventions of Human Rights and the European Social Charter, which refer to the right to unionize. Moreover, in Poland the right under discussion has been emphasized in statutory law. Article 18(1) §1 LC provides that employees and employers, in order to represent and to protect their rights and interests, have the right to establish organizations and to join them. Article 18(1) §2 LC indicates that the principles of establishing and operating the above-mentioned organizations are set out in the relevant provisions of law. The most important legal instruments in this field are the Trade Unions Act of 23 May 1991[88] and the Employers' Organizations Act of 23 May 1991.[89]

III. Right to Bargain

117. According to Article 59 item 2 of the Constitution, trade unions and employers and their organizations shall have the right to bargain, particularly for the purposes of resolving collective labour disputes and to conclude CLAs and other arrangements. Negotiations are a part of the procedure of resolving collective labour disputes under the Act of 23 May 1991 on settlement of collective labour disputes (CDSA). In addition, section IX of the LC (Articles 238–241(30)) provides a legal framework to conclude CLAs. It should be emphasized that only trade unions have the right to conclude a CLA. Moreover, Polish law provides several possibilities to conclude other collective arrangements by ad hoc employee representation (*see* Chapter 3, Part II).

IV. Right to Organize Workers' Strikes or Other Forms of Protest

118. Under Article 59 item 3 of the Constitution, trade unions shall have the right to organize workers' strikes or other forms of protest, subject to limitations specified by statute. For the protection of public interest, statutes may limit or forbid the conduct of strikes by specified categories of employees or in specific fields. The statutory regulations are subject to the Act of 23 May 1991 on settlement of collective labour disputes.[90]

88. Consolidated text *Journal of Laws* (2015), item 1881.
89. Consolidated text *Journal of Laws* (2015), item 2029; for a detailed analysis *see* Part II, Chapter 2.
90. Consolidated text *Journal of Laws* 2018, item 399; *see also* Chapter 4, Part II.

V. Employee Participation

119. The principle of employee participation does not enjoy constitutional status. However, it has been expressly mentioned in the LC. According to Article 18(2) LC employees may participate in the management of an undertaking as far as and in accordance with the principles specified in separate provisions. In addition, under Article 18^3 LC employers and administrative authorities have the duty to provide conditions to exercise the rights determined in Article 18^1 LC (right to coalition) and Article 18^2 LC (employee participation). Polish regulations on employee participation, to a large extent, have been influenced by the EU law.[91]

91. *See*, e.g., L. Mitrus, 'Works Councils in Poland: Problems of Informing and Consulting Employees', in: Blanpain (ed.), Lyutov (guest ed.), *Bulletin of Comparative Labour Relations - 85. Workers' Representation in Central and Eastern Europe. Challenges and Opportunities for the Works Councils' System* (The Netherlands, Wolters Kluwer Law & Business, 2014), pp. 151 et seq.; for further analysis, *see* Chapter 5, Part II.

Chapter 7. Equal Treatment and Protection Against Discrimination in Employment

L. Mitrus

§1. Introductory Remarks

120. Within the Polish legal system, the principle of equal treatment is well anchored in the Constitution. The Basic Law sets up a general rule of equality before the law and a prohibition on all forms of discrimination in political, social or business life for any reason whatsoever (Article 32). It also establishes the principle of equal treatment of women and men (Article 33). The issues of equal treatment have been also recognized as one of the basic principles of labour law listed in the LC (*see* the Introduction, Chapter 6 §3). Article 11^2 LC provides that employees enjoy equal rights on account of meeting the same duties, the rule holding true, in particular, as far as equal treatment of women and men in employment is concerned. Meanwhile Article 11^3 LC states that any discrimination in employment, whether direct or indirect, particularly in respect of sex, age, disability, race, religion, nationality, political views, trade union membership, ethnic origin, creed, sexual orientation, employment for a definite or indefinite period, full- or part-time employment, shall be unacceptable. In addition, Chapter IIa 'Equal treatment in employment' (Articles 18^{3a}–18^{3e} LC) provides, in detail, for the issues of prohibition of discrimination in employment relationships. More attention has been devoted by Polish legislators to equal treatment in employment than any other labour law principle.[92]

121. Of particular importance to the current shape of legal regulations concerning equal treatment in employment are the amendments to the LC of 14 November 2003.[93] In connection with Poland's accession into the EU, a number of EU directives were transposed into the country's national law, Chapter IIa 'Equal treatment in employment' having been considerably changed at that occasion. The provisions in question were also amended by the Act of 21 November 2008.[94] It should be stressed that Polish regulations concerning the prohibition of discrimination in employment have been, to an essential extent, influenced by the EU law, the LC accomplishing the principles of Directives 2000/43, 2000/78 and 2006/54. The issues of equal treatment in employment are one of those spheres of Polish labour law which have undergone the farthest-reaching transformation in order to be the aligned with the EU law standards. The matters are the object of a considerable body of judicial decisions, the Polish courts of law following the pro-EU interpretation of national legislation.

92. *See also* M. Kuba, *Zakaz dyskryminacji w zatrudnieniu pracowniczym*, (Prohibition of Discrimination in Employment) Wolters Kluwer, Warszawa 2017, pp. 48 et seq.
93. *Journal of Laws* (2003), No. 213, item 2081.
94. *Journal of Laws* (2008), No. 223, item 1460.

122. The LC regulations on equal treatment concern matters of employment relations. The concept of equal treatment goes, however, well beyond the narrowly termed employment as it pertains also to other forms of gainful activity. The Act of 3 December 2010 on the Implementation of Certain EU Regulations on Equal Treatment[95] should be mentioned at that occasion. It deals with the areas and ways of responding to the breaches of the rule of equal treatment based on race, ethnic origin, nationality, religion, beliefs, disability, age or sexual orientation, providing also for the authorities competent in that respect. It is also applicable to, *inter alia*, vocational training and retraining, as well as to the conditions of the establishment and maintenance of business or professional activity, to work done in the employment relationship and that performed under civil law contracts as well. In addition, the Act pertains to membership of and activity in trade unions, employers' organizations and professional associations. The rule of equal treatment is also directly expressed in the legislation on combating unemployment. Article 2a of Employment Promotion Act 2004 (EPA) clearly states that its provisions are aimed at ensuring the observance of the principle of equal treatment in the access to and use of labour market services and instruments, regardless of sex, race, ethnic origin, nationality, religion, creed, beliefs, disability, age or sexual orientation (*see* Chapter 15, Part I).

123. As mentioned above, the regulations on equal treatment in employment have been directly influenced by the EU legislation. Moreover, Poland is a party to the international labour law instruments concerning equal treatment in labour law. Poland has ratified the ILO Convention concerning Equal Remuneration for Men and Women Workers for Work of Equal Value of 29 June, 1951[96] and ILO Convention No. 111 of 25 June 1958 concerning Discrimination in Respect of Employment and Occupation.[97]

§2. Scope of the Principle of Equal Treatment

124. Pursuant to Article 18^{3a} §1 LC employees should be treated equally in respect of the establishment and termination of the employment relationship, terms and conditions of employment, promotion and access to training in order to improve their occupational qualifications, regardless of – in particular –sex, age, disability, race, religion, nationality, political beliefs, trade union affinity, ethnic origin, creed, sexual orientation and, also, regardless whether they are employed for a definite or indefinite period or whether they are full- or part-timers. Indicated by the legislator are, thus, employee characteristics, not related to performance of work, which may not constitute the grounds for differentiation of the employees. Given the requirements of Directives 97/81 and 99/70 a prohibition of discrimination of those employed under atypical contracts of employment has also been set by Polish legislators since it is unacceptable to differentiate the situation of employees on the

95. *Journal of Laws* (2010), No. 254, item 1700.
96. *Journal of Laws* (1955), No. 38, item 238.
97. *Journal of Laws* (1961), No. 42, item 218.

grounds that they are employed for a definite or indefinite period or as persons employed full- or part-time. The issue has been further specified by Article 29^2 §1 LC stating that conclusion of a contract for part-time employment with an employee may not result in his or her terms and conditions of employment being set in a way less favourable than those concerning employees doing the same or similar work as full-timers, account being taken, however, of the proportionality of remuneration for work and other work-related benefits to the employer's length of working hours. In addition, pursuant to Article 67^{15} §2 LC, an employee may not be discriminated in any way whatsoever due to being employed on a teleworking scheme or a refusal to take up such employment (*see* Part I, Chapter 7, §4).

125. The notions of 'equal treatment' and 'non-discrimination' are used by Polish legislator interchangeably. The discussed legal regulations are focused on the prohibition of discrimination in employment and claims available to the victims of unequal treatment. Pursuant to Article 18^{3a} §2 LC, equal treatment in employment means non-discrimination in any form, direct or indirect, for reasons specified in §1. No characteristics covered by the prohibition of discrimination may serve as the grounds for differentiation of employees' situations, nor is it allowed to place discrimination-fostering regulations in the legislation, CLAs or workplace regulations. The characteristics covered by the prohibition to discriminate may not be the basis of the decisions made by the employer. However, it is permitted to differentiate the situation of employees using fair and objective criteria, e.g., those of qualifications, skills, workload, quality of the work done or the length of service. It is well worth adding that Articles 18^{3b} §§2–4 directly allow the employee situation to be differentiated in particular situations. In the case of doubt it is the employer's duty to prove that the rule of equal treatment was not violated (*see* above §5 and §6).

126. In the light of the judicial decisions discrimination consists in unlawful deprivation or limitation of the rights following from the employment relationship or unequal treatment of employees in respect of a discriminatory criterion, and also in granting to certain employees, for those reasons, more limited rights than those enjoyed by other employees being in the same factual or legal situation.[98] Provisions contained in Chapter IIa of the LC, just like the EU law, do not include a norm requiring that all employees of a particular employer should be treated equally. The regulations do, however, set the criteria according to which the situation of those employed may not be differentiated.[99] The rule of non-discrimination in employment can only be breached where the differentiation of the situation of the employees results solely from the application of a criterion not allowed by law.[100] Where

98. Supreme Court judgment of 10 Sep. 1997, I PKN 246/97.
99. Supreme Court judgment of 14 May 2014, II PK 208/13.
100. Supreme Court judgment of 28 May 2008, I PK 259/07, Supreme Court judgment of 5 May 2011, II PK 181/10.

an employee complains that the employer has breached the prohibition of discrimination in employment, he or she should indicate the reason for the act of discrimination having been committed against him or her.[101] It is, thus, not sufficient to claim the existence of a 'discriminatory undercurrent'.[102]

127. The relation between the prohibition of discrimination within the meaning of Article 18^{3a} §1 LC and Article 11^{2} LC (establishing the rule of equal rights on account of equal meeting of identical duties) may seem confusing. The judiciary takes the view that a breach of the principle of non-discrimination is an aggravated form of unequal treatment of employees and means unacceptable differentiation of their legal situation in the sphere of employment, using negative criteria, forbidden by law.[103] Discrimination may not be equated with a 'regular' unequal treatment in employment.[104] In other words, discrimination takes place where non-justified differentiation of employees is based on one of the characteristics of the employee, those mentioned in Article 18^{3a} LC in particular. As opposed to it, the violation of the rule of equal rights on account of identical performance of the same duties within the meaning of Article 11^{2} LC does not necessarily involve the existence of a criterion forbidden by law.

128. The objective scope of the prohibition of discrimination is broad. According to Article 18^{3b} §1 LC a breach of the rule of equal treatment in employment is considered to have taken place if the employer differentiates the situation of the employee for one or a few reasons specified in Article 18^{3a} §1, the effect being, in particular: a refusal to establish or terminate an employment relationship, unfair remuneration for work or other conditions and terms of employment, omission when promoting or when granting the employee other work-related benefits, the employee's omission during the selection for participation in training courses aimed at improving professional qualifications, unless the employer proves objective reasons. The objective scope of the prohibition of discrimination, thus, covers all the phases of the employment relationship, i.e., the recruitment, conditions and terms of employment in the broad sense of the word, including the opportunities for promotion and training, as well as termination of the contract of employment.

129. Remuneration is just one of the elements of broadly termed conditions of employment, but Polish legislators, following the pattern of the EU law, devotes much attention to the issue. Pursuant to Article 18^{3e} §1 LC employees are entitled to equal pay for equal work or for the work of equal value. Under Article 18^{3c} §3 LC the work of equal value is the work, the performance of which requires from employees comparable professional qualifications confirmed by documents specified under separate provisions or occupational practice and experience as well as

---

101. Supreme Court judgment of 10 May 2012, II PK 227/11.
102. Supreme Court judgment of 23 May 2012, I PK 173/11.
103. Supreme Court judgment of 3 Dec. 2009, II PK 148/09.
104. Supreme Court judgment of 23 May 2012, I PK 173/11, Supreme Court judgment of 14 Dec. 2017, I PK 342/17.

comparable responsibility and amount of effort. Where the remuneration of employees doing equal work has been differentiated, the employer has to prove objective reasons. If different occupational qualifications and length of service are quoted by the employer, the latter has to prove that they were of importance for the accomplishment of the tasks entrusted to the employees.[105] The notion "'work of equal value"' has been determined by several factors (it is about comparable qualifications and professional experience) that focus on employee features. Apart from those, the legislature takes into account, also, employee efforts and responsibility that are connected to the particular post. All of these factors should be evaluated together in order to determine whether employees have the right to equal remuneration (the Supreme Court judgment of 14 December 2017, II PK 322/16).

130. Polish legal regulations concerning the prohibition of discrimination use a broad definition of 'remuneration'. In accordance with Article 18^{3c} §2 LC the remuneration mentioned in §1 includes all components of remuneration, regardless of their name and nature, as well as other work-related benefits granted to the employees in cash or in forms other than cash. The definition not only correlates with the strict meaning of the word (*see* §1 of Part I, Chapter 5) but also all other benefits provided under employment relationships. The definition of remuneration for the purpose of the regulations concerning the prohibition of discrimination reflects the content of Article 157 of the Treaty on the Functioning of the European Union.

131. The amount of the remuneration is determined by the parties to the contract of employment and may not – in principle – be altered by a court of law. An exclusion concerns violation of the prohibition of discrimination. Pursuant to Article 18 §3 LC, stipulations of the contracts of employment and other acts on which an employment relationship is based, violating the rule of equal treatment in employment, are void. Instead of such stipulations relevant labour law provisions are applicable and, should such provisions be lacking, they are to be replaced with appropriate provisions, non-discriminatory in nature. In the light of the judicial decisions a labour court judgment, whereby stipulations of a contract of employment have been replaced with relevant provisions of non-discriminatory character, may shape the content of the existing employment relationship for the future. And if the equal treatment in employment rule was violated, regarding the remuneration for work, in the past (after termination of the employment relationship in particular), the employee may seek damages in the amount being the difference between the remuneration which he or she should have received, if the equal treatment in employment rule had not been violated, and the remuneration actually received.[106]

105. Supreme Court judgment of 22 Feb. 2007, I PK 242/06.
106. Supreme Court judgment of 22 Feb. 2007, I PK 242/06, Supreme Court judgment of 9 Jun. 2016, III PK 116/15.

§3. Forms of Discrimination

132. Polish legislation provides for various forms of discrimination, reflecting in that respect the assumptions adopted by the relevant EU law. According to Article 18^{3a} §2 LC equal treatment in employment means lack of any discrimination, whether direct or indirect, for the reasons mentioned in §1. Article 18^{3a} §3 LC provides that direct discrimination occurs where the employee is or could be, for one or more reasons specified in §1, treated, in a comparable situation, in a way less advantageous than other employees; §4 meanwhile states that indirect discrimination exists where, owing to a seemingly neutral provision, applied criterion or action taken, there occur (or there could occur) unfavourable disproportions or a particularly unfavourable situation as regards the establishment or termination of an employment relationship, conditions and terms of employment, promotion and access to training for improvement of occupational qualifications towards all or a considerable number of employees distinguished for one or several of the reasons listed in §1, unless the provision, criterion or action is objectively justified, considering a legitimate aim which is to be achieved, the measures serving the attainment of the aim being appropriate and necessary. Indirect discrimination, thus, means a situation where the applied criteria of differentiation are seemingly neutral and legitimate but where they, nevertheless, result in a less favourable treatment of a specified group of employees distinguished using one of the prohibited characteristics.

133. Under Article 18^{3a} §5 LC discrimination is manifested by behaviour that consists in enticing another person to infringe the equal treatment in employment rule or ordering him/her to violate the rule in question. It also consists in unwanted conduct, the aim or effect of which is violating the dignity of the employee and creating an intimidating, hostile, degrading, humiliating or offensive environment to the person (harassment). Harassment can be a one-off incident. As such, it should be distinguished from mobbing, being a long-term action, not related to the prohibition of discrimination.[107] Article 18^{3a} §6 LC provides that, as far as sex-based discrimination is concerned, the discrimination also includes any unacceptable conduct of a sexual nature or reference to the sex of an employee, aimed at or resulting in the violation of the dignity of or creating an intimidating, hostile, demeaning or humiliating atmosphere towards an employee; the conduct may comprise physical, verbal, or non-verbal elements (sexual harassment). Both harassment and sexual harassment involve violation of the worker's dignity. The incidents in question are to be 'unacceptable', thus, being, to a certain degree, subjective in nature. According to the position taken by the Supreme Court, however, of crucial importance for the assessment of the validity of the claim that personal rights have been infringed is not so much the subjective perception of the person requesting legal protection as the reaction evoked by the infringement within the society.[108] In other words, it is the objective criteria that play the role of key factors in the assessment of whether an instance of harassment or sexual harassment has occurred.

107. *See* Chapter 3, §3, point XIII.
108. Supreme Court judgment of 17 Sep. 2004, V CK 69/04.

§4. Criteria Covered by the Prohibition of Discrimination

134. The prohibition of discrimination takes place where the situation of employees is differentiated for the latter's personal characteristics not related to the work done. The above quoted Article 18^{3a} §1 requires that employees be treated equally in terms of establishment and termination of employment relationships, terms and conditions of the work done, promotion and access to training in order to improve their occupational qualifications, regardless of – in particular – sex, age, disability, race, religion, nationality, political beliefs, trade union affinity, ethnic origin, creed, sexual orientation and, also, regardless whether they are employed for a definite or indefinite period or whether they are full- or part-timers. Considering the use of the 'in particular' expression, the prevailing opinion of the judiciary is that the catalogue of the reasons for which the employee situation may not be differentiated is just illustrative. For instance, the Supreme Court took the view that the rule of equal treatment was violated by differentiation of employee tasks due to the appearance of a particular person.[109]

135. It is sex that Article 18^{3a} §1 LC points out to in the first turn. As mentioned above, the rule of equal treatment of men and women is anchored in the Constitution; moreover, equal treatment on account of equal fulfilling of the same duties concerns, in particular, equal treatment of men and women in employment (Article 11^2 LC). Sex must not, thus, be a factor whereby the situation of employees could be differentiated, whether at the stage of acceptance to work, terms of employment or termination of the labour contract. In addition, sexual harassment, within the meaning of Article 18^{3a} §6 LC, as a form of discrimination, has been directly associated with sex. The Supreme Court has ruled that acceptance of the view that absence of a female employee from work, caused by a threat to pregnancy followed by miscarriage and related health complications, may justify giving a notice to terminate a contract of employment and be the reason for a refusal to reinstate the person at work on the grounds that it is inappropriate, is a violation of the rules concerning protection of maternity and can even be recognized as sex-based discrimination.[110] At the same time it should be noted that the application of measures differentiating the legal situation of the employee on the grounds of parenthood protection is permitted (Article 18^{3b} §2 item 3 LC), which the facilitations, in practical terms, can be enjoyed, to a wider extent, by women. The prohibition of discrimination on the grounds of sex is not violated by the prohibition of employment of women in the work which is particularly onerous and hazardous to health (Article 176 LC). It is worth adding that, given the EU prohibition of discrimination on the grounds of sex, Poland has terminated ILO Convention 45 concerning the Employment of Women on Underground Work in Mines of all Kinds.[111] The move was taken in a reaction to the EU Court of Justice judgment in C-203/03 *Commission of*

---

109. Supreme Court judgment of 4 Oct. 2007, PK 24/07.
110. Supreme Court judgment of 8 Jul. 2008, I PK 294/01.
111. The Act of 28 March, 2008, *Journal of Laws* (2008), No. 72, item. 418.

the European Communities v. Republic of Austria, in which the Court found the prohibition of employment of women in underground work to be contradictory to the prohibition of discrimination on the grounds of sex under the then effective Directive 76/207.

136. A direct prohibition of discrimination on the grounds of age has been established by Polish law. At the same time it is permitted to differentiate the situation of employees on the grounds of the length of service (Article 18^{3b} §2 item 4 LC), a length which grows with employees' age. Meanwhile, there are a number of legal regulations determining the status of particular categories of employees separately. The LC sets up specific regulations concerning the situation of young workers, between 16 and 18 years of age (*see* §2 of Chapter 9, Part I). On the other hand, a prohibition is established on termination of a contract of employment, with notice, of an employee lacking four years to reach retirement age (Article 39 LC). Apart from this, the regulations on the promotion of employment provide for differentiation of the situation of the unemployed depending on their age, this holding true both as far as the young unemployed and the people at more advanced age are concerned. Solutions of that kind, providing for differentiation of the situation of workers and labour market organization, should be regarded as in conformity with Directive 2000/78.[112] The employee's age can be of importance as regards termination of the contract of employment. Viewed as well-established should be the position taken by the Supreme Court that the reaching of the retirement age and becoming entitled to an old-age pension may not be the sole reason for the employer to give the employee a notice to terminate the employment contract.[113] At the same time, where the employee meets the conditions for retirement, it is a socially justified reason for his/her being chosen to be made redundant under an employment restructuring scheme,[114] nor does the employer apply a discriminatory criterion to an employee's dismissal, owing to poor business standing, when it is the youngest employee that is made redundant, the one who will find it easiest to get a new job.[115] In other words, the retirement age must not be the grounds for termination of an employment contract due to reasons concerning an employee. But reaching retirement age, combined with the employee having become entitled to social security performances, may be a criterion for selection of the employee to be dismissed under a mass layoff scheme.

137. Of a particular nature is the prohibition of discrimination on the grounds of disability. It is focused on providing equal opportunities to the disabled in the labour market and imposes duties to adapt working conditions to the needs of that category of persons. Particularly important in that respect is the Act of 27 August 1997

112. For a broader discussion, *see* L. Mitrus, 'Age Discrimination and Labour Law in Poland', in Nummhauser-Henning, Rönnmar (ed.), *Age Discrimination and Labour Law. Comparative and Conceptual Perspectives in the EU and Beyond* (The Netherlands, Wolters Kluwer Law & Business, 2015), pp. 249 et seq.
113. Supreme Court resolution of 21 Jan. 2009, II PZP 13/08.
114. Supreme Court judgment of 3 Mar. 2003, I PK 80/03.
115. Supreme Court judgment of 7 Apr. 2011 r, I PK 238/10.

on Occupational and Social Rehabilitation of the Disabled.[116] Besides that, Article 18^{3b} §2 LC directly provides that differentiating the situation of employees for their disability is not allowed.

138. Also, a prohibition of employee discrimination on the grounds of religion and creed has been established by Polish legislation. In general, differentiation of the situation of employees in respect of those elements is inadmissible. At the same time Article 18^{3b} §4 LC provides that limitation of access to employment on the grounds of religion, creed or outlook does not violate the rule of equal treatment if practised by churches and religious associations or other organizations whose ethical principles are based on religion, creed or outlook, provided that the type or nature of the activity carried out by the churches and religious organizations makes the religion or creed a genuine and critical occupational requirement to be met by employees, proportionate to the achievement of the legitimate differentiation of the situation of the persons. The same remains valid as far as the requirement that the employees should act in good faith and loyalty to the ethics of the church, other religious association and organization whose ethical principles are based on religion, creed or outlook is concerned. Consequently, certain organizations, due to their nature, are allowed to set the requirement of a particular religion or creed as a precondition of employment (e.g., church institutions or parish offices). The provision should be interpreted restrictively.

139. Article 18^{3a} §1 LC establishes a prohibition of discrimination due to nationality. It does not refer to the condition of citizenship though. Given, however, the free movement of workers within the EU, citizens of other Member States should be treated on par with the citizens of Poland, although the taking up employment by citizens of third countries may be subject to additional specific conditions (*see* Part I, Chapter 16). Certainly, discrimination on the basis of nationality may also involve less favourable treatment due to race and ethnic origin.

140. Yet another forbidden criterion of discrimination is political belief. Not all kinds of employee beliefs are addressed by Polish legislators, but the above-mentioned is a specific category. As regards discrimination on the ground of trade union membership, it has been forbidden under Article 3 of the Trade Union Act (*see* Part II, Chapter 2). In addition, direct prohibition of discrimination due to sexual orientation has been set by Polish legislation.

§5. Permitted Differentiation of the Situation of Employees

141. As mentioned above, the situation of employees may be differentiated by the employer for justified and substantive reasons. The legislators point to certain instances where such differentiation may take place. Pursuant to Article 18^{3b} §2 LC the rule of equal treatment in employment is not violated by actions proportionate

116. Consolidated text: *Journal of Laws* (2018) item 511, with further amendments; for a broader discussion, *see* Chapter 8, §3.

to the achievement of a legitimate purpose of differentiation of the employee's situation consisting in a refusal to hire the employee for one or more reasons specified in Article 18^{3a} §1, if the kind of work or conditions of doing it make the reason(s) mentioned in the provision a genuine and material occupational requirement for the employee. It is, thus, clear that the employer may establish specific requirements which the applicants for a job are expected to meet.

142. A notice to terminate the terms and conditions of employment, regarding the length of the working time, does not constitute an act of discrimination where it is justified by reasons not concerning the employee, other reason(s) stated in Article 18^{3a} §1 LC not being quoted. Additionally, it is allowed to apply measures differentiating the legal situation of the employee for parenthood protection due to disability. The LC directly allows the criterion of length of service to be applied when setting the conditions of employment and dismissal of employees, rules for their remuneration and promotion and access to training for improvement of occupational qualifications (the factors justifying the varied treatment of employees due to age). Consequently, a greater length of service may entail growth of employee benefits, the length of service concerning – as applicable – both the period of service in general or that with a particular employer. The Supreme Court has, however, expressed the view that the length of service at a specific employment' must not be the only criterion for the selection of employees for dismissal under the so-called mass layoffs.[117] A separate issue is the earlier-mentioned legal possibility for particular institutions to require that employees should represent a specific creed or outlook.

143. Under Article 18^{3b} §3 LC, no actions shall be considered a breach of the principle of equal treatment in employment if taken for a limited time and aimed at providing equal opportunities to all or a substantial number of employees distinguished due to one or several reasons provided for in Article 18^{3a} §1 LC by decreasing, in favour of such employees, the factual inequalities, to the extent specified in the provision. In other words, programmes of equalization of opportunities (also referred to as affirmative actions) may be launched for groups distinguished by specific characteristics. Programmes of that kind are not, however, popular in Poland.

§6. Protection Against Discrimination

144. Following EU patterns, a number of regulations concerning protection against discrimination, and the opportunities to seek claims if the rule of equal treatment in employment has been violated, have been enacted by Polish legislators. First of all, a model of apportionment of the burden of proof, differing from the standard one, has been established in that respect. As the earlier-mentioned Article 18^{3b} §1 LC provides, a breach of the rule of equal treatment in employment is considered to be taking place if the employer differentiates the situation of the employees

117. Supreme Court judgment of 16 Sep. 1997, I PKN 259/97, Supreme Court judgment of 29 Aug. 2017, I PK 269/16.

for one or a few reasons specified in Article 18^{3b} §1, unless the employer 'proves objective reasons'. In the opinion of the judiciary, the employee should indicate facts that make the accusation of unequal treatment in employment plausible, and the burden of proof of the existence of the objective reasons is then transferred onto the employer.[118] The employee should also indicate the reason, which – in his or her opinion – is the reason for the less favourable treatment. Should the employee be able to plausibly demonstrate the fact of discrimination, the employer that has been sued is expected to provide evidence that the unequal treatment – if any – was objectively justified and did not result from reasons giving it the character of an action discriminating against the claimant.[119] It should be added that no duty is imposed by Polish legislation on the employer to provide information on the situation of other employees, the assessment of which information could allow it to be discovered, without taking legal action, whether discrimination has taken place.

145. The basic claim available to victims of discrimination in employment is the claim for compensation. As Article 18^{3d} LC stipulates, the person in relation to whom the employer has infringed the rule of equal treatment in employment shall have the right to compensation in the amount not lower than the minimum remuneration for work established on the basis of separate provisions. The Article quoted above uses the general term of a 'person', meaning that it is not only the actual employee who may claim compensation from the employer but entitled to do so is also a candidate for a job or a former employee. The LC determines the minimum amount of the indemnification, which should correspond with the statutory minimum salary. The legislators have not established the criteria for the determination of the compensation, however, or its maximum limit. In the opinion of the Supreme Court, the monetary performance should cover both personal and material damage inflicted on the employee. In conformity with the European labour law, the compensation should be duly 'effective, proportionate and deterrent' in nature.[120] As legal scholars stress, not only should the amount provide a relevant compensation to the employee but it also should exert a preventive effect. In the opinion of the Supreme Court, claims on account of unequal treatment may not be waived, even though the compensation is not an element of remuneration for work in the legal meaning of the term.[121] It is worth adding that Polish law does not provide for a claim to the establishment of an employment relationship if the discrimination took place at the stage of recruitment. Also, in that case it is only the claim for compensation that is available to the affected person.

146. The Polish legislation directly stipulates that under specified situations the employee may not bear negative consequences of discrimination-related actions. As Article 18^{3a} §7 LC provides, the employee's exposure to harassment or sexual

118. Supreme Court judgment of 9 Jun. 2006, III PK 30/06.
119. Supreme Court decision of 7 Jan. 2014, II PK 218/13.
120. Supreme Court judgment of 17 Jan. 2009, III PK 43/08.
121. Supreme Court judgment of 2 Jul. 2012, I PK 48/12.

harassment, as well as the actions taken to oppose the harassment or sexual harassment, must not cause any negative consequences to the employee. In addition, pursuant to Article 18^{3e} §1 LC, the employee's exercise of the rights resulting from the infringement of the rule of equal treatment in employment must not be the basis for unfavourable treatment of the employee nor may it entail any negative consequences to him/her; it must not, in particular, be the reason for the notice to terminate the employment relationship with the person, nor for such termination without notice. In the light of §2 the provision should be applied, by analogy, to an employee who has provided, in any form, support to the employee exercising the rights on account of infringement of the rule of equal treatment in employment. Taking into account opinions of the judiciary, the phrase, 'exercising the rights' must not be identified solely with the employee raising claims against the employer. The notion undoubtedly covers also the employee's actions aimed at confirmation of the grounds for the claims, such as evidence-gathering.[122] The employer is, thus, not allowed to apply penalties for a breach of order of work or terminate a contract of employment due to the employee taking lawful actions aimed at protection of the employee's rights or providing assistance to another victim of discrimination. Equally unacceptable would be, also, a situation of the employer indicating – as the reason for a notice to terminate the employment contract – a motive different from the actual one (i.e., the employee exercising his or her rights discussed in this chapter). And, disclosing, to other employees, information on the employee's salary (a move prohibited by a so-called confidentiality stipulation) in order to prevent infringement of the rule of equal treatment and further instances of employee discrimination in the field of remuneration for work may not be a reason whereby termination of a contract of employment without notice could be justified.[123]

147. Regardless of the regulations contained in the discussed Chapter IIa 'Equal treatment in employment' of the LC, Polish legislation provides for a number of other measures aimed at preventing discrimination. The autonomous sources of labour law and contractual stipulations must not be lost of sight in that respect. Pursuant to Article 9 §4 LC, provisions of CLAs and other collective accords based on statutes, workplace regulations and articles of incorporation specifying the rights and duties of parties to the employment relationship, which infringe the rule of equal treatment in employment, are not binding. And under Article 18 §3 LC, also, similar stipulations of the contracts of employment and other acts on which the employment relationship is based are void; instead, relevant labour law provisions are applicable, and – absent such provisions – the stipulations should be replaced by appropriate provisions not being discriminatory in nature. An example of the operation of the rule contained in Article 18 §3 LC is the earlier-mentioned way in which terms of remuneration can be determined if an infringement of the rule of equal treatment has occurred.[124]

---

122. Supreme Court judgment of 15 Jul. 2011, I PK 12/11.
123. *Ibid.*
124. *See above* §2.

148. Fighting discrimination is one of the employer's duties. Moreover, the employer is obliged to make the regulations concerning equal treatment in employment available to the employees, in writing, by placing the information in the workplace premises or by providing access to the provisions in some other way accepted at the employer's (Article 94^{1} LC). It is worth noting that infringement of the prohibition of discrimination does not fall within the category of petty offences against employee rights as provided for by the LC.

Part I. Individual Labour Law

Chapter 1. Individual Employment Relationship

Z. Hajn

§1. Characteristics of the Individual Employment Relationship

I. Basis of the Employment Relationship; Freedom of Establishing and Determining the Content of the Employment Relationship

149. The employment relationship may arise on the basis of a contract of employment, an appointment, election or nomination or a cooperative contract of employment. The vast majority of workers are employed under an employment contract. The other grounds for employment relationship create specific groups of employment relations (for more *see* Part I, Chapter 10). An appointment, election or nomination is formally a unilateral act, yet the employment relations based on them do not lose the nature of voluntary obligations. Consequently, irrespective of the legal basis for the employment relation to be established and for the terms of work and pay to be fixed, a prior joint declaration of the will of an employer and of an employee is required (Article 11 LC).

150. The shaping of the contents of the employment relationship is based on the principle of employee privilege and the freedom of contract rule. Thanks to the operation of the two principles, the parties are free to determine their rights and responsibilities (the freedom of contract), provided that the situation of the employee is not worsened compared to what follows from the labour law provisions (Article 353(1) CC in conjunction with Article 300 LC and 18 §1 LC). The principles are applicable both to the contract of employment and to the employment relationship established on the basis of an appointment, election or nomination or a cooperative contract of employment. However, especially in the employment relations in public administration, based on appointment and nomination, the terms and conditions of employment are, to a greater extent, determined by the imperative (*iuris cogentis*) provisions, the freedom to determine the content of the employment relations by its parties being limited.

II. Characteristic Features of the Employment Relation

151. According to Article 22 §1 LC 'by establishing the employment relationship an employee undertakes to carry out work of a specified kind for the benefit of and under the control of an employer, in a place and at time designated by the employer, and the employer undertakes to employ the employee in return for remuneration.'

This legal definition of employment relationship is supplemented by judicial decisions and jurisprudence by further features following from the provisions of law and the nature of employment relations. As a result, a commonly held opinion is that the employment relationship is a bilateral and mutual labour law obligation, characterized by personal performance of work by the employee provided against payment, continuity of work performance, subordination of the employee to the employer as far as the performance is concerned and performance of the work on behalf of the employer and at his risk.

152. Some explanation should be provided as regards the concept of the employer's risk, well-developed in the judicature and legal writing. The risk is an element of uncertainty related to the running of a work establishment. It is borne mostly by the employer, as the organizer and main beneficiary of the business conducted there. In particular, the employer is burdened with the adverse effects of the employee's incapacity for work for technical or organizational reasons (technical risk), economic losses (business risk), errors in the employee's performance of work, not occurred through his/her fault (personal risk) and non-performance of work for social reasons specified in legal provisions, e.g., owing to incapacity for work resulting from illness, time off being afforded to the employee to do certain public tasks (social risk), etc. As a result, the employee is entitled to remuneration for work despite the work not being actually done owing to circumstances on the employee side or specific social reasons, and also because of business losses sustained by the employer. Similarly, poor performance of the work resulting from ineffectiveness not attributable to the employee's fault does not provide grounds for reduction of his/her the remuneration, nor can the employer claim a full compensation for a loss not caused by the employee intentionally.[125]

III. Employment Relation and Civil Law Contracts for Performance of Services

153. The above-indicated features of the employment relation make it possible to distinguish the contract of employment from civil law contracts for performance of services.[126] The importance of the issue results from the problem of employers

125. *See* more at Ł. Pisarczyk, *Ryzyko pracodawcy* (Warsaw, Wolters Kluwer Poland, 2008), passim.
126. When in doubt whether the concluded contract is a contract of employment or other contract for performance of services, the evaluation of the nature of the contract is done using the so-called 'typological method of legal qualification of contracts'. This consists in comparing the features specific of the employment relation with those present in the examined contract. Should the features

moving away from the labour law application. In order to conceal the actually existing employment relations, agreements of the above-mentioned kind are concluded, especially contracts for performance of services, contracts similar to the latter and contracts for performance of a specified task or work. A special type of problem related to the diversion from labour law schemes is cases of fake self-employment, i.e., situations when subordinate work is done by a person acting, formally, as one doing business on his/her own.[127] To counteract the phenomenon, a provision was incorporated into the LC (Article 22 §1 LC) in 1997 stating that employment on the terms which are characteristic of the employment relationship means the existence of employment relationship regardless of the name of the contract concluded by the parties.[128] In addition, in case of a civil law agreement being signed in order to conceal the actually concluded contract of employment, the employer is guilty of a petty offence (Article 281 point 1 LC). The same objectives are pursued by other legal measure provided for by the regulations on labour inspection, civil law proceedings as well as social insurance and tax law. In particular, the labour inspector is authorized to verify the legal basis of the employment of workers, as declared by the employer, for compliance with law and facts of life. The inspector may also bring an action to a labour court to establish that a specific person is employed under an employment relationship (Article 63 CPC). At the same time the Personal Income Act of 1991 attempts to prevent fake self-employment by stating that a specific work must not be qualified as a business activity where it is the ordering party that is liable towards third parties for the result of the work, the activities are performed under the guidance of the ordering party at the place and time indicated by the latter, with the work performing party not bearing the business risk (Article 5b). Recently, due to a heated social debate on 'junk contracts' conducted particularly intensively since 2013, further decisions have been taken. Among other things, starting from the beginning of 2016, social security contributions will have to be paid on all civil contracts for performance of services, up to the amount of the minimum remuneration for work. Subsequent changes took place from the beginning of 2017 by way of an amendment to the Act on the minimum remuneration for work (*see* paragraph 288). The essence of this amendment is the introduction (with some exceptions) of a minimum rate of remuneration for persons providing work on the

---

of the employment relation prevail, the contract is deemed to be a contract of employment. It is, by the way, the intensity of the essential characteristics of the employment relation that counts rather than their quantitative predominance. As regards judicature, the most essential factor taken into account in the process of qualification is the observance by the employee of the instructions given to him/her and personal performance of the work. The method of typological qualification was duly justified in the Supreme Court judgment of 20 Mar. 1965, III PU 28/64 as has been commonly used by courts of law ever since.

127. In its judgment of 24 Jul. 2001 the Supreme Court claimed that 'filing an application for entering a business (the intermediation in sales services on a fee or contract basis) into the municipal business activity register (and having the business registered), and then concluding an agreement on provision of such services does not preclude the ascertainment and legal assessment that parties to the agreement were actually bound by an employment relation under a sales assistant's contract of employment'.
128. The provision, incorporated at the request of trade unions, does not establish a presumption of the existence of a contract of employment. Its role consists in clearly stating, in the LC, what the effects of concluding an apparent civil law agreement, in order to conceal a contract of employment, are.

basis of contracts of mandate or contracts for the provision of services similar to a mandate. Self-employed workers (entrepreneurs) have been also included to these persons, provided that they do not employ employees or contractors. What is important, the amount of the minimum rate is the same as for employees. The entitled persons cannot waive the right to remuneration in the amount equal to the minimum rate or transfer it to another person. Inspection of respecting new regulations has been entrusted to the National Labour Inspectorate extending, thus, its control competences beyond the area of employment relations. It is worth adding that the same amendment introduced the obligation to verify contracts for the implementation of public procurement in terms of the parties' application of minimum rates of remuneration for workers employed in their implementation.

§2. The Employee

154. An employee is a person employed under an employment contract, appointment, election, nomination or under a cooperative employment contract. A legal capacity to be an employee is generally restricted to persons who have reached 18 years of age. However, on the terms laid down in provisions on employment of young persons, a person who has not reached 18 years of age may also be an employee (*see* Part I, Chapter 8, §2).

A person with limited capacity to effect transactions in law (e.g., adolescent) may, without the consent of his or her legal representative, establish an employment relationship and effect transactions in the law which relate to it. Where the employment relationship is contrary to the good of that person, the legal representative, with the permission of the custody court, may terminate the relationship.

§3. The Employer

I. The Notion

155. According to the LC an employer is an organizational unit (even if not vested in legal personality), as well as a natural person, if it employs employees (Article 3 LC).

Most frequently, the employer is a legal person (the examples being a joint-stock company, limited liability company, foundation, etc.) or a natural person. Employers can, however, include also so-called imperfect legal persons, i.e., independent organizational units not being legal persons though vested by law in certain legal capacity (e.g., a general partnership, professional partnership, limited partnership), to which entities provisions on legal persons are applicable appropriately (Article 33^1 CC). A peculiarity of Polish labour law is that counted among employers can also be internal organizational units of legal persons on which the right to hire and fire is conferred by provisions of law or statutes of legal persons. As a general rule, however, any legal person is the employer for those employed by it unless, from the provisions regulating its internal organization, it follows that for some of them it is one of the legal person's component units that is the employer.[129] The category of internal organization units of legal persons that can be employers includes, in particular, units of the State Treasury and municipalities (e.g., governmental and municipal agencies, public schools, courts of law), plants, branches as well as well as subsidiaries of companies and enterprises. The above-described legal architecture makes it possible to attribute the status of an employer to the organizational unit that has certain autonomy regarding its management though lacking civil law capacity. On that ground it is referred to as the managerial theory of employer.[130]

Certain specific provisions adopt their own notion of the employer. For instance, the Act of 13 July 2006 on the Protection of Employees in the Event of the Insolvency of Their Employer[131] narrows the notion down to the entrepreneurs that have the capacity to be declared insolvent.

II. Representation of the Employer in Labour Law Matters

156. According to Article 3^1 LC, on behalf of the employer being an organizational unit, legal actions in labour law matters may be executed by a person or a body managing such an organization or by another person designated to do this. For instance, legal actions in labour law matters on behalf of a limited liability company are executed by its managing body, i.e., the management board and, in certain, specific situations, the managing person (the liquidator, official receiver, trustee). It is, however, possible for the company to entrust the powers, in whole or to a specified extent, to 'another person designated to do this', e.g., the president or one of the other members of the management board instead of the entire board or an employee indicated in internal regulations of the company or authorized by the management board.[132]

The above rules of representation of the employer in legal actions apply *mutatis mutandis* to an employer who is a natural person if the employer does not personally execute the actions (Article 3^1 §2 LC). This means that the employer in question can perform the actions himself/herself or through a manager (director) being in charge of the work establishment or designate another person to perform all or only certain acts in labour law.

129. *See* the Supreme Court judgment of 6 Nov. 199, I PRN 47/91.
130. The adoption of the doctrine by the legislator is criticized by a considerable portion of the legal scholars.
131. Consolidated text: *Journal of Laws* (2014), item 272.
132. The above-mentioned system of employer legal representation was introduced by the amendments to the LC made in 1996 and keeps raising interpretative doubts dealt with in scholarly writing and judicature.

§4. WORK ESTABLISHMENT

I. Notion

157. No definition for work establishment has been provided by the LC. In legal writing work establishment is defined as a technical and organizational unit being an organized complex of tangible and intangible assets, composed, in particular, of material resources, property, structure of management, tasks and staff. Usually, it is the tangible assets, such as the offices, site, machinery and plant, etc. that form the most visible part of the work establishment. They are not necessary for its existence, though, or can play just a minor role in its operation, as the case may be, for instance, with small employment agencies, accountancy or advertising offices, the basic components of which are clients, trading contacts, business name and a team of employees. It is usually indicated that the work establishment is used by the employer to accomplish the objectives of the business run by the latter. At the same time it is the institution where the personnel are employed. The notion is, thus, similar to that of an enterprise, in the 'objective' meaning of the word, as used in civil law (Article 55^1 CC). It is, however, broader since a work establishment can be also used for the attainment of non-business purposes. The role of a work establishment is further specified by law in whose provisions the concept is used to denote an entity being the object of management (Article 18^2 LC), the place where the work process is carried out (Article 104^1 §1, Article 128, Article 207 §1, Article 283 §1 LC), the area of operation of a work establishment trade union organization, the area covered by a workplace CLA, the object of a transfer to another employer, etc. The work establishment is also the object of responsibilities of an employee, who is obliged to care for its interests (Article 100 §2 item 4 LC).[133]

II. Work Establishment and Employer

158. Characteristic of Poland's labour law is the dependence of the notion of work establishment on the notion of an employer, consisting in the fact that the work establishment must be an entity that has the quality of an employer. Other entities, regardless of their size and the degree of separation within the employer's structure, are regarded as parts of the work establishment.[134]

133. In the opinion of the Supreme Court the responsibility should be understood as the care for the work establishment viewed as an organizational unit being the workplace and, consequently, a common value, a 'good' owned, as it were, not only by the employer but the employees as well; e.g., Supreme Court judgments of 9 Feb. 2006, II PK 160/05; 20 Mar. 2007, II PK 214/06. In some other judgments the duty is, however, identified with taking care for the employer's interests. Opinions of legal scholars are divided in that respect.

134. Cf., e.g., the Supreme Court resolution of 21 Sep. 1990, III PZP 4/90; resolution of 23 Jul. 1993, I PZP 30/93; resolution of 22 Feb. 1994, I PZP 1/94.

III. A Part of Work Establishment

159. The notion of a part of a work establishment is essential for the safeguarding of employees' rights in the event of transfer of an establishment or a part of work establishment onto another employer. A part of work establishment has, as a rule, just as the work establishment regarded as a whole does, the nature of a set of tangible and intangible assets intended for the attainment of specific objectives of the employer. Most often, however, the objectives are not identical with the general objective of the entire work establishment, but are subsidiary (like the running of a canteen being part of the enterprise) or fragmentary objectives (like the maintenance of a school workshop belonging to a group of vocational schools operating under a joint management). Usually, a part of a work establishment can be identified with those components of the work establishment which are crucial for the latter's operation as the employing entity.[135] In the judicature it used to be assumed that a component such as that could also be the tasks undertaken by the work establishment (e.g., the task of a school to provide pre-school preparation, chores, etc.).[136] Finally, however, in cases concerning transfer of part of an undertaking to a new employer, the Supreme Court adopted the concept of a part of an undertaking as a business entity, developed in the case law of the Court of Justice since the *Süzen* case.[137] As a result, it is now accepted, in principle, that in sectors where the operation is mostly based on manpower, a part of a work establishment can be constituted by a team of workers conducting, on a permanent basis, joint activities. Meanwhile, in case of entities predominantly based on tangible assets, it is those resources that prejudge its identity.[138]

§5. Transfer of Work Establishment or a Part of it to Another Employer

I. Legal Regulation

160. A special connection between the employee and the work establishment is apparent in legal regulations concerning the transfer of work establishment to another employer. In the times of the centrally planned socialist economy the issue

135. In the opinion of the Supreme Court, relevant to identification of a part of work establishment, just like the identification of the work establishment itself, within the meaning of Art. 23(1) LC, are those elements (whether tangible or not) which make it possible for employees to perform work, thus making the establishment an employing entity and which – if taken over by another entity (another employer) – allow it to carry out the same or similar activity, the workers related to that part of the work establishment being able to continue their employment; *see* the Supreme Court judgment of 29 Nov. 2005, II PK 391/04; the Supreme Court judgment of 13 Apr. 2010, I PK 210/09.
136. For example, a resolution of the Supreme Court of 19 Jan. 1993, I PZP 70/92; sentence of 16 Mar. 1994, I PRN 4/94.
137. Court of Justice judgement of 11 Mar. 1997, C-13/95 *Ayse Süzen v. Zehnacker Gebäudereinigung GmbH Krankenhausservice*, [1997] ECR s. I-1259.
138. *See*, for instance, sentences of the Supreme Court of: 29 Mar. 2012, I PK 150/11; 11 Apr. 2012, I PK 155/11 and 17 May 2012, I PK 179/11; 14 Jun. 2012, I PK 235/11.

was of minor importance. Transformations of state-owned enterprises and other work establishments were mostly effected by means of administrative rulings which also provided for matters of employment relations. As far as transformations in other sectors are concerned, pre-war regulations concerning the matters were applicable, and after those were repealed in 1975 it was considered justified to assume continuity of employment relations by law, well-grounded – in the opinion of the scholars – in the whole body of the LC provisions; otherwise, Civil Code rules were applied on a subsidiary basis.

161. A new regulation of the transfer of work establishment, contained in Article 23^1 LC, was enacted in the breakthrough year of 1989 (*see* Chapter 2 of the Introduction). While the regulation has been amended a number of times since then, its relevance has been confirmed by numerous court decisions and academic papers. The reasons for it have been indicated by the Supreme Court indicating that changes of the parties to the employment relationships resulting from the disposal of the whole work establishment or part of it is an inherent feature of socio-economic relations in the market economy and that a change of the employer, the identity of the work establishment being preserved, does not justify termination of employment relationships with the employees nor deterioration of their working conditions.[139]

162. Unlike the Directive 2001/23/EC of 12 March 2001 on the safeguarding of employees' rights in the event of transfers of undertakings, businesses or parts of undertakings or businesses does, Poland's legal regulations do not limit the effects of the transfer to business entities but extend the effects on to the reorganization of public administrative authorities or the transfer of administrative functions between public administrative authorities, unless such changes are provided for by specific legal regulations.[140]

II. Notion and Effects

163. Transfer of work establishment or a part of it to another employer is a legal event resulting in taking over the rights and obligations of the transferor (the current employer) by the transferee. The main reason for the regulation of the issues related to such a transfer was to safeguard further employment to the employees, under the same terms and conditions, despite the transfer of the work establishment to a new employer.

A precondition for the effective transfer is the identity being preserved by the work establishment put to the takeover. In the light of the current decisions of the Supreme Court, legal assessments in that respect should take into account the rules set by the European Court of Justice, in the *Spijkers*[141] and *Süzen* cases in particular. Specifically, depending on whether the operation of a business entity is mostly

139. Supreme Court judgment of 7 Feb. 2007, I PK 269/06.
140. Supreme Court sentences of 22 Jan. 2004, I PK 288/03; 11 Apr. 2013, I PK 247/12.
141. Judgment of 18 Mar. 1986 on case C-24/85 *Jozef Maria Antonius Spijkers v. Gebroeders Benedik Abattoir CV et Alfred Benedik en Zonen BV.*

based on manpower or other assets, it is necessary to find out if the transferee has taken over a part of the employees or assets essential for the preservation of the identity.

164. Transfer of work establishment or a part of it to another employer can take place as a result of legal transactions (like those of a sale or lease) or other legal events (e.g., an administrative ruling). In such a situation the transferee becomes, by virtue of law, the employer to the employees working at the acquired entity. No new contracts of employment have to be concluded by the transferee.[142] The change of the employer occurs as soon as factual control is assumed over the work establishment by the transferee, understood as the new employer being actually able to manage the establishment and exercise authority over its staff.[143]

165. The primordial effect of the transfer of the work establishment is the transferee's entry into the rights and obligations of the current employer, derived from the employment relationships. For a period of one year, provisions of the current CLA are also applicable to the taken over employees unless more favourable terms of employment are to be applied to them by the new employer. After that time, terms and conditions following from the CLA remain applicable until they are terminated with notice (Article 241^8 LC). In addition, the effects of the transfer in certain other spheres are provided for by law. This concerns, in particular, the rules for the further operation of the company welfare fund and employee pension schemes.[144]

166. Article 23^1 is an imperative provision of law (*ius cogens*). The automatism of the change of the employer means that any other agreements and employers' decisions are void.[145] Neither is it permitted to make the legal effectiveness of the change of the employer conditional upon the employee's consent or objection.[146]

167. Provisions of the LC concerning transfer of work establishment are also applicable in case of employer's liquidation entailing transfer of the whole or part of the work establishment run by the employer to another employer, the operation of the establishment being then pursued or a similar activity undertaken.[147] Where the transfer takes place under bankruptcy proceedings, the application of the provisions is, however, disputable. Doubts are raised, in particular, in case of so-called liquidation bankruptcy aimed at the disposal of the bankrupt enterprise and satisfying the creditors from the thus acquired funds. As far as the so-called bankruptcy, with a possibility to make an arrangement is concerned, where the aim is to allow the debtor to continue operation through the conclusion of an arrangement covering the restructuring of his debts, the heavily prevailing opinion is that the transfer of

142. Supreme Court sentence of 20 Sep. 1990, I PR 251/90.
143. *See* the Supreme Court judgment of 29 Nov. 2005, II PK 391/04/.
144. *See* the Act of 4 Mar. 1994 on the Company Welfare Fund, consolidated text: *Journal of Laws* (2012), item 592, as amended; the Act of 20 April, 2004 on Employee Pensions Schemes, consolidated text: *Journal of Laws* (2014), item 710.
145. Supreme Court sentence of 6 Jan. 1995, I PRN 116/94.
146. Supreme Court resolution of 19 Jan. 1993, I PZP 70/92; sentence of 14 Jun. 2012, I PK 235/11.
147. Supreme Court judgment of 19 Aug. 2004, I PK 489/03.

work establishment or a part of it to another employer under such proceedings triggers the protection of employee rights attached to it, as specified in Article 23^{1} LC.[148]

III. Safeguarding Employee Rights

168. As already mentioned above, the aim of Article 23^{1} LC is to protect employees against the loss of jobs and deterioration of working conditions in the situation where the legal successor of the current employer taking over the work establishment or a part of it keeps running the same or similar activity there, there existing, as a result, a possibility to continue the employment of the staff.[149] For this reason a transfer of the work establishment or a part thereof to another employer may not justify termination of the employment relationship with notice by the employer (Article 23^{1} §6 LC). In the judgment of the Supreme Court, also, an agreement terminating the employment relationship with the aim of excluding the automatic continuation of the latter in case of transfer of work establishment or a part of it to another employer is void considering its contradiction with the mandatorily binding provision of Article 23^{1} §1 LC. The transferee is not allowed to change the working conditions of the employee for the worse owing to the transfer of the work establishment alone, regardless of whether the employee consents to such a change or not.[150]

IV. Transferee Liability for Debts

169. The transferee assumes liability for the current employer's debts to the employees, i.e., for the obligations emerged under the employment relationship prior to the transfer of the work establishment and not fulfilled until the time of the transfer. However, where the subject of the transfer is a part of the work establishment, the current employer is also, jointly and severally, liable for the debts (Article 23^{1} §2 LC).

V. The Right of the Employee to Terminate the Employment Relationship

170. Within two months of the transfer of the work establishment or a part thereof to another employer, an employee may, without notice, and upon seven days' prior notification, terminate the employment relationship. For the employee, termination of the employment relation in accordance with this procedure bears the same consequences as those envisaged under labour law for termination of the employment relationship with notice by the employer (Article 23^{1} §4 LC).

148. Supreme Court judgment of 28 Jun. 2013, I PK 34/13.
149. Supreme Court judgment of 19 Aug. 2004, I PK 489/03.
150. Supreme Court judgment of 7 Feb. 2007, I PK 269/06.

VI. The Duty of the Transferor and Transferee to Provide Information to Employees

171. The transferor and the transferee alike are obliged to notify, at least thirty days before the expected date of transfer, the trade union organizations active in their establishments, of the expected date of transfer, the reasons and the legal, economic and social consequences of it for the employees, as well as of the proposed action with respect to the terms of employment for the employees, in particular the terms of work, pay and change of qualifications. Where any of the employers intends to take up actions concerning terms and conditions of employment of the employees in question, the issues should be put by the employer to negotiations with the trade union organizations and an agreement in that respect should be concluded within thirty days of the providing of the information. Should the negotiations fail, the employer may, however, set the terms and conditions of employment independently, account being taken of the arrangements made in the course of the negotiations (Article 26^1 of the TUA).

If no trade unions are active at the work establishments of the employers involved in the transfer, information on conditions of the transfer, similar to that described above, should be presented directly to the employees. The duty should be met in writing.

Chapter 2. Conclusion of the Employment Contract

Z. Hajn

§1. The Beginning, the Form and the Language of the Employment Contract

I. The Beginning of the Employment Contract

172. The employment relationship is established on the date specified in the contract as the date for the commencement of work, and if no such date is specified, then on the date on which the contract is concluded (Article 26 LC). If no day is indicated, then the employment relationship is deemed established at the time the employee has been admitted to work.

II. The Form

173. The contract of employment should be concluded in writing. The written form requirement, as set in that respect, is not one of *ad solemnitatem* or *ad probationem* nature since a contract of employment concluded orally or *per facta concludentia* is valid and its existence may be confirmed by the testimony of witnesses. Failure to observe the written form can be purged by the employer by confirmation, in writing, of the arrangements made on the type of the contract and its conditions and terms. This should be done before the date of commencement of work by the employee (Article 29 §2 LC). Non-observance of the requirement to confirm the conclusion of the contract within the said time limit is an offence (Article 281, point 2 LC), the employment being illegal (Article 2 part 1, point 13 of the EPA). Even, however, in such case, the contract of employment gives rise to all legal effects of an employment relationship, including the establishment of an employee social insurance relationship.

III. The Language

174. The contract of employment on the territory of the Republic of Poland should be concluded in Polish if the employee has the place of residence in Poland and the contract is to be performed in the Republic of Poland. The same principle is also applicable to other documents related to carrying out labour law provisions. The contract of employment or other documents may be executed in a foreign language at the request of the employee who has a command of that language, who was earlier instructed on the right of development of the contract or document in

Polish. In case of future interpretations, the Polish version is an overruling version if the employee is a citizen of Poland (Articles 7 and 8 of the Polish Language Act of 1999).[151]

§2. Content of the Employment Contract and Information Related to the Employment Relationship

I. Content of the Employment Contract

175. Provisions of the LC concerning the content of the contract of employment and additional written information about certain engagement terms have been aligned, through the amendments made in the years 2004 and 2006, to the requirements of the Information Directive (91/533/EEC).

An employment contract should specify its parties, the type of contract, the date on which it is made, and the terms of work and pay, in particular: (1) the kind of work, (2) the location where the work is to be performed, (3) remuneration corresponding to the type of work, together with the components of the remuneration, (4) length of working time, (5) the date when the work ought to commence (Article 29 LC). For a valid conclusion of the contract of employment it is, however, sufficient to specify in the contract the kind of work which the employee undertakes for the benefit of the employer.[152] Other conditions and terms of work stem, as a rule, from the provisions of labour law, CLA or workplace regulations, and, in case of a dispute, can be determined by court.

The above-mentioned conditions and terms do not exhaust the content of the contract of employment. The parties may, enjoying the freedom of contract, provide for other issues unless such stipulations would place the employee in a position worse than that resulting from the applicable legal provisions.

II. The Duty of the Employer to Provide Information Related to the Employment Relationship

176. Regardless of the information contained in the content of the contract of employment, the employer should notify an employee in writing, not later than within seven days of the date on which an employment contract is made, of the: (1) applicable daily and weekly norm of working time, (2) frequency of the payment of the remuneration for work, (3) length of annual leave, (4) period of notice of termination of the contract, (5) collective agreement applied to an employee and – where the employer is not obligated to set out work rules – also of the night time,

151. *See also* the Constitutional Tribunal judgement of 13 Sep. 2005, K 38/04.

152. Where a few kinds of subordinate work are to be done by an employee for the benefit of the employer, it should be assumed that there exists a single employment relationship between the parties (the Supreme Court judgment of 14 Feb. 2002, I PKN 876/00. Concluding another (second) contract of employment, for regular remuneration, with the employer's current employee is permitted by the judicature only exceptionally, if the kind of work is markedly different from that agreed on within the basic working time (Supreme Court resolution of 12 Apr. 1994, I PZP 13/94).

the place, date and time of the payment of the remuneration and of the manner in which the employees should confirm their arrival and presence at work, as well as how they should excuse their absence from work. An employee may be notified about the conditions of employment mentioned in items 1–4 above by being indicated, in writing, relevant labour law provisions (Article 29 §3 and §3(1) LC).

III. The Duty of the Employee to Provide Information Related to the Employment Relationship

177. According to Article 51 part 1 of the Constitution, no one may be obliged, except on the basis of statute, to disclose information concerning his/her person. A principle of the individual's autonomy is established by the provision of law concerning all cases where the individual is obliged to disclose information about himself/herself to other subjects of law, including private entities.[153] Guarantees of compliance with the principle are contained in specific provisions.

178. The right of the employer to request the person seeking to be employed to provide information is, first of all, restricted by personal data protection provisions. Collecting personal information in connection with employment is regulated by the Personal Data Protection Act, 1997,[154] and by the LC. The employer may process only the data which are necessary for his/her/their justified aims and provided that the processing does not violate the rights and freedom of the person concerned. Processing of sensitive data, listed in the Personal Data Protection Act, as for instance sexual orientation, is forbidden. Still, the employer is allowed to process the sensitive data if it is indispensable for performing his/her/their tasks and the scope of the processed data is specified by the statute (Article 27). For instance, on the ground of the Civil Service Act, 2008[155] the employer is allowed to ask questions about candidate's membership with a political party, as a civil servant should be apolitical. Also, employers falling within the category of what is termed as tendentious establishments are free to process such data under specified conditions.

179. Further protection of employee privacy has been granted by the LC, which the piece of legislation specifies precisely the list of questions which the employer is allowed to ask the candidate (Article 22^1). According to this provision the employer may request the person to provide personal data, including: (1) name (names) and surname, (2) names of parents, (3) date of birth, (4) place of residence (address for correspondence), (5) education, (6) career to date. Other personal data may be requested by the employer if special provisions impose an obligation to provide them. An employer may also request an employee (but not a candidate) to provide other personal data, as well as the names, surnames and dates of birth of the children of the employee if it is necessary to provide such data in order for the employee to avail special benefits guaranteed by labour law, as well as the PESEL

153. *See* the Constitutional Tribunal judgment of 19 Feb. 2002, U 3/01.
154. Act of 29 Aug. 1997, consolidated text: *Journal of Laws* (2014), item 1182, as amended.
155. Act of 21 Nov. 2008, consolidated text: *Journal of Laws* (2008), item 1111, as amended.

number of the employee, issued by the Government Information Centre of the Common Electronic System for Registration of the Population (Article 22^1 LC).

§3. TYPES OF EMPLOYMENT CONTRACT

I. Introductory Remarks

180. An employment contract may be concluded for an indefinite period, for a definite period or for the period needed to complete a specific piece of work. Each of the contracts may be preceded by an employment contract for a trial period. In principle, parties to the contract are free to decide about the type of the concluded agreement, but legal limitations are imposed on the contracts for a definite period and for a trial period.

181. Notwithstanding this, labour law provides also for other categories of contracts of employment. These are, in particular, the employment contract for vocational training and employment contracts which provide for part-time work, telework and temporary work. The agreements, as related to protection of the work of the juvenile and atypical employment, will be discussed further on (*see* Part I, §7 and §8).

182. The preliminary contract of employment is not counted among employment contracts. The agreement is not regulated by the LC, yet the judiciary accepts its application under provisions of the Civil Code (Articles 389–390). A preliminary contract of employment is deemed concluded when parties thereof have agreed on the substantive stipulations of the future employment contract. The consequence of a failure of the obliged party to conclude, within the specified time limit, the promised contract of employment is the entitlement of the other party to claim for compensation in respect of the damage suffered as a result of the party counting on the conclusion of the contract. The employee may also seek conclusion of the promised labour agreement. The employer, however, may not demand that the contract be concluded, having only the right to seek compensation. An employee may request the signing of the promised agreement also when the contract of employment was actually concluded, but its conditions and terms substantially differ from those set in the preliminary contract of employment.[156]

II. The Contract for an Indefinite Period

183. The contract for an indefinite period is regarded by the LC as a typical contract, as opposed to other types of labour agreements, which may be concluded in particular situations or be subject to legal limitations. In the opinion of the Supreme Court, a standard labour law solution is employment under the contract for an indefinite period, as the latter – considering the mode and scope of protection

156. *See*, e.g., the Supreme Court judgment of 2 Sep. 1975, I PRN 21/75.

against termination thereof – respects the justified needs of the employee to the highest possible extent. Unlike the discussed agreement, fixed-time contracts are exceptional solutions which have to be duly justified by the interest of both parties and must not be misused by the employer for circumvention of the provisions on the protection of permanence of the employment relationship. No presumption of the conclusion of a contract of employment for an indefinite period is, nevertheless, conferred by labour law provisions. Where the parties have not specified the type of the employment contract, their statements of will should be interpreted in a way conforming to the rules of social conduct and established customs, taking into account the circumstances in which the contract was executed, joint intentions of the parties and the objective of the contract itself.[157] Usually, however, in a situation such as that, a contract for an indefinite period is deemed to have been concluded since it is only in the case of such contract that no additional stipulations are required.[158]

III. The Contract for a Definite Period

184. The duration of the contract is determined by the parties indicating the final date of the contract, the period for which the contract is concluded or an event, bound to take place, which brings the contract to an end. As a rule, the contract lasts until the end of the period fixed by the parties, yet it may not exceed the time prescribed by the law. It should be noted, however, that in certain cases long-term contracts for an indefinite period help strengthen the stability of employment. It is for those reasons that, for instance, the chief physician and the chief nursing officer at a public healthcare centre are employed for a period of six years.[159]

Considering the practice of repeated use of successive employment contracts for a definite period in order to deprive employees of the protection afforded to those employed for indefinite time, the freedom to conclude such contracts is limited by law. The limitations in question were introduced by the LC in 1996 and took the shape of a rule stating that once a third subsequent contract for a definite period had been signed, it was deemed to have become an indefinite term contract if the time between the termination of the previous contract and the conclusion of a subsequent one was not longer than one month. In order to prevent circumvention of the rule, in 2004 a provision was added stating that an agreement between the parties, concluded in the course of the duration of an employment contract for a definite period, concerning an extension of work under this contract, was considered to be a conclusion, from the day following after its termination, of a succeeding employment contract for a definite period. It was also decided that the above regulations would not be applicable to contracts concluded in order to replace an employee during his/her justified absence from work or to perform casual work, seasonal work or the tasks realized cyclically (Article 25^1 LC).

157. Supreme Court judgment of 17 May 1995, I PRN 11/95.
158. Supreme Court judgment of 26 Aug. 1999, I PKN 215/99.
159. Article 49 of the Act of 15 Apr. 2011 on Therapeutic Activities (*Journal of Laws* (2018), item 160, as amended).

185. Unfortunately, the rules did not turn out to be very effective, for at least two reasons: The allowed duration of subsequent contracts of employment was not specified while the break, after which another contract for a definite period could be concluded, proved to be too short. In practice, the legal limitations of periodical employment were, thus, relatively easy to circumvent, and counteracting the practice boiled down to courts of law interventions undertaken *ad casu.*[160] For those very reasons, the Act of 25 June 2015[161] introduced changes supposed to refine the system of workers' protection against the abuse of contracts of employment for a definite period, the amendments coming into force on 22 February 2016.[162] The changes consist in the specification of the allowed total period of employment under contracts for a definite period, namely thirty-three months. Within the period no more than three such contracts may be concluded and if the parties should arrive at an agreement on the extension of the duration of a specific contract, reaching the agreement is considered equivalent to concluding a new contract for a definite period. Where the period of employment for a definite time exceeds thirty-three months or where more than three contracts were concluded during that period, the employee is regarded as one employed for an indefinite time.

186. The above-mentioned limitations of employment under a contract (contracts) for a definite period are not applicable to the contracts concluded in order to replace an employee during his or her justified absence from work or to perform casual work, seasonal work or work done for a specific term of office, nor do they concern the cases where objective reasons are quoted by the employer, indicating the employer's genuine demand for a work done periodically and necessary to the agreed extent. The information on the reasons justifying the conclusion of a contract violating the above limitations has to be included in the content of the agreement. Moreover, if concluded due to objective reasons concerning the employer, the contract has to be reported by the employer to the regional labour inspector, the reasons for the conclusion being indicated (Article 25^1 and Article 29 §1^1 LC).

187. Employees hired for a definite period must be informed of any vacancies (Article 94^2 LC).

160. According to the Supreme Court, setting a long duration of the contract without proper justification could have been considered *in concreto* as circumvention of law or seen as in contradiction with the rules of social conduct. *See*, e.g., the judgement of 5 Jun. 2014, I PK 308/13 and the judgements quoted in its grounds.
161. The Act Amending the Labour Code and Certain Other Acts of Parliament, *Journal of Laws* (2015), item 1220.
162. The move was triggered by, *inter alia*, the proceedings instituted by the European Commission against Poland concerning non-conformity of Poland's Labour Code with Council Directive 99/70/EC (letter no. 2013/4161 of the European Commission), criticism of previous regulations expressed by legal scholars and a broad public discussion in which the contracts for a definite period were counted among the 'junk contracts'.

IV. The Contract for a Trial Period

188. The contract for a trial period may precede any other contract of employment. It is primarily aimed at checking the employee's capacity for work and this is why it is almost exclusively the employer that initiates the conclusion of such a contract. It may be signed at the employee's initiative as well, though. The contract may be concluded for a period not exceeding three months. Work interruptions caused, e.g., by the employee's illness do not result in an extension of the originally determined trial period. The contract enjoys high popularity, being applied very widely.

Finding out that the contract for the trial period was concluded in order to circumvent law results in the invalidity of the stipulation providing for the type of the contract. Consequently, the contract should be regarded as a contract concluded for an indefinite period unless both contracting parties intended concluding a fixed-time contract of employment.[163]

189. The contract for a trial period is not a fixed-time contract within the meaning of the LC and, as such, is not counted against the limit of such contracts, as established in Article 25^1 LC.[164] The contract may be concluded only once with a specific employee. The parties may, however, conclude a subsequent contract of that type after at least three years from the date of termination of the previous one or even at once if the aim of the contract is to assess the employee's suitability for a work of another kind (Article 25 §3 LC).

190. It is the objective of the contract of employment for a trial period that is crucial for its essence, not the limited duration of the agreement. Hence, unlike other contracts of limited duration, it may be, at any time, terminated with notice.

---

163. Judgment of the Supreme Court of 26 Aug. 1999, I PKN 215/99.
164. Judgment of the Supreme Court of 7 Feb. 2001, I PKN 229/00.

Chapter 3. Rights and Duties of the Parties to the Employment Relationship

L. Mitrus

§1. Introductory Remarks

191. Article 1 LC states that the LC defines the rights and duties of employees and employers. Numerous statutory provisions expressly determine those duties. Several of them were established under the previous political and economic system, but new ones were also introduced in order to meet the requirements of the free market economy or to implement the directives of the EU. Several employer's duties are regarded as 'basic principles of labour law' (*see* Introduction Chapter 6). In addition, rights and duties of the parties can be a subject matter of CLAs and work regulations. Certainly, an employment contract constitutes the major source of rights and duties in a particular case. Moreover, rights and duties of the parties can arise out of a separate contract concluded among the parties to the employment relationship, e.g., a contractual covenant of non-competition (Article 101^1–101^2 LC, Chapter 11), or an agreement between an employer and employee that determines certain aspects of telework (Article 67^{11} §2 LC, *see* Chapter 7, §4).

192. By establishing an employment relationship parties create a comprehensive set of obligations between them. We can say that rights and duties constitute the content of an employment relationship. Those rights are mutual but not always equivalent. For example, the employer is obliged to provide a remuneration for a period of annual paid holidays. He is also responsible for safe and healthy working conditions, even where an employee does not perform work conscientiously and scrupulously. In the recent literature it has been submitted that employers carry out public tasks of social policy.[165]

193. The major duties are connected to the legal nature of the employment relationship. According to Article 22 §1 LC, by establishing an employment relationship an employee undertakes to perform specified work for the benefit of an employer and under his supervision, in a place and at the times determined by the employer, the employer undertakes to employ the employee in return for remuneration. The employee's basic duty is to carry out work for the benefit and under the supervision of the employer. The employer is obliged to employ an employee (i.e., to provide work) and to pay remuneration. Further labour law provisions also constitute a source of rights and duties of the parties to the employment relationship. Articles 94 LC and 100 LC are of major importance since they expressly provide an exemplary list of duties of an employer and an employee. We can classify the duties of the parties as basic and ancillary. Under Article 52 §1 point 1 LC, an employer

165. *See* A. Sobczyk, *Prawo konstytucyjne w świetle Konstytucji RP. Tom I. Teoria publicznego i prywatnego indywidualnego prawa pracy* (Warsaw, C. H. Beck, 2013), pp. 105 et *seq.*

can terminate an employment contract without notice, due to employee's fault in the event of a serious violation of the employee's basic duties. According to Article 55 §1[1] LC, an employee can terminate an employment contract where an employer has committed a serious violation of his/her/their basic duties towards an employee. Therefore, from a practical point of view it is of major importance to determine in particular cases whether the duty of an employer or an employee can be regarded as 'basic'.[166]

§2. Duties of the Employee

I. Duty to Perform Work Conscientiously and Carefully

194. As already indicated, under Article 22 §1 LC the most important duty of an employee is to perform a specified work for the benefit and under subordination of the employer. According to Article 100 §1 LC the employee is obliged to perform work conscientiously and carefully, and to comply with the instructions of superiors that relate to work, as long as they are not contrary to the provisions of law or the employment contract. This provision determines the mode of work performance and introduces the limits of employee's subordination.

195. An employee is obliged to perform work 'conscientiously' and 'carefully'. There is no single universal measure to evaluate whether the work has been carried out 'conscientiously' and 'carefully', which could be applied to all employees. Particular measures can be applied in order to evaluate the work performance of particular professional categories. In principle, higher criteria of evaluation apply to employees who occupy managerial or independent positions. Each employee is obliged to carry out his/her duties with a relevant degree of diligence, to act according to individual's knowledge and experience, to follow employer's instructions, to take initiative in order to complete work, etc.

II. Duty to Follow Employer's Instructions

196. Under Article 100 §1 LC, the employer's instruction should relate to the type of the work agreed in the employment contract as long as they are not contrary to the provisions of law and the employment contract. The employer's instructions, e.g., can determine the mode of work performance. The instructions can also concern the functioning of the undertaking, e.g., following health and safety rules, ban on smoking, etc. The employer's managerial power contains also the competences to evaluate employees, to grant awards and distinctions or to apply penalties in case of violation of rules on maintaining order at the establishment. The employer's instruction should be consistent with the provisions of law (not only 'labour law').

166. *See also* D. Dörre – Kolasa, Rights and Obligations of the Parties to an Employment Relationship, (in:) K. W. Baran (Ed.) Outline of Polish Labour Law System, Wolters Kluwer, Warszawa 2016, pp. 256 et seq.

Therefore, an employer cannot go beyond his competences, e.g., cannot demand the employee to provide personal data not indicated in Article 22^1 LC or to assign a female employee to perform work prohibited for women. On the other hand, several statutory provisions provide the basis for employer's competences to decide unilaterally on particular matters, e.g., the employer enjoys the competence to order overtime work (Article 151 §1 LC) or to recall the employee from holiday leave (Article 167 §1 LC), subject to statutory requirements.

197. In particular cases provided by the LC, an employer can order the performance of another type of work than that agreed in the employment contract. Under Article 42 §4 LC, the termination of work and remuneration conditions is not required if the employee is assigned, where it is justified by employer's needs, work other than that specified in the employment contract, for a period not longer than three months in a calendar year, if it does not reduce the remuneration of the employee and corresponds with his other qualifications. In addition, according to Article 81 §3 LC, the employer may, for a duration of a work stoppage, assign an employee to another appropriate work. In such a situation the employee should receive remuneration corresponding with that work. Where a work stoppage results from an employee's fault, he/she should have the right to remuneration only for the work performed. Thus, in the above-mentioned cases the employer is competent to change work conditions by a unilateral decision, for a definite period of time. The permanent change of employment conditions requires the agreement of the parties or a changing notice (Article 42 §§1–3 LC, *see* Chapter 6, §4).

198. No special form of employer's instruction is required by the law. The employee is bound only by those employer's instructions that fulfil the criteria indicated in Article 100 §1 LC. Refusal to follow the instruction that goes beyond these criteria does not constitute a breach of employee's duties. However, an employee who refuses to follow the instruction bears the risk of the wrong evaluation. If the instruction meets statutory criteria, the employee can be penalized for breach of maintaining order or even can be dismissed without notice. On the other hand, the employee's duty to carry out work conscientiously and carefully excludes uncritical compliance with illegal employer's instructions.[167]

III. Duties to Observe the Order at the Establishment

199. According to Article 100 §2 point 1 LC, the employee is obliged to comply with working time established in the undertaking. Under Article 128 §1 LC, a working time is the time when the employee remains at the disposal of the employer in an undertaking or in any location designated by the employer.[168] Thus, an employee is obliged to remain at the employer's disposal within the period set out as working

167. Supreme Court judgment of 10 Sep. 1997, I PKN 244/97.
168. *See* Chapter 4, §1.

time at the particular undertaking and should be ready to undertake work and follow employer's instructions. He/she should also abstain from taking care of matters not connected with the employment contract. According to Article 104[1] §1 point 9 LC, the workplace regulations should determine the method adopted by the given employer to confirm the time of employees' arrival at work, their presence at work and the procedure for justifying an absence from work.

200. Article 100 §2 point 2 LC provides that the employee should observe the workplace regulations and order adopted at the undertaking. The workplace regulations set out the organization and order in the work process and related rights and duties of the employer and the employees. Thus, the employee is obliged to comply with the rules that regulate the functioning of the undertaking, the work process included. For example, the workplace regulations can determine the rules of access to the employer's premises, ban on smoking or procedure of control of employees upon the leaving the undertaking.

IV. Duty to Observe Health and Safety Regulations

201. Under Article 100 §2 LC, the employee should observe the provisions of law and principles of health and safety at work as well as provisions on fire protection. Rights and duties of the employee are subjects of Chapter II, section Ten LC (Articles 210–212). Particular duties are also imposed by separate statutes. The employee has the right to refrain from work if the conditions of work do not correspond with provisions on health and safety and pose a direct danger to the health or life of the employee or if a work performance presents a threat to other people. The employee is obliged to notify this fact to his/her superior immediately. He/she also retains the right to remuneration (Article 210 LC). Article 211 LC expressly provides that observing the provisions and principles of health and safety at work constitutes a basic duty of the employee. For example, the employee must be familiar with the relevant provisions and principles on health and safety, to carry out work in a manner that complies with the provisions and principles of health and safety at work, to care about the proper condition of machines, devices, tools and equipment. Persons managing employees are subject to additional duties, e.g., with regard to organizing job positions in accordance with provisions and principles on health and safety, care about the efficiency of measures of individual protection, to execute the observance of the relevant rules by employees (Article 212 LC).

V. Duty to Care for the Interest of the Work Establishment

202. Article 100 §2 point 4 LC provides that an employee should care for the interest of the work establishment, protect its property and keep confidential any information, the disclosure of which could cause damage to the employer. Thus, the employee is obliged to be loyal to the employer and to act with a purpose to care for the interest of work establishment. The Supreme Court emphasized that the provision under discussion refers to the 'interests of work establishment' understood as an organizational unit, which is also a workplace, and constitutes a common value, a 'good' not only for the employer but also employees employed at the workplace.[169]

203. On the basis of Article 100 §2 point 4 the employee can be expected not only to perform the work agreed but also to undertake action in the interest of the employer or to abstain from activities that could violate employer's interest, even where a particular behaviour is not expressly provided in the employment contract. For example, the employee can be obliged to undertake additional effort if it is necessary to substitute an unexpectedly absent co-employee. The employee can be expected to undertake actions that divert the threat of the damage in the employer's property or to strive to reduce the scope of damages. The employee should abstain from any actions or activities that could put the employer's repute in question. Although there is no statutory ban to enter into an additional employment relationship with another employer, the employee should not undertake competitive actions against his/her employer. Even where there is no separate contractual covenant on non-competition among parties, such action could be regarded as a violation of Article 100 §2 point 4 LC.

VI. Duty to Respect Confidentiality

204. As mentioned above, Article 100 §2 point 4 LC obliges the employee to keep confidential any information the disclosure of which could cause damage to the employer. Moreover, Article 100 §2 point 5 LC provides the duty to respect confidentiality determined in separate provisions. Thus, employees are obliged to keep in secret the sensitive information that they obtain in the course of performing duties arising out of the employment relationship. Article 11 item 4 of the Suppression of Unfair Competition Act of 16 April 1993[170] refers to undisclosed technical, technological, commercial or organizational information, where the entrepreneur undertook necessary actions to keep their confidentiality. In addition, the Protection of Classified Information Act of 5 August 2010[171] relates to state and professional secrecy. Particular obligations can be imposed on particular professional groups, e.g., those employed in the banking sector or healthcare institutions.

VII. Duty to Respect the Principles of Social Coexistence

205. Article 100 §2 point 6 LC states that the employee is obliged to respect the principles of community coexistence in the work establishment. Thus, the employee should not only observe law provisions, but he/she should also comply with moral,

169. Supreme Court judgment of 2 Oct. 2012, II PK 56/12.
170. Consolidated text *Journal of Laws* 2018 item 419 with further amendments.
171. Consolidated text *Journal of Laws* 2018 item 412 with further amendments.

social and ethic norms. He/she should act in a proper way towards other employees, with the purpose of proper cooperation and avoiding conflicts in the undertaking. For example, an employee who, in the framework of procedure following an accident at work, testifies untruth with regard to commonly known facts violates the duty to care for the interest of the establishment and the duty to respect the principles of social coexistence.[172]

§3. Duties of the Employer

I. Duty to Provide the Employee with Work

206. Under Article 22 §1 LC, the employer 'undertakes to employ the employee in return for remuneration'. Thus, the employer is obliged to provide the employee with work of a specified type, agreed in the employment contract. The employer does not fulfil his/her/their contractual obligations only by paying remuneration. On the basis of Article 22 §1 LC, the employee can claim to be provided with work and to effectively perform agreed work.[173]

207. The amendment of 25 June 2015[174] introduced the new Article 36^2 LC. The new regulation provides that upon the termination of the employment contract, the employer can exempt the employee from the duty to perform work until the end of the period of notice. During this period the employee retains the right to remuneration. Thus, under the amendment, the exemption from the duty to perform work falls within the scope of managerial prerogatives of the employer. The possibility to exempt the employee from work performance refers to the period of notice only. The type of the terminated employment contract, the length of the period of notice or the fact which of the parties terminated the contract are irrelevant and do not affect employer's discretion to exempt the employee from work. The exemption from work performance can cover the entire period of notice or its part. Since there are no further statutory conditions, it seems that the employer can unilaterally change his/her/their decision and call the employee to take up work until the end of the period of notice. Before the above-mentioned amendment took effect, the possibility to exempt the employee from work had not been regulated. However, the Supreme Court accepted that parties could agree on the exemption from work performance during the period of notice.[175]

172. Supreme Court judgment of 12 Jan. 1998, I PKN/458/97.
173. For example, the Supreme Court judgment of 14 May 1999, case I PKN 50/99.
174. *Journal of Laws* (2015), item 1220.
175. Supreme Court judgment of 20 May 1998, I PKN 137/98.

II. Information Duties

A. *Information on the Content of the Employment Relationship*

208. One of the basic duties of the employer is to provide the employee with the information on the substantial elements of the employment relationship (more *see* above Chapter 2, §2).

B. *Making Employees Familiar with the Scope of Their Duties*

209. Article 94 point 1 LC states that the employer is obliged to make new employees familiar with their duties, the manner of performing work at particular posts and their basic rights. The provision refers to a one-off duty to provide specific information to the employees starting work at the undertaking. No particular form is required. Providing such information is also important for the protection employer's interest, e.g., since he/she is responsible for the damages caused by the employee to the third party (Article 120 LC). The employee can be held liable for breach of his/her duties committed only through his/her fault. The lack of proper information can exclude the employee's fault and, as a consequence, his liability for damages. The present regulation does not determine the scope of rights that should be subject to employer's information duty. The employee can claim the access to the information that is substantial to determine his/her employee status.[176]

C. *Other Information Duties*

210. There are several further provisions that impose on the employer information duties in particular situations. For example, the employer is obliged to inform employees about a planned transfer of the work establishment (Article 23^1 §3 LC), the right to lodge a claim to a labour court in case of termination of the employment contract (Article 30 §5 LC), possibility to change the length of working time, i.e., from part-time to full-time or vice versa (Article 94^2 LC), the content of the workplace regulations (Article 104^1 §2 LC), dangers to health and life in the work establishment (Article 207^1 §1 LC) or occupational risks related to the work performed (Article 226 point 2 LC). Thus, in general, employers are subject to extensive information duties concerning various aspects of employee situation.

III. Duty to Organize the Work Process

211. The employer is obliged to organize work in a manner that ensures the effective use of working time as well as achieving high efficiency and appropriate

176. Supreme Court judgment of 16 Sep. 1999, I PKN 331/99.

quality of work through the use of the capacities and qualifications of the employees (Article 100 §1 point 2 LC). The duty implies also providing the employee with adequate equipment; it is not enough to pay the financial equivalent for the use of private employee's equipment.[177] In addition, the work should be organized in a manner ensuring a reduction in the strenuousness of work, in particular with regard to monotonous work and work of a determined pace (Article 100 §1 point 2a LC). The latter duty was introduced in order to meet the requirements Article 6 of the Council Directive 89/391/EEC of 12 June 1989 on the introduction of measures to encourage improvements in the safety and health of workers at work[178] and Article 13 of the Directive 2003/88 of 4 November 2003 concerning certain aspects of the organization of working time.[179]

IV. Duty to Counteract Discrimination

212. Polish labour law introduced the extensive regulations on the prohibition of discrimination in employment (*see* Chapter 7 of the Introduction). Article 94 point 2b LC obliges the employer to act against discrimination in employment, in particular with respect to sex, age, disability, race, religion, nationality, political belief, trade union membership, ethnic origin, belief, sexual orientation as well as on the ground of employment for a definite or indefinite period of time, or in full-time or part-time employment. The employer should also provide employees with the text of the legal regulations on equal treatment, the information in written form announced at the undertaking. Alternatively, the employer must ensure that employees have the access to these provisions in another method that is used by the given employer (Article 94^1 LC). This provision was introduced by the amendment to the LC of 14 November 2003 in order to meet the requirements of EU Directives on the prohibition of discrimination in employment. It should be also recalled that the employer is obliged to respect the employee's dignity and other personal rights (Article 11^1 LC) and should act against mobbing in the work establishment (Article 94^3 LC).

V. Duty to Ensure Safe and Healthy Working Conditions

213. Employers' duty to ensure the health and safe working conditions for their employees belongs to the basic principles of labour law (Article 15 LC). Moreover, Article 94 point 4 LC states that the employer is obliged to ensure healthy and safe working conditions for employees and to provide systematic training on health and safety at work. Further obligations of employers are subject to section 10 Chapter I of the LC (Articles 207–209^3) and numerous separate legal Acts. It is the employer who is responsible for health and safety in the work establishment. The employer is obliged to protect the health and life of employees by ensuring conditions of health

177. Supreme Court judgment of 7 Nov. 1978, I PZ 21/78.
178. *Official Journal* L 183, 29 Jun. 1989, pp. 0001–0008.
179. *Official Journal* L 299, 18 Nov. 2003, pp. 0009–0019.

and safety at work by an appropriate use and application of the achievements of science and technology (Article 207 LC). For example, the employer should organize work in a manner ensuring health and safety at work, ensure that instructions on that issue are observed, reacting to needs in relation to ensuring health and safety. Thus, the employer is obliged to ensure safe working conditions in practice, according to current needs, by the application of all means that remain at his disposal. The employer is obliged to ensure safe and healthy conditions to individuals who carry out work on a basis other than employment relationship in the work establishment or another location designated by the employer, as well as to persons who perform business activity on their own account, in the work establishment or a location designated by the employer. The same duty relates to students and pupils who are not employees (Article 304 LC).

VI. Duty to Pay Remuneration Timely and Correctly

214. The employee always performs work in return for remuneration (Article 22 §1 LC). The employer is obliged to pay remuneration timely and correctly (Article 94 point 5 LC). Thus, the employer should pay the agreed amount of remuneration at least once a month. The delay in paying remuneration constitutes the ground for claiming interests by an employee. The employer is not entitled to reduce the amount of remuneration or cannot unilaterally enforce the deductions. In addition, it constitutes an offence against employee rights (Article 281).

VII. Duty to Facilitate the Improvement of Professional Qualifications

215. The employer is obliged to enable employees to improve their professional qualifications (Article 17 LC and Article 94 point 6 LC). However, statutory provisions do not constitute the ground of an enforceable claim, i.e., the employee cannot demand that a particular form of training (e.g., computer training) should be organized in the work establishment.[180]

216. The professional qualifications of employees are regulated by the Chapter 3 of the LC (Articles 102–103^6 LC). Improving professional qualifications means acquiring or supplementing the knowledge and skills of the employee, upon the initiative of the employer or his/her/their consent. The employee who improves his/her qualifications has the right to a training leave, release from work for a period necessary to participate in obligatory classes. The training leave amounts to six days or twenty-one days, the latter option relates to the preparation of graduation thesis and final exams. The employee retains the right to remuneration for that period. The employer can also grant additional benefits, e.g., can cover education fees or travel or accommodation costs. The employer and the employee should conclude an agreement determining their mutual rights and duties relating to the improvement of qualifications. Such an agreement should be made in writing and cannot be less

180. Supreme Court judgment of 20 May 2000, I PKN 657/99.

favourable to the employee than the LC provisions on the improvement of professional qualifications. There is no obligation to conclude such an agreement where the employee does not intend to oblige the employee to stay in employment after completing the improvement of professional qualifications. In certain situations the employee is obliged to return the costs reimbursed by the employer. This duty lies on the employee who will not start the improving qualifications or disrupt it, who will be dismissed without notice through his/her fault within the period of three years after completing the improvement of qualifications or who will terminate an employment contract within this period. Moreover, the employee can be granted release from work without retaining the right to remuneration or an unpaid leave, according to the stipulations in an agreement between the employer and the employee.

VIII. Duty to Create Favourable Conditions for Employees Starting Work

217. The employer is obliged to create for employees taking up employment after graduation from a vocational school or a school of higher education conditions favourable for their adaptation to an appropriate work performance (Article 94 point 7 LC). Thus, the employer has particular duties of care towards employees who start their professional career after completing the education. In addition, the employer is obliged to ensure care and help for minor employees, as necessary, for them to adapt to proper work performance (Article 192 LC).

IX. Duty to Satisfy the Social Needs of Employees

218. The employer's duty to satisfy the welfare, social and cultural needs of employees, in accordance with possibilities and conditions, belongs to the basic principles of labour law (Article 16 LC). In addition, according to Article 94 point 8 LC the employer should satisfy, through the means available, the social needs of the employees. These provisions do not constitute the ground for an enforceable claim. Further duties can arise on the basis of the Company's Social Fund Act of 4 March 1994.[181] According to this Act, social activities carried out by the employer refer to various forms of rest, social and educational activities, sport and recreation activities, taking care of children in a crèche or day care centre, providing material assistance, in money or in kind, as well as financial help dedicated to housing purposes. The company's social fund should be created by employers who employ at least twenty employees, calculated on the basis of full-time employment. For example, holiday allowances can be financed by the Fund.

---

181. Consolidated text *Journal of Laws* 2017, item 2191, with further amendments.

X. Duty to Apply Objective Criteria when Evaluating Employees

219. The employer is obliged to apply objective and just criteria for evaluating employees and the effects of their work (Article 94 point 9 LC). Thus, the employer's decisions affecting employees should be based on objective criteria, e.g., work effectiveness, professional qualifications, etc. The evaluation should be connected to the employee's duties and the employer's demands. Employer's expectations which were not communicated to the employee upon concluding the labour contact or within its duration cannot constitute a ground for employee evaluation.[182] There are no statutory criteria of evaluation enshrined in the LC. However, quite often, employers introduce in a work establishment an internal procedure for evaluating employees on a regular basis. Where the employer introduces a collective redundancy, he/she has the competence to select employees to be dismissed, according to criteria indicated in Article 94 point 9.[183] A period of employment at the given undertaking cannot constitute the only criterion to select the employee for dismissal in the framework of collective redundancies.[184] Thus, under Polish labour law there is no principle of 'last in, first out'.[185]

XI. Duty to Keep Documentation in Matters Connected with the Employment Relationship

220. The employer is obliged to keep documentation in matters connected with the labour relationship as well as personal files of employees (Article 94 point 9a LC). In addition, he/she is obliged to keep records in matters concerning the labour relationship and personal files of employees is such a condition that are not threatened by damage or destruction (Article 94 point 9b LC). The new rules on the scope of employer's obligations have been introduced by the Act of 10 January 2018 on the amendment of some acts in connection to shortening of the period of keeping employee files and their electronization (Journal of Laws 2018, item 357). The new provisions (Article 94^4 – 94^{15} LC) take effect on 1 January 2019. The employer is obliged to keep personal employee files in paper or electronic form for a period of ten years. The employer is entitled to change the mode of keeping the files. He should also inform employees about the possibility to collect their documentations. If an employee does not reclaim the files, the employer is entitled to destroy them after the statutory period has elapsed.

XII. Duty to Influence the Rules of Social Coexistence

221. The employer is obliged to influence the establishment of rules of social coexistence in the undertaking. (Article 94 point 10 LC). Thus, the employer should

182. Supreme Court judgment of 10 Nov. 1998, I PKN 428/98.
183. Supreme Court judgment of 19 Dec. 1997, I PKN 422/99.
184. Supreme Court judgment of 16 Sep. 1997, I PKN 259/9.
185. *See* P. Walorska, *Staż pracy* (Warsaw, Wolters Kluwer Business, 2014), pp. 245 et seq.

support and promote ethical and moral behaviour of employees. He/she/they should also respect employees' dignity and react to any negative outcomes that can arise at the work establishment. Employees are subject to this duty as well.

XIII. Duty to Counteract Mobbing

A. Definition of Mobbing

222. The duty to counteract mobbing is relatively new. The regulation relating to this phenomenon was introduced into Polish law by the amendment to the LC of 14 November 2004.[186] Under Article 94^3 1 LC an employer is responsible for counteracting mobbing (Article 94^3 §1 LC). In the light of the definition contained in the Code, mobbing means actions or behaviour relating to an employee or directed against an employee, consisting in persistent and prolonged harassment or intimidation of the employee, provoking in the employee a low assessment of his/her professional usefulness, causing or intended to cause humiliation or ridiculing the employee, causing his/her isolation or elimination from the team of employees (Article 94^3 §2 LC). The statutory features of workplace bullying defined in the LC must be met jointly.[187] The definition does not explicitly state this, but nevertheless it should be assumed that mobbing covers unlawful actions and involves infringement of an employee's dignity. Mobbing, within the meaning of the code, refers only to the employment relationship and it does not concern civil law contracts. The definition of workplace bullying comprises a number of vague and evaluative elements, which causes practical problems. Workplace bullying is the subject of a great many court rulings.

223. When judging whether in a given situation we are dealing with mobbing, we have to take into account that the employer exercises management in the labour process. The employer has the right to give instructions and make sure that they are carried out. Certainly, not every conflict situation or unpleasantness experienced by an employee can be considered as mobbing. For example, a job appraisal will not be mobbing even if it involves the stress of the appraised person or criticism of a person's achievements. In the light of court rulings, by mobbing is meant unlawful, methodical and prolonged behaviour (action and omission) of persons who are members of a certain group, taken for no reason or for an evidently trivial reason, directed against other members (member) of the team harming their legally protected interests and aimed at forcing the victim(s) outside a given group. Unfavourable assessment of an employee's work cannot be considered as mobbing unless the supervisor's intention is to humiliate the employee. If the supervisor's intention is aimed at assuring the execution of a plan or proper organization of work, such an action is not workplace bullying. The notion of mobbing does not cover an employer's actions allowed under law.[188]

---

186. *Journal of Laws* (2003), No. 213, item 2081.
187. Supreme Court judgment of 11 Feb. 2014, I PK 165/13.
188. Supreme Court judgment of 22 Apr. 2015, II PK 166/14.

224. Mobbing includes persistent and continuing persecution. The code regulations do not indicate the time period in which the occurrence of workplace bullying can be found. One-off behaviour does not meet the definition of this phenomenon according to the opinion prevailing in the literature of the subject. In the light of court rulings the long-lasting character of persecution or intimidation of an employee within the meaning of Article 94^3 §2 LC has to be examined individually and should consider the circumstances of the particular case. Therefore, it is not possible to indicate a fixed minimum period required for workplace bullying to occur. Article 94^3 §2 and §3 LC implies that the moment of occurrence of the effects of harassment and intimidation indicated in these regulations and the persistence and the intensity of such actions is important for the assessment of the long-lasting character.[189] At the same time the examination and assessment of the subjective feelings of a person who believes that his/her superior is harassing him/her cannot be the basis for establishing responsibility for mobbing. A judgement about whether there was harassment and intimidation of an employee and what as the purpose of those actions must be based on objective criteria.[190] In other words, apart from the need to individually examine each case, the assessment of the occurrence of the effects of mobbing should be based on objective criteria.

225. Mobbing can be similar to harassment referred to in Article 18^{3a} §5 point LC. In practice, both can take the form of identical actions which violate an employee's dignity. The basic difference is that harassment can be a one-time action whereas workplace bullying is a process stretching over a period of time. In addition, harassment is regulated in the chapter of the LC dealing with the equal treatment of employees.

B. Liability for Mobbing

226. The code definition does not describe the perpetrator of mobbing but indicates that the regulation deals with 'action or behaviour concerning the employee' or 'directed against the employee'. Thus, the bully can be the employer, superior or fellow workers of the victim. According to Article 94^3 §1 LC, the person responsible for counteracting mobbing is the employer; therefore, workplace bullying claims can be made against him in the first place. In the light of the rulings of the Supreme Court the duty to counteract mobbing consists in acting with diligence. The employer should, therefore, counteract mobbing, in particular, by staff training, by informing employees about the dangers and consequences of workplace bullying or by applying procedures which will enable the detection and ending of this phenomenon. If, in a lawsuit based on the employer's liability for mobbing, the employer proves that he/she/they took real actions to counteract mobbing and, judging those actions from an objective point of view, their potential effectiveness can

189. Supreme Court judgment of 17 Jan. 2007, I PK 176/06.
190. Supreme Court judgment of 19 Mar. 2012, II PK 303/11, Supreme Court judgment of 23 Jan. 2018, III PK 13/17.

be confirmed, the employer can release himself from liability.[191] Consequently, in such a situation the perpetrator of workplace bullying can be called into account.

227. The LC gives the victims of mobbing the right to specific claims. First, it should be noted that under Article 94^3 §3 LC an employee to whom workplace bullying caused bodily or mental harm may demand an appropriate sum as monetary compensation for incurred damage from the employer. The necessary prerequisite for the award of the compensation is, therefore, an effect of mobbing in the form of bodily or mental harm. The injured employee is charged with the burden of proof in this respect.[192]

228. LC regulations do not indicate any criteria which should be taken into account when fixing the amount of the compensation. Court rulings favour the view that mobbing is a qualified offence under labour law, and the sanction for committing it are labour law events which are judged by courts primarily on the basis of Article 94^3 LC, though taking into consideration the achievements of jurisprudence concerning compensation for incurred harm as well as compensation for damage caused by bodily or mental harm.[193] In other words, it is allowed to use the achievements of civil law when determining the amount of compensation for bodily or mental harm caused by mobbing. According to the opinions expressed in the doctrine, the amount of the compensation should not be a token gesture but it should have a notable economic value, adequate to the circumstances of the case and to the consequences of the workplace bullying.

229. The employee is entitled, also, to other benefits which result from the termination of an employment contract without notice due to mobbing. According to Article 94^3 §4 LC an employee who terminated his or her contract of employment on account of workplace bullying has the right to sue the employer for compensation for not less than the minimum wage fixed by separate regulations. Thus, an employee who has been forced to leave a job because of mobbing is entitled to compensation. The Act specifies only the minimum level of compensation without defining its upper limit. The employee's declaration about the termination of his or her employment contract due to workplace bullying should be made in writing and should give the reason for the termination (Article 94^3 §5 LC). This regulation is exceptional in Polish labour law since, in principle, an employee who terminates his employment contract by notice does not have the duty to justify his/her decision.

230. Workplace bullying can be also classified as a gross breach of employer's duties towards the employee. That is why workplace bullying justifies termination of the employment contract by the employee, which can be construed from Article 55 $§1^1$ LC.

191. Supreme Court judgment of 3 Aug. 2011, I PK 35/11.
192. Supreme Court judgment of 7 May 2009, III PK 2/09, Supreme Court judgment of 23 Jan. 2018, II PK 333/16.
193. Supreme Court judgment of 29 Mar. 2007, II PK 228/06, Supreme Court judgment of 8 Aug. 2017, I PK 206/16.

XIV. Duty to Issue a Work Certificate

231. Upon the termination or expiry of the employment relationship, the employer is obliged to issue, immediately, a work certificate to the employee (Articles 97–99 LC). *See* Chapter 6, §6.

XV. Other Duties

232. Although it is not expressly stated in the statutory provisions it is accepted in the doctrine, and the employer should care for the employee's welfare. Thus, an employer should take action in favour of an employee even where this is not expressly provided in labour law provisions. For example, according to the judiciary, the general duty to take care for of employee's good implies the duty to inform employees and ex-employees about their rights connected to the process of privatization of a state-owned enterprise.[194]

233. According to the judiciary, the employer is responsible for the employee's belongings. Upon concluding an employment relationship the employer undertakes to safeguard the appropriate working conditions, which implies *inter alia* the duty to take care for employees' things which were brought to the work establishment in connection with work.[195] However, the employer is not responsible for a golden ring which was left in a locker in a cloakroom.[196] In addition, according to Article 237^1 §2 LC an employee who has suffered from an accident at work is entitled to compensation from the employer for any loss or injury connected to a damage to his personal items or items necessary to perform work, except for a loss or damage to vehicles and money.

194. Supreme Court judgment of 17 Feb. 2004, I PK 386/03.
195. Supreme Court judgment of 17 Oct. 1977, I PR 89/77.
196. Supreme Court judgment of 26 Jul. 1979, I PRN 76/79.

Chapter 4. Working Time

Z. Hajn

§1. Legal Notion of Working Time

234. Observance of working time established at the work establishment is one of the employee's most important duties (Article 100 §2 point 1), being part of his/her general duty to do work. Meanwhile, the employer is obliged to organize work in a manner which ensures that working time is used in full (Article 94, point 2), the obligation being part of the duty to employ the worker and secure the cooperation of the parties in fulfilment of what they are expected to undertake. The working time is also the measure of the length of work and – indirectly – of the amount of labour and the remuneration payable. Nevertheless, the essence of the working time legal regulation lies in the protection of the employee's safety and health and his/her right to rest. The fact is stressed by the LC, which lists the right of an employee to enjoy a rest ensured by 'regulations on working hours, days free of work and holidays' among fundamental principles of the labour law (Article 14). A similar regulation of working time issues is provided by the Constitution, according to which, 'An employee shall have the right to statutorily specified days free from work as well as annual paid holidays; the maximum permissible hours of work shall be specified by statute' (Article 66, part 2).[197] It is also worth mentioning that the Working Time Directive 2003/88/EC concerning certain aspects of the organization of working time looks on the issue as a measure of improvement of workers' safety, hygiene and health at work.

235. The general regulation of working time is provided by Division 6 of the LC. For certain categories of employees, of importance is, however, specific legislation whereby considerable differences from those general rules have been introduced. The legislation includes, in particular, the laws that provide for the working time of drivers, teachers, university lecturers, health professionals, public officials (whether of the central or regional/local government), judges and public prosecutors.

236. According to Article 128 LC, working time is the time when an employee remains at the disposal of the employer in the work establishment or in another place where work is to be performed. Remaining at the disposal of the employer means that the employee is actually prepared to do work and intends to perform it. As the Supreme Court indicated in its judgment of 2 September 2003, I PK 345/02, it is the condition in which the employee may, when called upon by the employer, begin working without delay. The fundamental part of working time is the time of exercising genuine work. The legal concept of working time includes, however, also

197. The Constitutional Tribunal in its judgment of 24 Sep. 2000, K 12/00, stated that appropriate regulation of working time was one of the elements of the safe and hygienic conditions of work within the meaning of Art. 66 part 2 of the Constitution.

certain periods when work is not performed, provided that the employee remains at the disposal of the employer. Counted towards the working time is, *inter alia*, the time of waiting for assignment of work, downtime, i.e., the time when work is stopped owing to unforeseen able disturbances, most often concerning technology, organization or weather conditions (Article 81 §§2–4 LC),[198] periods of rest at the workplace, breaks for nursing a child, periodic and control medical check-ups, safety and hygiene training courses, medical checks relating to pregnancy, the schooling time of a young employee and others.

§2. Length of Working Time

I. Basic Working Time

237. As a rule, normal working time (overtime hours not being taken into account) may not be longer than eight hours in a twenty-four-hour period starting with the hour on which the employee begins work and an average of forty hours in an average five-day working week in any applicable reference period of not more than four months (Article 129 LC). The definition means that an employee may work, on certain weeks, for a greater number of days, provided that the extension is compensated for by relevant shortening of the working time in another part of the reference period.

238. In the agricultural and breeding sectors, as well as in the services of surveillance of property or persons, a reference period of not more than six months may be introduced, and if this is also justified by unusual organizational or technical conditions which affect the working process, a reference period of not more than twelve months.

II. Length of Weekly Joint Working Time

239. The average working time for each seven-day period, including overtime, may not exceed forty-eight hours in any applicable reference period (Article 131 §1 LC).

III. Reduced Working Time

240. In instances indicated in law, the working time gets shortened. For instance, the working time of a young person of less than 16 years of age may not be longer

198. For the time of waiting for assignment of work and downtime the employee is entitled to remuneration in accordance with his/her individual scale, calculated at an hourly or monthly rate, and where this component of remuneration was not singled out when the terms of remunerating were established as 60% of the remuneration.

than six hours in a twenty-four-hour period. Disabled persons with severe or moderate disability may not work longer than seven hours in a twenty-four-hour period, and thirty-five hours a week. The reduction of the working time of employees who are employed in particularly onerous conditions or in conditions which are particularly harmful to health may consist in providing for breaks from work which are counted as working time, or in reducing such norms, and in the case of monotonous work or work in a set pace it consists in introducing breaks from work which count as working time. A statutorily based reduction of working time also concerns certain groups of professionals, e.g., some healthcare professionals.

Each public holiday which falls on a day other than Sunday reduces the length of working time by eight hours.

Working time reduction may be also provided for by CLAs and work rules. So far, the possibility has been used occasionally.[199]

IV. Extended Working Time

241. Extension of working time may concern, as a rule, only the working time in a twenty-four-hour period, provided that the maximum weekly working time of forty hours in the reference period is retained. Only when it comes to work in activities involving continuity of operation is it admissible to extend the working time to an average of forty-three hours per week in a reference period for not longer than four weeks.

§3. Rest Periods

I. Daily and Weekly Rest Periods

242. An employee is entitled to a minimum of eleven hours, per a twenty-four-hour period, of uninterrupted daily rest and to at least thirty-five hours per week of uninterrupted weekly rest. The weekly rest should fall on a Sunday, but when work on Sunday is allowed it may fall on another day.

II. Break from Work

243. Where the working time of an employee in a twenty-four-hour period is at least six hours, the employee is entitled to at least a fifteen-minute break from work counted as the working time.

---

199. *See Sprawozdanie Głównego Inspektora Pracy z działalności Państwowej Inspekcji Pracy w 2013 r.* (Warsaw, 2014), p. 28.

§4. Organization of Working Time

I. Systems and Schedules of Working Time

244. The freedom of the employer (or parties to a CLA) to organize working time is limited by the requirement of compliance with the working time schedules applied at the work establishment with systems of working time authorized by the LC (or other pieces of legislation). Both the system and schedule of working time should be established by the CLA, work rules, announcement made by the employer or be agreed upon in the contract of employment. It is only the working time system respecting the rules of the basic working time provided for in Article 129 §1 LC (and described above) that does not have to be expressly established. Where such a system is adopted, it is sufficient to set the schedule determining the hours in which the employee is obliged to remain at the disposal of the employer within a twenty-four-hour period, week and reference period. Other systems aim at the flexibility of working time, allowing specific exceptions from the basic working time within the twenty-four-hour period, length of the reference period, prohibition of work on Sundays and public holidays, etc.

245. The LC provides for following working time systems:

- Equivalent working time – under this system it is admissible to extend the daily working time within a reference period on condition that the extended daily working time is offset by a shorter working time on some other days or by days off in a reference period not exceeding, as a rule, one month (Articles 135–137 LC). In particularly justified cases the reference period may be extended up to three months, and in case of work dependent on season or weather conditions (e.g., construction, winter maintenance) up to four months. Generally speaking, this working time system may be applied in situations justified by the type of work or its organization. In such cases the daily working time may be extended to a maximum of twelve hours. Yet, as regards work that consists in surveillance of equipment or is connected with partial standby (as the case is, *inter alia*, with emergency technical services) the daily working time may be extended up to sixteen hours. But, the daily working time of those employed as security guards to protect property or people, as well as employees of company fire brigades and company rescue teams, may be extended up to twenty-four hours.
- Working time in continuous work processes is applied to work in activities involving continuity of operation due to the technology of production; the rules are also applicable if work cannot be discontinued considering permanent attendance to the needs of the public. Under this system it is allowed to extend the working time up to forty-three hours per week, on average, within the reference period not longer than four weeks; on one day in certain weeks of the period the daily working time may be extended up to twelve hours. For each working time over eight hours a day on the day when work is done under the extended working time scheme the employee is entitled to and supplement to remuneration, yet the work is not considered to be overtime work (Article 138 LC). The system may

not be applied when, given production technologies, the device can be deactivated. Continuous work supposed to meet the needs of the public is performed, for instance, in the field of healthcare, water and power supplies or passenger transport.[200]

- Interrupted working time allows the employer to introduce not more than one break from work in a day, not counted as working time. Application of the system is allowed if justified by the type of work or its organization. The breaks have to be set in the working time schedule in advance and must not exceed five hours. They are not reckoned towards working hours, but for the time of the break the employee is entitled to remuneration amounting to half the remuneration for downtime (Article 139 LC). Besides, one break not exceeding sixty minutes, not reckoned against working hours, may be introduced by the employer. This may be destined for the employee having a meal or handling his/her personal matters (Article 141 LC).
- Working time defined by tasks is the working time determined by reference to the tasks of an employee, provided that they may be performed within the basic time limits (Article 140 LC). The working time is, thus, set not by means of determining the working hours but the tasks to be done by the employee, the latter being able to independently decide on the length of the working day, number of the working days or number and length of breaks from work. The system may be applied where it is justified by the type of work or its organization or the place where the work is to be done. In practice, the work in question is usually one that does not involve team collaboration. If the tasks have been determined properly, work exceeding the basic working time is not deemed overtime work. Otherwise, additional remuneration may be claimed by the employee.[201]
- A compressed working week scheme allows the employee to work for fewer than five days per week, while the daily working time is extended to not more than twelve hours in a reference period not longer that one month (Article 143 LC);
- Weekend work is a system whereby work is performed exclusively on Fridays, Saturdays, Sundays and on public holidays. Under this system, the maximum daily working time may be extended to more than twelve hours in a reference period not longer than one month (Article 144 LC).
- Different hours of starting work – an employee may decide when to commence work on a given day within the time range specified in a working time schedule (Article 140^1 LC).

Shift work is admissible irrespective of the working time system being applied.

II. Establishing Systems and Schedules of Working Time

246. The systems and schedules of working time and the reference periods are determined in a collective agreement or in work rules. Employers not bound by a

200. In its judgment of 5 May 1999, I PKN 671/98, the Supreme Court stated that work of that kind does not include the running of fuel pump stations.
201. Supreme Court judgment of 4 Aug. 1999, I PKN 181/99.

collective agreement or not obliged to set out workplace regulations determine these matters in a written notice.[202] The reduced week and weekend work systems may be introduced by employment contract only. In any case, upon a written request by an employee, the employer may set out an individual schedule of working time for that employee within the framework of the system of working time applicable to the person in question.

§5. Overtime Work and Other Activities Beyond Normal Working Hours

I. Overtime Work

247. At the employer's request the employee is obliged to do overtime work.[203]

248. Doing such work may be ordered by the employer in two situations. First, when there is a need to mount a rescue operation to save human life or health or to protect property or the environment or to repair a breakdown. Second, in the case of special needs of the employer. In practice, overtime work is most often ordered for reasons of the employer's special needs. It is for the employer to judge whether such needs exist, on the understanding that such situations must be unforeseeable. Work planned ahead does not come within this scope.

249. Overtime work may not be done by pregnant employees, young persons and employees who are employed at work posts where the maximum admissible concentration and intensity of agents harmful to human health have been exceeded. As a rule, prohibitions are also applicable to employees who take care of a child below 4 years of age and to disabled employees. They may, however, do such work if they consent to. In case of a disabled employee, also doctor's authorization is required.

250. The number of overtime hours may not exceed 150 annually, the limit not being applicable to the work ordered to hold a rescue operation. In addition, in the CLA or work rules or in the contract of employment (where an employer is not bound by a collective agreement or obliged to the set-out work rules), a higher number of overtime hours may be prescribed (Article 151 §3 and §4 LC).

251. For overtime work done an employee is entitled, besides regular remuneration, also to extra pay. The extra pay amounts to 100% of remuneration calculated as the downtime remuneration – for the overtime work done at night, on Sundays

202. The notice enters into force two weeks from the date on which it was communicated to the employees in the manner customary at a given work establishment.

203. The judiciary allows, to be recognized as overtime work, also the work done without the instruction of the employer but with the latter's knowledge and agreement, and – exceptionally – also the work done without the employer's knowledge where, considering circumstances of the case, doing the work was objectively necessary for reasons of interest of the work establishment; *see*, e.g., the Supreme Court judgments of: 26 May 2000, I PKN 667/99; 3 Oct. 1978, I PRN 91/78.

and public holidays (not being days of work for the employee) and on a day off granted to the employee for work on those days, and 50% of such remuneration – for the work done on any other day (Article 151^{1} §1). At the employee's request, made in writing, or at the initiative of the employer, time off may be also taken in lieu of remuneration for the overtime hours. In the former case the proportion of the time off to the time worked is 1:1, in the latter 1.5: 1 (Article 151^{2} LC).

252. In part-time work the parties ought to agree an admissible number of working hours above the working time set out in the employment contract which – if exceeded – entitle the employee to be paid the overtime extra payment (Article 151 §5 LC).

II. Other Activities Beyond Normal Working Hours

A. *Introductory Remarks*

253. The employee is also obliged to take, in the interest of the employer, other than overtime work, actions beyond regular working hours. These include duty shifts and business trips. In scholarly writing and among practitioners doubts are voiced whether the time spent on activities of that kind should be the reckoned towards working hours and to what extent. Some uncertainties also arise as far as the qualification of the time of job-related employee training is concerned.

B. *Duty Shifts*

254. According to Article 151^{5} LC, a duty shift is characterized by the fact that the worker must be present at a place determined by his/her employer and must keep himself/herself available to take up his/her duties stipulated in the employment contract, if so requested by the employer. This may cover different situations:

- a duty time, when the employee is obliged to remain continuously attentive in order to be able to act immediately, should the need arise;
- on call duty when, being present at a place determined by his employer, the employee is authorized to rest or occupy himself/herself as he/she sees fit as long as his/her services are not required;
- a standby shift served at home, when, in practice, the worker is not obliged to remain waiting in a place designated by the employer but it is sufficient for him/her to be reachable at any time so that he/she may be called upon at short notice to perform his/her professional tasks.

255. The time of performing duty may not prejudice the employee's right to daily or weekly rest. Meanwhile, the LC expressly provides that the duty time is not counted as working time.[204] For the time in question the employee is entitled to time off equal to the length of the duty, and where time off may not be granted, the employee is entitled to remuneration counted like for the downtime. The effective working time when on duty is, however, reckoned towards the working time and is, as a rule, overtime, with all the consequences of the fact.[205]

256. For a standby shift served at home the employee is entitled neither to time off nor remuneration, unless the right to compensation stems from the CLA, workplace pay rules or contract of employment.

C. *Business Trips*

257. Employee duties performed beyond the regular working hours also include business trips, i.e., situations in which the employee, acting upon instructions of his/her employer, performs business duties outside the location of the seat of the employer or outside of the place where he/she normally performs work. The issue whether the time of a business trip should be reckoned towards the working time is controversial. The judiciary has, however, adopted a rule that it is only the time devoted to the performance of a business task and the time of the travel falling to the regular working hours of the employee that is counted as the working time.[206] Besides remuneration for work, the employee is entitled to reimbursement of costs related to the trip.

D. *Training Courses*

258. As a rule, the time of work-related training is not reckoned towards the working time. There are, however, certain exceptions from the rule. In particular, time of the occupational safety and health training course is counted as the working hours (Article 237^3 §2 LC) and so is the time of vocational training attended at the employer's instruction within the working hours, as specified by the schedule of the latter. The arguable issue whether the time of vocational training attended after working hours should be reckoned towards the working time has not been so far resolved by the judiciary.

§6. Night Work

259. A night worker is an employee whose working time schedule includes, in every twenty-four-hour period, at least three hours of night work or a quarter of

---

204. Medical duties have been provided for differently. These are reckoned towards the working time (Art. 95 of the Act of 15 Apr. 2011 on Medical Activity; *Journal of Laws* (2013), item 217, as amended).
205. *See* Supreme Court sentence of 31 Jan. 1978 r., I PRN 147/77.
206. *See*, e.g., Supreme Court judgements of: 27 Oct. 1981, I PR 85/81; 23 Jun. 2005, II PK 265/04).

whose work within the reference period falls during night-time. Night-time, within the meaning of the LC, is a period of eight hours between 2100 and 0700 hrs., as set in the work rules. The working hours of a night worker may not exceed eight hours per each twenty-four-hour period if the employee does a particularly hazardous work or one requiring high physical or mental efforts. The night worker is entitled to an extra pay for each hour of night work, amounting to 20% of the hourly rate following from the minimum wage (Article 151^7–151^8 LC).

260. Young workers and pregnant women may not be employed at night. Employees who take care of a child below 4 years of age and disabled employees may do such work only if they consent to.

§7. Work on Sundays, Public Holidays and Saturdays

261. Sundays and public holidays listed in the Act of 18 January 1951 on Days Free of Work[207] are days off. For that reason work on those days is not allowed, as a rule, save for the exclusions provided for in law (Article 151^{10} LC). There is a general consensus that these exemptions should be interpreted in a restrictive way. Such an interpretation is, unfortunately, difficult to apply as the exemptions are numerous and formulated in a wide and flexible way.

Article 151^{10} LC provides that work on Sundays and public holidays is permitted: (1) when rescue operations need to be conducted to protect the life and health of human beings, property, environment or to remove a technical problem; (2) in a continuous process work; (3) in shift work; (4) when necessary repair work is going on; (5) in transport and communication services; (6) in company fire brigades and rescue teams; (7) when guarding property or people; (8) in agriculture and animal husbandry; (9) when performing work that has to be done on account of its social utility and the daily requirements of the general public; in particular, in services, gastronomy, hotels, municipal services, healthcare organizations and other healthcare establishments taking care of people whose condition requires around-the-clock or daily care, social welfare and organizations for young people offering cultural, educational, tourist and leisure services; (10) in weekend working hour system, i.e., with respect to employees working only on Fridays, Saturdays, Sundays and holidays; (11) in services with the involvement of means of electronic communication received outside of the territory of the Republic of Poland, if days off by Polish law are days of work for those receiving the services.

262. Restrictions in performing work in retail sales shops on Sundays and public holidays and on 24 December and on Saturday immediately preceding the first day of Easter are determined by the provisions of the Act of 10 January 2018 on the limitation of trade on Sundays and public holidays and on certain other days. According to the Act, the ban on work on Sundays is to be introduced gradually during 2018–2020 to cover, from 2020, all Sundays with certain derogations (Article 151^{9b} LC).

207. Consolidated text: *Journal of Laws* (2015), item 90.

263. Priority is given to the rule of compensating holiday or Sunday work with a day off. Hence, for such work the employee is offered, first and foremost, a day off on another date indicated in the LC within the same reference period. An employee is entitled to a full day off, independently of how long he/she worked on a Sunday or on a holiday.[208] When an employee cannot take advantage of a day off on a given date, he/she is entitled to extra pay to the amount of 100% of remuneration, calculated as for overtime, for each hour worked on a Sunday or a public holiday. Regardless of the reasons for doing work on those days, the employee should have Sunday off at least once every four weeks (Articles 151^{11}–151^{12} LC).

264. The right to be free from work on religious holidays is also (besides the above-mentioned Act of 1951) provided for by the Act on the Freedom of Conscience and Religion of 1989[209] and by-laws determining the legal status of various churches and religious denominations. In general, according to those provisions, days off for members of churches and other religious communities whose religious holidays are not public ones may, upon their request, be established on the days celebrated as holidays in their respective religion. However, a day off may be offered, on condition, that is offset by another working day. So far, there have been no serious indications of difficulties or conflicts relating to the implementation of the right to celebrate holidays for these minorities.

265. The other day off, besides Sunday, in a week including five working days, may be any day from Monday to Saturday. Usually, however, the day is Saturday. The work on such a day may be ordered subject to general conditions concerning overtime work, although it should be compensated for by, first of all, granting the employee another day off within the reference period. Only where the employee is unable to benefit from the solution is he entitled to remuneration with the extra pay for overtime work (Article 151^3 and Article 151^{11} §3 LC).

§8. Working Time of the Management Staff

266. Essential derogations from the working time protective regulations concern employees who manage the work establishment on behalf of an employer, i.e., employees who manage the work establishment themselves and their deputies or employees who are members of the body managing the work establishment and chief accountants (Article 128 §2 point 2 LC).

267. The weekly working time of the employees may exceed the average standard of forty-eight hours within the adopted reference period (Article 131 §2). Neither are they covered by the guarantee of eleven hours of uninterrupted daily rest. If not enjoying such a rest they are, however, afforded an equivalent period of compensatory rest within a specific reference period. No records of their working hours

208. Resolution by the Supreme Court of 4 Jun. 1982, III PZP 17/82.
209. Act of 17 May 1989; consolidated text: *Journal of Laws* (2005), No. 231, item 1965, as amended.

are kept. While being on duty they have neither the right to time off nor remuneration. The hourly limits of night work are not applicable to them. As a rule, the employees in question perform work, should the need arise, outside of normal working hours without being entitled to a remuneration and the extra pay for overtime work.

§9. Annual Vacation Leave

I. The Right to Annual Leave

268. The employee is entitled to annual, uninterrupted, paid vacation leave.

269. The employee may not waive the right to annual leave (Article 152 LC). Payment of money equivalent for the unused vacation leave is only allowed in case of termination of an employment relationship (Article 171 LC).

II. The Length of Annual Leave

270. The length of annual leave depends on the length of service and amounts to twenty days – when the employee has been employed for less than ten years, and twenty-six days – when he/she has been employed for at least ten years (Article 154 §1 LC). Leave is granted so that it falls on days which are working days for the employee in accordance with the schedule of the working time (Article 154^2 §1 LC). Periods of previous employment are included in the period of employment which determines the right and the length of the leave. Counted against the period is also a certain number of years on account of graduation from specific types of schools, e.g., eight years for graduation from a higher education institute (Articles 154, 154^1 and 155 LC).

III. Rules for Granting Annual Leave

271. Annual leave should be granted to the employee by the employer in the calendar year in which the employee becomes entitled to it (Article 161 LC). Where the employee has not worked all months in a specific year, he/she is entitled to leave in proportion to the number of the months worked (Article 153 §1 and Article 155^1 LC). Leaves should be granted in accordance with the schedule of leaves or in consultation with the employee (Article 163 §1(1) LC). Initially, fixed dates of the annual leave may be changed, the leave may be divided into parts or the employee may be recalled from the leave only in exceptional cases, owing to unforeseen needs of the employer or for reasons concerning the employee (e.g., due to an illness). Besides those cases the annual leave may only be divided at the employee's request (Articles 162–167 LC).

IV. Leave on Request

272. A specific solution provided for by Poland's labour law is the so-called leave on request. The employer is obliged to grant such a leave at the time specified by the employee. The request ought to be made on the day on which the leave is to begin, at the latest. The employee is entitled to no more than four days of such a leave in each calendar year (Article 167^2 and 167^3 LC). The legal regulation, incorporated in the LC as of the beginning of 2003 following an agreement between the government, trade unions and employers' organizations gave rise to many complications, gradually resolved by courts of law. (For instance, in its judgment of 15 November 2006, I PK 128/06, the Supreme Court explained that the application to grant leave 'on request' should be made before the expected time of commencement of work by the employee, unless making the application later is allowed by the work rules or the adopted work establishment custom.) Leave on request is also used by the employees as a form of collective protest action.

V. Remuneration for the Time of Leave

273. The employee is entitled to the remuneration for the time of leave as which he/she would have received if he/she had worked during that time (Article 172 LC).

§10. Special Leave and Exemptions from Work

I. Introduction

274. Besides the annual vacation leave the employee can enjoy other leave and exemptions from work for purposes other than annual rest. These include unpaid leave, educational leave and exemptions from work, occasional exemptions from work, instances of justified absence from work and other leave and exemptions from work. Within the scope of the group also fall parenthood-related leave, as discussed in §1 of Chapter 8, Part I.

II. Unpaid Leave

275. Unpaid leave is a period of employment relationship suspension as agreed upon by the parties (Article 174). An agreement concerning the unpaid leave may only be concluded at the written request of the employee.[210] The employer may recall the employee from unpaid leave only when the agreement on the leave provides so and the leave lasts longer than three months. The period of the unpaid leave

210. For that very reason unpaid leave granted at the initiative of the employer and with no request of the employee, in writing, has no effect in the light of Art. 174 § 1; *see* judgment of the Court of Appeals of Łódź of 15 Oct. 1996, Aua 34/96, concerning the case in which the employer would give the employee unpaid leaves depending on the financial standing of the work establishment.

is not reckoned towards the length of service which determines employee rights. Upon completion of the leave the employer is obliged to employ the person again, on the same conditions as those preceding the leave.

276. Labour law also provides for other unpaid leave. These are, in particular, leave granted to allow the employee to hold elected offices outside the work establishment (e.g., to perform a trade union function, be a Member of Parliament or a senator) – Article 74 LC. The length of such leave is counted as the time of service at the work establishment where the leave was granted, if the provisions state so.

III. Educational Leave and Exemptions from Work

277. Employees improving their qualification at the initiative of the employer or with his/her/their consent are entitled to educational leave and exemptions from work (more *see* above §3 in Chapter 3).

IV. Occasional Exemptions from Work

278. Occasional exemptions from work are exemptions which the employer is obliged to grant to the employee in connection with his/her personal and family-related situation or event, performance of public duties or community/civic engagement of the employee.[211] The employee remains entitled to remuneration for the time of those exemptions where the law expressly provides so.[212]

V. Sick Leave and Other Justified Absences from Work

279. The employee's justified absence from work takes place as a result of obstacles preventing his/her attendance at work. The employee should notify the employer about his/her inability to come to work in advance, or – if not practicable – *ex post*, and justify his/her absence in each case. Remuneration for the time of justified absence from work is payable to the employee only where the law expressly provides so (Article 80 LC). In particular, the employee remains entitled to such remuneration for the time of incapacity for work resulting from an illness which lasts in total up to thirty-three days in a calendar year.[213] It is for that time that the

211. For example, the marriage of the employee, birth of his/her child, death and funeral of the closest family members, a need to obey court summons, participation in actions of the volunteer fire department.
212. *See* Ordinance of the Minister of Labour and Social Policy of 15 May 1996 Concerning the Way of Justifying Absence from Work and Granting Exemptions from Work to Employees, *Journal of Laws* (1996) No. 60, item 281, as amended.
213. Up to fourteen days in case of an employee who has completed 50 years of age. Such a differentiation was introduced as of 1 Jan. 2009 as part of changes of the law aimed at support of employment of the 50+ people.

employee remains entitled to 80% (exceptionally, e.g., where the illness occurs during pregnancy, to 100%) of his/her remuneration. Where the incapacity lasts, in total, longer than thirty-three days during a calendar year, the employee is entitled to a sickness benefit on the terms specified in social security provisions (Article 92 LC).

280. The employer has the right to check if the employee, while declared incapable for work owing to illness, does not use the sick leave contrary to the purpose of the leave, e.g., by being engaged in another gainful employment.[214]

VI. Other Leave and Exemptions

281. Interruptions in the performance of work may also result from the employee being engaged in military service, military training or military drills. Employee rights related thereto are provided for, in detail, in the Act of 21 November 1967 on the Universal Duty to Defend the Republic of Poland.[215] The time of military service is reckoned towards the length of service as regards any rights of the employee, and upon completion of the service the employee has the right to re-employment in a post equal to that occupied before the break, as far as the type of the work and remuneration are concerned.

---

214. Rules for the control are set by the ordinance of the Minister of Labour and Social Policy of 27 Jul. 1999 on Detailed Rules for and Mode of Control of Proper Use of Sick Leaves and Formal Verification of Medical Certificates, *Journal of Laws* (1999), No. 65, item 743.
215. Consolidated text, *Journal of Laws* (2015), item 144, as amended.

Chapter 5. Remuneration and Other Payments

Z. Hajn

§1. Notion of Remuneration

282. The remuneration for work, in the strict meaning of the word, means mandatory, periodic, financial performance provided by the employer to the employee under an employment relationship, against the employee doing work, which the performance should correspond to the type of the work, its amount and quality (Article 22 §1 in conjunction with Article 78 §1 LC). The remuneration for work *sensu stricto* most often is not a uniform consideration but one composed of many partial considerations.

283. A broader concept of the remuneration for work is used by the provisions prohibiting employment discrimination. According to Article 18^{3c} LC concerning the right to equal remuneration for the same work or for work of the same value, the remuneration, in the meaning of the provision, includes all components of the remuneration, regardless what they are called and of what nature they are, as well as other work-related benefits, granted to the employees in cash or in a form other than cash. Consequently, certain payments like reimbursement of training costs of the employee or per diem payment for business trip reimbursement is not remuneration in the strict meaning of Article 78 §1 LC, but it is considered remuneration within the meaning of Article 18^{3c} LC.

284. It should be also noted that in certain cases provisions of the labour law, social security law or tax law define what is to be understood as being the 'remuneration' for their specific purposes.

285. Remuneration, in the strict sense, is due for work actually performed. For the inadequate performance of work by the employee owing to the latter's fault, the remuneration is not payable or is reduced accordingly (Articles 80 and 82 LC).

286. Only exceptionally, in cases indicated in law, the employee is entitled to remuneration for the time of non-performance of work. The instances include work not being performed for reasons attributable to the employer – Article 81 LC (e.g., in case of downtime and certain breaks, leaves and exemptions from work). The payments are referred to as guarantee consideration (payments). While not being payments for the work actually done they nevertheless form, through the legislator's will, a constituent part of the remuneration.

§2. The Amount of Remuneration

287. Minimum pay is guaranteed by the Constitution, which provides that a minimum level of remuneration for work, or the manner of setting its levels, is to be specified by statute (Article 65, section 4). Article 13 LC sounds more encouraging, establishing the employee's right to decent remuneration, although stating that the conditions for the exercise of the right are specified in the provisions of labour law and by remuneration policy of the state, in particular as regards the statutory minimum wage. The wording of the provision offers but a false promise. As legal scholars and the judicature conclude in almost perfect unison, under the decent remuneration doctrine the employee has no entitlement to claim a wage raise other than up to the level of minimum wage.[216]

288. Remuneration for work may not be lower than the minimum wage fixed in accordance with the Minimum Remuneration for Work Act, 2002.[217] During the employee's first year of work, however, his/her remuneration may be lower, though not less than 80% of the minimum wage. The amount of the minimum wage is, every year, negotiated at the Social Dialogue Council. Failure to fix it in the aforementioned mode within the required time limit results in the wage being determined by the Council of Ministers (government).

289. Subject to negotiations in the Social Dialogue Council are also the average annual rates of salary growth in the state-budget sector.

Since 2000, statutory constraints have been put on the remuneration of top-level management of undertakings, companies and certain other organizational units controlled by the state and local government. A statute, commonly referred to as the 'Salary Cap Act', provides for constituent elements and maximum level of salaries of the persons in question. As the rule adopted by the law holds, contractual stipulations fixing the salary at a level higher than the maximum allowed by the statute are automatically void as regards that portion thereof which exceeds the maximum amount specified in the law.[218] The act was partly replaced in 2016 by a new law with respect to companies in which public entities have shares or stocks. The new law sets out the rules for determining the remuneration of persons managing such companies. At the same time, however, it provides that members of their management boards may be employed only on the basis of contracts for the provision of services.[219]

216. For instance, the Supreme Court judgment of 29 May, 2006 I PK 230/05. As the Constitutional Tribunal has indicated, it is only the minimum remuneration that is guaranteed to the employees by Art. 65 part 4 of the Constitution. The state has no obligation to secure appropriately high wage to its citizens, nor does a right to pay increase follow from provisions of the Constitution (judgment of 21 April, 2004, K 33/03); similarly, the Supreme Court resolution of a panel of seven judges of 17 Nov. 2011, III PZP 4/11.

217. Act of 10 Oct. 2002; *Journal of Laws* (2002), consolidated text: *Journal of Laws* (2017), item 847.

218. The Act of 3 Mar. 2000 on the Remuneration of Managers of Certain Legal Entities, consolidated text: *Journal of Laws* (2017), item 1222.

219. The act of 9 Jun. 2016 on the rules for determining the remuneration of persons managing certain companies; *Journal of Laws* (2017) item 2190.

§3. Fixing the Remuneration for Work

290. Fixing the remuneration for work consists in determining its conditions and terms, i.e., the constituent parts of the remuneration, the way of its calculation (pay system) as well as the date, place and form of payment.

291. Those fixing the remuneration for work, i.e., social partners and parties to the employment relationship, should follow the general rule, according to which the remuneration ought to be determined in such a manner so as to correspond to, in particular, the type of work provided and qualifications needed to do such work and should reflect the amount and quality of the work (Article 78 LC). In addition, employees have the right to equal remuneration for the same work or for work of the same value, and fixing the remuneration may not lead to the establishment of unfavourable terms of remuneration or other work-related benefits, in particular on grounds of gender, age, disability, race, religion, nationality, political convictions, union membership, ethnic origin, creed, sexual orientation, nor due to being employed for a fixed-term or in part-time work (Articles 18^{3e} and 18^{3b} §1 point 2 LC).

292. The remuneration for work is fixed, in principle, in the contract of employment (or other acts whereby employment relationship is created), directly or by making reference to pay provisions. The contract of employment should stipulate, at least, the remuneration corresponding to the type of work, together with its components (Article 29 §1 point 3 LC).

Terms and conditions of remuneration and granting of other payments, which have to be observed by the parties when fixing the remuneration for work in the contract of employment, are set up by CLAs or pay rules and (as far as the date, place and form of payment are concerned) workplace rules.

In accordance with the LC rules, determining remuneration for work and other work-related payments (Article 77^1 and 77^2 LC) should be done mostly by means of CLAs. The role of workplace pay rules in the shaping of salaries/wages should be limited to the situations where the work establishment is not covered by a CLA or where the CLA does not allow establishing individual terms of employment contracts under its provisions. In practice, considering the reasons mentioned in Part II, Chapter 3, §1, II, it is the workplace pay regulations that play the most prominent function in setting up the terms and conditions of remuneration. At unionized work establishments the workplace pay regulations have to be established through a process of negotiations between the trade unions and the employer. The regulations may not determine the terms of employment of the employees who manage the work establishment on behalf of the employer, i.e., the employees who, by themselves, manage a work establishment and their deputies or employees who are members of a body managing the work establishment, as well as chief accountants.

At the same time, there is the Act of 23 December 1999 on the Wage Determination in the Public Sector[220] which provides for wage increase indicators. Secondary legislation is also of significance. According to Article 77^3 LC the conditions of

220. Consolidated text *Journal of Laws* (2011), No. 79, item 431, as later amended.

remuneration for work and award of other benefits related to work for employees of the state public sector, if they are not covered by a collective agreement, will be determined – within the scope not reserved in other Acts for other authorities – in an ordinance by the minister responsible for labour issues on a proposal from the relevant minister. This ordinance should, in particular, specify the basic pay, as well as other components of the remuneration, including also other benefits associated with employment, such as the jubilee award and the one-time retirement gratuity. Therefore, if a given professional group employed in the public sector is not covered by a collective agreement, its detailed remuneration principles are determined by the ordinance of the minister responsible for labour issues.

§4. Components of Remuneration

293. The main component of all remuneration is basic remuneration, the fundamental equivalent of the work rendered by the employee. This is the only mandatory part of remuneration which can, at the same time, be its only component. The basic remuneration has the closest connection with the kind of the work done, making up the direct payment for the latter and the qualifications required to do it. The basic remuneration is calculated according to time or effects (under the piece rate system or commission system). Mixed systems can be encountered as well. If payment is chosen according to results, the employee is entitled, at least, to the basic remuneration regardless of what the outcome of the work may be.

294. Unlike basic remuneration, other (additional) components do not constitute direct payment for the work of a specific kind and the qualifications related thereto, but the employee becomes entitled to them upon meeting additional conditions. These are premium payments (bonuses) for the attainment or additional work results and wage supplements, paid, for instance, to compensate the worker for doing work in hazardous working environment, or to reward him for the length of service, the efforts undertaken at a managerial position, command of foreign languages, overtime work etc. As a rule, basic remuneration serves as the basis for the calculation of the additional components, which may be regulated by statutes (as is the case with, for instance, overtime pay, night work supplements, allowances paid to pregnant women relocated to work which they are capable of doing but which is paid at lower rates) or CLAs and workplace pay rules (as regards, e.g., the length-of-service allowances).

§5. Protection of Remuneration for Work

295. According to provisions of the LC, protection schemes in that respect include, first of all, restraints of the employee's liberty to dispose of his/her remuneration. In connection with this, the employee may not renounce his/her right to remuneration or transfer that right to another person (Article 84 LC). Actions taken by the employee contrary to the prohibition are void, and the employer is expected to pay the remuneration, the right to which was renounced by the employee or transferred by him to another person.

296. Employee remuneration is also protected through detailed rules regarding the determination of the date, time, place, mode and form of payment of the remuneration, set forth in the LC (Articles 85–86 LC), limitations imposed on deductions from remuneration (Articles 87–91 LC) and the employee's right to review the documents which served as the basis for calculating his/her remuneration (Article 85 §5 LC). According to Article 282 §1 point 1 LC, a person who, in breach of duty, fails to pay, on due time, remuneration for work or another benefit to an entitled employee or his/her family member, or reduces the amount of such remuneration or benefit without proper cause, or makes unauthorized deductions, is liable to a fine amounting from PLN 1,000 to PLN 30,000. It is worth noting at this occasion that under the provisions of the Civil Code the employee may seek compensation for the employer's delay in payment of the remuneration.

297. Literal interpretation of the legal provisions leads to the conclusion that the protection of the remuneration for work is applicable to the remuneration in the strict meaning of the term. However, court decisions, concerning the employee's renunciation of the right to remuneration and deductions from remuneration, in particular, have gradually extended the scope of the protection. In the Supreme Court's opinion, while certain payments under the employment relationship (like money equivalent for unused vacation holiday, retirement and disability severance pay, redundancy pay, jubilee award) do not have the nature of remuneration for work *sensu stricto*, they are, nonetheless, covered by the protection schemes just as the remuneration is.[221] Recently, however, in the controversial issue of the qualification of the compensation for unlawful termination of employment relationships, the Supreme Court (in a panel of seven judges) advocated adopting a strict interpretation of the term 'remuneration for work' in the provisions concerning the protection of the remuneration. Consequently, the Court found that the above-mentioned compensation is not remuneration for work within the meaning of the provisions securing protection against deductions from the remuneration.[222]

298. Remuneration for work is also protected by legal regulations other than those described above. Of special importance in that respect is the protection of employee claims in the event of the employer going bankrupt, provided for by the Act of 13 July 2006 on Employee Claims Protection in the Case of Employer's Insolvency,[223] having replaced an earlier Act of 1993, concerning the issue.

221. *See*, for instance, the Supreme Court judgment of 17 Feb. 2004, I PK 217/03, and of 20 Jun. 2006 and the judgments cited in their grounds.

222. The compensation fulfils, as a rule, functions not attributable to the remuneration in the strict meaning and, at the same time, does not reveal traits characteristic of the remuneration (*see* the resolution of seven judges of the Supreme Court of 17 Jan. 2013, II PZP 4/12). The resolution was passed with two votes against.

223. Consolidated text: *Journal of Laws* (2014), item 272.

§6. Other Payments

299. Besides remuneration, in connection with work the employee is paid, also, certain other benefits not being remuneration for work within the meaning discussed above. These include, in particular, compensation payments (e.g., to cover the costs connected with a business trip), commuting to work, use of personal car by the employee, retirement and disability severance pay, death grant, damages payments (e.g., for unlawful termination of an employment contract), dividends paid from employer's profits on account of the securities held by the employee and benefits from the company welfare fund. The legal nature of some of the payments is disputed, but the dominating opinion is that they do not form remuneration for work, not being an equivalent for the work provided by the employee. Neither is rewards for work (or achievements related to it) the remuneration. Such payments are not mandatory, but granting them is left to the discretion of the employer.

Chapter 6. Termination and Change of Employment Contract

Z. Hajn

§1. Ways of Termination

I. General Characteristics

300. The contract of employment comes to an end by dissolution or expiry.

301. The dissolution results from an act of will expressed by legal actions undertaken by one or both of the parties to the employment relationship. As opposed to the above, the expiry of a contract of employment takes place, by virtue of law, in the events specified by the LC and special provisions.

Bilateral legal transactions whereby a contract of employment may be terminated include, first of all, an agreement between the parties aimed at ending the employment relationship through mutual consent. Also, the duration of the employment contract is determined mutually by the parties to it. For that very reason the end of employment relationship owing to the lapse of the time for which the employment agreement was made is treated as dissolution and not expiry of the relationship.

The employment relationship can be terminated unilaterally by giving the other party a notice to terminate, without giving such notice and without notice but upon prior notification.

II. The Form and Content of the Declaration Concerning Termination

302. Any declaration to terminate a contract of employment should be made in writing. Failing to observe the written form does not, however, result in the declaration being null and void. However, violation of the rule entitles the employee to assert claims related to the wrongful termination of the employment relationship.

303. Both the declaration of an employer giving a notice to terminate an employment contract made for an indefinite period and his/her/their termination of an employment contract without notice should provide the reasons for the termination as well as advise the employee of his/her right to appeal the termination decision to the labour court (Article 30 §4 LC). An employee is obligated to specify the reason justifying his/her termination of the employment contract only in case of termination without notice. A notice to terminate the contract by an employee does not require justification.

304. A correct statement on the reason within the meaning of Article 30 §4 LC consists in the indication of the circumstances which, in the employer's opinion, justify termination of the contract. The reason should be concrete, i.e., indicate the nature, place and time of the circumstances so that the employee could be aware of the allegations he or she is to rebut. It should, thus, clearly stem from the employer's statement about the essence of the allegations. However, while assessing if the reason quoted by the employer meets the requirements outlined above, the conditions in which the statement are made must be taken into account. In the opinion of the judicature, if the reason for the termination clearly stems from facts well known to the employee, the requirements specified in Article 30 §4 LC are met even if the wording whereby the reason is explained, contained in the employer's letter conveying the declaration to terminate, is rather general.[224]

III. Dissolution of Employment Contract by Mutual Consent

305. The contract of employment may always be terminated by mutual consent of the parties. Such an agreement may be initiated by either party, yet neither of them is entitled to a claim for termination of the contract in such a mode. Both the contract of employment for an indefinite period and any fixed-time contract may be terminated by mutual consent. In their agreement, the parties may stipulate not only the mode of contract termination but also other issues related to the contract coming to an end. The employment contract terminates as of the date specified by the parties. Should no date of termination of the employment relationship be fixed by the parties, it ends as of the date of conclusion of the agreement.[225]

IV. Dissolution of Employment Contract with Notice

306. According to the LC, a notice to terminate is a unilateral statement of will leading to termination of the contract of employment upon the lapse of the period referred to as the period of notice. The period of notice must not be shorter than that provided for in the LC. Its length depends on the type of the contract.

307. The periods amount to:

- in the case of a contract for a trial period, three working days if the trial period is not longer than two weeks, one week if the trial period exceeds two weeks and two weeks if the trial period is three months;
- in the case of the contract for an indefinite period or a contract for a definite period, two weeks if the employee's length of service at a given employer's is less than six months, one month if the length of service is at least six months and three months if the length of service is at least three years (Article 36 LC).

224. For instance, in its judgment of 2 Sep. 1998, I PKN 271/98, the Supreme Court stated that the assessment whether the reason for the termination of the employment contract (Art. 30 §4 LC) was exact enough should take into account other circumstances explaining the reason, the employee being aware of.
225. Supreme Court judgment of 11 Jan. 2001, I PKN 844/00.

308. If a contract for an indefinite period or a contract for a definite period is terminated due to a declaration of the employer's bankruptcy or liquidation, or for other reasons not attributable to employees, the employer may reduce the three-month period of notice in order to terminate the contract earlier, but to no shorter than one month. If this is the case, the employee is entitled to payment in lieu of notice equal to the amount of remuneration due for the remaining part of the period of notice. The period of entitlement to compensation counts towards the length of service of the employee who is not employed during that period (Article 36^1 LC).

309. In connection with a notice to terminate, the employee may be released by the employer from the duty to do work until the expiry of the period of notice. While released from the duty, the employee retains the right to remuneration for work (Article 36^2 LC).

310. Since, traditionally, employees used to be hired as of the first day of the month or week, the period of notice of termination of an employment contract covering a week or a month, or a multiple thereof, ends on a Saturday or on the last day of the month, respectively. The requirement may result in the extension of the period of notice in specific cases.

311. During the period of notice, lasting at least two weeks, if the notice to terminate was given by the employer, the employee is entitled to paid time off to look for another employment (Article 37 LC).[226]

V. Termination of a Contract of Employment Without Notice

A. *Termination Without Notice by the Employer*

312. The employer may terminate an employment contract without notice, through the fault of the employee, if the employee grossly violates his or her basic duties, if he or she commits, while the employment contract continues, an offence which renders impossible his or her further employment at a specific position (provided that the crime is evident or has been declared by a final court judgement) or when the employee, through his or her own fault, loses the qualifications necessary to perform work at his or her position. Termination of an employment contract without notice, through the fault of an employee, may not take place after one month from the date on which the employer learned of the reason justifying termination of the contract (Article 52 §1 and §2 LC).

313. The employer may also terminate an employment contract without notice and without any fault of the employee when the employee's absence from work due to illness is of a long duration. The termination is allowed when the absence lasts more than three months (if the employee's period of service with a given employer

226. The amount of the time off is two working days during a period of notice of two weeks or one month, and three working days during a three-month period of notice.

is less than six months) or more than the total period of receipt of remuneration and benefits on account of the absence (if the period of service is at least six months or where the inability to work has been caused by an industrial accident or an occupational disease).[227] An employment contract may also be terminated after an employee's sixty-day absence caused by caring for a child or quarantine ordered in connection with an infectious disease or, finally, in the event of justified absence from work due to other reasons, if the absence lasts for over one month. In the case of the employee's justified absence from work for reasons other than listed above the employer may terminate the employment relationship without notice when the absence lasts longer than one month (Article 53 LC).

314. The employer should, as far as practicable, reinstate the employee, dismissed without his/her fault, who – within six months of termination of the employment contract without notice – reports to work immediately after the reasons for the termination cease to exist.

B. Termination Without Notice by the Employee

315. An employee may terminate the employment contract without notice if a medical certificate stating a harmful effect of the work performed by the employee on his/her health was issued and, if, within the time limit indicated in the certificate, the employer failed to transfer him to another job appropriate for his health and vocational skills. He/she may also terminate the employment contract without notice in case of violation of the employer's basic duties towards him/her. In such a case the termination may not take place after one month from the date on which the employee learned of the reason justifying it.

Termination of an employment contract without notice for the reasons specified above bears the same consequences as those provided for by the law in case of termination of an employment contract by the employer with notice (Article 55 LC).

VI. Termination Without Notice but upon Prior Notification

316. It is only the employee that can terminate a contract of employment without notice but upon prior notification. This option can be exercised solely in two situations. First, in the case of a transfer of work establishment or a part of it to another employer, the employee may, under the procedure, terminate the contract of employment upon a seven-day notification. Second, the employee, who – prior to being reinstated to previous work – has begun employment with another employer

227. The period for the receipt of sick pay amounts up to 33 days per year and for sickness benefit – up to 182 days or – where the incapacity to work has been caused by tuberculosis or takes place during pregnancy – does not exceed 270 days. In the case of incapacity to work resulting from an industrial accident or occupational disease, not more than three months during which the rehabilitation benefit is received by the employee are added to the aforementioned periods.

may, without notice and with a three-day prior notification, terminate the employment contract with the other employer within seven seven days of being reinstated (Articles 48 §2 and 57 §4 in conjunction with Article 48 §2 LC and Article 67 LC in conjunction with Article 48 §2 LC). In both situations termination of the contract entails the same consequences as those provided by law for the termination of an employment contract by the employer with notice.

VII. Expiration of an Employment Contract

317. As has been stated above an employment contract expires only in cases specified in legal provisions (Article 63 LC). Where such a case occurs, the employment relationship is terminated by law (*ipso jure*), no declarations of the employer or employee being able to reverse that effect. The parties may not, in particular, reverse the contract of employment expiration by mutual consent.

318. The expiration results, among others, from the death of the employee or employer,[228] at the end of a three-month absence of an employee due to his/her being detained for a period awaiting trial, from an employee's failure to notify his employer of his/her intention to return to work within thirty days of completing military training, from calling the employee into professional military service, etc.

§2. Protection of an Employee Against Dismissal

I. General Remarks

319. The essence of the protection of an employee against dismissal consists in constraints of the employer's liberty to terminate a contract of employment with or without notice. Consequently, the protection entails restriction of the freedom of contract and freedom of business, imposed for vital social reasons. It can take the shape of either general or special protection.

320. The general protection includes making the admissibility of termination conditional upon the existence of the cause justifying it. It also involves trade union control of termination reasonability. As regards the notice to terminate, general protection pertains to contracts of employment concluded for an indefinite period. This protection does not apply to fixed-term contracts. The lack of general protection of these contracts was understandable under the provisions of the Labour Code, before it was changed in 2015 (see paragraph 185), which did not allow the notice to terminate them during their duration, except in exceptional situations. However, this

228. Unless the work establishment was transferred to another employer or taken into succession management. The succession management can be established for the time necessary to settle inheritance matters, no longer than two years; see: Article 63^2 LC and the Act of 5 July 2018 on the management of the successive enterprise of a natural person; *Journal of Laws* (2018), item 917 as amended.

ban has been repealed. As a result, the protection of employees against the termination of a fixed-term contract has been radically weakened. In the case of termination without notice, covered are all types of employment contracts.

321. As opposed to the above-said, special protection consists in the prohibition to terminate a contract of employment even where the termination would be justified. The protection concerns all types of employment contracts but is provided only in situations indicated in law and for a period set up in legal regulations. Covered by it are the employees whose particular situation justifies, in the legislator's opinion, a limitation of the employer's right to decide on the composition of his/her staff going that far.

322. Provisions on the general and special protection of employees against termination of an employment contract with notice are not applied when bankruptcy or liquidation of an employer is declared. The protection is also subject to limitations in case of mass redundancies provided for in the Employment Termination Act 2003 (*see* below §5).

II. General Protection Against Dismissal

A. Grounds for the Notice to Terminate a Contract of Employment

323. No catalogue of reasons justifying a notice to terminate has been set up by the LC, the fact reflecting a long-established view that providing such a catalogue is not actually possible. Neither would the catalogue be expedient for striking a reasonable compromise between the employer's right to select employees and the employees' protection against unfair dismissal.[229] Rather than offer such a catalogue, the Code makes the employee, in case of an unjustified termination of a contract of employment concluded for an indefinite period, entitled to assert the rights provided for in the law (Article 45 §1 LC). The term of 'unjustified notice' is a general clause taking flesh (only) in a specific case, the circumstances accompanying the notice not being lost from sight. Such a concept of the justification of a notice to terminate allows for a flexible assessment of whether the notice was, in fact, grounded. Meanwhile, the justification is subject to strict limitations following from abundant court decisions on the issue. Current understanding of the term is based on the conviction that in the assessment of the justification both the legitimate interest of the employer and the employee's suitability for work should be taken into account. Other employee-related circumstances, such as the person's personal, family or financial situation are not relevant for the assessment of the notice itself, while

229. A link between the admissibility of a notice to terminate and the existence of expressly named circumstances (reasons) can be found in the provisions on employment relations of public servants (*see*, for instance, Art. 41 part 1 of the Civil Service Act, 2006).

not being ones to be neglected. A specific situation of the employee can give rise to finding the notice, though justified, to be contrary to the rules of social coexistence (Article 8 LC).[230]

324. As a rule, the notice to terminate is deemed to be a regular way of the termination of employment relations, allowing the employer to select the employees in order to secure the best performance of the operation of the work establishment.[231] Hence, where the employer is able to prove that the dismissal suited the purpose, it should be found justified. The duty of the employer to provide a justification of the notice to terminate is, however, one which is rigorously controlled by courts of law.

325. The reasons justifying a notice to terminate are divided into those on the side of the employer and those employee-related. The former include, *inter alia*, bankruptcy declaration or liquidation of the employer, staff reduction, job shedding (or other changes of the organizational structure of the work establishment), change of business objectives or reduction of the funds available for salaries/wages. A court of law is not authorized to examine whether the actions of the employer are purposeful. It may, however, verify the accuracy of the employer's statements and assess whether they justified the employee's dismissal. Reasons concerning the employee may stem from the latter's infringement of his/her duties or his/her unsuitability for doing the agreed job (owing, for instance, to his/her health status or loss of qualifications). The employer may name a few reasons for giving the notice to terminate. Taken separately, none of them may – in a specific case – justify the notice in itself, only the entirety of them providing sufficient justification.[232]

The distinction in reasons to terminate between those concerning the employer and those referring to the employee is essential where the dismissal is subject to provisions of the Employment Termination Act 2003. In other situations the nature of the cause is legally irrelevant.

B. Justification of Contract of Employment Termination Without Notice

326. Unlike in the case of termination with notice, the LC exactly states a majority of the reasons justifying termination of the contract of employment without notice. In practical terms, however, the most common reason for termination effected that way is the 'gross violation of basic employee duties', mentioned in Article 52 §1 item 1 LC, a term rather vague in itself. Putting it generally, the term means a violation of basic duties involving a considerable degree of the employee's fault (wilful misconduct or gross negligence), posing a threat to the employer or

230. *See* resolution of the Entire Composition of the Supreme Court Labour Law and Social Security Chamber of 27 Jun. 1985, III PZP 10/85, recapitulating earlier decisions of the judiciary in that respect.
231. Supreme Court judgment of 2 Oct. 1996, I PRN 69/96.
232. Such is the position taken by the Supreme Court in the judgment of 8 Jan. 2007, I PK 187/2006.

affecting the employer's interests.[233] It should be added, in passing, that termination of a contract of employment without notice through the employee's fault, being an extraordinary way of a contract of employment termination, should be applied by the employer in exceptional cases, prudently, and should be justified by special circumstances.[234]

C. Trade Union Control of the Justification of Contract of Employment Termination

327. The employer willing to dismiss an employee is obliged to notify of his/her/their intention to the trade union organization representing the employee, together with an indication of the reasons justifying the termination. Within five (and in the case of termination without notice, three) days the organization may communicate its objections concerning the justification of the intended termination. The objections are not binding on the employer, but the need to follow the procedure of the consultation is, in itself, a factor protecting the employees against hastily made decisions. Failing to undergo the consultations means that the termination of the employment relationship is wrongful, even if justified. It should be observed, though, that the importance of the trade union's control has been reduced now, owing to a majority of work establishments being non-unionized entities.

III. Special Protection Against Termination of Employment Relationships

A. Special Protection Against a Notice to Terminate

328. Prohibitions to give a notice to terminate are set up mostly due to the employee's personal or family situation or considering the function performed by the person. It is the personal or family situation that lies at the basis of, *inter alia*, the prohibition to give a notice to terminate during the employee's excused absence from work not exceeding the time limit specified in law (Article 41 LC), within the period of four years preceding the reaching of the retirement age, within the period of two years before an employee being a combatant reaches the age entitling him/her to early retirement, during an employee's pregnancy, maternity and paternity leave and the leave to raise a child, within the period of the employee's compulsory military service or during the time when the husband of a female employee undergoes compulsory military service. Protection of unlimited duration is enjoyed by war invalids. As far as performance of certain functions is concerned, the protection is extended onto, first of all, members of employee bodies of all kinds (i.e., trade union bodies, as indicated in law, works' councils, European works councils, employee representatives sitting on supervisory boards, employees being members of the bodies of professional associations (e.g., the Chamber of Physicians), etc.

233. For instance, the Supreme Court sentence of 21 Jul. 1999, I PKN 169/99; of 19 Aug. 1999, I PKN 188/99.
234. For instance, the Supreme Court judgment of 2 Jun. 1997, I PKN 193/97.

Protected are, also, members of work establishment conciliation commissions and social labour inspectors. In addition, entitled to special protection are employees performing certain public functions (the MPs, senators and counsellors of regional/local assemblies).

329. Altogether, special protection is enjoyed by more than thirty groups of employees, the fact stirring up protests of the employers.

330. The mode and scope of the limitation of the employer's freedom, resulting from the special protection, depends on the nature of the prohibition to terminate. Narrower and broader prohibition, just as absolute and relative protection schemes, can be distinguished. A narrower prohibition consists in the employer not being allowed to give a notice to terminate within the period of protection. For instance, the employer may not terminate the contract during the employee's excused absence from work. The prohibition does not apply, though, if the employer gave the notice earlier, the termination taking place during the employee's absence. Where a broader prohibition is applicable, wrongful is not only the notice to terminate given in the period of protection but also one served earlier, if termination of the contract of employment should take place, owing to the notice, within the period in question. For example, when serving a notice of termination to a female employee not being pregnant, the employer does not infringe the special protection scheme. But should the woman employee get pregnant during the notice period, the notice becomes objectively wrongful. As far as an absolute prohibition is concerned, its essence lies in unconditional inadmissibility of giving a notice. As opposed to it, a relative prohibition can be lifted, a relevant body mentioned in provisions of law consenting. For instance, the consent of the board of a company's trade union organization lifts the prohibition to serve a notice to terminate to a trade union activist. In the situation of protection conditioned upon the employee's personal or family situation, the body authorized to give or refuse the consent is the trade union organization representing the employee. Where the protection follows from the function performed by the employee, the authorization is vested in the relevant body of the institution where the function is performed by the employee (e.g., the municipal council, works' council, etc.).

B. *Special Protection Against Termination of an Employment Contract Without Notice*

331. The list of persons covered by the protection is shorter than that concerning employees covered by special protection against the notice to terminate.[235] The prohibition against termination without notice can be either absolute or relative. In principle, the protection provided on account of the employee's personal or family situation is absolute, if the termination should take place without the employee's

235. The major difference lies in the employees in the pre-retirement age, as well as those on a vacation leave and during an excused absence from work, not being protected against termination without notice.

fault and relative as regards reasons occurred through his/her fault. To quote an example, the termination of a contract of employment during pregnancy, maternity leave and other parenthood-related leave is unconditionally forbidden. The termination is, however, allowed through the employee's fault, at the consent of the trade union representing the employee. As regards protection offered to those performing specific functions, it is of relative nature, which means that termination both through the employee's fault and without it is allowed at the consent of the body indicated in law.

§3. Legal Sanctions for Defective Termination of an Employment Relationship

I. Sanctions for Defective Termination of a Contract of Employment by Consent of the Parties

332. The LC does not regulate sanctions for wrongful termination of a contract of employment by consent of the parties. Consequently, applicable in that respect are general provisions on contracts; in particular, provisions of the Civil Code on defects in a declaration of will and Article 58 CC (according to which a legal transaction aimed at circumvention of the law or infringing the rules of social coexistence is void). As a rule, it is most often the employees that file actions for the revocation of an agreement on termination of a contract of employment, claiming that the statement on termination of the contract was made by them under the influence of error or under the threat of the employer. The said holds true, for instance, about women who terminated the contract of employment not being aware of their pregnancy.[236] A second group of actions concerns the annulment of a contract of employment where, in connection with a transfer of the work establishment to another employer, the existing employment relationship was terminated with an agreement of the parties and the employee concluded a contract of employment with the new employer on terms less favourable than the preceding ones.[237]

II. Employee Claims in Case of Wrongful Termination of a Contract of Employment with Notice

333. The LC has departed from the sanction of absolute invalidity of a wrongful termination of the contract of employment by giving a notice or without a notice to terminate, as applicable before the Code's entry into force. The previous legal scheme created confusion as to the moment of the termination of the contract of

236. The Supreme Court resolved that a female employee who, without realizing that she was pregnant, made a declaration of will aimed at the termination of the contract of employment may evade legal effects of the declaration; e.g., the Supreme Court judgment of 19 Mar. 2002, I PKN 156/01.

237. The Supreme Court finds an agreement to terminate an employment relationship, aimed at exclusion of the legal automatism of employment relationship continuity in the situation of a transfer of work establishment to another employer, to be void by law as contrary to a mandatory legal rule of Art. 23(1) LC – *see*, e.g., the judgment of 7 Feb. 2007, I PK 269/06).

employment and delayed the possibility for the employee to contest the correctness of the notice of termination. The sanction was also conducive to the emergence of fictitious employment relationships, as on many occasions the employees did not contest the wrongful termination of the contract, which the fact led to serious complications regarding the determination of rights and duties of parties to the employment relationship and social security benefits.

As a result, the sanctions for wrongful termination of the employment contract with and without notice have been provided for in the LC in a way differing from the general rules stemming from civil law. At the heart of the regulations lies the assumption that termination of the contract of employment would be deemed effective regardless of its conformity with law. The effect can only be put into question by the employee turning to the labour court with relevant claims.[238]

334. Claims available to employees in case of wrongful termination with notice are provided for in Articles 44–51 LC. An action should be filed within twenty-one days of the date of the delivery of the letter to the employee, unless the employee failed to observe the time limit without any fault on his/her part.[239] If it has been determined by the court that the notice of termination was wrongful, the court, upon the request of the employee, declares the notice to terminate ineffective and, if the contract has already been terminated, orders that the employee be reinstated on the previous terms or rules that compensation is due to the employee. However, the court may reject the employee's request to declare the notice ineffective or to order reinstatement to the job if it finds it impossible or pointless to grant such a request. In such case the court awards compensation. Even then, however, the employee enjoying special protection has to be reinstated, unless it is impossible to grant the employee's request owing to the employer's bankruptcy or liquidation having been declared (Article 45 §3 LC).

335. An employee hired under a contract of employment concluded for a trial period or a definite period may only claim compensation. Yet, a female employee who is pregnant or on maternity leave, a male employee who is a father taking care of a child during maternity leave and an employee whose employment relationship is protected under the provisions of the Trade Unions Act may also claim for reinstatement to the job.

336. The employee who has resumed employment as a result of reinstatement has the right to remuneration for the period during which he/she was out of work, in the amount limited to the remuneration for two months, or one month if the period of notice was three months (Article 47 LC). The employee should report, being ready to begin work, within seven days of the reinstatement, or else the employer may refuse to re-employ him/her. The period of the reinstated employee

238. *See*, for instance, the Supreme Court judgment of 9 May 2006, II PK 270/05, on the grounds to which judgment the Court presents evolution of the law and court decisions regarding the issue.

239. Before 1 Jan. 2017, this time limit was seven days. The courts of law, considering it as too short, took an extremely liberal attitude to such failures; *see*, for instance, the resolution of the Supreme Court of 14 May 1986, III PZP 8/86; judgments of the Supreme Court of 13 May 1994, I PRN 21/94 and of 29 Mar. 2000 II PK 224/06).

being out of work and the period for which the compensation was awarded is reckoned towards the period of service according to the principles laid down in Article 51 LC.

337. The amount of the compensation payable in case of wrongful notice to terminate given by the employer is statutorily limited. As regards termination of a contract of employment for an indefinite period the compensation is paid as the amount of remuneration due for the period from two weeks up to three months, but not lower than the amount of payment in lieu of notice. In case of a fixed-term contract the compensation is equal to the amount of remuneration for the agreed term of the contract, but not more than for three months (Articles 47^1 and 50 LC).[240] Suggestions are made by labour law scholars to raise the upper limit of the compensation for wrongful termination of a contract of employment with notice. The principle, itself, of statutory limitation of the amount of the compensation, as well as that of limiting the amount of the remuneration for the time of being out of work, paid to the employee reinstated to the job is, however, not contested by a majority of those debating. There is also a dominating view that the issue has been sufficiently provided for in the LC and no supplementary compensation may be sought by the employee in court under civil law provisions. This is also the position that, for many years, has been taken by the Supreme Court.[241] Its conformity with the Constitution has been confirmed by the Constitutional Tribunal. The situation, however, is not that clear-cut any more since, in its judgment of 27 November 2007, SK 18/05, the Constitutional Tribunal found the exclusion of the right to full compensation under Civil Code provisions in case of wrongful termination of a contract of employment without notice to be non-constitutional. Some legal scholars believe that the arguments quoted in the grounds to the judgment speak in favour of departing from the principle of limited compensation also in other cases of wrongful termination of the employment relationship.[242]

III. Employee Claims in Case of Wrongful Termination of a Contract of Employment Without Notice

338. Claims available to the employee in case of a wrongful termination of a contract of employment without notice are provided for in Articles 56–61 LC. Where the immediate termination was made unlawfully, the employee may demand reinstatement to work or compensation. The claims should be filed with the labour court within twenty-one days of the service of a written communication that the employment contract is terminated without notice (Articles 264 §2 and 265 LC). Otherwise, the assertion of the claims has been provided for in a manner similar to

240. The limitation does not apply to a female employee when pregnant or on a maternity leave, and to an employee being a father raising a child in the period of enjoying the maternity leave.

241. The position was confirmed by the Supreme Court in the resolution of a panel of seven judges of 18 Jun. 2009, I PZP 2/09.

242. Cf., for instance, K. Jaśkowski, 'Wpływ wyroku Trybunału Konstytucyjnego z 27 listopada 2007 r. na odpowiedzialność pracodawcy za rozwiązanie umowy o pracę', *Praca i Zabezpieczenie Społeczne*, vol. 2 (2009), 9.

that concerning termination with notice, except that reinstated to work may be also an employee working under a fixed-term contract, should the court find it expedient.

339. According to Article 58 LC, the compensation is paid as the amount of remuneration due for the period of notice. In case of a fixed-term contract the compensation is equal to the amount of remuneration for the agreed term of the contract, but not more than for three months. However, as it has already been mentioned above, the Constitutional Tribunal, in its judgment of 27 November 2007, SK 18/05, found such reduction of compensation to be non-constitutional. Consequently, if affected by the wrongful termination of a contract of employment without notice, employees are entitled to full compensation under Civil Code provisions.

IV. Employee Claims in Case of Wrongful Expiration of an Employment Relationship

340. Where regulations concerning the expiration of an employment relationship have been violated by the employer, the above-mentioned provisions on sanctions for unlawful termination of a contract of employment without notice are applicable to the employee claims accordingly.

V. Legal Effects of Termination of a Contract of Employment Without Notice by the Employee

341. Legal effects of the termination of a contract of employment without notice by the employee depend on whether the termination was justified. Where the employee has immediately terminated a contract of employment for gross violation of basic duties of the employer towards him/her, the employee is entitled to compensation, and the termination of the contract entails the same legal effects as the termination of a contract of employment with notice by the employer does (Article 55 §1^1 and §3 LC). Should, however, the termination prove unjustified, the employer may seek compensation from the employee (Article 61^1–61^2 LC).

§4. Change of the Terms of the Employment Contract

I. Ways of Change

342. The contents of a contract of employment may be changed through a notice to change the existing terms of work and pay or by way of an agreement between the parties. In addition, in certain situations strictly specified by law, such a change may be unilaterally ordered by the employer.

II. Notice to Change the Existing Terms of Work and Pay

343. A notice to change the existing terms of work and pay (the so-called notice of change) is a unilateral legal transaction whereby notice is given by the employer to terminate the existing terms of work and pay as provided for in the contract of employment and an offer is made to the employee to continue to work under new terms and conditions after the lapse of the period of notice. The notice may be served solely by the employer. Change of the terms of work and pay occurs upon the lapse of the period of notice unless the offer of new terms of employment has been rejected by the employee by the mid-point of the period. If the employee rejects the new conditions of employment offered to him/her, the employment relationship is terminated upon the lapse of the period of notice. A notice to change may, thus, not result in the change of the contract of employment without the employee's consent, yet the lack of consent brings about the termination of the employment relationship.

344. Provisions on contract termination are applicable, accordingly, to a notice to change the existing terms of work and pay. This means, in particular, that the notice should be submitted in writing and that the employee is subject to the general and special protection schemes, in accordance with the principles set out in the provisions on termination of the contract of employment.

345. Changed through a notice of change are only the terms of work and pay specified in the employment contract, such as the amount of salary/wage or kind of work. This is why it is not allowed to change, for instance, the type of employment contract following that path.[243]

346. Considering its *ratio legis*, the notice of change is, in principle, used to make changes that are unfavourable to the employee. If, however, the employee refuses to accept the more favourable terms of employment (e.g., a pay raise), such a change may be made by the employer using a notice to change the existing terms of work and pay.[244]

III. Unilateral Change of the Content of a Contract of Employment

347. Under strictly defined circumstances labour law provisions authorize (and in some cases actually oblige) the employer to unilaterally change the content of the employment relationship, which the change may be effected without obtaining the consent of the employee. Changes of this kind are, as a rule, of a periodical nature.

243. Supreme Court resolution of 28 Apr. 1994, I PZP 52/93.
244. For instance, in the case of 21 Oct. 2003, I PK 512/2002, considered by the Supreme Court, the employee did not give consent to a raise of pay as the move would have resulted in his right to old-age pension being suspended.

348. The first group of situations concerns the employee being entrusted, for a certain period, with the performance of a work other than that agreed on.

The broadest authorization of that kind is provided by Article 42 §4 LC, allowing the employer, in situations justified by his/her/their needs, to entrust the employee with another work for a period not exceeding three months in a calendar year, provided that this does not result in a reduction of the employee's remuneration and that the work corresponds to the employee's qualifications. Assignment of another appropriate work is also allowed in the case of a downtime if relevant remuneration is secured to the employee.

349. The remaining cases concern the situation when the employer is obliged to relocate the employee to another job, appropriate to the health condition of the employee or adequate to the person's specific status. The employee is obliged to submit to such an order. This concerns the transfer to another job of a pregnant woman or one who is nursing a child, a young person, an employee who shows symptoms of a developing occupational disease or one who has become incapable of performing the existing job as a result of an accident at work or an occupational disease but has not been held incapable of working within the meaning of the provisions on old age and disability pensions. It is usually a medical certificate that provides the basis for the decision on such a transfer.

IV. Change of the Content of a Contract of Employment by Mutual Consent

350. The broadest opportunities for a change of the content of the employment relationship are offered by the mutual consent of the parties. By means of a mutual agreement, parties to a contract of employment may not only modify the content of the latter but also change the type of the contract itself. The agreement may either improve or deteriorate terms of employment, provided that the principle of employee privilege is not violated by the same and that the contract of employment may be changed for the good or only for a specified time. The admissibility of changing the contract of employment by mutual consent follows from the principle of freedom of contract. The LC does not provide for the issue.

§5. Dismissals for Reasons Not Related to Workers (Collective Redundancies)

I. Introductory Remarks

351. Unlike Directive 98/59 EC on collective redundancies of 20 July 1998, the Polish Employment Termination Act 2003 (ETA), which replaced the 1989 law on the same subject, addresses both group layoffs and individual redundancies. The Act, applicable to employers that have at least twenty employees, concerns dismissals, the reasons for which are not attributable to the employees. Smaller employers are not governed by the Act.

352. Reasons not attributable to employees are those which are not connected with the employee as a person (his/her body and mind) or the way in which he/she does the work and meets his/her employee duties. Instead, they cover reasons attributable to the employer, such as financial difficulties, organizational and technical changes, etc., and those not related to any of the parties, such as deterioration of the market situation, force majeure events and the like. In particular, further consequences are provided for by the law as regards the employer's bankruptcy and liquidation.

353. Dismissals covered by the ETA may be carried out through a notice to terminate or by an agreement between the parties.[245]

354. The Act is applicable to all employers having at least twenty employees, regardless of the type of activities conducted. Provisions of the Act do not cover those whose employment relationship is based on the act of nomination.

355. The main objective of the ETA is to make it easier for employers to carry out redundancies caused by restructuring or poor business standing of companies and other work establishments and to protect the interests of employees in such situations.

II. Collective Redundancies

A. The Concept of Collective Redundancy

356. A collective redundancy occurs where, owing to the reasons mentioned above, within a period not exceeding thirty days, made redundant are:

- 10 employees, where the employer has less than 100 employees;
- 10% of employees, where the employer has at least 100 but fewer than 300 employees;
- 30 employees, where the employer has at least 300 employees or more.

Employees dismissed by mutual consent of the parties are reckoned towards these numbers if there are at least five cases of such termination.

245. An issue of debate is whether dismissal, within the meaning of the discussed Act, includes a notice to change the existing terms of work and pay as well. A positive position on the matter was taken by the Supreme Court in its judgment of 17 May 2007, III BP 5/07. As opposed to the ruling, in the judgment of 30 Sep. 2011 (III PK 14/11) the Court stated that the dismissal does not include notices to change the terms of employment, unless the content and circumstances of the notice indicate that the employer intends to terminate the employment relationship with the employee.

B. Procedure for Collective Redundancy

357. The employer is obliged to consult, on the intention of carrying out collective redundancy, with the work establishment trade unions. To that end the employer should notify the trade unions, in writing, not later than thirty days before the date of serving the notices to terminate. The notification should include information concerning the reasons for the redundancy, the number and professional profile of the employees to be laid off, the period of redundancy, the criteria for selecting the employees to be laid off, the order in which the dismissals are to be implemented and any additional employee rights connected with the redundancy, e.g., the right to retrain in another profession or receive compensation. The trade unions may require that further information needed in order to conduct consultations and conclude an agreement with the employer be provided to them. The consultations concern, *inter alia*, ways and means of avoiding the redundancies, or reducing their scope, and employee issues related to the redundancies (the opportunities for occupational retraining of the employees made redundant or assistance in finding them another job in particular). Trade unions may submit proposals on the avoidance of the redundancy or the reduction of its size.

358. Within a time limit, not longer than twenty days of the notification on the contemplated layoffs, the employer and trade unions should conclude an agreement specifying the rules for collective redundancy and the redundancy-related employer's duties. The agreement should be concluded by all or at least the representative trade union organizations operating at the work establishment. In practice, a typical agreement determines the number of the laid-off employees, the criteria for the selection of the employees to be made redundant, the sequence and terms of the notices to be given, the rights of the dismissed employees exceeding the levels established by the statute (e.g., payment of higher severance pay to the employees). Where no agreement has been concluded, it is the employer that resolves the issues that should be provided for in the agreement, by means of setting up rules for the collective redundancies, taking into account, as far as practicable, the proposals submitted by the work establishment trade unions in the course of the consultations. At a non-unionized work establishment principles of the redundancies are laid down by the employer in the rules made after consultations with employee representatives appointed in the way adopted at the work establishment (Article 3).

359. A notification on the contemplated redundancies and the content of the agreement or rules providing for collective redundancies is also sent to the county (*powiat*) labour office. The notification allows the office to take the relevant actions related to the redundancies. The office may not, however, stop or delay the decision on collective redundancy.

360. Upon notifying the labour office the employer may give notices to terminate employment contracts. Termination of employment relations may not, however, occur before the lapse of thirty days from the notification.

361. The judicature has consistently held that infringement of these requirements means violation of legal provisions on the termination of employment contracts with notice within the meaning of Article 45 LC and makes the employee entitled to assert the claims that can be raised in case of an unlawful notice to terminate a contract of employment.[246]

C. Limitations of Employee Protection Against Termination of the Employment Relationship under the ETA

362. Concluding an agreement on collective redundancies results in limitations of the individual protection against termination with notice. Effecting the dismissals in accordance with the rules laid down in the agreement relieves the employer of the obligation to consult the intention to terminate contracts of employment, on a case-by-case basis, with the trade union representing the employee. Notwithstanding this, the employer is still obliged to give the reasons for the termination to each dismissed employee and the employee is allowed to assert his/her rights in court, claiming lack of justification or unlawfulness of the notice to terminate. In the situation of no agreement having been reached, individual notices to terminate are subject to general protection against termination, in accordance with the general rules.

363. The most essential deviation from the general rules of protection against dismissal consists in limitation of the special protection. In case of collective redundancies the protection is, in principle, excluded by the ETA, limited protection being retained only as regards certain groups of employees. This holds true as regards employees on vacation, holidays or during other excused absence from work not exceeding the time limit specified in law, within the period of four years preceding retirement age, pregnancy or maternity leave, performance of military service or training, as well as employees, mentioned in the Act, being members of employee representation bodies and social labour inspectors. The employer is not allowed to terminate the contract of employment with these persons, although a notice may be given to change the existing terms of employment they are subject to. Other employees, normally enjoying special protection, have been excluded from the coverage in case of collective redundancies.[247]

246. Supreme Court judgment of 23 Jan. 1991, I PR 450/90, OSP of 1992, no. 3, item 57.
247. For instance, trade union activists performing their functions outside of the work establishment, members of trade union bodies, MPs, senators, members of local/regional assemblies, employees on leave to raise children and others.

III. Individual Termination

A. *Conditions of the ETA Application to Individual Termination of the Employment Relationship*

364. The ETA is applicable to instances of individual termination where the employment relationship termination takes place for reasons mentioned in the Act but the number of the dismissed employees is lower than that required for the redundancy to be deemed collective. Another precondition for the application of the Act to individual dismissals is that the reasons should be the sole ground for the termination of the employment relationship (Article 10 part 1 ECTA).[248]

B. *Limitation of Protection Against Dismissal*

365. Employees dismissed under the individual procedure, for reasons non-attributable to employees, are covered by the rules of the general protection scheme. It is the special protection that is modified, though. While granted by the ETA to the same categories of employees, and on the same terms as in the case of collective redundancies, it nevertheless displays two differences. First, protected against individual dismissal are senators, MPs and members of local/regional assemblies. Second, as regards other situations, in place of 'regular' prohibitions of dismissal, the work establishment trade union organizations are empowered to oppose to a notice of termination contemplated by the employer. The employer is not allowed to dismiss the employee in the face of the opposition, although a notice may be given to change the existing terms of his/her/their employment. In a majority of work establishments no special protection is actually provided, though, there being no trade union organization that could voice the objection.

IV. Special Rules for Dismissals in the Event of Employer Bankruptcy and Liquidation

366. Where bankruptcy has been declared or liquidation started regarding an employer covered by the provisions of the ETA, both in case of collective and individual redundancy the protection is reduced to a mere requirement of justification of the notice to terminate. Certainly, grounds for the notice can be questioned by the employee in court. As far as collective redundancies are concerned, however, the above-described procedure involving information and negotiations has to be observed and the principles of dismissals ought to be laid down in an agreement with trade unions or in the employer's rules.

---

248. According to the Supreme Court this means a situation in which, the reasons not existing, the employer would not have made a decision to dismiss the employee. There can, thus, exist also other circumstances, which the circumstances themselves, however, without the reasons mentioned in Art. 1 part 1 of the Act, would not have resulted in the decision on the employment relationship termination; Supreme Court judgment of 10 Oct. 1990, I PR 319/90.

V. Benefits to Employees Made Redundant for Reasons Not Attributable to Employees

367. The benefits may follow, from the ETA, other statutes and the agreements or rules concerning the collective redundancy.

368. All employees made redundant on the terms prescribed by the ETA are entitled to a severance pay amounting to one, two or three months' remuneration (payable to employees who have worked for a given employer for two, between two and eight and over eight years, respectively). The employees dismissed under a collective redundancy scheme are also entitled to re-employment if the employer should again hire employees from the same occupational group, the dismissed employee reporting his/her intention to take employment within a year of the date when the employment relationship with him/her was terminated. The obligation to employ lasts for fifteen months from the date of termination of the employment relationship.

369. Further rights of the employees are based on other pieces of legislation. Of particular importance in that respect is the Employment Promotion Act 2004 (EPA). This provides for the funding, from the resources of the Labour Fund, of the costs of training the employees, allows them to receive unemployment benefits on preferential terms, grants to those meeting relevant conditions the right to pre-retirement benefits, secures assistance to start-up a business of their own, etc. The EPA also imposes on the employers intending to dismiss at least fifty employees a duty to agree, with the county *(powiat)* labour office, terms of assistance provided to the employees made redundant in the field of job matching or vocational counselling and training (Articles 62, 70).

370. Rights going beyond those established by statutory law can follow from agreements and rules concerning collective redundancies. These may include, e.g., higher severance payments, the right to the funding of training courses or receipt of job offers from an agency hired by the employer. Relatively often, in order to avoid conflicts and tensions brought about by collective redundancies, employers launch programmes encouraging their employees to leave voluntarily by offering high severance payments and other benefits.

§6. Employer's Duties Related to the End of the Employment Relationship

371. In connection with the termination or expiry of an employment relationship the employer is obliged to immediately issue to the employee an employment certificate. The certificate should include particulars concerning the period during which the work was performed, the type of work done, position(s) occupied, the manner in which the employment relation was terminated or circumstances in which it expired as well as other information necessary for its determination. The employer is also expected to include a note on a seizure (if any) of the remuneration for work in accordance with the provisions on executive proceedings. At the request of the employee, the work certificate should provide information on the amount and components of the remuneration and on the qualifications obtained (Articles 97– 99 LC).

Where the employment relationship ends in connection with the employee's retirement or his/her becoming entitled to disability pension, the employer should develop, in consultation with the employee, the claim for old-age or disability pension and pay the severance pay equal to the employee's one-month remuneration (Article 92^1 LC).

372. In case of the employee's death the employer is obliged to inform his/her family about the conditions of entitlement to the survivor's pension, develop a claim for the pension and file it with the relevant social security authority. The employer should also pay the death payment to the family of the deceased (Article 93 LC).

Chapter 7. Atypical Employment Contracts

Z. Hajn

§1. Introductory Remarks

373. The concept of 'atypical forms of employment' is based on the juxtaposing of the phenomenon so described with what is termed as the typical employment, i.e., a full-time job, done under a contract for an indefinite period, in one place and at the employer's premises.

374. The development of legislation concerning the atypical contracts of employment had become the element of employment policy in Poland even before the country joined the EU in 2004.[249] The perspective of the country's accession to the EU injected more dynamism into the process while forcing the legislator into observing standards contained in the Community (EU) directives.

375. The following forms of atypical work are discussed below:

- part-time work;
- temporary work;
- telework;
- workers put at the disposal of another employer.

The issue in relation to the contract for a definite period has already been discussed (*see* Part I, Chapter 2, §3, III and IV).

§2. Part-Time Work

I. Equal Treatment

376. A fundamental change in the regulations concerning part-time work was made on 1 January 2004. Until that time, characteristic of Polish law was rather casual regulation of that form of work.

Of particular meaning was the fact that from that time on, the list of the grounds of discrimination, as contained in Article 11^3 of the LC, was extended to include the criterion of part-time work. According to Article 29^2 §1 of the LC the terms of a part-time contract of employment may not be less favourable than the terms of contract of a comparable full-time employee who is engaged in the same or a similar work. The principle of *pro rata temporis* may, however, be applied in fixing the remuneration and other payments. An even more striking change is the extension of the full protection against non-discrimination, as embodied in Articles 18^{3a-3e} of the

249. It was contemplated, *inter alia*, in the programme National Strategy of Employment Growth and Development of Human Resources (point II, 5a) (2000).

LC, to part-time workers. This means covering the workers by legal guarantees of equal treatment identical with those pertaining to other workers (as regards concluding and termination of the employment relationship, fixing the pay and various conditions of employment, granting other benefits connected with work, promotion, training courses, etc.). The workers in question have also been granted access to instruments of protection against unequal treatment, like the right to claim equal pay for equal work, the right to make an accusation of harassment, reversing of the burden of proof in court proceedings concerning discrimination and the right to compensation. Guarantees going that far and putting the protection against unequal treatment of part-time workers on par with protection against sex discrimination go beyond the requirements to align Polish law with the EU standards, as contained in the part-time work Directive 1999/70/EC.

II. Limitation of the Number of Working Hours Permitted above the Agreed Duration of Working Time

377. An issue of practical importance is the obligation to establish, in the contract of employment, the number of hours permitted above the agreed duration of working time, the excess of which qualifies the part-time worker to get extra pay for working overtime (Article 151 §5 of the LC). The aim of the regulation is to prevent a situation in which the employee would be forced, permanently and without pay increase, to work overtime in excess of the working hours agreed. The current regulations also comprise duties of the employers concerning part-time workers. The obligation of an employer to inform the employees of the possibility to do full-time or part-time work (Article 94^2 of the LC) is essential for making the discussed form of employment better available. As far as practicable, employers should also give consideration to requests by workers to be transferred from full-time to part-time work and vice versa (Article 29^2 §2 LC).

III. Work-Sharing

378. Part-time work is also applied as a measure whereby jobs are protected under the work-sharing scheme. The company suffering from a fall in sales may, on terms specified in law, receive assistance, from public funds, to partly compensate their employees for a drop in remuneration resulting from reduced working hours.[250]

250. *See* the Act of 11 October, 2013 on Particular Measures for Job Protection, *Journal of Laws* (2013), item 1291.

§3. Temporary Work

I. Introductory Remarks

379. The initial Polish legal regulations concerning temporary work, enacted in 2001, established minimum standards for that form of employment, limited to the issue of safety and health at work and certain information duties on the part of the user employer.[251] Then, as of 6 February 2003, temporary work agencies were recognized by the Act on Employment and Prevention of Unemployment of 1994 as employment agencies to which the general rules of the operation of such agencies were applied. The object of their activity was described by the Act as services consisting in employing workers with a view to make them available to a third party, a natural or legal person, called the user employer. Provision of services of the type was clearly reserved for temporary work agencies, giving them exclusive rights to maintain employees in order to provide labour force for the benefit of a third party. At present the matters are regulated in a similar way in the Employment Promotion Act 2004.[252] The operation of temporary work agencies needs to be registered. A new and extensive regulation of temporary work was introduced by the Temporary Workers Employment Act 2003.[253] In June 2017, important amendments were introduced to this law to eliminate the abuse of some of its provisions and to increase employee protection.

II. Legal Model of Temporary Work

380. Temporary work is based on a tripartite relationship between the temporary worker, temporary work agency being its employer and the user employer benefiting from the services of the agency that directs the worker to do the job specified by the user. A temporary employment agency can only be the employment agency that meets the tasks of a labour market institution, as specified in the Employment Promotion Act 2004,[254] entered in the register of the agencies.

381. A temporary employee may be employed by a temporary work agency exclusively for the purpose of performing temporary work for the benefit and under the management of the user employer (Article 1). The agency employs temporary employees on the basis of an employment contract concluded for a definite period. The rights and obligations of the user employer and the temporary work agency, including charging the fee for the agency services, are defined in the agreement concluded between them.

382. Temporary work may be performed by the same worker for the benefit of a given user employer over a total period not exceeding eighteen months in any

251. *See* Art. 298^3 LC, now repealed.
252. Article 6 and Chapter 6.
253. Act of 9 Jul. 2003; *Journal of Laws* (2018), item 594.
254. Article 6 part 4 of EPA.

thirty-six succeeding months regardless of the number of agencies employing him/her at that time (Article 20). The temporary agency work may not go beyond the performance of tasks of a seasonal, periodic or ad hoc nature, or ones the timely performance of which by employees of the user employer would not be possible, or those the performance of which belongs to the duties of an absent employee of the user employer.

383. A temporary employee may not be entrusted with performing work:

- which is particularly hazardous;
- at a position occupied by an employee of the user employer during participation of that employee in a strike;
- to replace a full-time employee made redundant for reasons not attributable to the employee within three months of such redundancy being made;
- requiring the arming of a worker with a weapon of which the possession requires obtaining a permit.

384. An agreement between the temporary work agency and the user employer not to hire the temporary employee by the user employer after the completion of temporary work is null and void. The user employer is obliged to inform the temporary employees of any vacancies that the employer intends to fill.

385. The user employer should notify the representative trade union of the intention to engage a temporary worker as well as and provide it with information about his/her work. However, in case of an intention to engage such an employee for a period exceeding six months the employer is obligated to take steps aimed at arriving at an agreement on this intention with the union.

III. Rights and Duties of the Parties

386. The rights and duties of the parties to the said tripartite relationship are provided for, on the one hand, by an agreement between the agency and user employer and, on the other hand, by a contract of employment between the agency and the employee.

387. In order to conclude an employment contract between a temporary work agency and a temporary employee the user employer must agree with the agency on basic terms of the employment (such as the type of work, expected duration of work, working hours and the place where the work is to be performed) as well as other matters required by law, such as the scope, term and method of providing information to the agency by the user employer on the course of work and the scope of the obligations of the user employer regarding work safety and hygiene. The user employer must also notify the agency, in writing, of the remuneration for the work to be entrusted to the employee, determined in its pay regulations. It is also obliged to keep and transfer to the temporary work agency a record of temporary workers and periods of their work.

388. The temporary employee must be informed by the work agency of the above arrangements prior to the conclusion of the employment contract. The contract is similar to a typical one, with certain obvious peculiarities, such as an indication of the user employer and of the agreed duration of temporary work.

389. It is the work agency that, as the employer of a temporary worker, pays his/her remuneration, while the user employer performs duties and exercises rights of the employer to the extent necessary to organize the work. The user employer sets tasks for the employee placed by the temporary work agency and checks their execution. He/she is obliged to provide the employee with safe and hygienic working conditions and to keep working time records concerning the employee. The temporary employee may not be treated less favourably – as regards working conditions and other terms of employment – than permanent employees employed in the same or similar positions.

IV. Temporary Work Based on a Civil Law Contract

390. When the conditions of performing work are not typical of the employment relationship, the temporary work agency may delegate persons who are not employees of such an agency to perform temporary work on the basis of civil law contracts. In such a case the provisions of the Temporary Workers Employment Act 2003 are applicable only to a limited extent (Article 26). In particular, the worker may not be assigned to do the work which a temporary worker employed under a contract of employment is not allowed to do. The agency and the user employer cannot prohibit an employee from concluding an employment contract between the employee and the user after finishing agency work. Last but not least, the above-described limitation of the maximum working period of eighteen months must include both the work provided on the basis of employment and civil law contracts

§4. TELEWORK

I. Regulatory Framework

391. The legal regulation of telework was provided in Poland in 2007 by adding a new chapter titled 'Employment in the form of telework' (Article 67^5–67^{17}) to the LC. The new provisions fall in line with the 2002 EU social partners framework agreement on the regulation of telework. As some other EU Member States did, Poland chose to implement the agreement via national legislation. However, the way for doing this was paved, in 2005, by an autonomous bipartite agreement between representative social partner organizations participating in the negotiations of the Social Dialogue Roundtable for European Integration. After a deadlock in the process, caused by a refusal of the All-Poland Alliance of Trade Unions (*Ogólnopolskie Porozumienie Związków Zawodowych* (OPZZ)) to sign the agreement, the organization altered its position and declared that the agreement might be used as a basis for future legislation. Eventually, the draft legislation prepared by the government as a result of the agreement was approved by the Labour Law and Collective Bargaining Team of the Tripartite Commission in March 2007 and, further on, submitted to the Parliament, where it was successfully passed into law.[255]

392. The conditions under which telework is to be performed in a work establishment are to be determined in the agreement between the employer and the workplace trade union organization. If no consensus is struck with all the organizations, the accord may be concluded with representative workplace-level organizations (as defined by Article 241^{25a} LC). Only if the agreement cannot be concluded either way, the employer is entitled to make the regulations on telework independently. In the case of non-unionized workplaces, the regulations should be made after consultation between the employer and employee representatives selected in a way 'adopted at specific employer's' (Article 67^{6} LC).

393. Making an arrangement between the employer and the employee that the work will be performed under the telework scheme may take place either at the conclusion of the contract of employment or during the employment, both parties consenting. Notwithstanding this, the parties may, in a separate agreement, determine, in particular, rules for the use, by the employee, of his/her own equipment, ways of communication between the two parties, including the way of confirmation of the employee's presence at the workplace, the manner and form in which the employee's work would be supervised (Article 67^{11} §2 LC).

II. Legal Notion and Main Principles of Legal Regulation of Telework

394. The LC defines telework as a work performed outside the work establishment, on a regular basis, using means of electronic communications. Consequently, a teleworker is defined as an employee performing work on the terms specified above and reporting on the outcome of the work to the employer, in particular, by means of electronic communications (Article 67^{5} LC).[256]

395. The choice of telework is voluntary for the worker and employer. Accordingly, an employment relation in the form of telework can only be established with the mutual consent of both parties. In the case of an employee already working under a 'typical' employment contract and expressing a willingness to undertake telework, the employer is supposed to acquiesce to this request 'when feasible' (Articles 67^{7} and 67^{8} LC). No contract of employment may be terminated due to the employee's refusal to undertake telework (Article 67^{5} LC).

---

255. For more, *see* J. Czarzasty, *Telework in Poland*, Institute of Public Affairs, www.eurofound.europa.eu/eiro/2007/11/articles/ pl0711019i.htm.
256. Unlike the EU social partners' framework agreement, the LC does not require that the subject matter of the agreement with the teleworker be only the work that could also be performed at the employer's premises.

396. With due regard to peculiarities of telework, the teleworker may not, as far as working conditions and other terms of employment (including access to training) are concerned, be treated less favourably than permanent employees employed at the same or similar positions (Article 67^{15} LC).

III. Rights and Duties of the Parties

397. The employer is obliged to provide the teleworker with necessary equipment, insure it, cover the costs related to its installation and use and ensure technical assistance and training to the employee, unless use of the employee's own equipment has been agreed on by the parties (Article 67^{11} §1 LC). The teleworker is obliged to comply with the data protection rules, set up by the employer (Article 67^{12} LC). The employer is generally authorized to exercise control over telework. However, the teleworker retains his/her right to privacy. Consequently, the control activities performed directly at home require a prior written consent of the worker concerned, and where such consent has not been given, the control may only be performed indirectly by means of electronic communications. The employer is obliged to make it possible to the teleworker to stay at the premises of the work establishment, communicate with other employees, use the rooms and equipment of the work establishment, its social facilities and benefit from the welfare activities of the employer (Article 67^{16} LC). The employer is responsible for occupational safety and hygiene of the telework, albeit, where the telework is performed at the employees' home place, certain regulations do not apply, including those which concern sanitary and safety requirements for work premises or access to sanitary facilities (Article 67^{17} LC).

§5. Putting an Employee at the Disposal of Another Employer

398. With an employee's consent expressed in writing, an employer may grant the employee unpaid leave so that he/she may work for another employer for the period stipulated in the agreement relating to that matter made between the employers (Article 174^{1} LC). For the time of work at the new work establishment, a contract of employment is concluded between the employee and the relevant employer. The period of the work is included in the period of service which determines the rights of an employee with respect to the employer granting the leave. The above-described regulation allows the employers to flexibly change the numbers of the staff, depending on the periodical fluctuations of labour demand. The form can be also used as a way to avoid making redundant valuable employees who can prove useful in future.

Chapter 8. Protection of Special Groups of Employees

Z. Hajn

§1. Women; Workers Taking Care of Children

I. Introductory Remarks

399. In 2001, Chapter 8 of the LC (Articles 176–189[1]), originally bearing the title 'Protection of Women's Work', was entitled 'Protection of Work of Women and Men Raising a Child'. In 2002 it was changed again to read 'Rights of Employees Relating to Parenthood'. The changes reflect the process of equalization of employment-related rights of women and men, enabling both genders to reconcile their occupational and family obligations. They do not, however, change the fact that the essence of the regulations lies in the protection of women, as a particularly sensitive risk group that must be protected against the dangers specifically affecting them.[257]

This process has resulted in the successful equalization of female and male employees as regards their family-related rights and duties. This has been achieved, first of all, thanks to the amendments to the LC made by the laws of 6 December 2008 and 26 July 2013. Given ever more frequent legislative changes, it is not much of an exaggeration to say that there is always a bill on the matters, awaiting consideration in the Parliament. The best proof of this is that the last extensive amendments to the LC have been in force since 2 January 2016.

II. Protection Against Hazardous or Onerous Work

400. In earlier periods prohibitions of employment, concerning women in general, were set up; these contained long lists of work-stands and types of work inaccessible to female workers. To justify the prohibitions, both psychophysical factors (like protection of prospective maternity) and moral arguments were quoted. The first to be lifted were, at the beginning of the 1950s, morality-based bans, such as the prohibition to employ women as waitresses at nightclubs licensed to serve alcohol. In 1951 women were also allowed to take night shifts in industry and trade. A dramatic shortening of the list of then bans took place in 1996. Since that time they had been limited, in general, to the prohibition of doing underground work and transport of weights, the scheme resulting from Poland's obligations assumed under ILO conventions (the Underground Work (Women) Convention, 45/1935 and the Maximum Weight Convention, 127/1967); the same holds true as far as manual

257. As stated in the preamble to Council Directive 92/85/EEC of 19 Oct. 1992 on the safety and health at work of pregnant workers and workers who have recently given birth or are breastfeeding, in conjunction with Art. 15 of Council Directive 89/391/EEC of 12 Jun. 1989 on the introduction of measures to encourage improvements in the safety and health of workers at work.

tasks exceeding the loads specified in law are concerned. However, it was considered that the list of jobs prohibited to all women constitutes their discrimination as regards access to employment due to the gender criterion. Therefore, from August 2016, bans refer only to work prohibited to pregnant women and during breastfeeding (Article 176 LC and the Regulation of the Council of Ministers of 10 September 1996 on the list of work particularly onerous or harmful to women's health)[258]

401. Pregnant and breastfeeding women may not be employed to do work which is hazardous to them, specified in the above-mentioned provisions of law or indicated in a medical certificate. Where a woman has been employed at such work, the employer should, depending on the situation, eliminate the hazards by appropriate adjustment of working conditions, reduction of the working time or relocation of the woman to another job and, if the latter is not practicable, release her from the duty to do work. In neither case may the remuneration of the woman be reduced as a result (Article 179 LC).

402. In addition, a pregnant woman may not be employed to do overtime work or night work and may not be delegated to work outside of her usual workplace without her consent, nor may she be employed under the system of interrupted working time. The employer is obliged to organize work in a way excluding night employment and – whenever it is not possible – to release a female employee from the obligation to perform work for as long as may be required (Article 178, 178[1] LC). Where a pregnant woman is employed under a working time schedule according to which the daily working time is extended, the number of her working hours is reduced to eight, the right to full remuneration being retained (Article 148 LC).

403. Pregnancy ought to be confirmed by means of a medical certificate (Article 185 LC).

III. Leave of Absence

A. *Right to a Break for Breastfeeding a Child*

404. A breastfeeding employee has the right to two-half-hour breaks included in the working time. Where more than one child is fed, the time of each break is extended by forty-five minutes. At the employee's request, the breaks may be granted at one time. The employee working less than four hours a day is not entitled to the break for breastfeeding a child, and where the working time does not exceed six hours a day, the employee has the right to but one break (Article 187 LC).

258. *Journal of Laws* (2016), item 2057.

B. Time off for Medical Examinations

405. An employer is obliged to grant a pregnant female worker a paid time off for medical examinations relating to her pregnancy as recommended by a doctor if such checks cannot be given outside working hours (Article 185 LC).

C. Other Instances of Family-related Leave of Absence

406. Employees, regardless of their gender, are entitled to a two-day time off, which can be used in parts (e.g., per hours), paid by the employer, for the settlement of any issues related to the raising of a child below 14 days of age. In addition, they have the right to childcare leaves regarding children up to 8 years of age or a sick child up to 14 years of age, financed from social security resources, if the employee's personal care of the child is required. Time off granted on account of such duties may not exceed sixty days a year. During the absence in question the employee is entitled to care allowance in the amount of 80% of his/her average monthly salary. Entitled to the time off and allowance are, on equal terms, mother and father of the child, although they may not use them at the same time.[259]

IV. Leave Related to Birth and the Raising of a Child

A. Types of Leave

407. In 1975, when the LC entered into force, women were entitled to a maternity leave amounting to sixteen weeks for the first birth, eighteen weeks for each subsequent birth and twenty-six weeks in the case of a multiple birth. Women adopting a child had the right to a fourteen-week leave. Besides that, a woman could take advantage of unpaid leave to raise a small child, up to three years. That situation lasted until the end of 2003, although the unpaid leave to raise a child was replaced, as of 1996, by a leave with the right to allowance.

The ensuing changes of the legal provisions have resulted in the emergence of a rather complex system of leave to which the employees are entitled in the case of the birth and raising of a child.

408. Currently, the following types of leaves are distinguished in the LC:

(1) maternity leave;
(2) parental leave;
(3) child-raising leave;
(4) paternity leave.

259. Articles 32–35 of the Act of 25 Jun. 1999 on Social Security Monetary Benefits in Case of Sickness and Maternity, consolidated text: *Journal of Laws* (2014), item 159.

409. Entitled to the leaves are both natural parents of the child and (albeit with appropriate modifications) adoptive parents and persons acting as a foster family (Article 182(4) and Article 183 LC).

B. Maternity Leave

410. Until the end of 1974, the length of the maternity leave, determined by the old Act of 1924 on the Work of Young Employees and Women, was twelve weeks. As of 1975 the time was extended, by the LC, to sixteen weeks for the first birth, eighteen weeks for each subsequent birth and twenty-six weeks in the case of a multiple birth. In the years 2001–2003 the duration of the maternity leave was twenty-six, twenty-six and thirty-nine weeks, respectively. Since the beginning of 2004 a return to the sixteen, eighteen, twenty-six pattern took place, and as of December 2006 the duration was eighteen, twenty, twenty-eight weeks. The law of 6 December 2008 made the length of the maternity leave conditional solely on the number of children delivered at a single birth. Currently, the employee is entitled to a maternity leave of twenty weeks where one child is born and to thirty-one, thirty-three, thirty-five and thirty-seven weeks if two, three, four or five children are delivered at a single birth, respectively. No more than six weeks of the leave may be used prior to the expected date of childbirth. After at least fourteen weeks, mothers may waive the right to the remaining portion of that leave. If this is the case, the portion not used by her is granted to the father taking care of a child, at his written request. Maternity leave may be granted to the father of the child also whilst the mother is in hospital or has died (Article 180).

In special cases, such as a stillbirth, delivery of a child needing hospital care or waiver of the right to parent the child, the maternity leave may not be shorter than eight weeks (Articles 180^{1} and 182 LC).

C. Parental Leave and Child-Raising Leave

411. Parental leave may be taken by the employee, mother or father, up to thirty-two weeks for one child and thirty-four weeks in the case of a multiple birth for the purpose of taking care of a child until the latter has completed 6 years of age. It may be granted at the employee's written request after using maternity leave wholly. Both parents may take the leave at the same time, yet its total length may not exceed the periods indicated above. The leave may be split into no more than four parts. When taking the leave, the employee may do a part-time job at his/her employer, limiting the use of the leave to the hours exceeding the working time agreed on by the parties, unless it is not possible owing to work organization or the position occupied by the employee. In such a case the leave is prolonged proportionally to the length of time of work done in the period of the leave but not more than to sixty-four or sixty-eight weeks depending on the number of children (Articles 181^{1c}–182^{1g} LC).

412. The parental leave should be differentiated from a child-raise leave (Article 186-186^{8} LC). The latter may be used after or instead of the former. This leave is granted to an employee (mother, father, guardian) at his/her request, for the purpose of taking personal care of a child until the latter has completed 6 years of age. The length of the leave may not exceed thirty-six months. It may be split into no more than five parts. Where the child is handicapped, however, the employee is entitled to a further thirty-six months of leave until the date of the child's 18th birthday. Two solutions have been developed to encourage fathers to take the leave. First, both parents may take the leave at the same time. In such a case its total length may not exceed thirty-six months. Second, each parent is exclusively entitled to one of the thirty-six months, which cannot be transferred to the other parent. During the leave, an employee is free to take a paid job with the existing or another employer or to pursue any other activity, to study or to follow a training course, if this does not make it impossible to take personal care of the child. An employee not making use of a child-raise leave may be granted a reduction of his/her working time (up to a maximum of half of the latter) in the period corresponding with the leave. The employee's request concerning the issue may not be refused by the employer (Article 186^{7} LC).

D. *Paternity Leave*

413. Since the beginning of 2010 a father taking care of a child has been entitled to a paternity leave of two weeks but, in principle, only until the child is 2 years old. The leave is granted at the written request of an employee (Article 182^{3} LC).

V. Guarantees of a Secure Use of Parental Rights

414. The secure use of the above-described rights is guaranteed by the following:

- In the period of pregnancy, as well as when making use of the leaves related to birth and raising of a child, and also in the period of working time reduction for raising a child (not exceeding in total, twelve months) the employee enjoys protection against unilateral termination of employment relationship by the employer and change of terms and conditions of employment unfavourable to the employee.[260]

260. The judiciary goes further, recognizing the right of a woman employee who gave a notice to terminate a contract of employment or agreed to its termination by agreement not knowing that she was pregnant, to evade of the legal effects of such a declaration of will, and if the contract has already been terminated – to demand that it should be reinstated; for instance the Supreme Court judgments of 7 May 1958, 2 CR 700/57; 29 Mar. 2001, I PKN 330/00; of 19 Mar. 2002, I PKN 156/01; of 11 Jun. 2003, I PK 206/02.

- As a rule, the employee may, at the time of his/her choice (but after an appropriate period of notification to the employer about the intent), waive the right of further use of the leave he/she was granted. The option does not concern the maternity leave mandatory for women.
- Upon completion of the leave the employee is guaranteed the right to return to the same position or, if this is not possible, to a position equivalent to the position held before the leave or another position that corresponds with the employee's professional qualifications.
- For the period of maternity leave, paternity leave and parental leave, the employee is entitled to maternity allowance.[261]
- During child-raising leave the employee is entitled to a dependent child allowance of PLN 400 for the time and on terms set up in Article 10 of the Act of 28 November 2003 on family benefits.[262]
- A contract of employment concluded for a definite period or for a trial period of more than one month that would be terminated after the third month of the employee's pregnancy extends until the date of childbirth.

VI. Equal Treatment

415. Unequal treatment of a woman because of pregnancy or breastfeeding is discrimination on the grounds of sex. From the rules preventing such discrimination and from the employee's information autonomy, it also follows that the employer is not allowed to ask the candidate, for a job, whether she is pregnant or not. The relevant information may be demanded after the woman has been employed if, to the work which the person is supposed to do, prohibitions or limitations contained in the provisions on the protection of maternity are applicable.[263] The prohibition goes, thus, further than the prohibition from requiring a test for pregnancy or a certificate of such a test when a woman is applying for employment (ILO Maternity Protection Convention, 2000).

---

261. The allowance is granted in the amount corresponding to the average monthly salary from the period of the last twelve months preceding the month when the leave started (Art. 184 LC and Art. 31 in conjunction with Art. 47 of the Act of 25 Jun. 1999 on Social Security Monetary Benefits in Case of Sickness and Maternity (consolidated text: *Journal of Laws* (2014), item 159). During the parental leave the employee is entitled to an allowance in the amount of 100% of the so calculated salary for not longer than the first six or eight weeks and for 60% for the rest of the period of the leave.
262. Consolidated text *Journal of Laws* (2013), item 1456.
263. It was for that reason that the Supreme Court reversed the judgment of the regional court which had held void a contract of employment concluded with an employee having concealed pregnancy. The Supreme Court rejected the regional court's position that the behaviour of the employee violated rules of social conduct; *see* the judgment of 17 Apr. 2007, I UK 324/06.

§2. Young Workers

I. The Approach to the Legal Regulation of the Work of Young Employees

416. The legal regulation of the work done by the young employees is based on an apparent assumption that people before 18 years of age are dependent on their parents and should study instead of being involved in gainful employment. For that very reason, taking up a job at that age should primarily serve the purpose of vocational training, and gainful employment, if any, should not interfere with school education.

II. Notion of Young Persons

417. Unlike Council Directive 94/33/EC of 22 June 1994 on the protection of young people at work Polish legislation does not use the generic term of 'young persons' but provides separately for the protection of juvenile workers, i.e., persons of at least 16 but less than 18 years of age and children as persons below 16 years of age.

III. Employment of the Juvenile

A. *Limitations of Employment of the Juvenile*

418. Only such adolescents may be employed who have completed at least eight years in elementary school and present a medical certificate stating that work of a given type is not hazardous to their health (Article 191 §1 LC).[264] They may not do types of work, listed in provisions of law, which are prohibited to the juveniles. Certain deviations from the pattern, specified in detail are, however, acceptable if doing work of such types is required for the completion of their occupational training (Article 204 LC). Besides that, prior to being admitted to work, the juveniles have to undergo medical examination and – while employed – are subject to periodic examinations and checks (Article 201 LC).

419. Juveniles are not allowed to do overtime work or night-time work. The night break, in their case, may not be shorter than fourteen hours (Article 203 LC). They are also entitled to vacation holidays during the time of school vacation (twenty-six working days) as early as after a year of work. However, already with the lapse of six months from the date when they started their first job they become entitled to twelve days of the vacation holidays (Article 205 LC).

264. Juveniles not having graduated from eight-year elementary school may be employed only exceptionally, on conditions stated by law.

B. The Basis for Employment of the Juvenile

420. The juvenile may be employed under an employment contract for vocational training or a 'regular contract of employment' concluded for gainful purposes.

C. Employment Contract for Vocational Training

421. The main idea of the employment contract for vocational training – the acquiring of vocational qualifications 'in connection with the work done for the employer' – was formed as early as in the pre-war labour law.[265] Actually, the contract is a type of a training agreement designed as a contract of employment (considering specific features of the training and the intent to guarantee to the juvenile the benefits resulting from his/her having the status of an employee).

422. The main purpose of the contract for vocational training does not include gainful employment but the acquisition of occupational qualifications by the juvenile. Differences between such a contract and the regular contract of employment can be easily discerned. When concluding it, the parties do not determine the type of work but the type, duration and place of occupational training and the way of theoretical education (Article 195 LC) of the person concerned. While remuneration for work is received by the juvenile, it is, in fact, more a kind of a 'pocket money' (4% to 6% of the average salary in the national economy, depending on the year of the training). Upon completion of the training by the juvenile (his/her passing the final exam), the employer has the right to partial reimbursement of the sustained training costs by the municipality.[266] The time of school activities of the juvenile is reckoned toward his/her working hours which must not exceed eight hours a day. The contract in question can only be terminated for reasons specified in the LC, related to occupational training (Article 196 LC).

423. The contract for vocational training is concluded for an indefinite period; hence, after the period of vocational training it is transformed into a regular contract of employment. Only exceptionally, where the number of the juvenile employed for the purpose of occupational training exceeds the number needed by the employer, the contract may be concluded just for the period of occupational training. The period of occupational training is reckoned towards the length of service and the period upon which social security-related benefits are conditioned. The vocational training includes vocational practice at the work establishment and theoretical education, the latter taking place at the school to which the juvenile is directed by the employer or right at the work establishment (Article 195 LC). The

265. Article 477 of the Code of Obligations of 1933. For a broader discussions *see:* A. Raczyński, *Polskie prawo pracy* (Warsaw, 1930), pp. 62 et al.

266. Article 70b of the Act of 7 Sep. 1991 on the System of Education, consolidated text *Journal of Laws* 2004, no. 256, item 2572, as amended.

employer is expected to follow the curriculum accepted for school use. The vocational training can take the shape of a training for a particular occupation, lasting from twenty-four to thirty-six months, or a training to do a particular job, from three to six months (ordinance of the Council of Ministers of 28 May 1996 on Vocational Training of the Juvenile and Remunerating Them.[267] Upon completion of the vocational training in the first of the above-mentioned forms the trainee is granted the title of a skilled worker, upon completion of the other one of a semi-skilled worker.

D. *Regular Contract of Employment*

424. Under a regular contract of employment concluded for gainful purposes the juvenile may only be employed to do light work, specified by the employer after winning the acceptance of a medical doctor and approval by the labour inspector. The work done by the juvenile must not interfere with the timetable of his/her school activities. Moreover, during the period when such activities take place it may not last longer than twelve hours a week, and on the day when school classes are run not longer than two hours. The working time of a juvenile during school holidays may not be longer than seven hours in a twenty-four-hour period and thirty-five hours per week (Article 2002 LC).

IV. Employment of Children

425. Permanent employment of children under 16 years of age is forbidden by the Constitution (Article 65 part 3). The prohibition has been reiterated by the LC (Article 190 §2). As the dominating opinion of the judiciary and the legal scholars holds, the hiring of a child violating age limitations does not result in the employment relationship being null and void, and the person hired should be regarded as an employee. However, where an employment contract has been concluded contrary to the limitations, the employer is obliged to immediately terminate it and pay compensation equal to the remuneration for the period of notice.[268]

426. The prohibition on employing children is not absolute, as Article 65 part 3 of the Constitution, quoted above, exceptionally allows arranging such employment in the forms and nature specified in law. It is permitted to employ children below 16 years of age for vocational training purposes in the situation where an early start of such vocational training is justified by graduation from *gimnazjum* or for other reasons clearly indicated in the provisions of law.[269] The working time of such a person may not be longer than six hours in a twenty-four-hour period.

267. Consolidated text: *Journal of Laws* 2014, item 278, as amended.
268. *See* Supreme Court resolution of 26 Jan. 1982, V PZP 8/81, in which the Court judged that the young person who was employed before the date of his 14th birthday and met with an occupational accident may assert claims available to workers in the case of such an accident.
269. *See* the Ordinance of the Minister of Labour and Social Policy of 5 December, 2002 Concerning the Cases When It Is Exceptionally Allowed to Employ the Juveniles that Have Not Graduated from

427. Since the date of Poland's accession to the EU (i.e., since 1 May 2004), the LC has also provided for employment of children for gainful purposes (Article 304^5 LC). The regulation, in accordance with Article 5 of the protection of young people at work, Directive 94/33/EC, limits such employment to the work for an entity involved in cultural, artistic, sports or advertising business. To employ a child, a prior consent of the legal representative or guardian of the child, as well as a permit by a competent labour inspector, is needed. The permit provides, in detail, for the period of employment, working hours and other necessary requirements related to the child's work. It is given upon an opinion of a psychological-and-pedagogical consultancy, a medical certificate and an opinion of the headmaster of the school attended by the child.

428. These requirements concern the work done both under a contract of employment and a civil law contract.[270]

§3. Disabled Workers

I. Legal Framework

429. The first legal provisions concerning the integration of disabled persons in occupational life, contained in the laws of 1921 and 1932, concerned war invalids. Later on, certain rights were granted to persons having developed disability in connection with employment. Since the 1960s there has been a gradual deviation from the cause–effect principle towards regulations focused on the final effects of disability and providing for benefits to the disabled regardless of the cause of the disability. The current approach, consistently assuming coverage of all disabled, regardless of the source of disability, by special, multi-aspect legal regulation, was only imposed by the law of 1991 and reinforced by the Disabled Persons Act 1997, now in force.[271] Notwithstanding this, pieces of legislation providing for further rights (including protection against work relationship termination) to war and military invalids[272] and (albeit to a smaller extent) to so-called occupational invalids (e.g., Article 231 LC), remain effective.

430. The objectives of the state policy towards the disabled were set up by the Sejm (Parliament) in the declaration of 1 August 1997. The document stated that the persons had the right to an independent, self-contained and active life and could not be exposed to discrimination. Their right to work in the open labour market in

Gimnazjum, Persons Below 16 Years of Age Who Have Graduated from *Gimnazjum* and Persons Below 16 Years of Age Who have Not Graduated from *Gimnazjum*, *Journal of Laws* (2002), No. 214, item 1808.

270. *See*, more broadly, Z. Góral, 'Dopuszczalność pracy dzieci w polskim prawie pracy w świetle prawa międzynarodowego i europejskiego', *Monitor Prawa Pracy*, vol. 6 (2004).

271. The Act of 27 August, 1997 on Occupational and Social Rehabilitation and on Employment of the Disabled; consolidated text: *Journal of Laws* (2008), No. 14, item 92.

272. *See* the Act of 29 May, 1974 on Provisioning for War and Military Invalids and Their Families, *Journal of Laws* (1974), as amended.

accordance with their qualifications, education and capabilities and to the use of the services of vocational counselling and labour exchange (and – where necessary, given their disability and health status – also the right to work under working conditions adjusted to their needs) was declared.[273]

431. Legal protection of the disabled against discrimination in employment is secured by the LC (*see* Introduction, Chapter 7).

II. Rights of Disabled Employees

432. The Disabled Persons Act 1997 specifies the constitutional obligations of the public authorities to come to the aid of the disabled persons by ensuring their subsistence, adaptation to work and social communication (Article 69 of the Constitution). The Act comprehensively provides for the assistance to the disabled, the employment-related issues being just a single component of the aid. It is applicable to only to persons who have been formally found disabled by a special state-appointed body.[274]

433. The rights of the disabled specified by the statute are not, as a rule, conditional upon the cause of the disability but on its degree. As far as employment is concerned they include, in particular, shortened working hours, limited admissibility of night and overtime work, additional vacation holidays, leaves and rest periods at work as well as vocational courses and retraining. In addition, under the occupational safety and health rules, the employer that hires the disabled should adjust the work-stands (and access to them) to the needs and capacities of the persons.[275]

434. The implementation of tasks following from the Act by the public administration is supervised by the Government Plenipotentiary for Disabled Persons' Affairs. The National Consultative Council for Persons with Disabilities and the *voivodeship* (regional) and county (*powiat*) councils for the matters of the disabled operate in a consultative and advisory capacity. The councils are composed of representatives of public agencies and NGOs, including trade unions and employers' organizations. The activities for the benefit of the disabled are funded from the State Fund for the Rehabilitation of the Disabled Persons coming from, *inter alia*, contributions of the employers and budgetary subsidies. Employers with at least twenty-five employees should assign at least 6% of jobs to the disabled, or else they are burdened with payment of the amounts, specified in the Act, to the said Fund.

---

273. Resolution of the Sejm of the Republic of Poland of 1 Aug. 1997, Charter of the Rights of Persons with Disabilities, *Monitor Polski* (1997), No. 50, item 475.

274. As regards the legal notion of disability and its relation to similar legal notions, *see* the Supreme Court judgment of 20 Aug. 2003, II UK 386/02.

275. Ordinance of the Minister of Labour and Social Policy of 26 Sep. 1997 on General Rules of Occupational Safety and Health; consolidated text: *Journal of Laws* (2003), No. 169, item 1650, as amended.

435. Those employing disabled persons receive aid and enjoy facilitations provided for by law. Special rights in that respect are enjoyed by vocational development centres and sheltered employment establishments, i.e., the employers providing jobs, under statutorily determined working conditions, to a considerable degree, to the disabled. Occupational and social rehabilitation and reintegration is also dealt with by cooperatives of the disabled, cooperatives of the blind and social cooperative societies.[276]

§4. Posted Workers

L. Mitrus

436. The provisions on the posting of employees were introduced into Polish system by the amendment to the LC of 24 August 2001.[277] However, before those provisions took effect, they were changed by the amendment of 14 November 2003.[278] Regulations on the posting of employees entered into force on 1 May 2004, i.e., on the day of Poland's accession to the EU. Those provisions constitute a new institution of Polish labour law that were inserted into the national legal system in order to implement the Directive 96/71 on the posting of workers in the framework of the provision of services. The relevant provisions, previously, had been a subject of Chapter IIa of the LC, 'Conditions of employment for employees posted from a Member State of the European Union to work in the territory of the Republic of Poland' (Article 67^1–Article 67^2 LC). Currently, posting of workers to Poland is regulated by the Act of 10 June 2016 on posting of workers in the framework of providing services.[279] The above-mentioned Act took effect on 18 June 2016. Its main purpose has been to implement Directive 2014/67 on the enforcement of Directive 96/71 concerning the posting of workers in the framework of the provision of services and amending Regulation (EU) No. 1024/2012 on administrative cooperation through the Internal Market Cooperation System ('the IMI regulation').[280] In Poland, the implementation of Directives 96/71 and 2014/67 has been integrated into a single legal instrument.

437. The Polish law introduces the idea of Directive 96/71, i.e., it obliges foreign undertakings that post their staff to Poland to observe the set of national minimum rules on the protection of employee rights. Article 3 item 4 of the Act of 10 June 2016 provides that the employer posting an employee to the territory of Poland is an employer that posts an employee to perform work in Poland in the following cases: in relation to the performance of a contract concluded by this employer with a foreign entity, in a foreign branch of this employer, or as a temporary work agency.

276. The Act of 16 September, 1982 – Cooperative Law, consolidated text: *Journal of Laws* (2003), No. 188, item 1848; Act of 27 Apr. 2006 on Social Cooperatives, *Journal of Laws* (2006), No. 94, item 651.
277. *Journal of Laws* 2001), No. 128 item 1405.
278. *Journal of Laws* (2003), No. 213, item 2081.
279. Journal of Laws 2016, item 868.
280. O.J. of 28 May 2014, L 159/11.

The employee posted to Poland does not conclude an employment contract with a local employer. He/she remains in the legal relationship with the employer that sent him/her to Poland and, after completing the task, he/she comes back to the country of origin. The above-mentioned Act does not determine the maximum period of the posting of employees to Poland. In addition, Directive 96/71 can serve as a guideline for the interpretation of Polish labour law.

438. Article 4 of the above-mentioned Act expressly determines the scope of employment conditions that must be observed by employers sending staff to Poland. The minimum employment conditions concern: standards and length of working time as well as periods of weekly and daily rest, length of holiday leave, minimum remuneration for work, amount of overtime work bonus, health and safety conditions, employee rights connected to parenthood, employment of minor persons, as well as work and other paid activities performed by children, the prohibition against discrimination in employment, and performing work in accordance with the provisions on employing temporary workers. In fact, Polish regulations reflect the material scope of Article 3 of Directive 96/71. It should be emphasized that in Poland the minimum employment rights are determined by the LC and other statutes.[281] Certainly, the employer who posts employees to Poland is entitled to provide them with more favourable conditions, which is a regular case where an employee is sent from a country with a higher level of average remuneration.

439. Article 5 of the Act provides exceptions to the above-mentioned rules, i.e., in a situation where the employer is not obliged to meet minimum standards of Polish law. The duty to ensure minimum working conditions with regard to length of holiday leave, minimum remuneration and overtime work bonus do not apply to employees posted to Poland if, due to their qualifications, they work not longer than eight days a year on a given job position, performing initial assembly or installation works outside of the construction sector, as provided by the contract concluded by the employer with a foreign entity, provided that such a work performance is necessary to use the delivered good. Moreover, provisions on posting of employees do not apply to enterprises of the merchant navy in relation to the staff on merchant ships (Article 2 of the Act).

440. The Act of 10 June 2016 regulates also further issues, according to the requirements of the enforcement Directive 2014/67. Apart from the rules on posting of workers to Poland, the Act determines the observance of provisions on posting of workers and fulfilment of the information duties connected to posting of workers, cooperation between competent institutions from Poland and other Member States, protection of employees posted to and from Poland, proceeding on cross-border enforcement of financial administrative penalties and fines. The SLI constitutes a

281. *See* Introduction, Chapter 5.

competent authority to supervise the situation of posted workers. Moreover, new duties envisaged by the Directive 2014/67 have been imposed on employers that post workers from and to Poland.[282]

441. Article 1103^4 §1 of the Code of Civil Procedure provides that disputes arising out of labour law, where the employee acts as a plaintiff, belong to the national jurisdiction where the work usually is, was or should be performed in the Republic of Poland. Disputes initiated by an employee which concern the safeguarding of minimum employment conditions according to Article 67^1 LC and Article 67^2 LC belong to the national jurisdiction also where the employee is or was posted to perform work in Poland by an employer that has its seat in a Member State of the EU (Article 1103^4 §2) or in a third country (1103^4 §3). Thus, claims raised by employees posted to Poland concerning their employment conditions belong to the competence of Polish labour courts.

442. Directive 96/71 has been enacted in the context of freedom to provide services in the EU. Its main idea is to introduce the balance between fair competition and workers' protection in the common market. In other words, the Directive is intended to protect local labour markets and to combat social dumping, where posted workers would accept lower wages and introduce a risk of lowering employment standards of a host country. From this perspective it should be emphasized that Poland is 'sending country', i.e., Polish undertakings quite often post their workers to the 'old' Member States of the EU, while the number of employees sent to Poland in the framework of the freedom to provide services is substantially lower. The wages and labour costs in Poland are lower in comparison to the situation in the 'old' Member States. Therefore, it seems that currently there is no serious risk of social dumping by employees being sent to Poland. However, such a problem can arise in the future as the result of the sending of employees to Poland from the countries of Eastern Europe or Asia. Moreover, it seems unlikely that Polish trade unions would have to organize strikes in order to protect rights of employees sent to Poland from other Member States. For this reasons, the rulings in cases C-438/05 *Viking* and C-341/05 *Laval* did not imply a necessity to amend Polish labour law.[283]

443. Article 29 LC imposes on the employer the duty to inform employees about substantial conditions of their employment. In case of posting employees to a country not being a Member State of the EU, the Polish employer is obliged to provide further information. Under Article 29^1 §1 LC, the employment contract with the

---

282. (*See also*, K. Schiffter, *Praktyczne aspekty stosowania ustawy o delegowaniu pracowników w ramach świadczenia usług*, (Practical Aspects of Application of the Act on Posting of Workers in the Framework of the Provision of Services) "Monitor Prawa Pracy" 5/2017, pp. 241 i et. seq.; P. Wąż, *Polska ustawa o delegowaniu pracowników*, (Polish Act on Posting of Workers) "Monitor Prawa Pracy" 10/2016, pp. 511 et seq.).

283. *See* L. Mitrus, 'Poland', in Freedland, Prassl (eds.), *Viking, Laval and Beyond* (Oxford and Portland, Oregon, Hart Publishing, 2014), pp. 229 et seq.; A. M. Świątowski, 'Poland', in: Blanpain (ed.), Świątkowski (guest ed.), 'The Laval and Viking Cases. Freedom of Services and Establishment v. Industrial Conflict in the European Economic Area and in Russia', *Bulletin of Comparative Labour Relations*, vol. 69 (Kluwer Law International, 2009), pp. 139 et seq.

employee posted to work outside the EU for a period that exceeds one month, in addition to regular conditions specified in Article 29 §1 LC, should determine the duration of performing work abroad and the currency in which the remuneration will be paid while performing work abroad. In addition, prior to posting the employee, the employer must additionally inform the employee, in writing, about the benefits to which the employee will be entitled in respect to being posted abroad, including the cost of travel and accommodation expenses as well as the conditions of the employee's return to Poland (Article 29^1 §2 LC). The employee may be informed about his/her employment conditions in a letter indicating appropriate provisions. The employer is also obliged to inform immediately about any change of employment conditions, not later than within one month from the day of implementing those changes (Article 29^1 §§3–5 LC). Those duties refer only to posting employees to a third country and not to an EU Member State. It seems that such a solution is incompatible with Article 4 of Directive 91/533.

Chapter 9. Liability of Parties to the Contract of Employment

Z. Hajn

§1. Employee Liability

I. Types of Liability

444. For the infringement of duties resulting from the employment relationship the employee may bear liability for breach of the order of work and financial liability.

II. Liability for Breach of Order of Work

A. *Introductory Remarks*

445. Originally, the employee liability for breach of the order of work was based on work rules or contracts of employment. With time, however, it was statutory law that started determining the rules for and scope of application of disciplinary measures to employees.[284] Since the time when the LC entered into force (i.e., since 1975) the liability for breach of the order of work has been fully provided for by statutory law (Articles 108–113 LC). Meanwhile, the range of available penalties was restricted by the Code, the disciplinary dismissal having been removed from it, and the application of the penalties was limited to the public sector. It was only in 1996 that the measures were restored in private business.

446. Part of the scholars deem the disciplinary penalties to be a relic of the past, violating the rule of equality of the parties to the employment relationship and offending against the employee's dignity. The penalties are also viewed as measures that are not actually needed to keep order at the work establishment.[285]

447. Currently, the liability may be only borne where the employee has infringed order-related duties, i.e., the duties which, if not met, disturb the due course of work processes at the work establishment. This concerns the rules of organization and order of the working process, provisions on safety and hygiene of work, fire prevention regulations, the rules as to how employees should confirm their arrival and presence at work.

---

284. *See*, e.g., the Decrees of 1928 on Employment Contracts of Blue-Collar Workers and on Employment Contracts of White-Collar Workers.

285. For more, *see* Z. Góral, *Pracownicza odpowiedzialność porządkowa* (Łódź, Wydawnictwo Uniwersytetu Łódzkiego, 1987).

B. Penalties

448. For lesser breaches of work order the penalties of admonition and reprimand may be administered. For the more serious, including non-observance of OSH or fire prevention rules, leaving work without justification, reporting to work in a state of drunkenness or drinking alcohol at work, a fine can be imposed. A fine for one breach, as well as for each day of unjustified absence from work, may not be higher than one-day remuneration for work of the employee, and the fines in total may not be higher than one-tenth of the remuneration.

C. The Procedure of Penalty Administration

449. A penalty may not be applied later than two weeks after the employer learnt about the breach of the employee's obligation and after three months since the breach. The penalty may be administered only after the employee has been heard. The employer is obliged to notify the employee about the applied penalty, in writing.

450. An employee may lodge an objection to the penalty within seven days of being notified of imposing it. The employer may accept or reject the objection, having considered the position of the trade union which represents the employee.

451. After a year of faultless work a penalty is considered non-existent. An employer may consider the penalty as non-existent earlier.

D. The Right of Appeal to Court

452. For many years the issue whether the employee has a right to appeal to court against the employer's decision on the application of penalty was considered controversial. According to the Supreme Court, the powers of the head of the work establishment to administer penalties were not derived from the existence of the employment relationship but resulted from his responsibilities to direct the work processes and manage the work establishment. Given the said, the employee's right to lodge the objection exhausted, in the opinion of the Supreme Court, legal possibilities to contest the penalty.[286] That approach met with a strong criticism in legal writing, but the real change was brought only by the amendments to the LC of 1996 expressly providing for the employee right to appeal to court for revocation of the penalty. The precondition for the consideration of the issue by court lies, however, in exhausting the procedure of the earlier-mentioned lodging objection to the penalty. Moreover, powers of the court are limited to examine whether administration of the penalty was formally legal. Consequently, the court is not authorized to revoke the penalty on the grounds of its being groundless nor replace the penalty

286. *See* the resolution of a panel of seven judges of the Supreme Court of 28 Nov. 1975, V PZP 9/75, in which the Court's earlier approach to the issue was upheld.

with a milder one. The judicial oversight is also limited by inadmissibility of the cassation appeal in cases concerning penalties for the breach of the order of work.

III. Financial Liability of Employees

A. *Introductory Remarks*

453. The notion of 'financial liability', as adopted in the Labour Court, means liability for damages caused by an employee to the employer's property in connection with work.

454. Until the matter was separately provided for by the LC (Articles 114–127) (i.e., before 1975) the employees' liability for damages caused to the employer's property was based on the principles of civil law. Even at that early stage, however, the liability was considerably modified by court judgments. The modification concerned, in particular, rules for the apportionment of the burden of proof between the parties and establishment of the causal link (being originally a scheme unfavourable to the employee) and moderation of the compensation. Such an approach followed from the understanding that the employee was particularly exposed to the danger of causing damage to the employer's assets while having only a limited capacity to compensate it from his/her salary/wage. It was also noted that the employers themselves often did not attempt at seeking full compensation, fearing lest the employees should refrain from doing the work that entailed a high risk of causing a considerable damage.

B. *Special Rules on Employee Liability*

455. Taking account of specific features of employment relationships, the LC establishes special rules on employee liability for damages. These can be summarized as follows:

- The proof of burden that all the conditions of liability have been met rests with the employer.
- The employee is liable on account of the damage only to the extent of actual loss sustained by the employer/ (*damnum emergens*), liability for the lost profits (*lucrum cessans*) being ruled out.
- Compensation may not be higher than three months' remuneration due to the employee on the date on which the damage was caused. It may be also reduced under a settlement agreement entered into by the employer and an employee or by the labour court.
- The claims of an employer for redress of damage inflicted by an employee are barred by limitation after one year from the date on which the employer learnt of the fact that the employee inflicted the damage (but not later than after three years from the date on which it was inflicted) and not after ten years as the Civil Code provides.

- Where the loss was caused by a few employees the rules of joint and several liability are not applicable. In such cases each of the employees is liable for a part of the damage to the extent to which he or she contributed to the damage and the degree of his/her fault. Where it is not possible to establish the degree of the fault and contribution of each of the employees to the damage, they are equally liable.
- An employee is not liable for loss resulting from actions undertaken within normal economic risk, i.e., in the situation where the employee acts for the benefit of the employer and where, taking into account life experience and state of the art, a positive result of such an action could be expected, the possibility of a benefit being greater than the risk of occurrence of a loss.

C. Aggravated Liability

456. These special rules on employee liability are not applicable to the employees intentionally causing damage to an employer's property. In such a situation the perpetrator is required to redress the damage in full, following the principles of civil law.

457. As a rule, full liability is also borne by employees for the property entrusted to their personal care with the obligation to return it or to account for it, like: cash, securities or valuables, tools, work clothes, and other things. Such employees enjoy certain limitations of the liability, though, like the right to mitigation of the compensation by court or by way of settlement and a short period of limitation of the employer's claims for compensation. Neither do they bear liability for a loss resulting from actions within the boundaries of normal risk. Further-going limitations of liability for the entrusted property concern certain shop assistants and warehouse workers.[287] The employees who jointly exercise control over the employer's property entrusted to them may conclude an agreement on joint liability. In such a case their liability is borne in proportions set out in the agreement and according to the terms set up therein (Articles 125 and 126 §1 LC).

458. In practice, the employee liability for damages concerns mostly the entrusted property, as abundant judicial decisions confirm. Generally speaking, strictness of the liability in that respect is mitigated by the judiciary. *Inter alia*, following the position taken even before the LC entered into force, the Supreme Court found that the stringent rules of the liability are not applicable where the entrusted property has been damaged or lost by the employee unintentionally but the employee does return it or accounts for it (a resolution of the panel of seven judges of 18 December 1976, V PZP 6/76).

---

287. *See* the ordinance of the Council of Ministers of 10 Oct. 1975 on Financial Liability of Employees for a Loss in Entrusted Property, *Journal of Laws* (1996), No. 143, item 662.

D. Employee Liability for Damage Caused to a Third Party

459. Where an employee, while performing his/her employee obligations, causes damage to a third party, only the employer is liable to redress such damage. However, after redressing the damage, the employer may seek compensation from the employee for the losses sustained owing to the redressing. To seeking the compensation the above-described limitations of employee liability are applicable (Article 120 LC). If, however, the loss has been caused through the employee's intentional fault (e.g., due to the employee having installed non-licensed software on the computer) the employer may seek a full refund of the compensation paid. In such a case the aggrieved party may claim compensation not only from the employer but also directly from the employee.[288]

§2. Employer Liability

I. Liability for Damage

A. General Rule

460. The employer is obliged to redress any damages caused to the employee by a violation of the latter's rights following from the employment relationship. The liability is regulated, in principle, by labour law provisions concerning specific duties of the employer (e.g., the provisions determining the employer's liability for unlawful termination of the employment relationship, discrimination or mobbing). In matters not provided for directly by labour law, Civil Code provisions on contractual liability are applicable.

B. Liability for Damages Caused to the Employee by Tort

461. For damages caused to the employee by tort, the employer is liable under Civil Code tort provisions. This holds true, in particular, as far as liability for infringements of personality rights and the risk-based liability for damages caused to the employee by the operation of the enterprise is concerned.

288. The rule of the employer's liability for the damage caused by the employee to a third party is not absolute. The Supreme Court, recognizing primacy of the interests of the aggrieved party, stated that Art. 120 §1 LC concerns typical situations, i.e., ones in case of which the employer is capable of redressing the damage (cf. a resolution of the panel of seven judges of the Supreme Court of 7 Jun. 1975, III CZP 19/75). For that very reason Art. 120 §1 LC is not applicable where, owing to the insolvency or liquidation of the employer/work establishment, the aggrieved party cannot claim redressing the damage from the employer (Supreme Court judgment of 11 April, 2008, II CSK 618/07).

C. *Liability for the Employee's Personal Effects*

462. For the employee's personal effects which have been destroyed, lost or damaged in connection with work, the employer is liable, depending on the circumstances, under the Civil Code provisions on torts or under the rules of the LC, for a breach of the obligation of custody.

D. *Liability for a Loss Following from an Accident at Work or Occupational Disease*

463. Damage sustained by the employee as a result of an accident at work, or occupational disease, is essentially compensated under social security provisions.[289] However, the employee is entitled to compensation from the employer for loss of or damage to his/her personal items and items necessary for the performance of work which occurred in connection with the accident (Article 237(1) LC). Besides that, in conformity with the position taken by the judiciary, regardless of the social security benefits, the employee may seek to redress the loss not compensated for by the benefits directly from the employer under Civil Code provisions.[290] Under Civil Code provisions the employer is also liable for losses caused by para-occupational diseases, i.e., the diseases that are caused by the working conditions, though not placed on the list of occupational diseases.[291]

II. Liability for Offences and Petty Offences Against Employee Rights

464. As is stressed by labour law scholars, a characteristic feature of labour law are the great number of standards, the violation of which by the employer is threatened not only with private but also public law sanctions (*leges plus quam perfectae*). Liability of that kind is borne by the employers themselves or persons acting on behalf of the employers.

465. The most serious offences against the rights of the people involved in gainful employment are specified in Chapter XXVIII of the Criminal Code of 1997 (Articles 218–221). Instances of conviction under the provisions are, however, rare.[292]

---

289. Act of 30 Oct. 2002 on Social Insurance in Respect of Accidents at Work and Occupational Diseases, *Journal of Laws* (2002), No. 199, item 1673, as amended.
290. *See*, for instance, the Supreme Court judgments of 4 Nov. 2008, II PK 100/08, II PK 360/07.
291. *See*, e.g., the Supreme Court judgment of 2 Oct. 2008, I PK 57/08.
292. Liable under the provisions is the person who, while performing employment or social security-related actions:

- maliciously or persistently violates employee rights following from the employment relationship or social security;
- refuses to re-employ the employee reinstated to work;

466. In practice, of greater importance is the liability for petty offences, a long catalogue of which is contained in the LC (Articles 281–283). In petty offence cases it is the court that decides, the labour inspector being the public prosecutor. The labour inspector may, however, impose a fine himself/herself by handing a ticket to the offender, if he/she finds the penalty sufficient. Where the ticket has not been accepted, the labour inspector refers the case to court, to penalize the offender.

Liability for offences and petty offences related to infringement of duties provided for by labour law may be also borne under certain other statutes. The excessive number of those regulations, however, gives rise to doubts. Reflected in them is a belief (illusory though it may be) in the power of prohibitions supported by criminal sanctions.

- does not pay remuneration for work or other benefit under employment relationship, ordered by court;
- violates social security provisions by not reporting the required data or submitting false information thus affecting the right to benefits or the amount thereof;
- does not meet the requirements of occupational safety and health thus putting an employee to direct risk of loss of life or heavy detriment to health; does not report to the relevant agency, in due time, an accident at work or occupational disease or does not develop or submit the required documentation.

Chapter 10. Employment Relationships Based on Appointment, Election, Nomination or a Cooperative Contract of Employment

L. Mitrus

§1. Introductory Remarks

467. In Poland, the concept of an 'employment relationship' is broader than the concept of an 'employment contract'. Thus, the notion of 'employee' goes beyond an employment contract. According to Article 2 LC, an employee is a person employed on the basis of an employment contract, an appointment, an election, a nomination or a cooperative labour contract. They can be commonly labelled as 'non-contractual employment relationships'. The list provided by the above-mentioned provision is exhaustive. According to Article 11 LC, the consensus of both parties is required to create each labour relationship.[293] An act of appointment or a nomination can be regarded as a unilateral administrative decision of a relevant body or authority. However, the previous consent of an employee is a necessary pre-condition. Such consent can also be expressed by taking duties at the particular post.

468. An employment relationship based on a legal basis other than an employment contract shall arise only in cases specified in labour law. In other words, parties are not free to choose an appointment, an election, etc. The legal basis for concluding such an employment relationship is indispensable and mandatory. The situation of particular employee groups can be different, depending upon the legal basis of an employment relationship, the character of the job or functions performed, e.g., with regard to recruitment criteria, employee rights and duties or job security. According to Article 5 LC, where an employment relationship concerning a specific category of employees is regulated by special provisions, the provisions of the LC apply to the extent not regulated by those provisions. Thus, with regard to particular employee groups, other statues have priority over the LC.

§2. An Appointment

469. An employment relationship based on an appointment is regulated by Articles 68–72 LC and separate statutes. According to Article 68 LC, an employment relationship can be established on the basis of an appointment in the cases specified under separate provisions. In principle, an appointment refers to employees on managerial posts. An appointment implies creating an employment relationship and entrusting a post to the particular individual. For example, under Articles 33–34 of the State-owned Enterprises Act of 25 September 1981,[294] a manager of a

---

293. *See* Chapter I, §1.
294. Consolidated text *Journal of Laws* 2017, item 2152, as amended.

state-owned enterprise, his/her deputy and chief accountant shall be employed on the basis of appointment. In addition, several posts in self-government administration can be based on appointment, e.g., a deputy of a mayor of the city or a treasurer of a *voivodeship* (i.e., region) or local community.[295]

470. An appointment should be made in writing. Making an employment relationship on the basis of an appointment may be preceded by a competition. Under special provisions such a competition can be mandatory, e.g., with regard to the manager of a state-owned enterprise. An appointment can be established for an indefinite or definite period of time. As a rule, unless regulated otherwise, the provisions governing employment contracts for an indefinite period apply to the employment relationship established on the basis of an appointment, except for a provisions on the procedure of terminating an employment contract as well as the settlement of disputes arising out of an employment relationship in the part concerning to the invalidity of the termination and reinstatement.

471. In practice, an employment relationship on the basis of an appointment does not guarantee any job security. An appointed employee may be recalled from the post at any time, with immediate effect or at a certain date, by the body which appointed him or her. This rule applies also to an appointment for a definite period of time. The recall should be made in writing. The recall is equivalent to the termination of an employment contract with notice. Where the recall is based on reasons referred to in Article 52 LC (i.e., serious breach of basic duties or committing a crime) or Article 53 LC (i.e., long inability to work), it is regarded as equivalent to the termination of an employment contract without notice. Another position can be entrusted to such an employee within the period of notice. After that period an individual can be employed on other terms agreed upon by the parties. Where an employee is recalled during a justified absence from work, the period of notice begins after the end of the employee's absence. Should a female pregnant employee be recalled, the recalling body should assign her another work that corresponds to her qualifications. For a period equal to the period of notice the employee should receive the remuneration that is equal to the amount prior to the recall.

§3. An Election

472. The employment relationship based on election is subject to Articles 73–75 LC and separate statutes. Article 73 LC provides that an employment relationship can be established on the basis of an election, if the duty to perform work as an employee is a result of such an election. For example, according to the Self-government Employees Act, a *voivodeship* (i.e., region) marshal, a mayor of a city can be employed on the basis of an election. In addition, the internal regulations of social or political organizations can provide an election as a basis of an employment relationship.

295. Article 4 of the Self-government Employees Act of 21 Nov. 2008, Consolidated text *Journal of Laws* 2018, item 1260.

473. An employment relationship based on an election is terminated upon the expiry of the term of office. An elected employee can also resign or can be recalled from the post before that date. An employee who is on unpaid leave due to election has the right to return to work with the employer who employed him or her on the date of election (Article 74 LC). An employee who had not taken the unpaid leave connected to his or her election has the right to the severance payment that amounts to one month's remuneration.[296]

§4. A NOMINATION

474. The employment relationship based on nomination is not regulated by the LC. According to Article 76 LC, the employment relationship based on nomination is established in the cases specified under separate provisions. Thus, particular statutes have priority before the LC (Article 5 LC). An act of nomination is regarded as an act of an administrative law. Its purpose is to create an employment relationship and to entrust a particular individual a certain post in public service. It can be regarded as a unilateral act, but a prior consent of a candidate is required (Article 11 LC). The employment relationship based on nomination is used in the public sector. Thus, in principle, public entities act as employers with regard to nominated employees. For example, nomination at a particular post is provided by the Employees of State Offices Act[297] or the Civil Service Act.[298] Nomination is a basis of an employment relationship in the judiciary, i.e., with judges[299] and public prosecutors.[300] In addition, nomination is used in education[301] and higher education.[302]

475. The statutes concerning employment in the public sector introduce different regulations on particular categories of nominated employees. However, all employment relationships based on nomination share several common features. In order to be employed on the basis of nomination, particular recruitment criteria can apply. They can concern, e.g., full capacity to undertake legal action, Polish nationality, reputation, good character, minimum age, no previous criminal convictions for certain types of crimes. Nominated employees are subordinated to their superiors to a larger extent in comparison to an employment contract. For example, nominated civil service employees can be transferred to a position in another administrative entity. Nominated employees can be subject to special duties, e.g., observing the

296. *See* A. Giedrewicz-Niewińska, *Wybór jako podstawa nawiązania stosunku pracy z pracownikami samorządowymi* (Warsaw, Wolters Kluwer Business, 2008), pp. 56 et seq.
297. Employees of State Offices Act of 16 Sep. 1982, consolidated *Journal of Laws* 2017, item 2142, as amended.
298. Civil Service Act of 21 Nov. 2008, consolidated text *Journal of Laws* 2017, 1889, as amended.
299. System of Common Courts Act of 27 Jul. 2001, consolidated text *Journal of Laws* 2018, item 23.
300. Public Prosecutors Office Act of 28 Jan. 2016, consolidated text *Journal of Laws* 2017, item 1767.
301. Teachers Act of 26 Jan. 1982, consolidated text *Journal of Laws* 2017, item 1189, as amended.
302. The Higher Education Act of 27 July 2005, consolidated text *Journal of Laws* 2017, item 2183, as amended. *See also* J. Stelina, *Charakter prawny stosunku pracy z mianowania* (Gdańsk, Fundacja Rozwoju Uniwersytetu Gdańskiego, 2005), pp. 17 et seq.

Constitution and other provisions of law, protecting interests of the state and its citizens, dealing with matters on the basis of impartiality, proper behaviour in service and outside it. There can be, also, particular restrictions imposed on them, e.g., the ban on carrying out additional activities, duty not to express his/her political opinions, not to participate in strikes, not to create political parties or belong to them.

476. Employees employed on the basis of nomination are subject to a disciplinary liability. Disciplinary sanctions can cover an admonition, a reprimand, deprivation of promotion opportunities for a definite period of time, reducing a level of remuneration for a certain period of time, reassigning to a lower position. The most severe sanction is an expulsion from the office. The sanctions are sentenced, not by an employer but by an independent disciplinary commission, upon the motion of the disciplinary officer.

477. The major feature of the employment relationship based on nomination is job security. The protection against dismissal is much stronger in comparison to the employment contract for an indefinite term. In principle, a nominated employee can be dismissed only in cases expressly provided by the relevant statute. Such situations can refer, e.g., to repeated negative evaluation according to procedures established by a particular statute, loss of reputation, liquidation of an office, expulsion resulting from a disciplinary sanction. Thus, nominated employees are subordinated to their employers to a large extent and are obliged to observe particular duties, but in return they enjoy a strong protection against dismissal.

478. Nomination constitutes, also, a legal basis of service in law enforcement agencies, e.g., the Police, Internal Security Agency, Central Anti-Corruption Office, etc. Persons who serve in such institutions are not employees but functionaries. The level of their subordination in service is much more intensive in comparison to any employment relationship. Their situation is governed by administrative law.

§5. A Cooperative Employment Contract

479. Article 77 LC provides that an employment relationship shall be established between a labour cooperative and its members on the basis of a cooperative employment contract. Such an employment relationship is governed by Articles 181–203 of the Cooperatives Act of 16 September 1982.[303] Unless regulated otherwise by the Act, the provisions of the LC apply accordingly. The target of economic activities of labour cooperatives is to run a common enterprise based on the personal works of its members. With regard to cooperatives of disabled or blind persons, their professional and social rehabilitation is also of major importance. Such employment contracts arise, in practice, relatively seldom.

480. A labour cooperative and its members are obliged to establish an employment relationship based on a cooperative employment contract. Thus, membership

303. Consolidated text *Journal of Laws* 2017, item 1560, as amended.

of a labour cooperative is a precondition to making a cooperative employment contract. The termination of working conditions is admissible where commercial or organizational needs of a cooperative arise or where a member loses the capacity to carry out particular work. An employment contract with a member of a labour cooperative can be terminated with notice only in case of reducing the number of employees or obtaining the right to a retirement pension.

Chapter 11. Covenants of Non-competition

L. Mitrus

§1. Introductory Remarks

481. The LC does not introduce a statutory ban on competition in the framework of an employment relationship. In principle, additional employment is not prohibited, with several exceptions to public sector employees, especially those employed on the basis of a nomination (*see* above Chapter 9). However, section Four Chapter IIa 'Prohibition of competition' of the LC (Article 101^1 –101^4) provides a legal basis for making a contractual ban on competition between the parties to an employment contract. Under Article 101^1 §1 LC it is possible to agree on a prohibition of competition during an employment relationship. According to Article 101^2 §1 LC, parties can introduce a prohibition of competition after the expiry of an employment contract. There are big differences between both contracts. Both contracts must be made in writing, under pain of nullity (Article 101^3 LC). The provisions of the LC do not violate the ban on competition provided for in separate provisions (Article 101^4 LC). The chapter on the prohibition of competition was inserted by the Act of 2 February 1996 on the amendment of the LC.[304] The provisions under discussion are the subject of an extensive set of judicial decisions of the Supreme Court.[305]

§2. Prohibition of Competition During an Employment Contract

482. According to Article 101^1 §1 LC, within the limits specified in a separate contract, an employee may not carry out any activities competitive with the activities of an employer and may not perform work under an employment relationship or on another basis for an entity carrying out such activities (prohibition of competition). The substantial scope of activities prohibited to an employee should be determined by the parties themselves. The ban on competition should relate to activities pursued by the employer, both main and ancillary. Employee activities that could put an employer's interest in danger or cause damages can be expressly forbidden under the contract. The scope of prohibition should not go beyond the necessity to protect the employer's interests, but in practice its scope can be extensive. All details should be stipulated by the parties to an employment contract, e.g., subjective, temporal or geographical scope of non-competition. It would be inadmissible to introduce contractual prohibition of any additional activity by an employee.

483. The LC does not introduce further elements of a contract on the prohibition of competition during an employment relationship. Parties should specify the

304. *Journal of Laws* (1996), No. 24, item 110.
305. *See* M. Lewandowicz-Machnikowska, *Klauzula konkurencyjna w kodeksie pracy* (Warsaw, Wolters Kluwer, 2004), pp. 24 et seq.

type and scope of activities that an employee must not perform. There is no statutory requirement to grant an employee additional financial compensation in return for the prohibition of competition, although such a clause can be agreed to by the parties. Moreover, Article 101^1 §1 LC concerns various legal forms of paid activities. The prohibition of competition can cover an employment relationship with another employer as well as civil law contracts or self-employment.

484. Each prohibition of competition should be agreed on the basis of a 'separate contract'. Thus, a prohibition should be subject to additional agreement between an employer and an employee. However, it is generally accepted that a non-competition clause can also be a stipulation inserted into an employment contract.[306] We must emphasize that the ban on competition must be agreed upon individually with a particular employee and must be made in writing under pain of nullity (Article 101^3 LC). Therefore, it is not possible to make a contract on the ban of competition *per facta concludentia*. Customs cannot constitute a source of a prohibition of competition, either. Moreover, it is inadmissible to introduce a ban on competition by a CLA or work regulations.

485. Any employer, regardless of the type of pursued activity (e.g., commercial or not), and any employee can be a party to such a contract. The non-competition clause can be made at the moment of concluding an employment contract or can be agreed at the later stage, during an employment relationship, upon mutual consent of the parties. The employee's refusal to make a non-competition contract can constitute a ground for dismissal only where its concluding is justified by a legitimate interest of the employer.[307]

486. Article 101^1 §2 LC provides that an employer who suffers damage as a result of an employee's violation of a prohibition of competition stipulated in a contract may claim compensation in accordance to principles determined in the provisions of Chapter One I section V of the LC. Thus, provisions on employee's financial liability for material damages apply (Articles 114 LC et seq.). The basic precondition of liability is the fault of an employee who violated a prohibition of competition. In the event of unintentional guilt of an employee, compensation cannot exceed his/her three months' remuneration (Article 119 LC). Where an employee intentionally causes damages, he/she is obliged to provide full compensation (Article 122 LC). In addition, violation of a prohibition of competition can be regarded as a serious violation of basic employee duties and can constitute ground for the termination of an employment contract without notice due to employee's fault (Article 52 §1 point 1 LC).

487. The question arises what is the situation of an employee where an additional contract on non-competition has not been made. It is commonly accepted that the lack of such a contract does not imply the liberty to take up an activity that would constitute competition with an employer. Article 100 §2 point 4 LC states that

306. *See*, e.g., the Supreme Court judgment of 9 Mar. 2006, II PK 234/05.
307. The Supreme Court judgment of 24 Sep. 2003, I PK 414/02.

an employee is obliged to protect the interests of a work establishment. This provision is regarded as the source of the prohibition to take up any activities that would endanger employer's interests, a duty not to pursue competitive activity included. In other words, carrying out competitive activity is a violation of the employee's duty to respect and protect the interest of work establishments.[308] Thus, the contract on the prohibition of competition is not the only source of the employee's duty to abstain from competition with an employer, although the contractual ban on competition offers the possibility to determine precisely the scope of forbidden activities.

§3. Prohibition of Competition after the Expiry of an Employment Contract

488. According to Article 101^2 §1 LC, the definition of the prohibition of competition, as introduced by Article 101^1 §1 LC, apply also when an employer and an employee, who have access to particularly important information of which the disclosure could cause damage to the employer, conclude a contract prohibiting competition after an employment relationship has been terminated. Such a contract should determine the period of prohibition of competition and the compensation due to the employee from the employer. In addition, under Article 101^2 §3 LC, the compensation may not be less than 25% of the remuneration received by the employee prior to termination of the employment relationship for a period corresponding to the period of validity of the prohibition of competition. Such remuneration can be paid in monthly instalments. In the event of dispute the compensation shall be determined by a labour court. The contract on non-competition after an employment contract should be stipulated during an employment contract, not after its termination. An agreement on the prohibition of competition that would be made after an expiry of an employment contract would not be governed by the LC. Such a contract would be allowed in the framework of freedom of contracts and would be fully regulated by the Civil Code.

489. The above-mentioned provision constitutes a legal basis for concluding a specific type of a contract on the prohibition of competition, namely a contract on non-competition after the expiry of an employment contract. The personal scope of such a contract is limited by the LC. It can be agreed upon only with some specific employees, namely those who have access to particularly important information the disclosure of which could expose the employer to damage. There may be, e.g., top managers, highly qualified specialists, employees with access to sensitive information, and also all those employees who have knowledge of confidential technology or production details, etc. (Supreme Court judgment of 20 January 2016, II 108/15) It is an employer who evaluates whether an employee belongs to the group that has access to particularly important information. However, a contract with an employee who does not have access to particularly important information should be null and

308. Supreme Court judgment of 6 Nov. 2009, III PK 43/09.

void.[309] In the event of dispute, a labour court is competent to verify whether it was admissible to conclude a contract on the prohibition of competition after an employment contract has been terminated with a particular employee.

490. The ban on competition after an employment contract has been terminated implies that an ex-employee is prohibited from carrying out activities stipulated in an agreement. An employee is entitled to financial compensation. Article 101(2) §3 LC provides that it cannot be less than 25% of an employee remuneration received prior to the termination of an employment contract. Certainly, parties can agree on a higher level of the compensation. Where the parties did not include a clause on financial compensation, the contract on non-competition should not be regarded as invalid. Instead, the provisions on the statutory minimum level of compensation due to an employee apply.[310] In practice, usually, compensation is paid in monthly instalments. That also should be the case when parties did not include any provisions on the method of compensation payment.[311]

491. The contract on the prohibition of competition after an expiry of an employment contract needs to be made for a definite period. However, there is no statutory time limit for the duration of a non-competition clause after an expiry of an employment contract. It must be determined by the parties. Where such an element has not been agreed, the contract on a ban of competition shall be null and void.[312]

492. The prohibition of competition after the expiry of an employment contract remains in force until the date specified by the parties. Under Article 101^2 §2 LC, the prohibition of competition shall become invalid before the end of the agreed period, where the circumstances justifying such prohibition cease to exist or the employer does not pay compensation. Thus, in the two above-mentioned situations the contract expires by operation of law. The first one relates, e.g., to a situation where an employer changed the profile of his/her/their activities or where a confidential technology details were made public. The latter condition concerns a case where an employer does not fulfil his/her duties arising out of the contract on non-competition.[313]

493. The LC does not expressly regulate other forms of termination of a contract on the prohibition of competition after an expiry of an employment contract. However, there is no doubt that such a contract can be terminated upon mutual consent of the parties. The question arises whether an employer is entitled to terminate, unilaterally, the contract prior to the agreed date. According to the judiciary, such a

309. Supreme Court judgment 4 Dec. 2003, I PK 165/03.
310. Supreme Court judgment of 3 Dec. 2003, III PZP 16/03, Supreme Court judgment of 7 Feb. 2017, II PK 355/15.
311. Supreme Court judgment of 26 Jan. 2005, II PK 186/04.
312. Supreme Court judgment of 2 Oct. 2003, I PK 453/02.
313. *See* P. Prusinowski, *Zakaz konkurencji w prawie pracy* (Warsaw, Wolters Kluwer Business, 2014), pp. 133 et seq.

possibility can be stipulated in a contract on non-competition, provided that contracts indicate the ground for termination.[314] The possibility of earlier termination of a covenant on non-competition after the expiry of the labour relationship has to be expressly provided by that covenant.[315]

494. The liability of an ex-employee for a violation of a contract of non-competition is fully regulated by civil law and not by labour law on employee's financial liability. According to Article 471 CC, a debtor is obliged to remedy any damage arising from non-performance or incorrect performance of his/her obligation. An employee is obliged to compensate the damage in full, regardless of the degree of his/her guilt. The burden of proof lies on the employer.[316] In addition, it is admissible to agree that a damage will be remedied by a specific sum agreed by the parties, i.e., stipulated penalty.[317]

§4. Other Provisions on Prohibition of Competition

495. Under Article 101^4 LC, the provisions of the LC do not violate the ban on competition provided for in separate provisions. Therefore, regulations on the prohibition of competition regulated by other statutes are remained intact by the LC. Polish law introduces several statutory regulations that introduce such a ban. These separate rules have mandatory character. According to them, a person who occupies a specific post should be prohibited, by operation of law, to carry out certain kinds of professional activities. To provide several examples, according to the Act of 16 April 1993 on combating unfair competition,[318] it is prohibited to deliver, disclose or to use establishment's secrets. Such an action is regarded as unfair competition. An employee is obliged to keep the secret, for a period of three years after the termination of an employment contract, unless an agreement stipulates otherwise (Article 11). The Commercial Companies Code of 15 September 2000 (consolidated text *Journal of Laws* 2017, item 1577) provides that a member of the board of a joint-stock company or a company with limited liability cannot carry out competitive activities or become a partner of another company or entity without prior permission of the board (Article 211). Moreover, Article 15 point 2 of the Banking Law of 29 August 1997[319], as amended) expressly provides that a member of a management or a supervisory board of a bank is not allowed to pursue competitive activities.

---

314. E.g., the Supreme Court judgment 26 Feb. 2003, I PK 139/02; the Supreme Court judgment of 12 Mar. 2014, II PK 151/13.
315. Supreme Court judgment of 13 Mar. 2014, II PK 151/13.
316. For example, the Supreme Court judgment of 6 Apr. 2011, II PK 229/10.
317. Supreme Court judgment of 5 Apr. 2005, I PK 196/04, Supreme Court judgment of 14 Jun. 2017, II PK 179/16.
318. Consolidated text *Journal of Laws* 2018, item 419.
319. Consolidated text *Journal of Laws* 2015, item 2015.

Chapter 12. Inventions of Employees

L. Mitrus

§1. Introductory Remarks

496. The development of new technologies demands for ever-increasing competence, skills and self-reliance from workers in performing their duties. The role of creative work performed within an employment relationship is increasing, which applies especially to computer specialists, commercial artists or website creators. While carrying out employee duties, a worker may create a 'work' within the meaning of the copyright law, which justifies a special regulation of the situation of an employee-author. An employee always performs his/her duties in subordination, and the employer is entitled to possess the result of his work. At the same time the copyright law tends to leave freedom to decide about the content of creative work to every author. It is necessary to find a compromise between the principles of labour law and the principles of copyright law. The relevant regulations have been introduced by the Copyright and Neighbouring Rights Act of 4 February 1994.[320]

§2. Employee Work

497. According to Article 1 of the Copyright Act 'work' is any manifestation of the creative activity of an individual character, fixed in any form, irrespective of its value, purpose and the manner of expression. Article 8 section 1 enacts that a creator is entitled to copyright, unless the Act provides otherwise. Employee rights are regulated by relevant modifications. In the light of Article 12 section 1 of the Copyright Act, unless the Act or an employment contract provides otherwise, an employer whose employee has created a work as a result of carrying out his/her employee duties acquires author's economic rights within the limits resulting from the purpose of the contract of employment and the mutual intent of the parties, as soon as the work is accepted. Thus, the Act provides for the transfer, onto the employer, of the property rights to a work which is the product of an employee's activity, within the framework of the employment relationship. This regulation has a relatively binding character, so the parties may regulate the question of copyright differently. Court rulings confirm that if the performance of duties within the framework of an employment relationship is to consist in an employee's creative activity, the ownership of the author's economic rights depends on the will of the parties. Failure to determine the ownership of these rights in the employment contract causes that, within the limits resulting from the employment contract and the mutual intention of the parties, the author's economic rights to such works are acquired by the employer at the moment of their acceptance.[321] Exceptions to the above rule result also from statutory regulations (*see* below, §4). Article 12 of the Copyright

320. Consolidated text *Journal of Laws* 2017, item 880.

321. Supreme Court judgment of 26 Jun. 1998, I PKN 196/98.

Act is not applicable to works made to order, created under a contract for a specific work or a mandate contract, as well as works created within a framework of a competition.

498. The LC imposes an obligation on an employee to submit to the employer's orders, which applies also to employees-creators. In such cases submission manifests itself, first of all, in defining the employee duties. At the same time, an employee is entitled to a far-reaching freedom in the way of carrying out his/her duties.[322] The unique character of the employment relationship with a creator consists in the fact that the work comes into existence within the framework of the copyright law, without the employer's excessive interference. The Copyright Act does not define directly – 'employee work'. This concept can be defined on the basis of Article 1 and Article 12 of the Act. It is every manifestation of human activity which has an original and individual character and which, at the same time, came into being as part of duties carried out in an employment relationship. So we are talking about cases in which the creation of the work belongs to the employee's job description. Court rulings confirm that the intention to charge an employee with making works within the meaning of the copyright law should rise directly from the contract. Only if an employee has been charged in the employment contract with the duty to make a work within the meaning of the Copyright Act, the presumption from Article 12 section 1 of the Copyright Act will be applicable.[323]

499. Article 12 of the Copyright Act is not applicable to works made outside of the scope of employee duties. For example, this regulation does not apply to situations in which a work was produced only in connection (e.g., temporal or local) with employment or when working for the employer or owing to the employer's contribution. Use of equipment or materials belonging to the employer, preparation of the work during the creator's employment, financing of the creative work by the employer or participation of other persons employed at the workplace in the creative process as well as toleration by the author of the fact that the employer utilizes the work without consulting him/her is not enough to determine the 'employee character' of a work.[324] In other words, for applying Article 12 of the Copyright Act, the employee should have a contractual duty to perform creative work, and this activity must be connected with the type of work and duties emerging from the contract.

§3. Transfer of Economic Rights to the Employer

500. As already mentioned, as soon as the work is accepted by the employer, he acquires economic rights to a work created by an employee within the limits resulting from the purpose of the contract of employment and a mutual intent of the parties, unless they decide otherwise. Therefore, the acquisition of the author's

322. *See*, e.g., L. Jaworski, *Twórczość pracownicza* (Warsaw, Wolters Kluwer, 2003), pp. 109 et seq.
323. Judgment of Provincial Administrative Court in Warsaw of July 2009, III SA/Wa 34/09.
324. Judgment of the Provincial Administrative Court in w Katowice of 4 Oct. 2011, V ACa 422/11.

economic rights to an employee work takes place not at the time of creation of the work but only at the time of its acceptance by the employer. The employer acquires the economic rights to a work in a derivative way (*cessio legis*). Article 12 section 1 of the Copyright Act obligates an employee to transfer a work created within the framework of the employment relationship, and the employer to accept it. At the same time the employer does not have at his disposal any special measures to force the employee to submit the work except typical measures provided in the LC in case of breach of employee duties. It is, therefore, appropriate to stipulate in the employment contract the way of delivering the work as well as the consequences of a violation of this obligation by the employee. At the same time Article 13 of the Copyright Act says that if the employer fails to notify the creator within six months from delivering the work about its non-acceptance or that the acceptance is subject to making specific modifications within an appointed appropriate time, it will be considered to have been accepted without reservations. The parties may agree on a different time limit.

501. A contract of employment with a creator does not only cause that an employment relationship is formed but it constitutes, also, the basis for the transfer of the author's economic rights to the employer. Article 53 of the Copyright Act provides that a contract for the transfer of author's economic rights requires a written form without which it is null and void. This is a certain inconsistency with the LC which does not enact such a requirement for the employment contract itself. It should be also stressed that Article 12 of the Copyright Act applies only to economic rights. Only the author is entitled to the author's moral rights. This arises from Article 16 which says that the author's moral rights protect the bond between the author and the work, which the bond cannot be waived and which is not limited in time, unless the Act provides otherwise. The protection covers the right of *attribution*, the right to have a work published anonymously or *pseudonymously* and the right to the integrity of the content and the form of the work and to its honest use, as well as the right to dictate when the work is first displayed to the public.

502. A special regulation applies to a case where, due to the character of the work or the content of the contract, the work is to be distributed. In such a case the employer has special responsibilities. According to Article 12 section 2 of the Act, if the employer fails to start to distribute a work within two years from the date of acceptance of the work, if this work is intended for distribution according to the employment contract, the author may set, in writing, an appropriate deadline for the distribution of the work. The consequence of such an action by the author is that when the deadline has passed without result, the rights acquired by the employer together with the ownership of the object on which the work was recorded return to the author unless the contract provides otherwise. The parties may specify a different deadline for starting the distribution of the work. Moreover, as emerges from Article 12 section 3, the employer acquires the ownership of the object on which the work has been recorded with the acceptance of the work, unless the contract of employment provides otherwise. Therefore, the employer acquires also the ownership of the so-called work carrier.

503. An employee is not entitled to a separate remuneration for the creation of an employee work and its transfer to the employer.[325] This does not, of course, exclude the award of additional remuneration to the author on the basis of the contract or special provisions of the Act.[326] In other words, unless the contract of employment provides otherwise and if the creator's duties arising from the employment relationship consist in carrying out a creative activity or if they include it – the remuneration for work is, at the same time, the remuneration for the transfer of author's economic rights or for the use of the work within the scope provided by the contract. Furthermore, nonfeasance to pay remuneration under a contract of employment does not thwart the effect of the acquisition of the relevant rights by the employer within the framework of the concluded contract.[327]

§4. Special Regulations

504. The Copyright Act allows exceptions to the general rule indicated in Article 12 of the Copyright Act. The first of the exceptions concerns research activity. According to Article 14 of the Act, unless the contract of employment provides otherwise, a research institute is entitled to be the first to publish a piece of scholarship or a research work of an employee who created this work as a result of carrying out his/her duties arising from the employment relationship. The author is entitled to remuneration. The right of first publication expires if a publishing agreement with the author has not been signed within six months from the delivery of the work or if the work has not been published within two years from the date of its acceptance. What is more, a research institute may, without a separate remuneration, use the scientific material contained in such work and make it available to third persons if it is consistent with the agreed intended use of the work or if it was agreed in the contract. Thus, the basic right of the research institute is the right of first publication of a scientific work which was performed within an employment relationship. The limitation of the author's rights consists in the exclusion of the possibility to decide about the place and form of publication of the work.

505. Another exception concerns audiovisual works, including films. According to Article 70 section 1 it is presumed that the producer of an audiovisual work acquires, by virtue of the contract for the creation of a work or a contract for the use of an already existing work, exclusive economic rights to the use of these works as part of the audiovisual work as a whole. The exception to the general rules applies also to computer programs. Article 74 section 1 provides that computer programs are subject to protection like a literary work, unless regulations provide otherwise. Under the copyright law computer programs constitute, therefore, a separate category of works. The employer is entitled to the economic rights to a computer program created by an employee as a result of carrying out his/her duties arising from employment relationship, unless the contract provides otherwise. Therefore, if there

325. Supreme Court resolution of 14 Feb. 2012, III UZP 4/11.
326. Judgment of the Provincial Administrative Court in Warsaw of 11 Feb. 2011, III SA/Wa 1219/10.
327. Supreme Court judgment of 11 Jun. 1997, I PKN 146/97.

are no different contractual provisions, the employer acquires the entire author's economic rights to the program without the need to pay additional remuneration. The employer also has the right to distribute the program. Case law confirms that the owner of the copyright to a computer program developed as part of employee duties is the employer, unless the parties decided otherwise in the employment contract or a civil law contract.[328]

328. Supreme Court judgment of 9 Jan. 2001, I PKN 493/00.

Chapter 13. Limitation of Claims under the Employment Relationship

506. Polish labour law governs most problems connected with the statute of limitations. This question is addressed in Articles 291–195 of the LC. Use of civil law is necessary only in rare cases. It should be noted here that labour law regulations and civil law regulations relating to the statute of limitations are, in some cases, different, which provokes discussions about the application of the regulations of the statutes of limitations to the employment relationship. In every case the statutory regulations concerning limitation periods are absolutely binding. They must not be regulated differently, e.g., in a collective agreement or in work regulations. Moreover, the statutory time limits must not be reduced or extended by a legal action.

507. According to Article 291 LC the limitation period for employment claims is three years from the date they became due. However, an employer's claim for the repair of damage done by an employee because of failure to perform or inadequate performance of employee duties comes under a one-year statute of limitations from the day on which the employer discovered it or three years from the day it was done, whichever is earlier. This rule applies, also, to cases where the employer claims damages for unjustified termination of the employment contract by an employee without notice (Article 61^1 LC) or for violation of prohibition of competition during the employment relationship (Article 101^1 §2 LC). If an employee did the damage deliberately, the statute of limitations provided in the Civil Code would apply. Moreover, a claim confirmed by a legally valid ruling of an organ designated to settle disputes, as well as a claim confirmed by a settlement reached before such organ as provided in the Code, comes under a ten-year statute of limitations from the day on which the ruling or settlement became legally valid.

508. It should be noted, therefore, that, as a rule, the limitation period for employment claims is three years. Different time limits apply only as an exception in specified situations. In labour law, the claim refers both to pecuniary claims (e.g., for remuneration or compensation) and non-pecuniary claims (e.g., for granting annual leave). This is a certain difference compared to civil law in which only pecuniary claims come under the statute of limitations. The general three-year limitation period applies to claims for both one-time obligations and periodical obligations. The institution under discussion concerns both an employer's and an employee's claims. Statute of limitations begins to run from the date a claim becomes 'payable', i.e., from the date on which one may demand the fulfilment of an obligation of a specific type.

509. According to Article 292 LC a stale claim cannot be pursued in court unless the person against whom the claim is owned waives the right to enjoy the statute of limitations; a waiver done before the passage of the limitation period is null and void. In other words, a claim does not expire after the end of the limitation period but the debtor may refuse to satisfy such a claim. In the light of the rulings of the

Supreme Court, in employment relationship cases a court does not consider the limitation period ex officio.[329] This means that in the light of the court rulings the plea of limitations may be used only if the defendant invokes it, as it is done in civil law. It seems, however, that in employment relationships the statute of limitations should be applied ex officio. The same opinion is expressed in academic literature. Moreover, the Supreme Court takes the view that admission of a plea of limitations can be considered as infringing the principles of social coexistence only in situations justified by exceptional circumstances.[330]

510. In certain circumstances the law specially regulates when the statute of limitations begins to run, when it is suspended and when it ends. According to Article 293 LC, the statute of limitations does not start to run, and if started, it is suspended for the duration of an impediment if, due to *vis major*, the entitled person cannot pursue his or her claims before the appropriate organ designated to settle disputes. *Vis major* means an extraordinary event which is outside of human control, which could not have been foreseen or prevented even with utmost diligence (e.g., a natural disaster). According to established rulings, an employee's illness, his/her stay in prison or a trip abroad is not an occurrence of *vis major*.

511. Article 293^1 LC, added by the amendment of 26 July 2013,[331] provides that the statute of limitations for a claim for annual leave does not start to run, and if it has already started it will be suspended, for the duration of a childcare leave (i.e., unpaid extended post-maternity leave). This regulation applies to the run of the limitation period for a claim of only one type (for annual leave), only in one specific situation, namely while exercising the childcare leave. This regulation was introduced because of the requirement to implement Directive 2010/18/EU on parental leave, in the light of the interpretation made by the Court of Justice of the European Union in case C-486/08 *Zentralbetriebsrat der Landeskrankenhäuser v. Land Tirol*. There, the Court of Justice recognized that the Framework Agreement on parental leave must be interpreted as precluding a national provision under which workers exercising their right to parental leave of two years lose, following that leave, their right to paid annual leave accumulated during the year preceding the birth of their child. Even though the regulation was introduced because of the necessity to implement EU law, its accuracy raises doubts. The point is that the run of the statute of limitations for a claim for annual leave applies only to the childcare leave, not other leaves connected with parenthood. Therefore, a question of the infringement of the equality principle arises.

512. For certain categories of persons the Code provides that the end of the limitation period will be suspended until the coming of a specified event. As provided in Article 294 LC, for a person who does not have full legal capacity or for whom there is ground for total legal incapacitation, the statute of limitations cannot end

329. Supreme Court resolution of 10 May 2000 r., III ZP 13/00.
330. Supreme Court judgment of 11 Sep. 1997 r., II UKN 230/97.
331. *Journal of Laws* (2013), item 1028.

earlier than two years from the date of appointment of a guardian or the date of cessation of the ground for his/her appointment. If the limitation period is one year, it begins to run from the date of appointment of the guardian or from the day on which the ground for his/her appointment ceased. In addition, based on Article 295 §1 LC, the limitation period is suspended by any action taken to pursue or establish a claim before an organ designated to settle disputes, and also by the admission of a claim. Such an admission can be explicit or implied and it does not require any specific form. For example, it may be the instituting of an action or a call for settlement. After each, such, suspension the limitation period runs again (Article 295 §2).

513. As already mentioned, the standard statute of limitations for employment claims is three years. We should notice the difference between a statute of limitations as discussed above and the so-called final dates (statute of repose), i.e., dates whose expiry causes loss of possibility to perform legal actions that produce material and legal consequences. They have to be taken into account ex officio by organs which settle disputes. An example can be the fourteen-day deadline for taking legal action by an employee for lifting a disciplinary penalty (Article 112 §2 LC). Deadlines that set time limits for lodging an appeal to the labour court against termination of a contract of employment are of a similar character. They can be revived by the court if an employee has failed to comply with the time limit through no fault of his/her. Since 1 January 2017, the employee has twenty-one days for lodging an appeal against the termination of an employment contract by notice (Article 264 §1 LC), for lodging an appeal against termination of an employment contract without notice (Article 264 §2 LC) and also for making a demand for establishing an employment relationship (Article 264 §3 LC). The change has been introduced by the amendment of 16 December 2016 (Journal of Laws 2016, item 2255). Previously, the time limits to lodge a claim to a labour court amounted to seven days in case of termination of an employment contract with notice, and fourteen days in case of disciplinary dismissal and a claim to conclude an employment contract. In other words, regardless of the statute of limitations for pecuniary or non-pecuniary claims, an employee whose contract of employment has been terminated has a very short deadline for lodging an appeal to court.

Chapter 14. Settlement of Individual Labour Disputes

Z. Hajn

§1. Introduction

514. Characteristic of the settlement of individual labour disputes is a number of peculiarities resulting from the social nature of employment relationships, the power imbalance of the parties to the dispute in particular. The latter is confirmed by a notorious fact that in the vast majority of cases initiated by employees a lawsuit is lodged after or in the course of termination of the employment relationship, when the fear of the employer's advantage starts to fade. The traditional arguments put forward to justify separate regulation of the disputes in question remain, thus, valid also today. It is stressed that the employee, when asserting his/her rights, is restrained by the existence of the employment relationship. It is further observed that the issues are urgent as usually the claims raised against the employer concern provision of means of subsistence. And, finally, it should not be lost of sight that settlement of the disputes in question requires knowledge of many circumstances specific to the place where the dispute has arisen from.[332]

515. Poland has a tradition of individual labour disputes settlement before the court. A system like that was originally formed by the presidential decrees of 1926 and 1934, whereby labour courts were established operating as specialized courts until 1950. In the period 1950–1954 labour disputes were resolved by common courts of law (albeit under procedures that took account of the specificity of the cases tried by them). Next, until as late as 1974, labour law cases were examined by arbitration committees made up of half trade union, half management of the work establishment representatives. Appeals against judgments of the bodies were considered by competent general boards of trade unions, courts deciding where unanimity could not be reached by the arbitration committee or where its decision was quashed by the trade union board. From 1975 until the end of June 1985 a mixed system was in place, with arbitration committees and committees of appeal deciding in the first instance, as out-of-court system bodies, the appeals being examined by regional labour courts.

516. The current system of individual labour dispute settlement, as far as its main traits are concerned, took shape in 1985.[333] Within the system the main role is played by labour courts.[334] The out-of-court mechanisms of dispute settlement, as provided for by law, are of relatively small importance.

332. *See* M.Święcicki, *Prawo Pracy* (Warsaw, Państwowe Wydawnictwo Naukowe, 1968), p. 560.
333. The Act of 18 Apr. 1985 on Consideration of Labour Law and Social Security Cases by Courts, *Journal of Laws* (1985), No. 20, item 85, as amended and the Act of 18 April, 1985, on Amendments to the Act - Code of Civil Proceedings, *Journal of Laws* (1985), No. 20, item 86, as further amended.
334. More broadly, K.W. Baran, *Procesowe prawo pracy* (Kraków, Zakamycze, 2003).

§2. Settlement of Labour Disputes Before the Labour Court

I. Jurisdiction of Labour Courts

517. In Poland, labour courts operate within the structure of common courts. The Civil Procedure Code reckons labour law cases towards civil cases. Established for dealing with them are common courts and the Supreme Court (Article 1 and Article 2 §1 CPC).

518. According to Article 476 §1 CPC, labour law cases come within the jurisdiction of labour courts. Under the Code of Civil Procedure, these include cases concerning: (1) claims under an employment relationship; (2) claims related to employment relationship (e.g., claims of family members of the deceased employee for payment of the death grant); (3) claims for establishment of the existence of an employment relationship; (4) claims pursuant to other legal relationships to which, under separate regulations, labour law provisions are applicable (e.g., claims concerning home workers); (5) claims for compensation from the employer under provisions on accidents at work and occupational diseases. It should be noted that courts shift towards a broad interpretation of the notion of 'labour law cases'.[335]

519. Under separate provisions, also other cases concerning individual and collective labour law issues come within the jurisdiction of labour courts.[336]

520. Under labour law cases, the claim may be brought before the defendant's court of general competence, i.e., the court having jurisdiction over the place where the defendant has the registered office or place of residence, before the court having jurisdiction over the place where the work is, was or should have been performed or before the court having jurisdiction over the place where the work establishment is situated. Besides that, the competent court may, on a joint application by the parties, refer the case, for a ruling, to other equivalent labour courts if reasons of purposefulness so dictate (Article 461 §§1 and 3 CPC).

II. Characteristics and Organization of Labour Courts

521. Labour courts in Poland are organizational units of common courts of law. They operate as separate departments of district courts, regional courts and Courts of Appeal. Where they consider also social security cases, they are referred to as

335. For instance, the Supreme Court has reckoned towards the category in question the case of the heir of an employee against the State Treasury for compensation in respect of a loss of the right to gratuitous acquisition of shares of a company emerged from the transformation of a state-owned enterprises into a company fully owned by a State Treasury; *see* the Supreme Court resolution of 28 Apr. 2004, III CZP 19/04.

336. For instance, cases concerning compensation in respect of the ban on competition after termination of employment relationship (Art. 101(2) §3 LC); disputes regarding trade union claims for transfer of resources to the company welfare fund or the return of amounts unlawfully spent from the fund.

labour and social security courts. Appointed to hear the cases at labour courts are judges displaying particularly good knowledge of labour law issues. The judges do not hear other cases.

The district court is the Court of First Instance in all cases not reserved to the jurisdiction of the regional court. The regional court is the Court of Second Instance for the district court and the Court of First Instance in cases involving claims ensuing from non-property rights and claims ensuing from property rights asserted jointly with the former as well as property claims in cases where the value of the object of dispute exceeds PLN 75,000 (Article 17 and Article 461 §1(1) CPC). The Court of Appeal is the Court of Second Instance for the regional court. The regional court hears the case when an appeal has been lodged by a party not satisfied with the ruling of the first instance.

522. Against a legally valid ruling of the Court of Second Instance a cassation appeal may be lodged with the Supreme Court. In labour law cases the cassation appeal is allowed in respect of claims ensuing from property rights where the value of the object of cassation appeal amounts to at least PLN 10,000. The cassation appeal is not allowed in cases concerning penalties for breach of the order of work, work certificates and claims related to them, payments in kind or the equivalents thereof and in cases examined in summary proceedings (Article 398(2) CPC).

A party may also lodge a complaint for declaring a final judgment of the court of second instance unlawful with the Supreme Court, where a damage was done to the party by the judgment and the judgment could not and may not be amended or repealed through the remedies available to the party, e.g., the cassation appeal (Article 424^1 CPC).[337]

Both complaints mentioned above may be based solely on objections concerning infringement of law and may not be based on allegations concerning facts. Where the court of the second instance has violated essential rules of the legal order, the complaints in question may be also lodged by the General Prosecutor and where the violation hits the constitutional rights, they may be lodged by the Ombudsman. In the Supreme Court the labour law cases fall under the jurisdiction of the Chamber of Labour Law, Social Security and Public Affairs.

523. Labour law cases concerning: (a) the establishment of the existence, conclusion or expiration of employment relationship, declaring ineffectiveness of termination of an employment relationship with notice, reinstatement to work and restoration of previous conditions and terms of payment or employment along with claims asserted jointly with them and compensation for non-justified or unlawful notice to terminate or termination of employment relationship; (b) violation of the rule of equal treatment in employment and claims related thereto; (c) damages or compensation of moral injury for mobbing, are heard in the Court of First Instance

337. A judgment unlawful within the meaning of the regulations concerning the complaint is a judgment obviously contradictory to essential provisions of law and not lending themselves to different interpretations, a judgment contradictory with generally accepted standards of judicial rulings or one that was made as result of a particularly grossly erroneous interpretation or wrong application of law; *see*, e.g., the Supreme Court judgment of 7 Jul. 2006, I CNP 33/2006.

by a single career judge as chairperson and two lay judges. Other cases in the Court of First Instance are heard by a single career judge (Article 47 §1 and §2 CPC). In the Court of Second Instance the case is heard by three career judges (Article 367 §3 CPC).

III. Parties to the Proceedings Before Labour Courts

524. Cases brought in labour courts are both ones filed by employees and those lodged by employers.

525. Before courts of the first and second instance a party may represent his or her own cause independently or be represented by an attorney *ad litem*. The function of the attorney may be performed not only by an attorney-at-law or legal counsel but also a representative of a trade union or a labour inspector or an employee of the work establishment in which the mandator was or is employed (Article 465 CPC).

As regards proceedings before the Supreme Court, the parties must be represented by attorneys-at-law or legal counsels.

526. Trade unions and other civic organizations whose statutory objectives do not include business activity[338] may, at the employee's consent, given in writing, institute legal proceedings on behalf of the employee or intervene in the proceedings at any stage thereof (Article 462 CPC). The entities may not, however, without the employee's consent, dispose as to his or her claim, i.e., may not, on behalf of the employee, waive the claim, reduce its amount or make a settlement agreement. The trade union may also present an opinion essential for the case to the court (Article 63 CPC). In addition, in cases concerning the establishment of the existence of an employment relationship, labour inspectors may institute proceedings on behalf of citizens and intervene in the proceedings at any stage of them, the employee consenting (Article 63^1 CPC).

527. The provisions in force do not confer similar rights onto employer organizations in labour law cases. It is rather strange considering that powers of the kind have been granted to business associations in business cases (Article 479^6 and Article 479^{6a} CPC).

IV. Proceedings Before the Labour Court

528. As a rule, labour law cases are considered following the rules of procedure prescribed for civil law cases. The proceedings before labour courts are, however, proceedings of a separate nature. When dealt with by legal scholars, the specificity

338. For instance, NGOs operating for the benefit of the handicapped, war combatants, the elderly or active in promotion of equal opportunities.

is usually presented by indicating particular rules of such proceedings, justified by characteristic features of labour law disputes as mentioned at the beginning of the chapter.

529. The rule of amicable settlement of the dispute should be named first. The rule is a general principle of civil law proceedings and is reflected in the court's obligation to strive towards an amicable resolution of the dispute at any stage of the proceedings (Article 10 CPC). In labour law cases the rule has a special meaning, though. In particular, where the case has not been considered by the conciliation committee, the court should schedule an explanatory meeting aimed, *inter alia*, at explaining the positions taken by the parties and inducing them to reconciliation and settlement of the dispute. In addition, the defendant, usually the employer, should be, in every instance of his or her personal participation in meetings of the court, be represented by a person authorized to make a settlement agreement (Article 468 §2 item 2 and Article 470 CPC).

530. Of essence in labour law cases is also the rule of speed and simplification of procedure. An employee acting without the assistance of an attorney-at-law or legal counsel may orally state for the records in the relevant court the action raised by him or her, contents of the remedies and other written observations (Article 466 CPC). Where it is an employee that brings the action, immediately after submitting the case to the court the chief judge of the court division or the appointed judge examines it initially with a view to further proceed it. The objective of the examination is to find out whether the lawsuit, which may be drawn up by the employee himself or herself meets the requirements for the case to be continued and for actions allowing the case to be decided at the first meeting taken (Article 467 §§1–3 CPC). Should defects be found in the lawsuit, the chief judge (or the appointed one) may call on the plaintiff to eliminate them only when this cannot be done at the explanatory sitting. He/she may not, however, apply the rigour of return of the letter in case of the elimination not having been done on time. After initial investigation the court, composed of a single career judge, with no participation of lay judges, should undertake explanatory proceedings, unless they are obviously pointless. The explanatory sitting is aimed, as indicated above, at clarifying the positions of the parties and causing them to reconcile and settle the dispute. Where this has not been achieved, the sitting is supposed to clarify the circumstances of importance for proper and quick resolution of the matter and in order to make evidence-gathering orders (Article 468 CPC). The date of the hearing should be set not later than two weeks after completion of the explanatory actions or the date on which the lawsuit was lodged (Article 471 CPC). The court may summon the parties, witnesses, experts or other persons in the mode considered, by the court, most purposeful, even with the exclusion of the modes prescribed by general provisions, should the court find such a mode necessary to speed up the dealing with the case (Article 472 CPC).

531. The principle most widely reflected in provisions of law is the principle of enhanced judicial protection of employee interests. Its aim is to reinforce the employee's position in the proceedings and make it easier for the employee to assert his or her claims. The principle is, in fact, of primordial importance, as it is also other rules described above (and the peculiarities of court proceedings in labour law cases discussed above) that serve the same purpose. In order to implement the rule, lots of procedural remedies, applied only where the action has been brought by the employee, are used. Among other things, a court may not dismiss a suit of the employee on account of inadmissibility of suing but should refer the case to a competent public agency or examine it if the agency has found itself incompetent (Article 464 CPC). Procedural steps taken by the employee, such as a settlement agreement or withdrawal of the lawsuit, are controlled by a court of law and considered inadmissible if they violate the employee's legitimate interest (Article 469 CPC). Neither may application of the evidence by witnesses and evidence obtained by hearing the parties be limited (Article 473 CPC). The judge presiding over the sitting is obligated to instruct the employee on claims following from the facts quoted by the employee (Article 477 CPC). Where the employee has selected one of the claims he or she is alternatively entitled to and the selected claim has proven to be unmeritorious, the court may, *ex* officio, select the alternative claim (Article 477^1 CPC). It is also ex officio that the court calls on the person who should be the defendant in the case and the person against whom a lawsuit concerning the same claim may be still made (Article 477 CPC). Judgments awarding payments to the employee (his or her family) are, as a rule, immediately enforceable. However, the judgment of the Court of the First Instance is immediately enforceable in the portion not exceeding a full one-month remuneration of the employee (Article 477^2 §1 and Article 477^6 CPC).

532. Part of the above-discussed provisions protecting the interests of the employee in the civil law procedure is not applicable to minor cases heard under the summary proceedings scheme. The said concerns only the claims resulting from the contracts of employment (and not all labour law cases) with the value of the object of dispute not exceeding PLN 10,000. The application of the summary proceedings in the above-mentioned instances seems to contradict the purpose of separate treatment of labour law cases, though.[339]

---

339. According to Art. 505^{14} CPC, under summary proceedings in labour law cases, Art. 466, Art. 467, Art. 468, Art. 470, Art. 471, Art. 477 and Art. 477^1 CPC are not applicable. The opinion of a majority of legal scholars concerning the admissibility of summary proceedings in labour law cases is firmly negative. The issue has been, however, prejudged by the legislators in the amendments to the Civil Proceedings Code of 2 Jul. 2004, which entered into force as of 5 Feb. 2005. The same amendments also repealed earlier provisions requiring the court of law:

- to rule on claims resulting from the facts quoted by the employee, regardless of what he or she demands;
- to seek the objective truth, not restricting itself to the evidence provided by the parties;
- in cases concerning the establishment of the existence of the employment relationship, to carry out investigation ex officio;
- to instruct the employees appearing without an attorney-at-law or legal counsel on procedural steps; *see* criticism of the amendments: T. Liszcz, 'Kontradyktoryjne postępowanie sądowe w sporach pracowniczych', *Praca i Zabezpieczenie Społeczne*, vol. 3 (2005), passim.

V. Costs

533. Until 1 March 2006, the system of Polish law included a rule whereby the employee asserting labour law claims was, by law, fully exempt from court fees and both parties of the proceedings were exempt from the fees as regards cases concerning employee claims following from the employment relationship. That situation was changed by the new Act on Court Fees for Civil Cases of 2005,[340] which replaced the rule – as regards employees – with a scheme involving limited court fees in labour law cases. Exempt from the court fees, under the new Act, is only an employee lodging a lawsuit with the labour court (Article 96^1 item 4). Covered by the exemption are court fees, court registry charges (e.g., for excerpts from or certified copies of documents) and expenses (e.g., expert fees, witness expenses, etc.). The exemption is not complete, though, as certain small basic fees are borne by the employee. These fees amount to PLN 30 and concern appeals, complaints, cassation appeals and complaints for declaring a legally binding judgment unlawful. Moreover, in accordance with the prevailing interpretation, where the value of the object of dispute exceeds PLN 50,000, the employee is charged a proportional fee on pleadings which are subject to charges, including the lawsuit, amounting to 5% of the value of the object of dispute, not more, however, than PLN 100,000.

534. As regards cases brought before the court by the employer, costs of the proceedings are borne by both parties, according to general rules. However, where the value of the object of appeal does not exceed PLN 50,000, a basic fee of PLN 30 is charged on appeals, complaints, cassation appeals and complaints for declaring a legally binding judgment unlawful.

Labour inspectors and trade unions are exempt from court fees regarding labour law cases.

§3. Settlement of Disputes Under Workplace Procedures

I. Workplace Conciliation Proceedings

535. Proceedings in cases regarding employment relationship considered before conciliation commissions have been provided for in Chapter 12 of the LC (Articles 242–258). The main objective of the provisions is to prevent confrontation between the employee and employer in court and to secure amicable resolution of the dispute at the workplace. A conciliation commission may be established jointly by the employer and trade union organization. Where the workplace is non-unionized, the commission may be created by the employer upon winning a positive opinion of the staff. The expenses related to the operation of the commission are borne by the employer. In practice, conciliation committees are seldom established.

---

340. Act of 28 Jul., 2005 on Court Fees for Civil Cases, *Journal of Laws* (2005), No. 167, item 1398, as amended.

536. Proceedings of the commission are instituted at the application of an employee. The commission is not authorized to make decisions but may only induce the parties to a settlement agreement, i.e., to making mutual concessions. Settlement does not mean a final resolution of the dispute. If the employee believes that the settlement breaches his/her legitimate interests he/she may apply to the labour court, within thirty days of the date on which the settlement is made, that it be declared ineffective. The concluded settlement agreement should be voluntarily implemented by the employer. Otherwise, the employee may apply to the court to declare the settlement enforceable, following which step the settlement is enforced as provided for by the Code of Civil Procedure.

II. Workplace Complaint Procedures

537. Workplace complaint procedures consist in the employee lodging a claim with the employer. The latter is obligated to take a position on the claims filed within the time limit set by provisions of law and in the mode prescribed by them. This procedure for dealing with a dispute has been established by the LC as regards two situations. First, an employee may, within seven days of receipt of a work certificate, request that the employer correct it (Article 97 §2^1 LC). Second, an employee, who believes that the penalty for the breach of the order of work was imposed on him or her unlawfully, may lodge an objection to the penalty within seven days of being notified of imposing it. The employer may accept or reject the objection having considered the position of the trade union which represents the employee. Failure of the employer to accept the claims within the time limit set up by the LC makes the employee authorized to apply to a labour court for annulment of the penalty. Lodging a claim with the court is not allowed if the workplace complaint procedure has not been exhausted, The court may not reject the lawsuit in such a situation, though, but should refer it to the employer (Article 464 §1 CPC).

§4. Other Methods of Resolving Labour Cases

I. Introduction

538. Individual labour law disputes may also be resolved using other methods, viz. the judicial conciliation schemes, mediation and proceedings before the court of arbitration. In labour law cases the procedures, save for certain modifications concerning an arbitration agreement, are conducted following general rules concerning civil cases. Settlement agreements concluded under the proceedings have, however, to take into account the limitations following from labour law provisions, e.g., a prohibition to the employee to waive the right to remuneration for work (Article 84 LC).

II. Judicial Conciliation Scheme

539. Judicial conciliation schemes can be instituted prior to filing a lawsuit by calling the other party to a settlement trial, filed with the court of law. The procedure is fully optional to both parties, its aim being arrival at a settlement agreement. The proceedings are carried out by a court composed of a single judge, at an open sitting (Articles 184–186 CPC). Procedure of this kind is of limited use to labour law disputes since provisions concerning separate proceedings in such cases require the court to undertake explanatory measures aimed at reconciliation and concluding a settlement agreement.

III. Mediation

540. Mediation consists in resolving the dispute by conclusion of a settlement agreement before the mediator. Mediation may be initiated prior to the institution of court proceedings or in the course of the latter. It is based either on a mediation agreement or a court order made at the consent of both parties. In each case the mediator may only be the person accepted by both parties. Social and professional organizations are authorized to keep lists of regular mediators and establish mediation centres. Mediation proceedings are confidential and the mediator is obligated to keep secret the facts of which he or she learned in connection with conducting the mediation. Where a settlement agreement has been concluded, the court, at the request of a party, immediately conducts a procedure aimed at approving it. The court, however, refuses to approve the settlement agreement if it contradicts the law or rules of social coexistence or is aimed at circumventing the law and also if it is incomprehensible or contains contradictions (Article 183^{1}–183^{15} CPC).

IV. Arbitration Court

541. Since the amendments to the CPC, which entered into force on 17 October 2005, it is also possible to resolve individual labour law disputes before an arbitration court. The resolution provided by the arbitration court comes in the form of a judgment. Concluding a settlement agreement before such a court is also possible. Given the protection of employee rights, an arbitration agreement can be concluded only after the dispute has occurred and only in writing (Article 1164 CPC). It is, thus, not possible to include an arbitration agreement (taking the shape of an arbitration clause) in the contract of employment. When accepting the arbitration agreement, the parties consent to being bound by the judgment of the arbiters. The dispute is resolved by the arbitration court pursuant to the law applicable to the relationship concerned and if the court is expressly authorized to do so by the parties – according to the general rules of law or on the basis of general considerations of equity. In each case, however, the arbitration court takes into account contract stipulations and established customs applicable to the specific legal relation. The judgment of an arbitration court given in Poland may be overruled by courts only under proceedings initiated as a result of an application for the annulment of the judgment having been filed, in particular, where the judgment contradicts basic rules of the legal order of the Republic of Poland (the public order clause). The legal force of a judgment of the arbitration court or a settlement agreement is equal to the legal force of a judgment given by a court of law or settlement agreement concluded before it, after they are recognized by a court of law of the latter has stated their enforceability.

§5. Resolution of Labour Law Disputes Under Administrative Court Proceedings

542. Certain labour law matters, e.g., issues concerning the status of an unemployed, benefits and other entitlements of such a person, are dealt with in administrative proceedings. In cases like this the person not satisfied with the decision of an administrative agency may turn, with a complaint, to the administrative court. The applicant in such cases does not bear court costs.

Chapter 15. The Organization of the Labour Market and Combating Unemployment

L. Mitrus

§1. Introductory Remarks

543. Unemployment was formally non-existent in the socialist period. This phenomenon appeared on a large scale with the political turning point of 1989 and with the transition from a centrally planned economy to a market system. Looking from today's perspective we must note that too little attention was paid to the social consequences of the transformation and that the social policy, including that relating to unemployment, was far from satisfactory. These problems were addressed in several Acts of Parliament. These were in chronological order: the Act of 29 December 1989 on employment,[341] the Act of 16 October 1991 on employment and counteracting unemployment[342] and the Act of 14 December 1994 on employment and counteracting unemployment.[343] The currently valid Act is that of the 20 April 2004 on the promotion of employment and the organization of the labour market.[344] Thus, as can be seen, unemployment control regulations are unstable and are subject to frequent changes. Initially, the criteria for awarding unemployment benefits were very liberal but gradually they have been tightened. Gradually, more and more importance has been attached to the means of increasing chances for taking up jobs. The recent changes[345] place emphasis on increasing the effectiveness of the work of job centres and on an individual approach to the unemployed. More and more attention is given to the rise in the number of young people who are active in the labour market.

544. According to Article 65 point 1 of the Constitution of Poland, public authorities shall pursue policies aiming at full, productive employment by implementing programmes to combat unemployment, including the organization of and support for occupational advice and training as well as public works and economic intervention. As can be seen, combating unemployment has a constitutional basis and one of the duties of public authorities is to pursue an active labour market policy. Furthermore, according to Article 10 §3 LC the state conducts a policy aimed at full productive employment. Under Polish law, the right to employment does not have a claims character, but a person seeking a job may demand assistance of public authorities in finding an adequate employment. Therefore, we may conclude that combating unemployment is an element of a broadly understood social policy of the state.

341. *Journal of Laws* (1989), No. 75, item 446.
342. *Journal of Laws* (1991), No. 106, item 457.
343. *Journal of Laws* (2003), No. 58, item 514.
344. Consolidated text *Journal of Laws* (2018) item 12065.
345. The amendment of the EPA of 14 Mar. 2014, *Journal of Laws* (2014), item 598.

545. The tasks of the state relating to the promotion of employment, unemployment relief and labour market re-entry are carried out on the basis of the National Action Plan for Employment passed by the Council of Ministers, containing the rules of the implementation of the European Employment Strategy, and on the basis of the initiatives of the local government administration at various levels as well as the initiatives of social partners (Article 3 point 1 of the Act). The organization structure of institutions which combat unemployment is complex and complicated. In Poland, combating unemployment is decentralized and the relevant actions lie within the competence of various institutions. According to Article 2 point 17 of the Act, by 'employment authorities' are meant the ministers competent for employment issues and provincial governors, province marshals and district governors. In the light of Article 6 point 2 the public employment services, together with district and provincial job centres, the office supporting the minister competent for employment issues and the province offices, make up the employment authorities. The basic organization units are the district *(powiat)* job centres, which are supervised by the district governor (a local organ of government administration). They are responsible for, among other things, registration of the unemployed, employment agency services, payment of benefits, organization of training courses and vocational education of adults.

§2. Objective Scope of the Employment Promotion Act

546. The currently valid Act of 2004 is very extensive and its regulations concerning the organization of the labour market and combating unemployment are complicated. According to its Article 1, the Labour Market Organization Act defines the tasks of the state relating to employment promotion, relieving the effects of unemployment and raising the number of persons active in the labour market. These tasks are carried out by labour market institutions acting for a full and productive employment, development of human resources, the achievement of high quality of work, strengthening social integration and solidarity as well as to increase mobility in the labour market. Therefore, the act lays emphasis on the state's tasks relating to countering unemployment and not to the right to benefits, though actually the act concentrates on the entitlements of the unemployed and of persons trying to find a job.

547. The objective scope of the Act covers the following issues: labour market policy, labour market institutions, public employment services and their structure, commercial employment agencies, various forms of fighting unemployment, the notion and the status of an unemployed person and of a jobseeker, unemployment benefits, taking up jobs abroad by Poles and employment of foreigners in Poland and also the Labour Fund which finances benefits for unemployed persons. The excessive bulkiness of the act and too much detail of its solutions (e.g., bulky regulations concerning the unemployment administration) are criticized in academic literatures. It is also noted that combating unemployment within the framework of the existing structures is ineffective. Of course, the level of unemployment is related to the pace of economic growth. Labour law does not, by itself, create jobs, but it can remove barriers hindering the hiring of the unemployed. It seems that Polish labour law does not adequately fulfil those standards, and some solutions connected with the costs of labour plainly encourage small enterprises to flee to the grey area or to use civil law contracts instead of employment contracts.

548. The Employment Promotion Act dedicated to countering unemployment introduces the notion of 'illegal employment'. We are talking here about a phenomenon which, in many countries, is called 'unregistered employment'. According to Article 2 point 13 of the act, illegal employment or other illegal gainful work means the employment of a person by an employer without confirming the type of the concluded contract and its terms and conditions in writing and within the required time limit, failure to register the person employed or performing other gainful work for the national insurance and also taking up a job, other gainful work or activity without notifying the proper district job centre. Working a foreigner who is not authorized to work under the act and who does not have the proper permission is also illegal (Article 2 point 14).[346]

§3. Subjective Scope of the Employment Promotion Act

I. Introductory Remarks

549. The circle of subjects covered by the objective scope of the Employment Promotion Act is diverse. Not every person remaining without a job is unemployed within the meaning of the act. To exercise the rights under the Act one has to fulfil specific criteria and comply with formalities. The regulations differentiate between an 'unemployed' person and a 'jobseeker' and each of these categories is eligible for a different range of entitlements. Moreover, within the notion of an 'unemployed' person a number of categories are distinguished depending on the situation of a jobless person. The Act applies both to Polish and foreign nationals. Article 1 section 3 provides that the Act is applicable to Polish nationals seeking and taking up employment or other gainful work in the territory of the Republic of Poland and employment or other gainful work for foreign employers and, also, foreigners intending to work or already working in the territory of the Republic of Poland including, *inter alia*, nationals of the EU and the European Economic Area, possessing the status of a refugee or a residence permit, as well as their family members.

II. Unemployed Person

550. The notion of an 'unemployed' person is the subject of the extensive Article 2 section 2 of the EPA. To put it simply, a given person has the status of unemployed if he or she: was employed in the territory of Poland for a period of no less

346. *See* A. Drabek, *Nielegalne zatrudnienie w prawie polskim* (Warsaw, Wolters Kluwer Business, 2012), pp. 109 et seq.

than six months directly before the registration, is not employed and does not perform any gainful work, is able and ready to take up a full-time employment, is not in full-time school education or does not study in a higher education institution, is registered in a district job centre, is seeking employment or other gainful work. Furthermore, such a person is in the age bracket between 18 years of age and the retirement age, is not entitled to other national insurance benefits (such as a disability or retirement pension), and does not possess an arable farm. We can say that the above definition is based on three elements. The unemployed, within the meaning of the Act, are persons who are jobless, are actively seeking a job and ready to take it up.[347] There are certain duties that rest with the unemployed. An unemployed person has a duty to report to the proper district job centre, on the date indicated by the centre, in order to accept an offer of a suitable job or other forms of aid and also for other purposes, e.g., to confirm readiness to take up a job. Failure to do these duties can result in the loss of rights to benefits provided by the EPA.

551. One of the elements of the definition mentioned above is the requirement that the unemployed person is not employed or performing other gainful work. Therefore, it should be emphasized that according to Article 2 point 43 of the EPA 'employment' means performing work on the basis of an employment relationship, a service relationship or a home work contract. From Article 2 point 11 of the Act it also appears that 'other gainful work' means doing work or providing services on the basis of civil law contracts, including the agency contract, the civil law contract for providing services, the contracts to perform a specified task or work or during membership in a farming cooperative. In other words, the act addresses broadly understood gainful activity. Thus, an unemployed person is not only a person remaining outside an employment relationship but also a person who does not obtain income for work done on other legal bases.

552. Article 2 section 1ff. of the EPA introduces different categories of unemployed persons. The act distinguishes between the unemployed up to 25 years of age, above 50 years of age, the long-term unemployed, i.e., persons remaining without work for a total of twelve months over the period of the last two years, and also the unemployed without professional qualifications. The range of entitlements of all those persons can be different depending on how a given person is categorized. Then, Article 49 of the Act indicates persons in a special situation in the labour market. These are the unemployed up to 30 years of age, the long-term unemployed, the unemployed above 50 years of age, the unemployed receiving benefits from social aid institutions, the unemployed having at least one child up to 6 years of age or at least one disabled child up to 18 years of age and the disabled unemployed. Such persons are entitled to being preferentially referred to participate in special programmes organized by work centres. The principle of the model of vocational development is to indicate the priority groups to which the actions aimed at reducing unemployment should be addressed in the first place.

---

347. *See* Z. Góral (ed.), *Ustawa o promocji zatrudnienia i instytucjach rynku pracy. Praktyczny komentarz* (Warsaw, Wolters Kluwer Business, 2011), pp. 44 et seq.; E. Staszewska, *Środki prawne przeciwdziałania bezrobociu* (Warsaw, Wolters Kluwer Business, 2012), pp. 18 et seq.

553. As mentioned above, one of the elements of acquiring the unemployment status is to comply with the proper formal requirements. The act provides for the requirement of the registration of unemployed persons. According to Article 33 of the EPA, district job centres register the unemployed and jobseekers and keep a register of such persons. The amendment of the act of 2014 introduced three profiles of the unemployed, depending on the degree of the risk of remaining without a job. The purpose of these regulations is to match the aid to the needs of an unemployed person and to individualize the aid given by job centres. Persons for whom the appropriate form of aid is employment agency service and vocational counselling are categorized into profile I. Persons who should use the labour market services and instruments provided in the act, as well as development and integration actions, are categorized into profile II. Finally, profile III includes unemployed persons who are the most exposed to continuing joblessness (e.g., persons receiving social aid benefits). This category of persons should be covered by the Development and Integration Programme, which is to prevent social exclusion, and special programmes organized by job centres (such as employment in a social cooperative). It seems, however, that the first experiences with the profiling of the unemployed do not show a far-reaching qualitative change or a significant increase in the effectiveness of combating unemployment.

554. The Act regulates, in detail, cases in which an unemployed person may lose unemployed status. Such a loss of status requires the decision of the district governor, i.e., of the local organ of government administration who supervises job centres. The deprivation of the status of an unemployed person may be permanent or for a certain period of time. This refers mainly to situations where a given person ceases to meet the statutory criteria, does not agree to the identification of the support profile, obtain a loan for starting a business, fails to turn up at the district job centre on a set date without justifying the failure to turn up and also if such person interrupts a training course, a placement or the execution of an individual plan of exiting unemployment due to this person's own fault. Another cause for the deprivation of the unemployed status is an unjustified refusal to accept an offer of adequate employment. Even the first refusal results in the loss of the unemployed status.

III. A Person Seeking a Job

555. In the light of Article 2 section 1 point 22 of the EPA, persons 'seeking a job' are a separate category of persons covered by the provisions of the act. These are persons registered in the district job centre who are seeking employment, other gainful work or other forms of aid provided in the Act. This definition is more liberal than the definition of an unemployed person. By way of example, a person seeking employment within the meaning of the act can be a person attending school or university or someone already employed who wants to change his or her work or improve his or her qualifications. At the same time, the range of entitlements of persons seeking a job is narrower than the range of entitlements of unemployed persons.

§4. Active Methods of Combating Unemployment

556. Active methods of combating unemployment include all instruments that prevent unemployment and reduce its level as well as actions aimed at vocational development. Under Polish law, labour market services provided by public employment services include employment agency service, vocational development and organization of training courses (Article 35ff of EPA). The labour market instruments supporting the basic labour market services include various types of financial aid, e.g., covering the costs of travel or lodging, partial funding of a workplace or a refund on costs incurred in connection with the employment of an unemployed person referred to the employer by a job centre.

557. A form of vocational development is a placement for the unemployed. Article 2 point 34 of the EPA defines placement as the acquisition by an unemployed person of practical working skills by carrying out tasks in a workplace without establishing an employment relationship with an employer. According to Article 53 of the EPA, a person is referred to a work placement on the basis of an agreement between an employer and the district governor. A placement can last up to six months and, for an unemployed individual less than 30 years old, up to twelve months. A trainee does not receive remuneration directly from the employer, but he or she is entitled to a scholarship amounting to 120% of the unemployment benefit, paid by the district governor. The placement is, first of all, a form of vocational development of graduates and it often is an opportunity to gain first work-related experience. It should be emphasized that trainees are not employees despite the fact that their job description is basically identical with employee duties.

558. According to Article 2 point 29a of the EPA, the vocational education of adults is an instrument of vocational development in the form of apprenticeship for adults or learning a job for adults without establishing an employment relationship with the employer. It goes according to a programme consisting of the acquisition of practical skills and theoretical knowledge, ending with an exam. According to Article 53a, training programmes are initiated by a district governor. Such training may take place at the employer's plant or in training institutions. It takes place according to a predefined programme which is aimed at the acquisition of practical skills and gaining theoretical knowledge. The basic purpose of this form of combating unemployment is to facilitate re-entry to the labour market of persons who lost their jobs and whose qualifications are not adequate to the needs of the labour market.

559. As provided in Article 2 section 1 point 32 of the EPA, public works is the employment of a jobless person for a period not longer than twelve months at work organized by districts and proper non-governmental institutions, if such work is funded from budgetary means. In practice, this is a form of employment subsidized by the Labour Fund. The purpose of such actions is increasing, albeit periodically, the number of the unemployed having a job. Typically, this is short-term physical labour for persons with low professional qualifications. There is also intervention work, which according to Article 2 section 1 point 26 is the employment of a jobless individual by an employer on the basis of a contract with the district governor, and its purpose is to support the unemployed. According to Article 59a of the EPA, the district governor may refer unemployed persons to intervention work for a period of up to two or four years, depending on the status of the unemployed individual, and to refund costs of remuneration and national security contributions incurred by the employer. The aim of this form of actions is to support unemployed persons who are in an especially difficult situation.

560. The already mentioned amendment to the EPA of 14 March 2014 on the organization of the labour market added a number of new instruments. An employer can enter into a contract with an employee which will be the basis for awarding a grant for creating a workstation in the form of telework (Article 60a) or a development benefit for the full-time employment of such person (Article 60b). The mentioned instruments can be applied to parents or guardians who re-enter the labour market after an earlier resignation from employment and after a period of care of an infant or other dependent persons. Their purpose is to facilitate the return to the labour market by combining a career with family duties. As regards unemployed persons not older than 30 who take up a job for the first time, the district governor may refund the money paid by the employer as national insurance contributions (Article 60c). Partial funding of the remuneration of a jobless individual who has been employed after turning 50 is also possible (Article 60d). Moreover, the new Chapter 11b (Article 61e ff.) extends the possibilities of giving loans to employers for creating new jobs or loans for starting business activities by the unemployed, graduates and students in their senior year.

561. Some means of combating unemployment are addressed only to young individuals. The Employment Promotion Act singles out persons below 25 years of age as a separate category of the unemployed (Article 2 section 1 point 3). In addition, according to Article 49, one of the groups in a special situation in the labour market are the unemployed below 30 years of age. In Poland, as in other Member States, unemployment among young people is a major problem in the labour market. These people are referred to as NEET, or Not in Education, Employment or Training. Moreover, in Poland unemployment is the main cause of mass emigration for economic reasons to other Member States of the EU. Considering that, as a rule, those leaving the country are young, active and well educated, we can speak straight out about brain drain. Fighting unemployment among young people should, therefore, be a priority task of the public authorities. Unfortunately, the relevant efforts can hardly be considered as effective. Without a doubt, one of the causes of unemployment among young people is the fact that the education system is unadjusted to the requirements of the labour market.

562. According to Article 50 section 1 of the EPA, the district job centre should give unemployed persons under 25 years of age an offer of employment, other gainful work, training, placement, vocational education for adults, employment as part of intervention or public works or other form of aid provided in the Act, within a period of four months from the date of registration. The original version of the Act under discussion already contained this regulation, but the period in which an unemployed person should be given a suitable offer was six months. The realization of this regulation in practice could hardly be considered an effective instrument for combating unemployment. However, there is no doubt that the idea of the regulation corresponds to the actions proposed by the EU in the Council Recommendation of 22 April 2013 on establishing a Youth Guarantee (2012/C 120/01).

563. In 2014, the new Chapter 3d 'Additional instruments addressed to the unemployed younger than 30 years of age' was added to the EPA by an amendment. The instruments are nothing but a possibility to receive financial support in the form of vouchers by young unemployed persons. An individual action plan needs to be developed and an unemployed individual has to file an application to qualify. The district governor can award a training voucher which covers the cost of the training course chosen by the jobless individual up to the equivalent of 100% of the average wage. A person interested in the offer has to prove that such training will improve his or her chances of taking up employment or other gainful activity (Article 66k). The district governor can also award a placement voucher for spending half a year on a work placement with an employer who undertakes to employ the unemployed individual for another six months following the placement (Article 66l). Another benefit is the employment voucher (Article 66m); its purpose is to refund an employer a part of the cost of the remuneration and national security contributions if the employer decides to employ a jobless person for a period of eighteen months. The settlement voucher (Article 66n) has a somewhat different character from the above forms of aid. The district governor can award it on the basis of a contract with an unemployed individual who takes up employment, other gainful work or business activity. Thus, the purpose of the settlement voucher is to increase the professional mobility of young unemployed individuals. As these regulations have been in effect for a short time, it is difficult to assess, in practice, the functioning of the vouchers as a new form of increasing the number of young unemployed people who are active in the labour market.

§5. Public and Private Employment Agency Service

564. Under Polish law, an employment agency is classified as a labour market service. It is one of the basic forms of combating unemployment. First, it falls within the competence of the district job centres (Article 34 EPA). According to Article 36, employment agency service consists, in particular, in helping the unemployed and jobseekers to get a suitable job and the employers to acquire workers with suitable qualifications. Another function of this service is to distribute offers of employment and provide information about the situation in the labour market. Thus, under Polish law, employment agency service has a broad subjective scope. Employment agency service is run free of charge and it is based on availability for jobseekers and employers, voluntary character, equality and open nature.[348] If a district job centre is not able to provide suitable jobs, then it should provide vocational counselling, organize training courses, vocational education and placements, subsidize the creation of new jobs and grant benefits on account of unemployment. Furthermore, employment agency service connected with the free movement of workers in the EU can be carried out within the EURES network. In Poland, EURES services are provided by job centres, and they can be provided also by private entities that fulfil specified formal requirements.

565. As already mentioned, employment agency actions are the responsibility of public authorities. At the same time, Polish legislation allows private entities to run such business. The legal situation of employment agencies is dealt with in Chapter 6 of the Act under discussion (Article 1ff. EPA). According to Article 18 of the Act, business activity consisting in providing employment agency services, personal counselling, vocational counselling as well as temporary employment agency is permitted. Employment agencies are obliged to cooperate with employment authorities. Therefore, their activity complements the activity of the public employment services, and the aid provided by them should be individualized and at a high professional level. It is worth adding that on 1 August 2008 Poland ratified the ILO Convention No. 181 on Private Employment Agencies of 19 June 1997.[349]

566. According to Article 6, section 4 EPA, employment agencies are entities which provide employment agency services, agency services relating to employment abroad with foreign employers, vocational consulting, personal consultancy or temporary employment. Employment agencies assist in seeking work in Poland and with foreign employers; they also help employers to find workers with required qualifications. Personal consultancy agencies provide payable services for employers. Vocational consulting agencies provide assistance in selecting a suitable trade and place of residence, including posts requiring special psychological and physical predisposition. Temporary employment agencies refer their employees to work for a user employer.

567. The already mentioned amendment of 14 March 2014 changed the functioning of employment agencies. Under the new regulations, employment agencies that have been given accreditation may pursue tasks related to the movement of workers within the EU, within the EURES network (Article 36a ff. EPA). In this respect, Polish legislation implements the principles of the Regulation (EU) No. 492/2011 of the European Parliament and of the Council of 5 April 2011, on freedom of movement for workers within the Union, and the Decision of the European Commission of 26 November 2012 implementing the Regulation No. 492/2011 as regards the clearance of vacancies and applications for employment and the re-establishment of EURES. These actions are an element of the strategy – 'Europe 2020' executed by the EU, which aims at raising the employment rates in Member

348. M. Włodarczyk, *Pośrednictwo pracy. Studium prawno-społeczne* (Łódź, Wydawnictwo Uniwersytetu Łódzkiego, 2002), pp. 31 et seq.
349. *Journal of Laws* (2008), No. 222, item 1448.

States. In addition, the amendment added a new Chapter 13c 'Commissioning of development actions' (Article 66d ff.). Development actions are a package of actions aimed at taking up and keeping suitable employment or business activity by a jobless individual (Article 2 section 1 point 9aa). They can be addressed, first of all, to the long-term unemployed, including persons classified into the second or the third aid profile. Therefore, we may state that the legislators force employment agencies into more and more intensive involvement in the realization of undertakings connected with combating unemployment.

§6. Unemployment Benefit

568. Passive methods of combating unemployment do not have a pro-employment character. In practice, they are limited to money benefits addressed to the unemployed. Under Polish legislation, these are the unemployment benefit as well as scholarships and development bonuses. The most important is, without doubt, the unemployment benefit. According to Article 71 of the Act an unemployed person is entitled to the benefit when there is no offer of a suitable job or another form of combating unemployment, e.g., a placement, vocational education or intervention work. Moreover, during the eighteen months before registration the interested person should have been employed or should have performed other gainful work for a period of at least 365 days, and he or she should have also earned an income equivalent to at least the statutory minimum wage. The period of employment preceding the registration does not need to be uninterrupted. Of course, periods of gainful activity in EU Member States are taken into account when ascertaining the right to the benefit. Employment in third countries is taken into account, provided the Labour Fund has been paid.

569. The amount of the benefit is not related to the earlier income, but it is defined in the Act as a fixed amount. In 2018, this amount was PLN 831 (approximately EUR 200) over the first three months and PLN 652 (approximately EUR 160) over the subsequent months. Depending on the situation of the unemployed individual, the time of receiving the benefit is six or twelve months. The right to the benefit is lost, earlier, if the unemployed person has declined an offer for a suitable job, other gainful work or any of the forms of occupational development. When assessing the unemployment benefit we should note that the eligibility criteria are difficult to meet, and, in practice, only a small proportion of the unemployed are entitled to it. Moreover, the benefit does not cover the cost of living even at the subsistence level, which must be considered as contrary to the obligations under the European Social Charter. Actually, unemployed persons often have to use welfare.

Chapter 16. Employment of Foreigners

L. Mitrus

§1. Introductory Remarks

570. The employment of foreigners in Poland is regulated in different ways, depending on the country of origin of an employee. We should set apart two basic categories. First, Poland is fully included in the system of free movement of workers in the EU and the transition periods provided in the Treaty of Accession expired finally in 2011. That is why the nationals of the Member States of the EU, the European Economic Area not belonging to the Union and the states that signed international treaties with the EU on free movement of workers (which practically means the Swiss Confederation) may take up employment without a permit. They are protected by the EU prohibition of discrimination based on nationality. Thus, they are treated equally with Polish nationals, and restrictions may only apply to the access to employment at certain posts connected with exercising power, e.g., in the judiciary, in the civil service or in the state or local administration or in the uniformed services. Second, there are third-country nationals. As a matter of principle, they should meet formal requirements to take up work in Poland. This group is not homogenous, and the procedures of obtaining residence and work permits may differ depending on the country of origin of the candidate. The further discussion in this chapter focuses on this latter category of foreigners, i.e., on nationals of countries not belonging to the European Union.[350]

571. The issues connected with the employment of foreign nationals are addressed in the Act on the Promotion of Employment and Organization of the Labour Market (Chapter 16, Article 84ff.) of 20 April 2004[351] as well as in the secondary legislation based on this Act. Therefore, regulations addressing the status of foreigners are treated as an element of the organization of the labour market element, and restrictions concerning the employment of foreign citizens should be understood as a means of fighting unemployment among Polish citizens. The rules concerning employment of foreign nationals have been changed by the amendment to the Act on the Promotion of Employment of 20 July 2017 (Journal of Laws 2017, item 1543), that took effect on 1 January 2018. This amendment refers to seasonal work. We should also mention the Act on Foreign Nationals of 12 December 2013[352] which includes, among other things, the procedure for obtaining residence permit in Poland. On the other hand, the Act on the Consequences of Giving a Job

350. *See* E. Bielak-Jomaa, *Zatrudnianie cudzoziemców* (Warsaw, Wolters Kluwer Business, 2015), pp. 120 et seq.*;* E. Podgórska – Rakiel, M. Szypniewski, *Zatrudnianie w Polsce cudzoziemców spoza UE, Warsaw,* Wolters Kluwer, pp. 19 et seq.

351. Consolidated text *Journal of Laws* (2017) item 1065.

352. *Journal of Laws* (2017) item 2206, as amended.

to Foreigners Illegally Staying in the Territory of the Republic of Poland of 15 June 2012[353] concerns sanctions for illegal employment of foreign workers.

572. Now, Poland is gradually becoming a more and more attractive place for taking up work by foreigners. From a historical perspective, the regulations concerning the employment of foreigners have been undergoing frequent changes, and a tendency to simplify the procedures allowing taking up work can be observed. We can also expect that the protectionist policy aimed at protecting the domestic labour market will have to change due to the demographic processes. The Poles are among the fastest ageing societies in Europe, and the scant birth rate results in more and more unfavourable proportions between persons active on the labour market and those who have retired from the workforce. At the same time many Poles decide on permanent emigration for the purpose of employment within the EU, which applies mainly to young and well-educated people. Therefore, it is possible that the loss in the domestic workforce will have to be filled in by foreigners. Possibly, it will prove necessary to not only ease the restrictions but to encourage foreign nationals to take up work in Poland. The above-mentioned processes pose a serious challenge for the Polish migration policy. Therefore, we can expect that the importance of regulations concerning the employment of foreigners in Poland will grow.

§2. 'Foreigner' Status in the Light of the Employment Regulations

573. In the light of Polish law, a 'foreigner' is anyone who has no Polish citizenship (Article 3 point 2 of the Act on Foreign Nationals, and also Article 2 point 7 of the EPA). Thus, both the nationals of other states and stateless persons are considered as foreigners. Dual nationality, i.e., a simultaneous possession of Polish and alien nationality, is allowed. Of course, in Poland such persons are treated as Polish workers and not as foreigners. The availability of the Polish labour market to third countries' nationals is not uniformly regulated. This results from Poland's international obligations and from the preferential treatment of workers from the East European countries. The status of an individual may be affected, also by Polish ethnicity or individual situation, such as having the status of a family member of a Pole or the status of a foreigner with a Polish residence permit.

574. Polish regulations concerning foreigners use a broad concept of gainful work. 'Performing work by a foreigner' means employment, performance of other gainful work or sitting on the board of directors of legal entities (Article 2 section 1 point 40 of the EPA). On the other hand, by an 'entity entrusting performance of work to a foreigner' it means an organizational unit, even if it is not a legal entity, or a natural person who entrusts the performance of work to a foreigner under a contract or other legal relationships (Article 2 section 1 point 21b of the EPA). Therefore, the regulation of work of foreigners in Poland and the relevant restrictions concern not only employment within an employment relationship, but also other gainful activity, e.g., work based on a civil contract.

---

353. *Journal of Laws* (2012), item 769.

575. Article 18^{3a} §1 LC dealing with equal treatment in employment introduces *inter alia* prohibition of discrimination based on nationality.[354] It does not, however, enact the prohibition of discrimination on the grounds of citizenship understood as the legal bond between an individual and a state. As already mentioned, as regards the nationals of the EU Member States the prohibition of discrimination arises directly from the EU law. As to third-country nationals, the possibility of taking up employment in Poland can be subject to the requirement of obtaining the appropriate permits. Thus, with regard to access to employment, there is a clear-cut difference between Polish nationals and the third country nationals. As a rule, Poles and EU nationals have priority in taking up employment. Nevertheless, if a third country national enters into an employment relationship, then he or she must not be treated worse because of his or her citizenship. The principle of equal rights on account of equally carrying out of the same duties applies fully to foreigners (Article 11^2 LC). The same applies to the right to equal pay for identical work or work of equal value (Article 18^{3c} LC).

§3. Foreigners Taking Up Work Without a Work Permit

576. Certain categories of foreigners have the right to take up employment or other gainful work in Poland without the need to obtain permission. In any case, however, the interested person is obliged to obtain a document certifying the right to legal residence. As has already been mentioned, EU and EEA nationals and members of their families have the right to freely take up work. As regards third-country nationals, Article 87 section 1 of the EPA indicates *inter alia* that foreigners who obtained the refugee status, those who have a permanent residence permit, a residence permit due to humanitarian reasons, consent for tolerated stay, a temporary residence permit, are those who enjoy temporary protection in the Republic of Poland.

577. The EPA indicates also foreigners who are exempt from the obligation to possess a work permit (Article 87 section 2). For example, these are foreigners who apply for the refugee status or family members of Polish citizens. A special category is formed by foreigners who hold the Pole's card. The card is awarded on the basis of the Pole's Card Act of 7 September 2007.[355] This is a document which proves that the holder is a member of the Polish nation. It can be issued for descendants of Poles who, as a consequence of the twentieth-century historical processes (including, especially. deportations), found themselves in the territory of the then Soviet Union against their will. The Pole's Card may be awarded to the citizens of Armenia, Azerbaijan, Belarus, Estonia, Georgia, Kazakhstan, Kirgizstan, Lithuania, Latvia, Moldova, Russia, Tajikistan, Turkmenistan, Ukraine or Uzbekistan. The interested person has to demonstrate his or her connection with the Polish nation and Poland, which can be corroborated, e.g., by a fact that at least one parent or

354. Which, in this context, refers to an ethnic group.
355. Consolidated text *Journal of Laws* (2017) item 1459.

grandparent or two great-grandparents are or were of Polish nationality or were Polish citizens. Such persons should demonstrate at least a basic knowledge of the Polish tongue as well as the knowledge and cultivation of Polish traditions and customs. It is also required that such person makes a written declaration of belonging to the Polish nation. The Pole's Card is issued by a Polish consul for a period of ten years. Such document does not mean that the holder has obtained Polish citizenship. It does not give the holder the right to enter Poland or to settle in Poland. However, it is a source of specific rights during stay in Poland, such as exemption from the need to have a work permit, freedom to pursue business activities, as well access to education at all levels.

578. On the grounds of Article 90 section 4 of the EPA, the minister competent for labour issues may issue an ordinance specifying the cases in which entrusting performance of work to a foreigner is admissible without the need to obtain a work permit. While exercising his/her competence, the minister should take into consideration, among other things, international treaties and agreements, Polish foreign policy, the specific features of the profession or trade, the nature of work, the period of work and also the requirements concerning the entity that gives work to a foreigner. The relevant regulations are contained in the Ordinance of the Minister of Labour and Social Policy of 21 April 2015 on the cases in which entrusting performance of work to a foreigner in the territory of the Republic of Poland is allowed without the need to obtain a work permit.[356] In the light of the ordinance, persons exempt from the duty to obtain a work permit are *inter alia* persons conducting training courses or taking part in professional placements which are a part of the activities of the EU or other international aid programmes, foreign language teachers, regular correspondents of foreign media, students, foreigners working for research institutes. Also, persons covered by the Association Agreement between the European Economic Community and Turkey of 12 September 1963 can work without a permit. Sportsmen or artists, as well as persons delivering occasional lectures or reports of a special scientific or artistic value, may pursue their activities for up to thirty days in a calendar year. In addition, there are some particular rules on employment of the citizens of Armenia, Belarus, Georgia, Moldova, Russia and Ukraine. Their status is regulated by Article 87 item 3 and 4 EPA and the Ordinance of the Minister for Family, Labour and Social Policy of 8 December 2017 on the list of states, to which nationals apply some provisions on seasonal work and provisions on declaration to entrust work to a foreigner (Journal of Laws 2017, item 2349). With regard to citizens of the above-mentioned countries, the work permit is not required if work is to be performed not longer than six months within a consecutive twelve months. Instead, the employer is obliged to inform the district job centre about the intention to hire a national of one of these countries.

356. *Journal of Laws* (2015), item 588, as amended by the Ordinance of 8 Dec. 2017 [Journal of Laws 2017, item 2346.

§4. Foreigners Taking Up Work After Obtaining a Permit

579. Article 88 of the EPA specifies third-country nationals who are obliged to obtain a work permit. First, those are foreigners who are employed on the basis of a contract with an entity whose registered office, place of residence or branch is located in the territory of Poland. Second, foreigners sitting on the board of directors of a legal entity entered into the register of entrepreneurs, or one being a limited liability company, who stay in Poland for a period exceeding a total of six months within a successive twelve months. Third, foreigners employed by a foreign employer who are seconded to Poland for a period in excess of thirty days in a calendar year to a branch or plant of the foreign entity or its associated entity. Fourth, foreigners employed by a foreign employer who does not have a branch, a plant or other form of organized business in the territory of the Republic of Poland, who are seconded to Poland to provide a service of a temporary and occasional character (an export service). Fifth, foreigners employed by a foreign employer who are seconded to Poland for other purposes than those indicated above, for a period in excess of thirty days within six consecutive months. Next, the ordinance by the Minister of Family, Labour and Social Policy of 7 December 2017 on issuing a work permit for a foreigner[357] specifies various types of work permits depending on the classification of the foreigner to one of the above-mentioned categories. It should be emphasized that in each case the foreigner must have the right to legally reside in Poland. Since 1 January 2018, there is a new type of work permit concerning seasonal work (*see* below).

580. The procedure of issuing work permits is regulated, first of all, by Article 88a ff. of the EPA. A work permit is issued and extended on application by the entity entrusting the performance of work to a foreigner, e.g., an employer who intends to sign an employment contract with a foreigner. Thus, a foreigner is not a party to the administrative proceedings, although he/she should be informed about all actions and decisions. The organ authorized to issue the permit is the provincial governor (*wojewoda*), i.e., the organ of government administration at the regional level. The provincial governor will issue the permit if the foreigner's remuneration is not lower than the remuneration of workers performing comparable work or working at a comparable post. The application should include information from *starosta* (a local organ of government administration) about the impossibility to satisfy the employer's needs on the basis of the registers of unemployed and job seekers or about a negative result of recruitment organized by the employer. For posted workers the permit is issued if the expected working conditions will comply with Polish labour law standards, and the amount of the remuneration will not be less than 30% of the average wage in the province.

581. An important element of the permit issue procedure is 'labour market test' or statement by *starosta* that a given position cannot be filled by an unemployed person registered in the county job centre. In other words, Polish citizens seeking employment and those foreigners who may take up jobs without a permit (e.g., EU

357. *Journal of Laws.* (2017), item 2345.

nationals) have priority. According to Article 10 section 3 of the EPA it is the provincial governor who determines the criteria for issuing work permits to foreigners. It should be emphasized that the detailed criteria of the 'labour market test' are developed at the level of the provinces with a possibility of taking their specific features into account. The criteria determined by the province governor include a list of trades and professions, as well as types of jobs, for which a work permit may be issued without taking into account the *starosta*'s information and also cases where a work permit may be issued for a period shorter than that given in the application.

There are situations when it is not necessary to verify if a given post can be filled in the first place by a Polish national. These exceptions are established by the ordinance of the Minister of Labour and Social Policy of 29 January 2009 on defining the cases in which a work permit for a foreigner is issued regardless of the detailed conditions of issuing work permits for foreigners.[358] Such situation applies, e.g., to a foreigner who is a family member of an employee of a diplomatic mission, a consular office or an international organization, working in the Republic of Poland on the basis of international treaties and agreements, as well as a foreigner employed as domestic service of the employees of the above-mentioned missions. The above-mentioned ordinance of 29 January 2009 has been amended by the ordinance of the Minister of Family, Labour and Social Policy of 28 June 2018,[359] that took effect on 1 July 2018. According to the new regulations the work permit can be issued to foreigners, who exercise specific occupations, without the necessity to undergo 'labour market test'. The new procedure covers construction, health care, transport and informatics.

582. The work permit is issued for a limited period of time, not longer than three years, and it can be extended. The province governor may issue a work permit for a period not longer than five years for a person sitting on the board of directors of a legal entity. In the case of a secondment of a foreigner by a foreign employer for the purpose of delivering an export service, the province governor grants the work permit for the period of secondment. The work permit specifies the hiring entity, the post or type of the job, the foreigner, the lowest remuneration the foreigner can receive at the given post, full- or part-time and the expiry date of the permit. In other words, the permit is valid for the employment of a specific foreigner at a specific post. An employer may entrust a foreigner with work of a different character or at a different post than the one specified in the permit only for a period not exceeding thirty days in a calendar year. In such cases a work permit specifying new circumstances is not required. Moreover, a work permit does not release a foreigner from the duty to meet the requirements provided in separate regulations and needed to pursue regulated professions. These are professions requiring the necessary qualifications verified by appropriate degrees or certificates, e.g., the professions of a doctor, engineer, etc.

583. The entity entrusting the performance of work is obliged to include conditions from the work permit in the contract of employment with the foreigner. It

358. Consolidated text *Journal of Laws* (2015), item 97.
359. Consolidated text *Journal of Laws* 2018, item 1264.

also has a duty to conclude the contract with the foreigner in writing and, before giving the contract to the foreigner for signing, to show him/her its translation into a language he/she understands, give him/her a copy of the work permit, inform him/her about the actions undertaken in connection with the proceedings regarding the granting or extending of the permit as well as to exercise due diligence in work permit issue and extension proceedings. An entity entrusting the performance of work to a foreigner should inform the provincial governor of all significant circumstances concerning the employment of the foreigner, in writing, within seven days. The information duty includes, in particular, the taking up of work by the foreigner at a different post than that specified in the work permit, as well as a situation where the foreigner failed to take up work or interrupted it for a period longer than three months, or if the foreigner ended work more than three months before the expiry of the work permit.

584. The province governor issues a decision about the rejection of the request for a work permit for a foreigner when the entity entrusting the performance of work to the foreigner does not meet the statutory requirements, has provided false data or withheld relevant information and also if it was sentenced for illegally entrusting the performance of work to a foreigner. The request will also be rejected in a situation where the foreigner does not meet the qualification requirements, e.g., when he/she is not able to prove the qualifications necessary to perform work in a regulated trade or profession. Moreover, the province governor will revoke a permit if, *inter alia,* the circumstances or evidence related to the issued decision have changed, the reason for issuing the work permit has ceased, the hiring entity failed to fulfil its duties, the foreigner no more meets the statutory requirements and also if the governor received information that the foreigner had been put on a list of foreigners whose stay in Poland was undesirable.

585. As already mentioned, in principle, it is the entity which entrusts the performance of work to a foreigner that is a party to the proceedings to issue a work permit for such a person. The new Act on Foreigners of 12 December 2013 established new, alternative work permit extension procedures. They can be initiated by a foreigner who is legally residing in Poland. Article 114ff. of the Foreigners Act deals with a combined temporary residence and work permit. It can be issued if the purpose of the stay in Poland is employment and if all the following conditions are fulfilled: the foreigner has a health insurance, a source of stable and regular income sufficient to cover the cost of living of the foreigner and his/her dependants and is provided with accommodation in Poland. At the same time the hiring entity cannot satisfy its manpower needs on the local labour market and the foreigner's remuneration will not be lower than the remuneration of workers having a comparable job or a comparable position. These regulations implement Directive 2011/98/EU of the European Parliament and of the Council of 13 December 2011 on a single application procedure for a single permit for third-country nationals to reside and work in the territory of a Member State and on a common set of rights for third-country workers legally residing in a Member State.[360]

Moreover, Article 127ff. of the Foreigner Act establishes a similar procedure of granting a temporary residence permit for the purpose of employment in a trade or profession requiring high qualifications. The interested person must have the adequate professional qualifications and must sign an employment contract, a home work contract or a civil contract for a period of at least one year. These provisions implement Council Directive 2009/50/EC of 25 May 2009 on the conditions of entry and residence of third-country nationals for the purposes of highly qualified employment.[361] Both types of permits are issued for three years. Thus, the Foreigners Act provides a possibility to obtain the right to reside and work in one administrative proceeding for a foreigner who is already staying in Poland. The purpose of these regulations is to facilitate obtaining the required permissions, in particular, by speeding up the administrative procedure. The interested persons may choose if they want to use this uniform procedure or to apply separately for the temporary residence permit and work permit. The procedure of issuing a single permission for temporary residence and for work does not apply to workers posted by a foreign entity and temporarily residing in Poland.

The amendment to the EPA of 20 July 2017 introduced a new type of work permit that relates to seasonal work (Article 88n – 88z). The new regulations took effect on 1 January 2018. They implement Directive 2014/36 on the conditions of entry and stay of third-country nationals for the purpose of employment as seasonal workers.[362] The seasonal work of foreigners covers agriculture, horticulture and tourism sectors. It can be performed up to nine months within a calendar year. The work permit is issued by *starosta*, after evaluating the situation on the labour market and the possibility to take up a particular job by a Polish national. There is a preferential treatment for nationals of Armenia, Belarus, Georgia, Moldova, Russia and Ukraine. With regard to them, the work permit can be issued without the labour market test.

§5. Consequences of Illegally Entrusting Work to a Foreigner

586. The infringement of foreigner employment regulations is subject to criminal sanctions, and the consequences of illegal employment can hurt both parties. The EPA defines 'illegal performance of work by a foreigner' as the performing of work by a foreigner who has no right to perform work within the meaning of the act or who does not have a work permit, and whose basis for residence does not give right to perform work, or who is employed on different terms or at a different post than the one specified in the permit (Article 2 section 1 point 14). Entrusting work to a foreigner in the indicated circumstances, as well as admitting such person to work without concluding a contract of employment or a civil contract in the required form (Article 2 section .1 point 22a of the Act), is also illegal. In other

360. *Official Journal* L 343, 23 Dec. 2011, pp. 1–9.
361. *Official Journal* L 155, 18 Jun. 2009, pp. 17–29.
362. O.J. of 28 Mar. 2014, L 94/375.

words, employment of a foreigner or entrusting him/her with other activities in violation of the existing procedures is a type of illegal (unregistered) employment, or so-called 'black labour'. It is worth adding here that the competence of the State Labour Inspection (in Polish: Państwowa Inspekcja Pracy, PIP) includes, among other things, the inspection of the legality of employment, other gainful work and doing work by foreigners.[363] Within this scope the labour inspection cooperates with the relevant institutions, i.e., the Police, Border Guards, Customs Service, province governors and *starostas*. Besides the SLI, Border Guards may also inspect the legality of employment of foreigners.

587. Article 120 of the EPA enumerates petty offences punishable with fines. Such penalties can be inflicted on a person who illegally entrusts the performance of work to a foreigner and also on a foreigner who does work illegally. Also, he/she who makes a foreigner to illegally do work by misinforming the foreigner, taking advantage of his/her misapprehension, subordination or inability to properly understand his/her actions bears criminal responsibility. Demanding material benefit from a foreigner in exchange for undertaking actions aimed at obtaining a work permit is subject to criminal sanctions. Subject to punishment is also a person who fails to fulfil his/her duties to inform the province governor about employing a foreigner and about changes in the foreigner's status. The amount of the fine depends on the type of offence committed.

588. Separate regulations are contained in the Act on the Consequences of Entrusting the Performance of Work to Foreigners Staying Illegally in the Territory of the Republic of Poland of 15 June 2015.[364] The Act implements Directive 2009/52/EC of the European Parliament and of the Council of 18 June 2009 providing for minimum standards on sanctions and measures against employers of illegally staying third-country nationals.[365] It provides sanctions for entities entrusting the performance of work to a foreigner residing without a valid residence document as well as the principles of pursuing claims for remuneration and relevant benefits by a foreigner residing without a valid residence document. Within the meaning of the Act, foreigners are persons who are not nationals of a Member State of the EU, a Member State of the European Economic Area, Switzerland, or family members of such person.

589. The Act provides that an entity that entrusts the performance of work to a foreigner is obliged to demand from the foreigner the presentation of a valid document entitling to residence in Poland before starting work and also to keep a copy of such document. In addition, the Act confirms *expressis verbis* that a foreigner who stays in Poland without a valid document entitling residence, who was entrusted with doing work, may demand payment of the remuneration and the relevant benefits. In a case where a foreigner was employed under a contract of

363. Article 10 section 4 of the Act of 13 Apr. 2007 on the State Labour Inspection, consolidated text. *Journal of Laws* (2017) item 786.
364. *Journal of Laws* (2012), item 769.
365. *Official Journal* L 168, 30 Jun. 2009, pp. 24–32.

employment, when pursuing the right to the unpaid remuneration and the relevant benefits, the presumption is that the employment relationship existed for three months, unless the employer or the foreigner proves a different period of employment. The Act also provides legal sanctions. As provided in the Act, he/she who entrusts work at the same time to many foreigners staying in Poland without valid residence documents is subject to a fine or the penalty of restricted liberty. Subject to the same punishment is a person who entrusts work to a minor foreigner residing without a valid document. A person entrusting the performance of work to a foreigner residing without a valid document entitling stay in Poland in conditions of special exploitation is subject to a term of imprisonment of up to three years.

590. Sanctions connected with illegal employment are provided also in the Foreigners Act. According to its Article 302 section 1 point 4, one of the cases in which a decision obliging a foreigner to leave Poland may be issued is a situation where the foreigner did or is doing work without a work permit or without an employer's declaration about the intention to entrust work to the foreigner, which the declaration has been registered at the job centre. This sanction is also applicable if a foreigner is fined for illegally working. In such circumstances the costs connected with the issue and execution of the decision obligating a foreigner to return to his country of origin are paid by the entity entrusting the foreigner with work or a specific function (Article 337 section 1 point 3).

Part II. Collective Labour Law

Z. Hajn

Chapter 1. The Concept and Foundations of Collective Labour Law

§1. The Concept of Collective Labour Law

591. The objective of the collective labour law is to institutionalize the operation of employee and employer representations and the methods whereby trade unions (or other employee representatives) and employers (as well as their organizations) seek to preserve the employee and employers' advantages as inscribed in law (the collective protection of rights). It also provides for the mechanisms used by both groups to achieve new advantages (the collective protection of interests). Meanwhile, general public and social objectives are also pursued by the law, these including, in particular, stabilization of social relationships, public order protection, protection of interests of third parties, e.g., the citizens whose well-being is jeopardized by collective actions. Specifically, collective labour law serves the case of preservation of social peace and maintenance of sustainable economic growth.

592. The concept of collective labour law has filiations with an obvious need to regulate a special social phenomenon – workers standing up collectively to represent and defend their rights and interests. That very method of collective action, related to the rights and interests of the employees and employers, makes up the main criterion whereby the collective labour law is distinguished.

593. The collective labour law provides for: association of employees and other working people in trade unions, formation of employer organizations and the legal status of the bodies in question, collective bargaining and concluding CLAs and other accords whereby terms and conditions of employment are determined, resolving disputes related to collective bargaining and other conflicts relative to industrial relations, employee participation in work establishment and company management.

594. The fact that collective labour law is part of labour law, in general, is not called into question. It is being indicated, though, that covered by collective labour law are not only employees but also other people doing professional work gainfully (*see* below §2 in Chapter II).[366]

§2. Trade Union Freedoms

I. Legal Framework

595. Article 12 of the Constitution, placed in the chapter concerning the foundations of the political and socio-economic system of the Republic of Poland, guarantees freedom for the creation and functioning of trade unions and other voluntary associations. The guarantee is further specified in Article 59 of the Constitution providing for the freedom of association in trade unions, socio-occupational organizations of farmers and in employers' organizations, the right of trade unions and employers and their organizations to collective bargaining as well as the right of trade unions to organize workers' strikes or other forms of protest.

596. When enacting the trade union law in 1991 (in principle, from scratch, after fifty years of communism), the legislators adopted, as the main basis for the drafted Act, the standards well established in international law. That special role of international law has found its confirmation in Article 59 paragraph 4 the Constitution, according to which 'The scope of freedom of association in trade unions and in employer's organizations and of other union freedoms may only be subject to such statutory limitations as are permissible in accordance with international agreements to which the Republic of Poland is a party.' The limitations can be imposed, the rules of proportionality being observed (Article 31 paragraph the Constitution) (*see* Introduction, Chapter 5, §2). It should be noted in passing that the trade union freedoms can be subject to the limitations following from the rules that protect other constitutional goods.[367]

597. Detailed trade union freedom guarantees are inscribed in a number of pieces of legislation. The Trade Union Act and the Act on Employer Organizations provide for the autonomy and independence of their operation and guarantee judicial control over the formation and dissolution of trade organizations. The Trade Union Act secures protection to trade union representatives and facilitates trade union activities. The LC counts the right of employees and employers to associate in order to protect their rights and interests among the fundamental principles of labour law (Article 18^1).

366. It is worth adding that the Labour Law Codification Committee appointed by the government in 2002 worked out separate drafts of individual and collective labour law. However, the draft legislation was never passed. For more, *see* M. Seweryński, 'Pojęcie, zakres i próba kodyfikacji zbiorowego prawa pracy w Polsce', in: Goździewicz (ed.), *Aktualne problemy zbiorowego prawa pracy w Polsce i w Niemczech* (Toruń, Dom Organizatora, 2012), pp. 15 et seq.

367. *See* the Constitutional Tribunal judgment of 23 Oct. 2001, K.22/01, item III.1.

598. The freedom of employees and employers to associate includes, in fact, all kinds of individual and collective rights related to the protection of professional interests achieved through the creation of the organization.

II. Individual Rights

599. Among the individual rights the right of the working people and employers to establish and join organizations is one of fundamental importance. The establishment of a trade union or employer organization requires registration, the formality being done with a court of law and performed on the basis of clearly stated criteria. The right to be a trade union or employer organization member does not mean the right to join a particular organization, as the terms and conditions of admittance to membership are determined by the organizations autonomously in their by-laws. The conditions may not, however, be discriminatory. The membership is acquired through the submission of member's declaration and acceptance of it by the organization. Certain trade union by-laws prohibit dual affiliation.

600. The right to associate is also reflected in what is termed as the 'negative' trade union freedom. This consists in the individual's right not to be a trade union member (with no adverse consequences to the person) but also the freedom not to join a trade union or leave the organization. The principle, directly proclaimed by Article 3 of TUA, is a guarantee of the voluntary trade union membership recognized by Article 1 Part 1 TUA as a trade union feature.[368] In practical terms, however, the problem of violation of the freedom to join and leave a trade union is non-existent. Union security clauses are, in particular, unknown in Poland.[369]

601. The individual trade union freedom also covers the right to participate in the union activities. Its scope includes the affiliation to the organization itself, the right to be its representative and perform duties in the service in the organization, as well as participation in union activities, strikes in particular. Being a trade union member, staying outside a trade union or performing a union function may not entail negative consequences, as it has already been stressed. In particular, this may not constitute a reason for concluding the employment relationship, maintenance of one or promotion.

---

368. In the Constitutional Tribunal's view, the negative trade union freedom is anchored in the Constitution, even though it is only the freedom to associate in trade unions that is expressly guaranteed in its Art. 59 part 1. After all, once the freedom to associate is guaranteed, the freedom not to join a trade union is recognized by the same (the Constitutional Tribunal judgment of 1 Jul. 2008, K.23/07).

369. Even before WWII such clauses, if used in collective labour agreements, were put into question by the labour inspection as being contrary to the freedom of association. Such were also the views expressed in judicial decisions. *See* W. Masewicz, *Położenie prawne związków zawodowych w Polsce w latach 1919-1939* (Instytut Wydawniczy CRZZ, 1972), pp. 175–176. Under the existing law, in the case concerning a trade union having obliged its employees to join it, the Supreme Court considered the provision of the trade union statute proclaiming such a duty as an unacceptable violation of the freedom of association; Supreme Court decision of 3 Jul. 1991, I PRZN 2/91.

602. It is forbidden to discriminate against employees for their trade union affiliation (Article 11^3 LC). A similar prohibition concerning jobseekers is included in the EPA, 2004. Guarantees of the right to perform trade union functions are established by, *inter alia*, provisions protecting trade union activists against dismissal and deterioration of their employment conditions (*see* Part II, Chapter 2, §2, VI, F).

III. Collective Rights

603. From the freedom of association there follows the right of trade unions to establish and join federations and confederations and their right to affiliate with international organizations of workers and employers. Related to the freedom, as its necessary complement indicated by Article 3 of the ILO Convention 87/1948, is the right of trade unions and employers organizations to freely decide on their by-laws and bodies, manage their affairs, draw up their programmes and decide on the way in which their activities are pursued.[370] As far as the latter is concerned, of particular importance is the trade union right to conduct collective bargaining and engage in collective actions. According to Article 59 of the Constitution, trade unions and employers and their organizations have the right to bargain, particularly for the purpose of resolving collective disputes, and to conclude CLAs and other accords. As part 3 of the Article provides, trade unions have the right to organize workers' strikes or other forms of protest subject to limitations specified by statute (…).

§3. Social Partners' Dialogue

I. Constitutional Meaning

604. The principle of social partners' dialogue, as a rule pervading the system of labour relation, was established by the Constitution of 1997. In its preamble, the Constitution identifies itself as the fundamental law of the state, based, among others, on social dialogue. The notion should be understood as the so-called civil dialogue, a phenomenon going beyond the sphere of interests of employees and employers. It is in a separate provision that the Constitution touches the issue of solidarity, dialogue and cooperation between social partners (Article 20). The dialogue of social partners is, thus, according to the Constitution, an element of the broader notion of the civil dialogue.

605. As Article 20 of the Constitution provides, the foundation of the economic system of the Republic of Poland is a social market economy based on the freedom of economic activity, private ownership, solidarity, dialogue and cooperation between social partners. Within that constitutional context the above-mentioned

370. The Supreme Court, referring to the convention, resolved, *inter alia*, that regional federations can be established by trade unions, though only nationwide federations and confederations are mentioned by TUA in its Art. 11; cf. the resolution of seven judges of the Supreme Court of 15 Oct. 1992, I PZP 35/92.

phenomena (those of solidarity, dialogue and cooperation between social partners) are the instruments employed to modify market economy; the nature of the modifications consists in the conditions of employment being shaped through social partners' negotiations. Among the basic instruments of dialogue and cooperation between social partners the following should be named: mutual information and consultation, collective bargaining leading to the conclusion of CLAs and other collective accords and cooperation of the employers and representatives of employees in the management of the work establishment. The social partners' dialogue, as provided for in the Constitution, has, thus, the nature of a so-called autonomous dialogue.

606. The constitutional position of the dialogue and cooperation between social partners indicates their strong affiliation with the principles of business freedom, private ownership and solidarity. Solidarity means that the social partners, while meeting their fundamental tasks of representing employees and employers, should take into account the interests of the vulnerable social groups, i.e., the unemployed, the poor, the handicapped or the people being in a tough situation for reasons other than those mentioned. Following from the assumption is the imperative of the redistribution of wealth, meaning that certain rights and interests of employees and employers can (and should, in fact) be subject to limitations, part of the income of the groups in question being transferred to satisfy the needs of the less affluent social circles. As the Constitutional Tribunal indicated in one of its judgments, the reference made in Article 20 of the Constitution to the solidarity, dialogue and cooperation between social partners 'assumes striking a balance of the interests of the market actors, while respecting their autonomy. A constitutional guarantee for a negotiation-based way of resolving controversies is created by the same, allowing to overcome the tensions and conflicts that arise within economic processes. The sources of the values in question can be traced back to the social philosophy known as social solidarity'. From that very philosophical trend there follows a postulate that 'all social classes should be burdened with the consequences of the economic crisis' and a belief that 'it is social solidarity that lies at the foundation of the redistributive function of the social justice principle'.[371]

607. In legal writing and social discourse the above-mentioned notion of the 'social partners' dialogue' is seldom used. As far as the general constitutional notion of 'social dialogue' is concerned, it is mostly used in the context of employment relationships and, in practice, associates with that very sphere of social relations. Moreover, the term of 'social dialogue' is most frequently applied to denote all kinds of exchange of views and communication between the employers and trade unions or other employee representatives as well as between trade unions and public authorities.

371. *See* the judgment of 30 Jan. 2001, K17/00.

II. Tripartite Dialogue

A. *Social Dialogue Council*

608. Until September 2015, the most important general tripartite institution in Poland was the Tripartite Commission for Socio-Economic Issues. The Commission was established in 1994 (a year of heavy social tensions connected with the transformation of the socio-economic and political system after the breakthrough of the year 1989) as a result of an agreement concluded between major central trade union organizations, employer associations and the government. A statutory basis for its operation was provided in 2001.[372]

Over more than twenty years of the Commission's history, many a compromise solution was reached on the forum, concerning vital social issues. In practice, all important labour law amendments and changes of social policy had been preceded by arrangements made within the Commission. Not always, however, a compromise was arrived at. Still, the changes agreed on within the Commission were, as a rule, respected by the legislator and departure of the Parliament from the arrangements made at the forum of the Commission would meet with a strong resistance, especially on the part of the trade unions. In particular, the government was accused of breaking the arrangements concerning the so-called anti-crisis package, as contained in the Act that became effective in 2009.[373] The dialogue came to a standstill in 2013, when trade unions refused to participate in the Commission's proceedings. As they explained, the move was taken in a protest against, *inter alia*, the flexibilization of working time regulations, enacted without their consent. In addition, in their opinion, the dialogue in the Commission was actually simulated over past years, trade union suggestions not being taken into account by the government. Following the criticism, central trade union organizations having the right to sit on the Commission started drafting a new piece of legislation, the government declaring support to the efforts. A draft of their own was also developed by employers' organizations, and a joint team prepared, further on, a text presented to the government. The result of the work is the Act of 24 July 2015 on the Social Dialogue Council and Other Institutions of Social Dialogue (SDCA), having come into force on 11 September 2015.

609. The Social Dialogue Council (CDS) is composed of representatives of the government, the employees and the employers.[374] Representatives of the employees' and employers' sides come – respectively – from the trade unions and employers' associations, representative at the national level. Each of the sides has an equal

372. The Act of 2001 on the Tripartite Commission for Socio-Economic Issues and Voivodeship (Province) Social Dialogue Commissions (*Journal of Laws* (2001), No. 100, item 1080, as amended).
373. The Act of 1 Jul. 2009 on the Mitigation of the Impact of the Economic Crisis on Employees and Entrepreneurs (*Journal of Laws* (2009), No. 125, item 1035).
374. Currently, members of the CDS on the employee side are: *NSZZ 'Solidarność'* (Independent and Self-Governing Trade Union 'Solidarity'), *OPZZ* (All-Polish Alliance of Trade Unions) and *FZZ* (Forum of Trade Unions), the employer side being represented by: *PKPP Lewiatan* (Polish Confederation of Private Employers Leviathan), *Pracodawcy RP* (Employers of Poland), *ZRP* (Polish Craft Association) and *Związek Pracodawców BCC* (Business Centre Club Employers' Union).

number of representatives, and each of the trade unions and employer organizations has an equal number of representatives within a specific side.[375] The government side is composed of representatives of the Council of Ministers indicated by the President of the body (the Prime Minister).[376] Representatives of the President of the Republic of Poland, President of the National Bank of Poland and the President of the Central Statistical Office of Poland participate in the work of the Council in an advisory capacity. At the invitation by the Chairperson of the Council, participants in the work carried out by the body may also include representatives of other organizations and institutions. In addition, the employees' and employers' sides may invite representatives of trade unions and employer associations not being Council members, and representatives of other social and trade organizations, to take part in the activities of the Council, in an advisory capacity.

610. The Council is chaired, alternately, by a representative of the employees' side, the employers' side and the government. The chairperson's term of office is one year. Council meetings are held in public.

611. The Social Dialogue Council Act has assigned the Council the following tasks:

- to conduct a dialogue to secure conditions for socio-economic development, improvement of the competitive advantage of the economy and social cohesion;
- to take actions for a growth of participation and social solidarity in the field of employment;
- to adopt measures for better formulation and implementation of socio-economic policies and strategies and mutual understanding in that respect by promoting a dialogue of the organizations of employees, employers and the government;
- to support social dialogue at all levels of local/regional government.

612. First and foremost, the Council is a forum of direct consultations between the parties concerning, in particular, development of the central budget (and the draft budget act itself), government proposals regarding wage setting in the national economy (state-budget units in particular) as well as pensions paid from the Social Security Fund. Subject to consultation may be also other matters of considerable socio-economic significance, presented by any of the parties represented in the Council.

The decision-making powers of the Council concern setting of minimum wage, the salary indicators in state-budget sector, income-related criteria for the granting

375. At present, in accordance with the arrangements made by the parties in question, each of the three trade union organizations has eight representatives, each of the four employer's associations having six.

376. Currently, the government is represented in the Council by six ministers – of labour, finance, treasury, education, health and development, as well as vice-ministers of labour and finance.

of social security benefits as well terms and conditions for the granting (and determining the amounts) of family benefits. They are arrived at in the process of negotiations, but if the negotiations are not successfully concluded until a specified date, it is the government that sets the indicators.

The employees' and the employers' side of the Council are entitled to develop joint assumptions for and drafts of pieces of legislation or other legal acts or proposals to enact or amend an Act of Parliament or other legal acts concerning matters falling within the scope of powers of the Council; these are to be further presented to a relevant minister for submission to the Council of Ministers. Should the government refuse to accept the initiative or approve it with substantial amendments, its standpoint has to be justified in the way specified by law.

The employees' and employers' sides may also instruct the Chairperson of the Council to approach the Supreme Court with an application to resolve a legal problem related to divergence of opinions expressed in judicial rulings.

613. The Act also provides for the conclusion of accords between the employees' and the employers' sides and between all sides of the Council, as well as CLAs above the company level concluded by the Council's social (citizen) sides.

B. Voivodeship *(Province) Social Dialogue Councils*

614. The counterparts of SDCs at the level of Poland's *voivodeships* (provinces) are social dialogue councils – VSDC.

The composition of a VSDC includes: marshal of the *voivodeship* and his/her two representatives (the regional government side), the *voivode* (governor) and his/her two representatives (the government side) and representatives of trade unions and employers' organizations, representative within the meaning of the SDCA, in the numbers jointly agreed on by the organizations.

Powers of the VSDC include, first of all, providing opinions and taking standpoints on matters concerning tasks of trade unions or employers' organizations falling within the scope of responsibilities of central and regional/local administration operating in the *voivodeship.* In particular, the social (citizen) sides of the VSDC voice their opinions on draft development strategies of the *voivodeship* and action programmes (in the scope covered by the tasks of trade unions and employers' organizations) and reports on the implementation of those, submitted by the marshal of the *voivodeship.* Where the VSDC takes a standpoint on a specific issue, e.g., recommends making amendments to certain local legal regulations, the relevant public agency has to express its position, in writing, within thirty days. In matters covered by the scope of responsibilities of the VSDC the sides represented on the body may also conclude agreements determining their obligations related to the implementation of relevant tasks.

615. The VSDC may also examine social or economic issues resulting in conflicts between the employers and employees and initiate goodwill missions in order to resolve the conflicts.

C. Other Tripartite and Multipartite Bodies

616. The SDC and the *voivodeship* (province) social dialogue councils are bodies of general competence determined by the broadly termed tasks of trade unions and employer associations. Besides the commissions there exist, also, other tri and multipartite bodies of a specialized profile of operation.[377] These include, for instance:

- the Labour Protection Board, being the body supervising working conditions and the operation of the SLI;
- employment councils, established at the national, *voivodeship* (province) and county (*powiat*) level, as bodies operating in an advisory and opinion-giving capacity for the minister of labour, governor and head of the county administration (*starosta*);
- the Supervisory Board of the Social Security Agency (ZUS);
- the Commission for the Issues of CLAs;
- the Statistical Council as the advisory and consultative body to the Prime Minister in matters of statistics;
- the National Consultative Council for Persons with Disabilities and the *voivodeship* (regional) and county (*powiat*) councils for matters to do with the disabled.

617. The specialized bodies in question also include tripartite industrial committees dealing with the issues of specific trades (business lines). These have been gradually established since the early 1990s, at the request of social partners. The committees are mostly concerned about matters of state intervention in a specific industry. The composition of such a committee includes representatives of the minister in charge of labour issues or (albeit less frequently) minister responsible for other matters and representatives of trade unions and employer organizations operating in the industry. They aim, as a rule, at resolving the issues by means of seeking consensus among all the parties. Currently there are fifteen such committees.[378]

377. The composition of some of the bodies, e.g., the employment councils, includes also representatives of institutions and organizations other than trade unions and employers' organizations, such as farmer organizations, NGOs, units of local government, academic institutions.

378. http://www.dialog.gov.pl/dialog-krajowy/trojstronne-zespoly-branzowe/; accessed 11 Jan. 2015.

Chapter 2. Trade Unions and Employer Organizations; Ad Hoc Employee Representatives

§1. Legal Basis and Status of Trade Unions and Employer's Organizations

618. Trade unions operate under the Trade Union Act of 23 May 1991 (TUA). The Act is applicable to all trade unions save for the unions of self-employed farmers. Specific laws concerning some occupational groups (e.g., the policemen) provide for certain derogations from the rules set up in the TUA. The legal basis for the employers' associations is the Act of 23 May 1991 on Employers' Organization (the Employers' Organization Act, EOA). Only the organizations registered under the laws in question can be granted the status of trade unions or employer organizations.

619. In the light of the laws in question trade unions and employers' organization are social organizations of a special kind, differing from associations in a number of aspects. Their operation is provided for in special pieces of legislation. They also have a separate history, different objectives and means of operation and particular socio-economic and political importance. The laws of 1991 provide for all the fundamental aspects of their legal status, viz. the ways of their establishment, dissolution, internal structure, membership, powers, assets and legal responsibility. Consequently, it should be stated that trade unions and employer organizations are not associations but the organizations of a special kind, having a legal regime of their own. The latter results from the trade union freedom secured by the Constitution of the Republic of Poland and international law and from the Acts of Parliament mentioned above. Trade unions and employers' organizations are vested in legal personality which they gain upon their registration (Article 15 TUA and Article 10 EOA). The difference between trade unions/employer organizations and associations does not mean that there do not exist links between the two types of organizations. As the Act on Associations (Article 7 part 2 in conjunction with part 1 item 1 *ab initio*)[379] provides, the law is applicable, in matters not provided for otherwise, to social organizations operating under special Acts of Parliament or the international agreements to which the Republic of Poland is a party.

620. Besides the above-mentioned trade unions and organizations also trade unions of self-employed farmers operate in Poland.[380]

379. The Act of 7 Apr. 1989 on Associations (*Journal of Laws* (2001), item 855, as amended).
380. The legal status of the organizations in question is determined by: the Act of 7 Apr. 1989 on Trade Unions of Self-Employed Farmers (*Journal of Laws* (1989), item 106, as amended) and the Act of 9 Oct. 1982 on Socio-Economic Organizations of Farmers (*Journal of Laws* (1982), item 217, as amended). Major nationwide farmer organizations include: *Krajowy Związek Rolników, Kółek i*

§2. TRADE UNIONS

I. Notion

A. Introduction

621. A trade union is a voluntary and self-governing organization of the working people, expected to represent and defend their rights as well as occupational and social interests. In its operation, as conducted under its by-laws, the trade union is independent of employers, state administration, local government agencies and any other organizations (Article 1 TUA). In addition, it is a democratic, formalized and durable structure. No organization lacking the features may be registered as a trade union, the same being true also as far as trade union federations and confederations are concerned (members of the latter being trade unions themselves). Provisions of the Trade Union Act are applicable to the said federations and confederations accordingly (Article 38 TUA).

B. Membership Composition

622. Article 1 of the TUA defines trade union as an organization of the working people. It follows from the provision that it is not only employees who have the right to form trade unions and be their members. In fact the principle is carried into effect only in respect of specific groups of 'working people'. According to the literal wording of Article 2 of the TUA, the right to associate in trade unions is granted to employees (within the legal meaning of the word) and to categories of persons employed on other legal grounds enumerated in the provision. The most privileged group are employees who enjoy the rights in question, in general, with some exceptions set out in specific laws. Officers of the state uniformed services referred to in Article 2, i.e., officers of the Police, Border Guards, Prison Service and the State Fire Service may associate, subject to the constraints arising from separate laws. A similar rule applies to employees of the Supreme Chamber of Control. Legal regulations concerning the right to associate of other working people who are not employees are more complex. The TUA grants the right to form and join unions to members of agricultural cooperatives, persons performing work under an agency contract, unless they are employers, and persons performing alternative military service. On the other hand, home workers cannot form unions. They can only join a union operating in the business where they perform their work. The case is similar with pensioners who are entitled to remain members of their trade union and to join the existing trade unions. Unemployed people retain the right of union membership

---

Organizacji Rolniczych (National Union of Farmers, Machinery Rings and Agricultural Organizations), NSZZ Rolników Indywidualnych 'Solidarność' (Independent and Self-Governing Trade Union of Self-Employed Farmers 'Solidarity') and Związek Zawodowy Rolnictwa 'Samoobrona' ('Self-Defence' Farmers' Trade Union).

and may join unions in cases and on the terms defined in the unions' articles. Provisions of the Act concerning employees are applied according to the above-mentioned persons authorized by the law to associate. (Article 2 paragraph 7 TUA).

It is hard to resist the impression that the described regulation bears the traits of a legislative discretion and the criteria for granting the right of association to specific groups of working people or the scope of that freedom are not very transparent. Further-going reservations to the correctness of Article 2 of the TUA in the light of international law and the Constitution of the Republic of Poland were raised in legal doctrine.[381] It should be indicated that, following a complaint by the NSZZ 'Solidarność' on 28 July 2011, the ILO Committee on Freedom of Association questioned the conformity of the above provisions of the TUA to the ILO Conventions 87/1948 and 98/1949, recommending that the provisions should be amended accordingly. The Committee requested the government to take the necessary measures in order to ensure that all workers, without distinction whatsoever, including self-employed workers, home-based workers and those employed under civil law contracts, enjoy the right to establish and join organizations of their own choosing within the meaning of Convention No. 87.[382]

In practice, more important is that in the judgment of 2 June 2015 the Constitutional Tribunal stated that the provisions of the Law on Trade Unions that limit the rights of persons employed outside the employment relationship (persons performing gainful activity) are inconsistent with Article 59(1) in conjunction with Article 12 of the Constitution. The Tribunal ruled on the incompatibility of the statutory regulations on the right to unionize with the Constitution and the ILO Convention No. 87. In view of the Tribunal, the Supreme Law of Poland protects persons who: carry out paid work, remain in the legal relationship with a subject who is a beneficiary of work and have common interests that can be collectively defended. One may conclude then that the constitutional protection refers to all categories of persons who carry out paid occupational activity. As an immediate consequence of the ruling, Polish regulations on the right of association should be amended in order to safeguard the right to set up trade unions to civil law contractors and self-employed persons. As a further result, it is necessary to reconstruct the statutory framework of the right to associate in trade unions as well as other union freedoms.

C. *Special Tasks*

623. The basic task of any trade union is to represent and defend the rights and interests of the working people. It is being stressed that among the tasks of the trade

381. Z. Hajn, *Prawo zrzeszania się w związkach zawodowych - prawo pracowników, czy prawo ludzi pracy?* a paper given in 2010 at an International Conference devoted to the XXX Anniversary of Solidarity Trade Union. For the English version of this paper, *see:* Z. Hajn, 'The Right of Association in Trade Unions – the Right of Employees, or the Right of Working People?', in Stelina, Pisarczyk (eds.), *Studia Iuridica* vol. 60. *Collective Labour Law* (Warsaw, 2015), pp. 107 et seq.

382. *See Reports of the Committee on Freedom of Association. 363rd Report of the Committee on Freedom of Association.* International Labour Office, Geneva 2012, Case no. 2888, paragraphs 1066–1087 (www.ilo.org/gb/WCMS_176577/lang – en/index.htm).

union one of particular importance is the defence of the employee interests, understood as striving to improve working conditions of the people. The defence of rights (viewed as ensuring that employee rights already stemming from legal regulations are observed) is relatively less important as they are protected by the law enforcement bodies (e.g., courts) and the trade union actions in that respect are ones of supplementary nature. The Act also provides the necessary legal basis for trade union participation in company management by stating that the unions participate in the creation of favourable conditions of work, living and leisure (Article 6 TUA). The tasks are further detailed in the by-laws of specific trade unions.

D. Trade Union Self-Governance and Autonomy

624. Self-governance, as the trade union's right to decide, on its own, on the organization's affairs, concerns, in particular, the freedom to establish, by means of trade union by-laws and resolutions, the rules governing the membership and organizational structures of the unions, election of trade union bodies, development of action programmes and conducting of statutory activities (e.g., Articles 9, 10 and 13 TUA). When proclaiming trade union autonomy, the TUA makes reference to the organizations' relationships with the employers, central and local government agencies and other organizations, e.g., political parties (Article 1 part 2 TUA).[383] The autonomy means that the entities in question do not have control of trade union activities. The idea is clearly expressed by Article 4 EOA stating that employer organizations are not allowed to take actions aimed at establishing control over trade unions (Article 4 EOA). Also, the requirement of equal treatment of all trade unions by the state administration, local government and employers (Article 1 part 3 TUA) is expected to secure trade union autonomy.

625. The self-governance is limited, to a certain extent, by the provisions of law protecting democracy within the organizations and the requirement that the trade union should have the bodies prescribed by law: the general meeting (or a meeting of delegates), board and audit committee (Article 11 TUA in conjunction with Article 7 part 2 of the Act on Societies).

E. Voluntary Membership

626. The general feature of Poland's corporate-type legal persons (including – besides trade unions – also societies, cooperatives and bodies of business self-administration) is the voluntary membership in the organizations. The voluntary

383. In its decision of 26 Oct. 1999, II CKN 527/87, the Supreme Court stated that participation of the employer in the proceedings concerning the registration of a workplace trade union organization would contradict the principle of the freedom to form a trade union and the rule of trade union's independence against the employer. The employer is, however, entitled to a claim against a cross-workplace trade union organization for establishing whether he/she is covered by the scope of operation of the organization (judgment of 20 May 2011, II PK 295/10).

trade union membership directly follows from Article 1 TUA and the rule of 'negative' trade union freedom, as expressed in Article 3 of the Act.

F. Internal Democracy

627. The essence of trade union democracy lies in the formalized procedures whereby trade union members may have their say about the decisions of the organization. The measures that serve the objective include: the requirement that member rights and duties should be provided for in trade union by-laws, the principle that trade union bodies are to be elected for a specified term of office, the general meeting of members (or the meeting of delegates) being regarded as the trade union's supreme body, the presumption that it is the general meeting or meeting of delegates that has the powers to adopt resolutions on matters in which the by-laws do not specify the authorized body and the requirement that an internal audit body should be appointed within the organization (Article 11 TUA in conjunction with Article 7 part 2 of the Act on Societies).

628. The prevalent opinion of the judiciary is that claims based on the allegation of a violation of by-laws of associations and other similar unions can be asserted in judicial proceedings.[384] Yet, the issue of the judicial protection of the rights of trade union members is a matter of dispute in the scholarly writing, considering – in particular – the context of trade union autonomy. Neither has the issue been clarified by judicial decisions, owing to the scarcity of actions brought to court in the discussed respect.

G. Formalized Organizational Structure and Durability

629. The formalization of a trade union follows from the provisions of law. It is required by the latter that the organization in question should, *inter alia*, be a legal person and have relevant by-laws, bodies and a system of representation in financial matters. In principle, the organization and system of representation can be freely determined by means of trade union by-laws and resolutions. Nevertheless, as it has already been mentioned, it is a must for a trade union to have a general meeting (or a meeting of delegates), board and a body of audit.

630. Trade union durability is reflected in the union's existence despite changes in the composition of its membership (Article 2 part 1 in conjunction with the Article 7 part 2 of the Act on Societies).

384. *See* Supreme Court resolution of 1 May 2005, III CZP 16/05. The right of appeal to court against disciplinary measures applied to members in associations and similar unions was also confirmed by the Constitutional Tribunal judgment of 6 Nov. 2012, K 21/11.

II. Description and Structures

A. General Remarks

631. The Trade Union Act proclaims that trade union statutes and resolution shall freely specify the organizational structure of trade unions (Article 9 TUA). Both the Act and other provisions of law mention, nonetheless, certain trade union structures, assigning to them specific powers and duties. Vested in particularly numerous rights are the nation-wide intersectoral trade union organizations (umbrella organizations) and workplace organizations. The fact that the powers are assigned by law to trade union structures selected and named in it has a strong impact on the organizational shape of the trade union movement since, without creation of the structures, exercising the powers would be just impossible (*see* §5 below).

632. Three main types of trade union organizations can be distinguished. These are: nationwide intersectoral union organizations, multi-company regional and sector-based union organizations and workplace trade union organizations.[385]

B. Nationwide Intersectoral Union Organizations

633. At the national level there operates a certain number of organizations in which employees of various trades and occupations are associated. They have the nature of trade union associations or nationwide uniform and general unions. Among those, the most important role is played by the organizations of nationwide general representativeness (*see* §3, V, below). Currently, there are three organizations of the kind: *Niezależny Samorządny Związek Zawodowy 'Solidarność'*, in short NSZZ 'Solidarność' (Independent and Self-Governing 'Solidarity' Trade Union); *Ogólnopolskie Porozumienie Związków Zawodowych*, in short OPZZ (All-Polish Alliance of Trade Unions) and *Forum Związków Zawodowych*, in short FZZ (Forum of Trade Unions).

634. NSZZ 'Solidarność' was founded in September 1980 as a result of the workers' protests of August 1980. After the introduction of martial law, the union was banned in 1982. It was registered again in April 1989 following the Round Table negotiations. 'Solidarity' is a uniform and general union with a membership composed of people involved in various occupations. The union is one of a territorial/industrial structure; it is divided into thirty-eight regions and sixteen

385. According to the information furnished by the Department of Social Dialogue and Partnership of the Ministry of Labour and Social Policy, besides the three major central trade union organizations, i.e., NSZZ 'Solidarność', OPZZ and FZZ, in Poland there exist federations (about 300), nationwide trade union organizations (273) and local trade union organizations (ca. 24,000). Independently – with no relations to a large trade union organization and solely at a local level – there operate about 7,000 workplace trade unions, http://www.dialog.gov.pl/czym-jest-dialog-spoleczny/strony-i-instytucje-dialogu-spolecznego/zwiazki-zawodowe/; accessed 18 Jan. 2015.

industrial secretariats composed of a few or more than ten national industrial sections. At the local level there operate almost 12,000 workplace and multi-workplace organizations. In larger work establishments also departmental and sectional organizations are established, their scope of operation covering just some portion of the establishment. Meanwhile, workplace organizations are associated in the regions and national branch sections. By the trade union's own estimates, 'Solidarnośc' has 900,000 members in almost 120,000 workplace organizations mentioned above.[386] Bodies of the trade union include the National Congress of Delegates, meeting – as the general assembly of the union – at least once a year, National Commission operating as the union's management board and National Audit Committee. It is the territorial structures that play a dominant role in the union, whereas the existing regions and old branches get petrified, making it difficult for the trade union to adapt to the socio-economic changes. The dominance of the regions in 'Solidarity' is rooted in the trade union's history since the union was established as a counterweight to the communist party based on the territorial principle. The rule is still well anchored in the trade union's statute giving the regions a distinct advantage over the industries.[387] It is also the regions that are the main beneficiaries of the funds formed from the trade union member dues.

635. OPZZ is a nationwide inter-union organization of a confederate structure, established on 24 November 1984. Member organizations of OPZZ may include nationwide trade unions and trade union associations as well as workplace (multi-workplace) trade union organizations. Associated in OPZZ currently are twelve branches with ninety-nine nationwide trade unions (uniform trade unions and federations) and sixteen *voivodeship* (regional) councils. OPZZ also has internal territorial structures corresponding to the administrative division of the country. These are the said sixteen *voivodeship* (regional) councils and *powiat* (district) councils (240).[388] Registered with the territorial councils are workplace trade unions not being members of any of the trade union federations associated in OPZZ yet willing to be members of the confederation. The decision-making bodies of OPZZ are the Congress and Board (authorized to adopt resolutions between meetings of the Congress). Those sitting on the Board are representatives of the industrial and regional structures of the Confederation. The managing functions are exercised by the Presiding Body and the chairperson/vice-chairpersons of OPZZ. All the bodies are elected for a four-year term of office. By estimates, the total membership of OPZZ includes about 400,000 people.[389]

---

386. *Source*: information furnished by the Department of Social Dialogue and Partnership of the Ministry of Labour and Social Policy, http://www.dialog.gov.pl/czym-jest-dialog-spoleczny/strony-i-instytucje-dialogu-spolecznego/zwiazki-zawodowe/; accessed on 18 Jan. 2015.
387. For instance, out of 101 members of the National Commission, 85 represent regions, and only 16 industries.
388. Source: http://opzz.org.pl/, accessed on 4 Mar. 2011.
389. Source: information furnished by the Department of Social Dialogue and Partnership of the Ministry of Labour and Social Policy, http://www.dialog.gov.pl/czym-jest-dialog-spoleczny/strony-i-instytucje-dialogu-spolecznego/zwiazki-zawodowe/; accessed on 18 Jan. 2015; http://www.dialog.gov.pl/partnerzy/zwiazki, accessed on 23 Feb. 2011.

636. FZZ was registered on 31 January 2002. It was formed as a loose confederation of smaller central union organizations which, due to the adoption of the Act on Tripartite Commission, lost the seats earlier held with the Commission. When explaining the reasons for its emergence, the Confederation pointed out to the politicization of other central union organizations. Associated in FZZ are thirty-five national federations and uniform trade unions. Its membership includes also a certain number of workplace and cross-workplace organizations. The statutory bodies of FZZ are: the Congress, General Board, Presiding Body and National Audit Committee. The bodies are elected for a four-year term of office. The General Board is a supreme body of the Forum between the Congresses. The day-to-day management of FZZ between meetings of the Board is exercised by the Presiding Body, with the President at its head. According to its statements, FZZ counts to about 300,000 members.[390]

C. Supra-Establishment Regional and Sector-Based Organizations

637. Supra-establishment regional and sector-based organizations operate in various cross-sectoral settings and organizational forms. Most frequently they are nationwide industrial trade unions or the unions where employees of specific occupations are associated. There exist roughly 300 nationwide federations and 273 trade unions of an all-Poland outreach.[391] Some of them play a significant role in specific industries or occupational groups. For example, an important and independent role in the educational system is played by *Związek Nauczycielstwa Polskiego* (Polish Teachers' Trade Union), established in 1930, associated with OPZZ, whereas in the healthcare system *Ogólnopolski Związek Zawodowy Lekarzy* (All-Poland Trade Union of Medical Doctors), not related to any confederation, is a vital actor.

D. Workplace Union Organizations

638. Particular significance is attached by the legislator to the workplace trade union organization. An organization like that can take the shape of part of a supra-establishment trade union (e.g., a workplace union organization of NSZZ 'Solidarność') or can operate as an independent trade union, its activities being limited to just a single work establishment (e.g., a trade union associated in OPZZ). It is only through the creation of such an organization that the staff can benefit the workplace-related trade union powers, including the right of collective bargaining (regarding CLAs and company regulations), representation of members in their individual

390. Source: fzz.org.pl; accessed on 6 Apr. 2018.
391. *Source*: information furnished by the Department of Social Dialogue and Partnership of the Ministry of Labour and Social Policy, http://www.dialog.gov.pl/czym-jest-dialog-spoleczny/strony-i-instytucje-dialogu-spolecznego/zwiazki-zawodowe/; accessed on 18 Jan. 2015.

cases, etc. Also, the protection of trade union representatives and support provided for their operation depends on whether the workplace union organization has been established or not.

639. The law does not put any limitation on the number of union organizations operating at one workplace. Nevertheless, there can be only one workplace organization of a specific supra-establishment trade union in a single company.[392] To a certain extent the problems arising from an excessive number of organizations operating at one workplace are wiped out by the legal doctrine of workplace trade union representativeness.

640. The powers of a workplace trade union organization are vested in it only if the number of its members is at least ten. Making trade union activity at a work establishment dependent on a precondition that a formal union organization has to be established there, with at least ten members needed by the organization to have the rights to represent the staff, seems to be one of the reasons why trade unions are scarce in some sectors, the SME sector in particular.[393]

641. The powers of a workplace trade union organization are also enjoyed by a cross-workplace trade union organization made up of at least ten members (Article 34^2 TUA). Covered by the operation of such organizations are work establishments owned by more than a single employer. That very organizational form is successfully applied in case of interrelated work establishments (e.g., companies falling into one group). The solution does not prove workable, though, in case of smaller work establishments where having ten members, employed at the same entity, can be difficult to a single trade union. Obviously, the legislators wrongly assumed that the pattern of a workplace trade union organization could be successfully transferred onto a number of workplace establishments belonging to various employers.

E. Membership

642. As the results of the public opinion poll of 8–14 May 2014 show, trade union membership is declared by about 12% employees. A majority of them are trade union members of NSZZ 'Solidarność' (4%), OPZZ (4%) and *Forum Związków Zawodowych* (2%). Others (2%) are members of trade unions not associated with the above-mentioned central organizations. Of the employed, 39% (5% more than the year before) indicated that in the companies where they worked, trade

392. Resolution of seven judges of the Supreme Court of 24 Apr. 1996, I PZP 38/95.
393. In work establishments with fewer than 50 employees the unionization rate is 5%, in the establishments employing from 50 to 249 people the rate is 18%, whereas in work establishments whose staff exceeds 250 employees the trade union membership rate reaches 31% of those employed. Source: research of December 2008, similar figures resulting from the 2010 research. *See* M. Wenzel *Członkostwo w związkach zawodowych. Naruszenia praw pracowniczych i szara strefa w zatrudnieniu* (Warsaw, CBOS, 2009), pp. 3–5; *Pracujący w gospodarce narodowej w 2010 r.* (Warsaw, Central Statistical Office of Poland, 2011), p. 115.

unions were operating, 17% stating that there was more than one trade union organization. In the work establishments of more than a half of those polled (55%) there were no trade unions at all. The existence of trade unions at work establishments is a phenomenon more frequent in education and science, healthcare and administration, as well as – albeit to a smaller extent – in transport, communications and industry. As a rule, trade unions operate in state-owned enterprises and public institutions, in large work establishments and, only sporadically, can be found in private enterprises with smaller numbers of the staff.[394]

III. Establishment, Dissolution and Transformations of Trade Unions

A. *Establishment*

643. A trade union is formed upon a resolution on its establishment adopted by at least ten eligible persons. The statute is adopted by the persons afterwards. The issues that should be provided for by the statute are detailed in the TUA, leaving the mode of the regulation in the hands of the founders (Article 13), not without certain limitations, though. First, certain mandatory legal solutions have to be observed (concerning, e.g., an indication of the persons authorized, under civil law provisions, to assume obligations on behalf of the organization). A second group of the limitations concerns the issues of internal democracy, the fundamental rules for which have been laid down by the legislator himself in Article 13 TUA. After adoption of the statute, a founding committee of three to seven persons is elected by the founders and the trade union is subject to registration with the National Court Register.[395] Unless the application for the registration has been filed by the founding committee within thirty days of the date on which the trade union was established, the founding resolution becomes invalid. The court of registration verifies the documents attached to the application for compliance of their form and content with the provisions of law. It also checks if the submitted data are true, should grounded doubts in that respect arise.[396] The registration-related proceedings are free of charge (Articles 12–14 TUA). The registration itself entails twofold consequences. First, as of the date of the registration the trade union and its organizational units become vested in legal personality (Article 15 TUA). Second, as the *communis opinio* has it, it is only since that date that the trade union may be active within the sphere of the collective labour law. Until the registration, the founders may only

394. Public Opinion Research Centre (CBOS), *Związki zawodowe i prawa pracownicze* (Trade Unions and Employee Rights), CBOS Communication Research No. 106/2014, Warsaw, July 2014; available at: http://badanie.cbos.pl/details.asp?q=a1&id=5045; for a description of the situation in the preceding years *see:* P. Kikosicki, 'Związki zawodowe w zakładach pracy w Polsce w świetle badań opinii publicznej', in Hajn (ed.), *Związkowe przedstawicielstwo pracowników zakładu pracy* (Warsaw, Lex a Wolters Kluwer Business, 2012), pp. 59–66.

395. The system of registration reflects the desire by the trade unions, which – during the work done on the TUA – opted for it, rejecting the proposal that the foundation of trade unions be based on mere notification.

396. Article 9 part 3 and Art. 23 of the Act of 20 Aug. 1997 on the National Court Register, consolidated text: *Journal of Laws* (2013), item 1203, as amended.

take actions related to the establishment of the organization and preparation of the latter for future operation.[397] The statute of a trade union may be amended in the mode prescribed in it. Amendments to the statute should be immediately notified to the court of registration which verifies them for their compliance with law (Article 16 TUA).

Issues regarding the registration of trade unions (i.e., any cases regarding entries on the fact, amendments to the statute, removal from the statute and making other entries in the register) are considered by courts of law. Appeals against court decisions can be lodged subject to the general rules.

B. Dissolution

644. A trade union terminates its activity following its removal from the register. The removal takes place ex officio or at a request by the trade union:

- where the body indicated in the statute adopts a resolution to dissolve the union;
- where the number of trade union members remains fewer than ten for a period longer than three months;
- in case of the employer's bankruptcy or winding up, if the union operates in a single work establishment (Article 17 TUA).

A separate reason for the removal from the register is the activities of a trade union body contradicting the law (Article 36 TUA). The removal results in the organization being stripped of the legal personality and the capacity to conduct statutory activities. The trade union removed from the register should carry out its liquidation in the mode prescribed in its by-laws.[398]

C. Transformations

645. The law does not provide for trade union transformations. These may only take place under the provisions on the establishment and dissolution of the organizations.[399] It is only the impact which the transformation of a trade union may have on the concluded CLAs that has been provided for in the legislation (Article 241^{19} §1 and Article 241^{29} LC).

397. *See* the Supreme Court judgement of 16 Jan. 1996, I PRN 85/95.
398. For a broader discussion, *see* Z. Hajn, 'Rozwiązanie związku zawodowego i organizacji pracodawców', *Państwo i Prawo*, vol. 10-11 (1995).
399. Supreme Court resolution of 20 Sep. 2005, III SZP 1/05.

IV. Representation of Employees

A. *Individual Cases*

646. In individual cases trade unions represent, in principle, only their members (the specific representation rule). The trade union may, however, at the request of an associated member, take up the defence of his/her rights and interests in dealings with the employer (Article 7 and Article 30 part 1-2^2 TUA). In such an event the defence-undertaking organization is regarded in individual cases as if the person in question were its member. Where the law provides for cooperation between the employer and the workplace trade union organization in individual cases (e.g., under the procedure of employment contract termination with notice), the employer is obliged to cooperate with the union organization representing the employee whether the task has been undertaken by the organization owing to the person's membership with the trade union or at the employee's request to do so. Failure of the employer to follow the cooperation procedure prescribed by law results in the employer's legal transaction being defective (Article 23^2 LC and Article 30 part 1-2^1 TUA).

647. At the consent of the employee or an insured person given in writing, the trade union may also defend his/her rights in the proceedings before common courts as regards cases in the field of labour law and social security. In that respect the union is authorized to file a suit, make an appeal against a decision of a social security body, accede to the proceedings on the side of the employee or the insured in the proceedings that are already pending (Article 462 CPC). A trade union representative may also be an employee's plenipotentiary in labour law and social security cases (Article 465 CPC). A trade union which does not participate in a case is authorized to present a view of importance for the latter (Article 63 CPC).

648. A trade union may also defend the individual rights of the working people in administrative proceedings. As the Code of Administrative Procedure provides, trade unions (similarly to other social organizations) are authorized, whenever it is justified by their statutory objectives and the public interest speaks in favour of such a move, to request that administration proceedings be instituted, the trade union being allowed to participate, and then to take part in the proceedings with the rights of a party.[400] These rights become useful, especially as regards proceedings concerning social security and assistance, medical and rehabilitation services, legal status and rights of the unemployed. The trade union that took part in the administrative proceedings may then lodge a complaint with an administrative court on behalf of the defended person and, if no complaint has been lodged by the union, notify its intention to participate in the case with the rights of a party.[401]

---

400. Article 31 of the Act of 14 Jun. 1960 – the Code of Administrative Proceedings (*Journal of Laws* (2013), item 267, as amended).
401. Article 9, 33 §2 and Art. 50 §1 of the Act of 30 August, 2002 on Proceedings Before the Administrative Courts (*Journal of Laws* (2012), item 270, as amended).

B. Collective Cases

649. As far as collective rights and interest are concerned, Polish law keeps to the legal doctrine of general representation. According to the latter, all employees, regardless of their trade union membership, are represented by trade unions. Consequently, it is also non-unionized employees or ones being members of another trade union that are represented. Whenever a CLA is concluded or a collective dispute conducted by a trade union, the said is done *ex lege*, in the interest of all employees covered by the statutory scope of its operation.

650. Where the same group of employees is represented by more than a single trade union, e.g., where there are more than one trade union operating in the workplace, the trade unions should strive to reconcile their positions and represent the employees jointly (the cooperation principle). If an agreement on the issue has not been reached, the right to represent the employees is transferred onto the representative organizations (the representativeness principle). The legal concept adopted by Polish law is, however, one of non-exclusive representativeness. Considering that, where there exist a number of representative organizations at the workplace, the principle of cooperation takes precedence again. In such a situation, the inability of trade unions to reach a consensus in negotiations aimed at concluding a collective agreement or other collective accord results in a stalemate preventing the conclusion of the instrument in question. The situation looks different where representative organizations are supposed to cooperate in order to express their joint consent to the employer's making of workplace regulations, salary regulations, regulations concerning the company welfare fund, a staff leave planner and certain other matters specified by law (Article 30 part 5 TUA). The employer is authorized to make a discretionary decision if no joint position is presented to him/her/them on the matter within thirty days.

651. The issue is further complicated by the fact that the above-mentioned procedures for resolving conflicts related to the plurality of trade unions are not actually applicable to certain collective employment relationships. In particular, the legal doctrine of representativeness is not applicable in a situation of collective labour disputes. Unless a joint representation has been appointed by trade unions to conduct a collective dispute, the latter is conducted by the organization having started it, even if the organization is not a representative one. If the dispute was instituted by a number of organizations, it is conducted by each of them independently (Article 3 CDSA).

652. In certain collective relationships the right to represent employees is vested, from the very beginning, solely in representative organizations. This holds true, in particular, as far as participation in tripartite institutions and bodies is concerned.

V. Representativeness

653. As indicated above, Polish law keeps to the concept of non-exclusive representativeness, acknowledging the fact that under a specific collective employment relationship a few organizations may be representative at the same time. A weak point of the solution is that, when combined with the rule of general representativeness, it allows a few representative organizations to take actions concerning the same collective issue. As a result, the desired consensus between the organizations lacking, a specific collective action (e.g., concluding a CLAs) will simply not take place.

654. The concept of trade union representativeness has evolved since 1989, i.e., since the date of enactment of the democratic trade union legislation resulting in the gradual formation of the ideas presented further on. Of critical importance in that respect was the introduction of the concept of representativeness into legal provisions concerning CLAs and the Act on Tri-partite Commission on Socio-Economic Issues, replaced by the Social Dialogue Council Act of 2015. It is to the models of representativeness mentioned in the above legislation that legal rules providing for other collective labour law relationships refer.

655. Four levels of trade union representativeness can be distinguished:

(1) Representativeness at the national level, the concept being applicable to tripartite relationships and to collective bargaining on CLAs and other collective accords between the employee and the employer sides of the SDC. Representative at the national level are the organizations representative within the meaning of the Act on Social Dialogue Council (SDCA). These include nationwide trade unions, nationwide associations (federations) of trade unions and nationwide inter-trade union organizations (confederations) of employee membership exceeding 300,000, operating in business entities whose basic object of operation is specified in more than a half of the sections of the Polish Classification of Business Activities (Article 23 SDCA).
(2) Representativeness at the regional level (*voivodeship*, *powiat*) is applicable to tripartite relationships at the level of a region. At this level, considered representative are the organizations which are representative at the national level or their devolved (field) structures.
(3) Representativeness at the supra-establishment level concerns concluding CLAs. Representative at that level are supra-work establishment trade union organizations: (a) representative at the national level or (b) organizations of membership amounting to at least 10% of the total employees covered by the scope of operation of their statutes (not fewer, however, than 10,000 employees) or (c) representing the highest number of the employees for whom a specific CLA is to be concluded (Article 241^{17} LC).
(4) At the workplace level, representative organizations are those meeting the criteria set up in the law concerning workplace CLAs. The said are organizations which represent at least 10% of employees working for a given employer or at least 7% of the employees if they are members of a trade union organization

representative at the national level. Should the criteria be not met by any of the workplace trade union organizations, it is the organization representing the greatest number of employees that is representative (Article 241^{25a} LC). It should be also remembered that a precondition for the organization's capacity to take a position towards the employer on collective issues is to have a membership of at least ten persons (Article 25^1 TUA). The workplace-level representativeness is, thus, based also on the criterion in question.

The national and supra-work establishment representativeness has to be confirmed by a declaration of the Regional Court (*sąd okręgowy*) of Warsaw. In case of a workplace trade union organization a confirmation like that has to be sought if objections, in writing, have been raised by another union organization or the employer. It is, then, the competent district court (*sąd rejonowy*) which is authorized to declare that the organization is representative (Article 241^{25a} §4 and §5 LC).

656. In scholarly writings, doubts are raised concerning the above-described, lenient criteria of representativeness at the workplace level. A question arises if all the organizations meeting them are, in fact, capable of voicing the opinion of the staff.

VI. Statutory Competences

A. *Introduction*

657. A natural criterion for classification of the powers granted to trade unions is spheres of the trade union activity regarding representation and defence of employee rights and interests. Considering that, a distinction needs to be made between the competences related to collective bargaining, resolving of collective disputes and participation in workplace management. These will be discussed in the chapters to follow, whereas the subject of the considerations presented below is, thus, major powers, not described in other parts of this monograph.

B. *Participation in Law-Making*

658. Trade unions and employers' associations representative at the national level have the right to voice opinions on the assumptions for and drafts of legal acts concerning matters falling into the scope of trade union operation.[402] The powers concern the acts of any public agencies and bodies, those enacted by the local government being no exclusion. Some trade unions enjoy exceptional, further-reaching powers in that respect. In particular, governmental implementing regulations (ordinances and orders) for the Teachers' Charter (Act) are subject to consultation with

402. For a broader discussion, *see* G. Goździewicz, 'Rola związków zawodowych w tworzeniu prawa pracy', in Florek (ed.), *Źródła prawa pracy* (Warsaw, Liber, 2000), pp. 23–32 in particular, and the literature cited there.

teachers' trade unions.[403] The trade unions' opinion may be presented, as a rule, within thirty days, although the time may be reduced down to twenty-one days for reasons of important public interest. A rejection of the organization's position needs justification in writing. In case of divergent opinions, the trade union may present its opinion at the meeting of a relevant committee of the Sejm (the lower chamber of Parliament), Senate or a local government assembly. The organizations are also authorized to voice their opinion on consultative documents of the EU, especially as regards White Papers, Green Papers, communications and draft legal acts of the EU, as far tasks of the organizations in question are concerned. Trade unions may also address members of Parliament or the bodies entitled to initiate legislation requesting for the enactment of or amendment to an Act of Parliament or other legal Acts. The agency or body thus approached is obliged to present to the trade union its position, and – in case of the position being negative – also the reasons for it. The enforcement of the powers is secured by relevant procedures and sanctions.[404]

659. A frequently used way whereby trade unions can have an impact on the shape of the law in force is their right to make applications to the Constitutional Tribunal. Considering the political position of the latter, the Tribunal happens to be referred to as the 'negative legislator'. Its powers include ruling on the conformity of a legal act with the Constitution or other overriding legislation (Article 191 part 1 item 4 of the Constitution of the Republic of Poland). Vested in the right to approach the Tribunal are all nationwide trade union organizations, whether enjoying national representativeness or not.[405]

660. A special channel of the impact exerted by trade unions on law-making is tri-partite institutions and general accords (*see* Introduction, Chapter 5, §4, II, C).

C. Impact on Public Opinion

661. Nationwide trade union organizations are guaranteed the right to express their opinions and present their position on key public issues by means of public radio and TV. This is achieved, *inter alia*, by the obligation of the Polish (public) TV and Polish (public) Radio to duly analyse and fairly present the position taken by trade unions on the matters and to develop and broadcast programmes allowing union representatives to voice their opinions. The airtime destined to that purpose

403. Article 4 part 2 of the Act of 26 Jan. 1982 – Teachers' Charter. According to the Constitutional Tribunal judgment of 17 Mar. 1998, U 23/97, the provision does not require that the Minister's ordinance should be enacted jointly with trade unions nor does it make the enactment conditional upon their consent. It does, however, require that consensus, unification or mutual harmonization of standpoints should be sought.

404. Cf. Arts 19, 19(1) and 20 TUA and Art. 16, 16(1) and 16(2) EOA. As far as the standpoint of the Constitutional Tribunal on the violation of the duty to consult pieces of legislation with trade unions, *see*, more broadly, T. Liszcz, 'Zbiorowe prawo pracy przed Trybunałem Konstytucyjnym', in Wypych-Żywicka, Tomaszewska, Stelina (eds.), *Zbiorowe prawo pracy w XXI wieku* (Gdańsk, Fundacja Rozwoju Uniwersytetu Gdańskiego, 2010), pp. 116–122.

405. It is not sufficient for a trade union to declare that it has a nationwide structure but the structure has to actually exist; *see* the decision of the Constitutional Tribunal of 20 Jan. 2003, Tw 58/02.

(as the law provides in detail) is shared by trade unions with representatives of political parties and employer associations.[406]

D. Participation in Control of Working Conditions

662. The control rests with the hands of the state, as the subject responsible for supervision of the working conditions (Article 24 of the Constitution of the Republic of Poland). Delegation of part of the responsibilities to trade unions is a form of their participation in the wielding of relevant powers. The Trade Union Act confirms the right of trade unions to control the observance of legal provisions concerning the interests of employees, retirees, pensioners, the unemployed and their families. The control, in its strict legal meaning (the essence of which lies in the controlled entity's duty to make itself subject to it and allow the relevant body to carry out the control), is exercised by trade unions in compliance with legal rules in force. The available control measures include, in particular:

- guidance of the social labour inspection by the workplace trade union organization;
- cooperation with the SLI as regards control functions of the latter (Article 26 item 4 TUA and Articles 7, 14 part 1 and Article 29 of the SLI Act;
- initiating examinations where there are grounds to suspect that there exist hazards to employees' life or health at the workplace. In case of the request for inspection being rejected by the employer, the necessary examination may be carried out by the workplace trade union organization at the employer's cost unless the labour inspector should find such examination impracticable (Article 29 TUA);
- participation of trade union representatives in control bodies, such as the Labour Protection Board, Supervisory Board of ZUS (the Social Insurance Institution), National Consultative Council for the Handicapped.

E. The Right to Information

663. Under Article 28 TUA, the employer is obliged to provide, at trade union's request, the information needed to carry out trade union activity, that concerning working conditions and rules of remuneration in particular.[407] The provision is one of general nature and supplements the detailed rules on disclosure of the information in specific situations, e.g., in connection with collective redundancies, transfer of undertaking to another employer, hiring of temporary workers and in other circumstances provided for by law. Consequently, Article 28 TUA proves important

406. Article 19 part 4 TUA and Art. 23 of the Broadcasting Act of 29 December, 1992, *Journal of Laws* (2017), item 1414, as amended.

407. Trade unions are, however, not entitled to require from the employer that information about the remuneration of an employee be disclosed to them without the employee's consent being sought; cf. the resolution of seven judges of the Supreme Court of 16 Jul. 1993, I PZP 28/93.

mostly in the situations not covered by specific provisions, e.g., when it comes to the making of company regulations or trade unions taking position in individual cases of the employees.

F. Protection of Trade Union Representatives

664. The performance of trade union functions must not entail negative consequences for the employee (Article 3 TUA), dismissal from work and deterioration of employment conditions in particular. The protection of trade union representatives consists, thus, in the reinforcement of guarantees for their employment stability. In the opinion of the Supreme Court, the function of the guarantees is to defend the collective interests of employees, the individual interest of the protected union activist being a derivative of the protection of the collective one. Consequently, using the protection for personal purposes only would mean an abuse of the rights.[408]

665. According to Article 32 TUA, the protection concerns, in the first turn, members of the board of the workplace trade union's organization or other employees being members of the organization, authorized to represent the organization in its relations with the employer and named in the resolution of the organization's board. As regards the persons, giving a notice to terminate or termination of the contract of employment with them, just like a unilateral change of employment conditions to the employees' disadvantage may only be done at the consent of the board of the workplace trade union organization. The number of activists entitled to the protection depends on whether the organization is representative at the workplace level or not. A representative organization may indicate the representatives in the number not exceeding the number of persons being members of the managerial staff of the work establishment or a number of activists related to the numbers of the organization's membership, calculated following the rules set up by law. The choice of the method for determining the number of the protected activists is left to the decisions of the trade union. Should no representatives, covered by the protection scheme, be named, it is only the president of the organization that is covered. A non-representative organization may indicate only a single activist. The union activists are entitled to the protection for a period specified in the board's resolution and – after the expiry of that period – additionally for the time corresponding to a half of the period, but not longer than a year. Besides the above-mentioned persons, protected are also a maximum three members of the founding committee of the workplace organization named in a resolution of the committee; where no protected members of the committee have been indicated, covered is only the latter's chairperson. The protection lasts for a period of six months from the establishment of the committee. It also extends to the employees elected to perform a trade union function outside of the work establishment and entitled, for that reason, to unpaid leave or time off from work. Such a person is entitled to the protection for the period of the exemption from the obligation to work granted to him/her to perform the function throughout the period in question and for a year after completion of the

408. *See*, for instance, the judgments of 27 Feb. 1997, I PKN 17/97; 9 May 2006, II PK 260/05.

exemption. The protection in question may be precluded or limited in instances indicated by law. Specifically, in case of redundancies for reasons not attributable to employees, trade union activists are protected in conformity with the general rules specified in the Employment Termination Act of 2003 (ETA). The said does not concern only board members sitting on the board of the workplace trade union organization and the organization's members named as those authorized to represent the organization towards the employer; these may be dismissed by the employer only with the board's consent. The employer may, however, give them a notice to terminate the conditions of work and remuneration and pay to them (if the notice entails a reduction in salaries/wages) a compensatory allowance until the end of the protection period (Article 5 part 5 and Article 10 ETA).

G. *Trade Union Facilities*

666. Statutory-based facilities afforded to trade unions include time off granted to trade union representatives for the performance of trade union duties, provision of office space and technical equipment to trade unions by the employer, deduction of trade union dues from the employee's remuneration by the employer and the authorization to conduct business activity by trade unions.

667. Of particular importance is the exemption of trade union representatives from the duty to do work. Each employee has the right to time off from work to perform an ad hoc activity following from his/her trade union function if the activity cannot be undertaken in his/her free time; the employee's work to the salary/wages is in such case retained. The time off from the work is also granted to a member of the board of a workplace trade union organization. Such an exemption from the duty to work is granted at the request of the board, the number of the persons thus exempted and scope of the provided exemption being dependent on the number of members of the organization. If the board requests so, the employer is obliged to pay remuneration to the persons in question. The employee elected to perform trade union function outside of the work establishment has the right to unpaid leave from work.[409] In practice, it is the exemptions from work to perform an ad hoc activity following from the employee's trade union function, the right to remuneration being retained, that give rise to problems most frequently. As regards the matter, it has been explained by the Supreme Court that the exemption is not left to the employer's discretion. The exemption should be granted by the employer if the activity cannot be performed in the employee's free time and is an ad hoc activity or one that must not be postponed and performing it on a specific date is needed for the retaining of rights of the trade union, its members or other persons onto whom trade union protection is extended. Making use of the exemption is,

409. Articles 25 and 31 TUA and the Ordinance of the Council of Ministers of 11 Jun. 1996 on the Mode of Granting Unpaid Leave and Time Off From Work to Employees Elected to Perform Functions in Trade Unions and Rights Enjoyed by the Employees While on Unpaid Leave and Time Off From Work (*Journal of Laws*, 1996), No. 71, item 336).

however, conditioned upon the employer's consent, and a refusal to give such consent is subject to evaluation in the context of all circumstances of the case.[410]

668. Another facilitation consists in the provision of office space and technical equipment at the workplace to the workplace trade union organization. The facility is provided on conditions set up in an agreement between the organization and employer. Disputes, if any, related to the fulfilment of the duty, are subject to resolution by labour courts (Article 33 TUA). Space and equipment can be provided against payment, it being assumed, however, that the payment should be limited to the actual costs borne by the employer.

669. The employer is also obliged by law to deduct trade union dues from the employee remuneration and transfer them to the bank account indicated by the trade union organization (Article 33^1 TUA). The service is provided at the request of the trade union workplace organization, made in writing. The dues are deducted from the employee's remuneration in the amount declared by the person and at his/her consent, given in writing.

670. For the meeting of their statutory tasks, trade unions are also authorized to conduct business activities. The income from such activities is used for the fulfilment of their statutory tasks and must not be distributed among the trade union members. Considering that, the trade union is not allowed to conduct business activities that would serve as a source of income for its members.[411] Trade unions enjoy tax exemptions afforded to associations (Article 24 TUA).

671. Polish law does not provide, *expressis verbis*, for the right of trade union representatives to be present at the workplace. Neither does it expressly grant to them the rights – mentioned in ILO Recommendation 143 concerning Protection and Facilities to be Afforded to Workers' Representatives in the Undertaking – of access to all workplaces in the undertaking where such access is necessary to enable them to carry out their representation functions, access to the management of the undertaking and to management representatives empowered to take decisions, without undue delay or the rights to distribute news sheets, pamphlets, publications and other documents of the union among the workers of the undertaking. It seems that the provisions concerning the workplace trade union organization are based on a tacit assumption that trade unions are obviously entitled to be present at the workplace; just as obvious are the other mentioned rights. There are no signals indicating the existence of practical difficulties in making use of the rights.

672. Specific issues concerning the facilities afforded to activists of the cross-workplace trade union organizations are provided for by Articles 34 and 34^1 TUA.

410. Supreme Court judgments of 6 Jun. 2001, I PKN 460/00 and 18 Feb. 2011, II PK 196/10.
411. Supreme Court judgment of 14 Oct. 1997, II SA 193/97.

§3. Employers' Organizations

I. Notion

673. Provisions concerning the legal status of employers' organizations are analogous, to a high extent, to those concerning the status of trade unions. This holds specifically true about the legal notion of the organizations, their creation, termination of their operations, transformations and, finally, their rights and powers. This having been said, further remarks will be focused on the issues characteristic of the employers' associations.

674. The notion of an employers' organization differs from that of a trade union mostly in that the former – unlike the latter – is an organization representing employers and defending them. Membership of the organizations includes employers in the legal meaning of the word and not heads of work establishments or company managers. Since 2004, Polish employers' organizations may combine the functions of employers' and entrepreneurs' organizations. The amendment actually sanctioned the existing state of affairs, as many organizations had already represented their members in both spheres of interests. Nonetheless, in order to be recognized as an employers' organization, the entity has to embrace, as its members, employers, and represent their employment-related rights and interests. The organizations of entrepreneurs operating as associations or business chambers are not employers' organizations unless they are, at the same time, registered as such.

675. The fundamental task of employers' organizations is to protect the rights and represent the interests (including business interests) of their membership towards trade unions, governmental agencies and local government bodies (Article 5 EOA). The basic objectives and tasks of the organizations, as well as the modes and forms of their fulfilment, should be provided for in the organization's statute. The statutes of employers' organizations reveal the weight attached by the organizations to the services they perform to their members, in the broadly termed sphere of information, consultation and training in particular. A valuable activity of the organizations consists in supporting their members in the establishment of business contacts and exchange of opinions on matters of importance to the circles in question.[412]

II. Description and Structures

676. Polish employers' organizations are highly diversified. They represent their membership at various levels and are organized according to varied principles.

412. Services of the kind are provided for, as a rule, in the statutes of employers' organizations, as published on the websites of specific organizations.

677. Representative at the national level are four, largest, organizations: *Pracodawcy RP* (Employers of Poland),[413] *Polska Konfederacja Pracodawców Prywatnych Lewiatan*, PKPP Lewiatan (Polish Confederation of Private Employers Leviathan), *Związek Pracodawców BCC* (Business Centre Club Employers' Union), *Związek Rzemiosła Polskiego*, ZRP (Polish Craft Alliance).

678. *Pracodawcy RP* is an organization operating as a confederation, with industrial and regional organization and federations as well as single employers associated in it. The confederation was established in 1989. Currently, the organization represents 10,000 firms with total employment of about 5 million.[414] In the past, the confederation used to be considered a representation of the public sector. Today, however, 85% of its members come from the private sector, many of them being former state-owned enterprises, now privatized. Since 1990, the confederation has been representing Polish employers in ILO. It is also a member of the International Organization of Employers in Geneva.

679. *PKPP Lewiatan* is a confederation emerged in 1999 to represent the interests of private employers. It is now comprised of a few tens of federations, industrial and regional associations and twenty-three large enterprises being its direct members. The confederation represents over 3,900 firms, altogether employing more than 750,000 people.[415] It is involved, on a high scale, in expertise-providing activities. The confederation has also made successful applications to the Constitutional Tribunal and it was its efforts that triggered the Tribunal's judgment proclaiming, as non-constitutional, a provision prohibiting the employer to give a notice to terminate a CLA before a new CLA has been concluded. *PKKP Lewiatan* is a member of UNICE and BUSINESSEUROPE and runs an office of its own in Brussels.

680. As regards *Związek Pracodawców BCC*, it should be noted that the Business Centre Club, mentioned in its name, was created in 1991 as a business club taking the form of a company. BCC represents the overall interests of Polish business and offers professional lobbying to its members. It was in 2002 that the *Związek Pracodawców BCC* (Employers' Association BCC) was registered, which gave the organization the legal status of an employers' organization and vested it in the powers enjoyed by such organizations. Not all BCC shareholders are members of the *Związek Pracodawców BCC* but all members of the employers' organization are shareholders of the company. Thanks to the separation of the employers' association from the BCC, it can focus on social issues, leaving the protection of the business interests of its members to the parent company. Since 2002, the employers' organization has participated in the Tri-partite Commission for Socio-Economic

413. Until 2010 operating under the name of *Konfederacja Pracodawców Polskich* (Confederation of Polish Employers).
414. *Source*: http://www.pracodawcyrp.pl/o-nas/misja-i-dzialalnosc/; accessed on 14 Jan. 2015.
415. http://konfederacjalewiatan.pl/o_nas/o-lewiatanie; accessed on 14 Jan. 2015.

Issues (Social Dialogue Council since 2015). BCC has over 2,500 members – entrepreneurs and companies (chiefly private-owned), jointly employing 600,000 people.[416]

Związek Rzemiosła Polskiego, ZRP (Polish Craft Alliance) is a central organization of craftspeople operating since 1933 (and under the current name since 1989). The organization is, for the most part, an organization of the self-government of the crafts. However, it also operates as the employers' organization registered under EOA 1991. The structures of ZRP include regional, local and trade organizations of crafts (28 chambers of crafts, 477 guilds and 180 cooperative societies). Altogether the association embraces about 300,000 micro, small-and medium-sized enterprises. Besides the typical functions of a central organization of employers, training of craftspeople is arranged and supervised by ZRP (currently over 92,000 people are trained at craft enterprises, in more than 100 occupations). Since 1991 ZRP has been a member of the European Association of Craft, Small and Medium-Sized Enterprises (UEAPME) with the registered office in Brussels. As regards the Tri-partite Commission for Socio-Economic Issues, ZRP has been its member since 2001.[417]

681. Besides central organizations, there are numerous trade-based organizations of employers operating at the national or regional level[418] and regional organizations.[419]

III. Establishment, Dissolution and Transformations

682. The creation of employers' organizations, termination of their operation and their transformations are provided for in a manner analogous to those concerning trade unions.

---

416. http://www.bcc.org.pl/About-us-English.4389.0.html; accessed on 14 Jan. 2015.
417. *Source*: http://www.zrp.pl/Onas/OZRP/tabid/249/language/pl-PL/Default.aspx; accessed on 14 Jan. 2015.
418. For instance: *Związek Pracodawców Kolejowych* (Union of Railway Employers), *Federacja Związków Pracodawców Energetyki Polskiej* (Polish Power System Federation of Employers' Organization), Izba Pracodawców Polskich (Chamber of Polish Employers), in which exporters rendering services all over the EU, including temporary work agencies, are associated, *Polska Organizacja Handlu i Dystrybucji* (Polish Commerce and Distribution Organization) – employers' organization for large area shopping centres, *Polska Organizacja Przemysłu i Handlu Naftowego* (Polish Organization of Oil Industry and Trade), *Związek Pracodawców Przemysłu Piwowarskiego w Polsce Browary Polskie* (Union of Brewing Industry Employers Polish Breweries), *Federacja Pracodawców Przemysłu Lekkiego* (Federation of Light Industry Employers), '*Porozumienie Zielonogórskie*' - Federacja Związków Pracodawców Ochrony Zdrowia ('Zielona Góra Alliance' – Federation of Healthcare Employers' Associations).
419. For example, *Federacja Pracodawców Polski Zachodniej* (Employers' Federation of Western Poland), *Gdański Związek Pracodawców* (Gdańsk Employers' Association).

IV. Representation of Employers

683. Unlike a trade union, the employers' organization represents the employers, both in individual and collective cases, under the specific representation scheme. It may thus – with but a few exceptions – represent solely its members, as the Employers' Organization Act does not give the organizations the right to represent the employers *ex lege*. Their right to act on behalf of their members, both in individual and collective matters, has, thus, to be based on either a statute or a specific power of attorney since the organizations are, by nature, the organizations of market competitors voluntarily limiting their freedoms for the sake of their joint actions in the group. In addition, unlike an employee, each employer has a capacity of his/her/their own to act in the collective labour relations. A deviation from the rule of specific representation concerns only tripartite relationships, as provided for by law, and some other relations whereby the employers' organizations participate in public decision-making, such as the right of opining on draft legal acts (Article 16 OEA), in which only representative organizations may take part. It is only such cases that the organizations represent the interests of all employers, as the very essence of representativeness suggests. Similarly, in international relationships, e.g., in the activities undertaken on the forum of International Labour Organization, the employers' organization being a representative of Poland, represents the rights and interests of all Polish employers (Article 20 paragraph 2 EOA).

V. Representativeness

684. At the national level deemed representative are employers' organizations representative within the meaning of the Act on Social Dialogue Council (SDCA). The organizations have to jointly meet the following criteria: (1) their membership has to include the employers that altogether have more than 300,00 employees; (2) the organizations operate on a nationwide scale; (3) in the entities of the national economy, the basic type of operation of which is specified in more than a half of sections of the Polish Classification of Business Activities (Article 24 SDCA).

685. At the regional (province, *powiat*) level deemed to be representative are the organizations that are representative at the national level or their devolved (field) structures. The legal doctrine of representativeness of employers' organizations is applied in tripartite relationships and in the relations concerning their participation in law-making (Article 16–16^2 EOA). It is not applicable to collective bargaining, though, save for the – still hypothetical – situation of the conclusion of supra-work establishment CLAs by the employee and employer sides of the SDC (Article 15 SDCA). Compared to trade unions, the concept of representativeness applied to the employers' organizations has, thus, a much more limited meaning.

VI. Statutory Competences

686. The powers of employers' organizations allowing them to protect the rights and represent the interests of their members will be discussed further on in connection with their participation in collective bargaining on terms and conditions of employment of workers and resolution of collective disputes. Their competences regarding the influence on law-making and public opinion are similar to those enjoyed by trade unions, described above (Article 16–16^2 EOA). It is quite obvious, though, that the employers' organizations are not afforded any facilities similar to those granted to trade unions. The only right of the kind is to reckon the dues paid by members of the employers' organizations towards tax-deductible expenses, up to the amount specified by the ordinance of the Council of Ministers (Article 6 part 2 EOA). The employers' organizations may also run business activities, yet the income derived from them may be only destined to the purposes indicated in their statutes. For unclear reasons the law does not grant employers' organizations the right to appear, on behalf of their members, before common courts in cases in the field of labour law and social security, while such a right is enjoyed by trade unions. That deficiency seems to be merely a result of the legislator's oversight since the organizations are authorized to file a suit on behalf of their members or join the action in the proceedings that are pending in a dispute regarding claims derived from the conducted business activity (Article 61 §3 CPC).

§4. Employee Representatives Appointed Ad Hoc

687. A specific form of employee representation at non-unionized work establishments is employee representatives appointed ad hoc.[420] The main reason for the establishment of such a form of employee representation is to give the employees at a non-unionized place the opportunity to have a say on matters reserved to the competence of trade unions. The ad hoc representatives operate only in cases expressly mentioned in law and only extemporaneously, i.e., in order to perform a specific action indicated in the provisions in question. As the law states, they should be appointed or elected 'in the manner adopted at the employer's'. Representation of that kind is of subsidiary nature since it may exist, as it has already been mentioned, at the work establishments where no trade union is operating and perform certain actions assigned to trade unions. In certain situations the representatives act in a consultative capacity, in other are authorized to conclude collective accords, including those concerning working conditions and remuneration.

688. The ad hoc representatives are to be appointed, *inter alia*, in order to:

420. For a broader discussion, *see* J. Wratny, 'Rady pracowników. Przedstawiciele pracowników powoływani *ad hoc*', in Wratny, Bednarski (eds.), *Związki zawodowe a niezwiązkowe przedstawicielstwa pracownicze w gospodarce posttransformacyjnej* (Warsaw, Instytut Pracy i Spraw Socjalnych, 2010), pp. 129 et seq.; M. Latos-Miłkowska, 'Przedstawiciele pracowników wyłaniani w trybie przyjętym u pracodawcy', *Praca i Zabezpieczenie Społeczne*, vol. 10 (2010), passim.

- conclude an agreement on the suspension of the application of the autonomous labour law provisions;
- conclude an agreement on the application of working conditions less favourable than those stipulated in the contract of employment;
- extend the working time account period up to the maximum time of twelve months;
- introduce the interrupted working time scheme;
- introduce variable hours of starting the work;
- determine by the employer, in consultation with the representatives, a list of types of work particularly hazardous or involving strenuous efforts, concerning night workers;
- consult on the determination of a list of types of work particularly onerous or hazardous to health;
- conclude a company and an inter-company pension agreement;
- agree with the employer on the establishment of a company welfare fund and on the rules for use of the services and allowances financed from the fund;
- determine the company rules for the use of the company rehabilitation fund;
- provide the information and carry out consultations concerning redundancies;
- consult on the establishment of the rules for telework.

689. The above-discussed legislator's concept has been put to criticism in scholarly writings. The mode of appointment of the representatives, hardly clear, gives rise to doubts. The dominating opinion on the issue is that the representatives should, in fact, be elected, given the requirements formulated in Article 3 of ILO Convention 135/1971. A view is also expressed that the representatives are not duly protected and, hence, their autonomy and their capacity to express genuine employee interests can be questioned. Neither are they capable of enforcing the arrangements made by the employer with their participation. And it is also stressed that the expansion of the described form of employee representation (as reflected in the ever wider range of situations to which, through the legislator's will, the representation is applicable, including collective matters of considerable weight) indicates that there exists an urgent need to entrust all the powers in question to a stable, operating as a commonly accepted scheme, non-trade union body representing the staff.

§5. Structure of Interest Representation and the System of Collective Labour Relations

690. As it has already been indicated, the law vests particular rights in nationwide sector organizations and workplace organizations, the fact having a considerable impact on the organizational shape of the trade union movement (*see* §2, II above). The relevant provisions reinforce and perpetuate Poland's bipolar model of the movement, as evolving since the 1980s. Within that model, trade union operation is concentrated at the national and local (work establishment) level, the industrial-based activity being weak. The industry-focused trade union structures get marginalized as a result. As opposed to them, at the supra-work establishment level regional structures with workplace trade union organizations associated in them are ones of greater importance. For instance, Poland's largest central trade union organization, *NSZZ 'Solidarność'*, is based on a regional structure, petrifying the organization adopted by the trade union in order to confront the *voivodeship* (province) communist party committees in the 1980s. Its industrial structures play only a secondary role, have limited powers, are poorly represented in the trade union's central bodies and are underinvested.[421] The general picture does not change radically despite the existence of certain stronger and more active trade unions with memberships based on the industrial or occupational criterion, such as *Związek Nauczycielstwa Polskiego* (Polish Teachers' Trade Union) or *Ogólnopolski Związek Zawodowy Lekarzy* (All-Poland Trade Union of Medical Doctors), capable of taking effective trade-based actions. Considering the said, little role is played in Poland by industrial collective bargaining (*see* Part II, Chapter 3, §1, II). For the same reason, also the employers' sectoral (industry-based) organizations perform mostly coordination and service functions, in practical terms not taking part in collective bargaining. In fact, quite numerous industrial organizations, while registering as employers' organizations, concentrate on business issues. In this conjecture, the main actors of collective labour relations on the employer side are individual employers focusing on relations with trade unions and other employee representatives at their work establishment. Also, the central structures of employers' organizations play a conspicuous role. They defend employers' interests related to hiring employees through the impact exerted on statutory laws and public decision-making and by participation in the tripartite bodies.

421. Two per cent of the resources pooled from member dues are earmarked for the structures, as opposed to the 25% going to the regions. Out of 101 members of the National Commission 85 represent regions, against the mere 16 members representing industries; Resolution No. 5 of XIX All Polish Delegates Convention concerning financial management of the trade union (consolidated text) of 13 Oct. 2005; www.solidarnosc.org.pl/pl/uchwala-finansowa.html; §35 of the Statute of NSZZ '*Solidarność*'.

Chapter 3. Collective Bargaining

§1. General

I. Legal Framework

691. Article 59 part 2 of the Constitution provides that the 'trade unions and employers and their organizations shall have the right to bargain, particularly for the purpose of resolving collective disputes, and to conclude CLAs and other arrangements.' According to the Constitutional Tribunal, from the said Article 59 part 2 there follows, *inter alia,* a requirement to ensure that trade unions and employers' organizations should enjoy: (1) the right to take the initiative for concluding a CLA (CLA); (2) the right to participate in collective bargaining aimed at concluding a CLA; (3) the freedom to make a decision on becoming bound by the negotiated CLA; and (4) a possibly wide scope of freedom in shaping the content of a CLA. The Tribunal has also observed that the provision requires the legislator to recognize the binding force of CLAs concluded by social partners in accordance with the rules set up in law.[422]

692. Meanwhile, Article 59 part 2 of the Constitution should be viewed in conjunction with Article 9 LC. The latter expressly includes provisions of CLAs (just as other collective arrangements, regulations and statutes of employers that set out the rights and obligations of the parties to an employment relationship) into the labour law (§1). Article 9 LC also provides that the above-mentioned rules of the autonomous labour law may not be less favourable for employees than the provisions of the LC and other laws and executive provisions (§2). From Article 18 LC it follows, in addition, that the stipulations in contracts of employment which are less favourable for an employee than the provisions of labour law within the meaning of Article 9 should be regarded as null and void and automatically replaced by the corresponding stipulations of the collective agreement or other labour law Acts. In such a way the binding effect of CLAs and other autonomous legal acts is *expressis verbis* recognized and shaped by the legislator.

II. Existing System of Collective Bargaining; Levels of Negotiation

693. The existing system of collective bargaining has a close link with the structure of representation of collective interests of employees and employers, as described in Part II, Chapter 2, §5. An essential trait of the system is its focus on the workplace level. Bargaining at the supra-workplace level (*rokowania ponadzakładowe*) plays a secondary role in Poland. No information is available on coordination of company-level bargaining in specific industries by industry-based trade

422. Judgment of 23 Sep. 2001, K 22/01.

unions of employers' organizations. According to the information provided by the Ministry of Labour and Social Policy, on 31 December 2012 covered by the supra-workplace CLAs were about 390,000 workers (as opposed to nearly 1 million in 2002). On 15 April 2014 altogether 174 supra-workplace CLAs and 46 accords concerning the application, in whole or in part, of another concluded supra-work establishment CLA were registered.[423]

Covered by supra-company CLAs are, *inter alia*:

– local government workers not being teachers, local government workers of municipal utilities, social assistance workers employed by the local government;
– public sector workers employed in water management entities, military units and state-owned forests;
– workers of power industry, power engineering infrastructure, lignite mines, defence and aviation industry companies, 'Orange Polska SA' and those employed by members of the Construction Development Section of the Chamber of Polish Employers and the employers' organization referred to as Narodowa Kasa Urlopowa (Leave Allowance Union).[424]

The above information, while formally correct, may, however, be misleading. It should be noted that part of the CLAs that officially have the status of company-level CLAs actually provide for working condition in a greater number of work establishments defined as separate social and technical/organizational units. They thus have, in fact, the nature of supra-workplace or even branch agreements.[425]

694. It is also hard to determine precisely the scope of workplace-level bargaining. It is impossible to do so using solely the information on the concluded

423. However, information about notices to terminate or termination of seventy-four CLAs have been filed with the register by parties to the said collective agreements, while twelve collective labour agreements and forty-five accords on the application of another supra-workplace CLA can be deemed dead; no amendments may be made to the latter as the body that signed them on behalf of the employers has lost its powers.

424. *Source*: www.dialog.gov.pl/dialog-krajowy/uklady-zbiorowe-pracy/; accessed on 11 Jan. 2015.

425. Such is, e.g., the nature of company-level agreements at:

– *Zakład Ubezpieczeń Społecznych* (National Social Security Agency) with its 46,000 employees in 43 branches, 212 inspectorates and 70 field offices (information from the ZUS website, http://www.zus.pl/default.asp?p=2&id=2; accessed on 20 Jan. 2015);
– *PKP Polskie Linie Kolejowe SA* (PKP Polish Railway Lines) – 37,611 employees in 2013;
– *Lasy Państwowe* (Polish Forests) company – 470 entities with 24,820 workers in 2012; http://www.sejm.gov.pl/sejm7.nsf/InterpelacjaTresc.xsp?key=63BFB1FC;
– *Poczta Polska SA* (Polish Post Office) – about 80,500 employees, http://www.bankier.pl/wiadomosc/Poczta-Polska-redukuje-zatrudnienie-3149857.html, accessed on 23 Jun. 2014;
– coal mine companies, each of them embracing a few or a dozen or so mines and other sites (e.g., the largest of them, Kompania Węglowa, employed over 53,000 workers in the first half of 2014), as well as workplace CLAs in some other companies of nationwide scope of operation;
– *KGHM Polska Miedź SA* (KGHM Polish Copper) company dealing with copper extraction and processing – 20 entities, 18,000 workers;
– *Skanska SA* – four sites and 7,500 employees.

company-level CLAs, the low number of which has, for years, been indicated in the reports of the General Labour Inspector.[426] Terms and conditions of employment are also provided for in workplace regulations and rules of remuneration. These have to be made at the employers whose staff numbers at least fifty unless the matters covered by such rules and regulations are provided for in a CLA the employees are covered by. The workplace regulations, while providing for work organization and order, specify the rights and duties of the employer and employees related to it, including systems and schedules of working hours and the adopted account periods of the latter (Article 104–104^3 LC). The object of the rules of remuneration is the terms and conditions of remuneration for work and the granting of other work-related benefits (Article 77^2 LC). The rules and regulations can, thus, provide for the most essential terms and conditions of employment, replacing a CLA in that respect; this – in practical terms – happens quite often. Considering complex legal requirements concerning the conclusion and registration of a CLA, the regulations can provide an attractive alternative to the latter, from the perspective of both the employer and trade unions. Some sort of a distribution of matters between a workplace CLA and workplace regulations frequently takes place as well, the CLA providing for remuneration and other work-related benefits, the working time being the subject of the workplace regulations.[427] The employer is obliged to agree to the above-mentioned rules and regulations with the workplace trade union organization, the acts becoming ones that are negotiated on with the trade union. They can be, thus, referred to as the collectively negotiated acts of employers.[428]

695. In addition to the above-said, it is quite common to conclude various kinds of collective accords other than CLAs, the main subject matter of those being the terms and conditions of employment (for a broader discussion, *see*, §5 below).

---

426. Cf. the recent *Report of the General Labour Inspector on the operation of State Labour Inspection in 2013* (Warsaw, 2014), p. 27. As of 31 Dec. 2014 there were 8,173 effective and operating company CLAs and 167 accords on the application of another CLA, covering, in total, about 1,819,000 people (information gained by the author from the spokesperson of the State Labour Inspection on 23 Jan. 2015).

427. As the General Labour Inspector indicated in her report for 2013: 'The subject matter of CLAs included – similarly to the preceding years – mostly the issues of remuneration and other work-related benefits. Matters of OSH, working time or holiday leaves are seldom touched on'; *Report of the General Labour Inspector on the operation of the State Labour Inspection in 2013* (Warsaw, 2014), p. 28.

428. Regulations not agreed on with the trade union organization have no legal value; *see*, for instance, the Supreme Court judgments of: 21 March, 2001, I PKN 320/00; 12 Feb. 2004, I PK 349/03. In cases specified in law, the regulations may, however, be made by the employer acting independently (Art. 104^2 §2 and Art. 30 part 5 TUA). According to certain opinions, the agreed regulations are collective accords or sui generis collective accords. Better grounded seems to be the opinion that the regulations are actually acts of employers, negotiations on the working conditions being part of the mode in which the regulations are developed by the latter.

§2. CLAs

I. Legal Notion

696. The collective labour agreement is usually defined as a normative agreement between the employer or employers' organization and trade union organization(s), determining the terms and conditions, with which the content of employment relationships of the employees covered by the agreement should correspond, mutual obligations of the parties to the agreement as well as other matters that have not been provided for in law in a mandatory (unconditionally binding) way. The definition reflects the most essential trait of the CLA, viz. the fact that it contains what is referred to as normative provisions, i.e., provisions established in the course of bargaining between the trade union and the employer (or employers' organization), setting forth the rules of the behaviour for third parties, recognized by the legislator as labour law provisions (Article 9 §1 LC).

697. The LC makes a distinction between workplace CLAs and CLAs above the work establishment (supra-workplace) level. A special kind of a supra-work establishment CLA is an agreement between the employee and employer sides of the SDC, covering all or a group of employers associated in organizations represented in the Council and employees working for the employers in question (Article 15 of the SDCA).[429] The circle of employees covered by a supra-workplace CLA can be determined under the criterion of industry, occupation, region or other ones accepted by the parties. A company CLA covers the employees of a single work establishment. It can also cover employees of a greater number of work establishments if they are embraced by a single legal person (Article 241^{28} LC).

II. *Personal (Ratione Personae) Scope of Application*

698. By law, a CLA is applicable to all workers of the employers covered by its provisions unless the parties have agreed otherwise (Article 239 §1 LC). Where the parties to a CLA have expressly agreed so, covered by the CLA may also be persons doing work on legal bases other than employment relationship, e.g., under contracts for performance of services, home workers, agents, as well as retirees and pensioners.[430] Covered by CLAs are employees being trade union members and non-unionized workers alike, and it is forbidden to use the so-called differentiating clause that would allow to apply provisions of the CLA only to trade union members or to treat the latter in a preferential way. In 1994, CLAs were extended onto the public service, yet employees belonging to the civil service corps do not fall into

429. No such agreement has been concluded so far.

430. As the annual reports of the General Labour Inspector reveal, in practice the CLAs do not go beyond the regulation of working conditions of employees. A common opinion of the scholars has it that certain benefits can be afforded to persons not being employees. It is, however, a matter of dispute whether their working conditions can be provided for in accordance with the principle of employee's privilege and the principle of the most favourable provision.

the personal scope of CLAs. The agreements are not concluded for employees of state and local/regional offices employed by nomination, appointment or election; judges and public prosecutors neither (Article 239 §1 and §3 LC).[431]

III. Parties

A. *Employers' Side*

699. Vested in the capacity to conclude a workplace CLA are individual employers and employers' organizations as regards a supra-workplace CLA.[432] In the public sector a supra-workplace CLA may be also concluded by agencies of central and local/regional government (i.e., the relevant minister, head of the municipality board or a municipal association, head of a commune, mayor, head of the district (*powiat*) administration – *starosta*, marshall of the *voivodeship* or chairperson of the board of local government association).[433]

700. Authorized to conclude a workplace CLA is the employer (within the meaning of Article 3 LC) or a legal person composed of organizational units (work establishments) being employers (Article 241^{28} LC).

B. *Unions' Side*

701. A workplace CLA is concluded by the workplace or cross-workplace trade union organization, and a supra-workplace CLA – by a supra-workplace trade union organization.[434]

702. Having the ability to be a party to a CLA is, in principle, any trade union organization. Things get complicated, however, when the same group of employees is represented by more than one union organization. In such cases the negotiations are conducted by a joint representation of the authorized trade union organizations

---

431. It is recognized in scholarly writings that the exclusion goes beyond the limits sets by Art. 1 of ILO Convention No. 151 of 27 Jun. 1978 concerning Protection of the Right to Organise and Procedures for Determining Conditions of Employment in the Public Service (ratified by Poland in July, 1982 (*Journal of Laws* (1994), No. 22, item 78) and contradicts Art. 59 parts 2 and 4 of the Constitution of the Republic of Poland.

432. The law limits, however, the capacity of federations and confederations to conclude CLAs, as Art. 241^{14a} §3 of LC reserves that right for an organization with which those employers are directly associated.

433. Article 241^{14} in conjunction with Art. 1 item 1 of the Act of 28 Mar. 2008 Amending the Act on Amendments to Labour Code and Certain Other Acts of Parliament (*Journal of Laws* (2008), No. 86, item 523).

434. The ability to be a party is, in case of trade union federations and confederations, however, subject to considerable limitations set out in Art. 241^{14a} §1 and 2 LC, in the light of which provision a CLA can be concluded, in principle, only by organizations directly representing the associated employees. For criticism of the provision, *see* Z. Hajn, 'Nowa regulacja prawna zdolności układowej związków zawodowych', *Praca i Zabezpieczenie Społeczne*, vol. 4 (2001), 2–3.

or by individual organizations acting jointly. The CLA is concluded by all the organizations involved in the bargaining. The said is not, however, an absolute precondition; it is sufficient for the CLA to be concluded by all representative organizations. A non-representative organization may, thus, not block the bargaining (Article 241^{16} and Article 241^{25} LC). Concluding a CLA may be prevented, though, if not all representative organizations participating in the bargaining have approved it.

IV. Conclusion of CLA and Its Entry into Force

A. Conclusion of a CLA

703. A CLA is reached through bargaining. A party having the capacity to conclude a CLA is not allowed to reject the request of the other party to start the bargaining: (1) in order to conclude a CLA for employees not covered by it; (2) in order to amend a CLA owing to a substantial change in the business or financial situation of the employer or deterioration of financial situation of the employees; (3) where the request was made not earlier than sixty days before the end of the period for which the CLA had been concluded or after the date on which a notice to terminate was given (Article 241^{2} §3 LC). Each of the parties is obliged to conduct the bargaining in good faith, with respect for the legitimate interest of the other party (Article 241^{3} §1 LC). The employer is obliged to provide the trade union(s) with the information about its economic situation as far as the matters covered by the bargaining and necessary to conduct responsible negotiations are concerned. The trade union representatives, in turn, are obliged to keep confidential the obtained information, being business secrets. In the course of the negotiations the parties may agree on the mode of resolution of the disputes connected with the subject matter of the negotiations. The provisions on the resolution of collective disputes are, then, not applicable unless the parties should decide to apply them to a specified extent (Article 241^{3} §2). A CLA is concluded in writing, for a specified or for an indefinite time.

B. Entry into Force

704. A CLA enters into force on the date specified in it but no sooner than as of the date when it is registered (Article 241^{12} §1 LC). Entry into force means that the normative provisions of the agreement become labour law provisions within the meaning of Article 9 §1 LC. The purpose of the registration is to verify the CLA for its compliance with the law. Company CLAs are registered by the regional labour inspector, the supra-workplace ones by the minister of labour. Parties may appeal to court against a decision denying registration (Article 241^{11} LC). The employer is obliged to inform the employees about the entry of the CLA into force, amendments made to it, notice given to terminate the CLA and its dissolution.

705. The most essential consequence of a CLA becoming effective is changes in the content of individual contracts of employment arising from the most favourable provision principle. As soon as the agreement enters into force the more advantageous provision thereof replace, by virtue of law, current stipulations of the contract of employment (or other acts being the basis for the establishment of the employment relationship). The provisions of a CLA being less advantageous to the employees may be introduced by the employer into contracts of employment by a notice to terminate the existing terms and conditions of work or remuneration. Where this is the case, giving such a notice is not subject to any limitations to terminate the terms and conditions of such a contract of employment or other legal instruments upon which the employment relationship is based (Article 241^{13} LC).

C. Agreement on Application of Another CLA

706. A measure being a kind of a substitute to concluding a CLA is signing an agreement on the application of another CLA. Parties capable of concluding a CLA may reach an agreement on the application, in whole or in part, of a CLA to which neither of them is a party. Provisions concerning the CLA shall be applicable to the discussed agreement accordingly. The agreement is autonomous against the original CLA, and amendments to provisions of the CLA do not entail amendments to the agreement concerning its application (Article 241^{10} and Article 251^{6} LC). An opportunity like that is more readily used at the supra-workplace level than that of a workplace.[435]

V. Extended Application of a CLA

707. The application of the whole or part of a supra-workplace CLA may be extended onto employees not covered by any supra-workplace CLA, working for the employers whose business activity is identical or similar to the activity of the employers covered by the CLA. The extension is made by the minister competent for matters of labour, at a joint request by the organization of employers and supra-workplace trade union organizations having concluded the CLA. The extension concerns the application of the CLA (i.e., its normative arrangements). The minister is allowed to perform the extension if an important public interest speaks in favour of it. Prior to the extension the minister is expected to seek the opinion of the employer to be covered by the CLA or the employers' organization indicated by the employer as well as the trade union organization operating at the workplace. The extension stays valid until it is repealed by the minister but no longer than until the employer has been covered by another supra-workplace CLA (Article 241^{18} LC). The above-described option has not, however, been made use of so far.

---

435. As of 15 Apr. 2014 there were registered altogether 174 supra-workplace CLAs and 46 agreements on application of another CLA. As of 31 Dec. 2014 there existed 13,911 registered workplace CLAs and 253 workplace agreements on the application of another CLA (*see* above §1, II).

VI. Contents of a CLA

708. A CLA provides for the terms and conditions of employment relationships, mutual obligations of parties to the agreement and other matters not regulated by provisions of law in a mandatory (unconditionally binding) manner (Article 240 §1 and §2 LC).

709. The Constitution of the Republic of Poland proclaims, in its Article 59, the right of social partners to bargain collectively, without any reservations in that respect. Limitations concerning the content of the concluded CLAs can, however, be imposed by the legislators if found needed for the implementation of other constitutional values.[436] In principle, the LC does not limit the matters that can be provided for by a CLA. An exception is a prohibition to establish – by means of a company CLA – the rules for remuneration of persons managing the work establishment on behalf of the employer (Article 241^{26} §2 LC). Also, freedom of the parties concluding CLAs for employees of budgetary units and local government budgetary undertakings is limited. They can conduct bargaining on the terms and conditions of work and remuneration only within the limits of the financial resources being at their disposal (Article 240 §4 and §5 LC). A CLA may not provide for the matters regulated by the statutory legal provisions of a mandatory nature, e.g., for time-bar of claims arising from the employment relationship. Neither may it disturb the principle of equal treatment in employment, provisions of a CLA violating the rule being null and void (Article 9 §4 LC). In addition, third party rights may not be violated by CLA provisions and, for instance, it may not limit the allowed deduction of maintenance payments from the remuneration for work, amounts of advance payments on account of personal income tax, shareholder rights (Article 240 §3 LC). As mentioned earlier, a CLA may not be less favourable for employees than the provisions of the LC and other laws and secondary legislation are. Few exceptions from that rule can be found in Polish law. Among others, it is allowed by the LC to set up a rule in CLAs providing that part of the remuneration for work would be paid other than in cash (Article 86 §2). Similarly, an annual limit of overtime exceeding 150 hours can be set up by a CLA (Article 151 §4 LC). Another kind of deregulation is the option to depart from the creation of a company welfare fund in the CLA (Article 4 of the Company Welfare Fund Act 1994).

710. In connection with the above-indicated Article 240 §1 and §2 LC, three groups of provisions (often referred to as the three 'parts') of a CLA are distinguished: normative, obligating (defining mutual obligations of the parties) and those forming what is termed the third part of a CLA.

711. The essence of the CLA lies in its normative provisions, setting up terms and conditions of the employment relationship. In practice, the normative part is mostly about employee remuneration. It is, for the most part, the systems of remuneration, remuneration components and their amount, as well as the rules for the assignment and payment of non-obligatory remuneration components and other

436. The Constitutional Tribunal ruling of 18 Nov. 2002, K 37/01, part IV item 1 of the reasons to it.

benefits, such as bonuses, awards, long-service awards, supplementary damages that are subject to regulation. The CLAs also provide, albeit to a lesser extent, for the time off from work, additional guarantees and benefits related to the termination of the employment relationship, additional vacation leaves, etc.[437]

712. In its binding part the CLA provides for mutual obligations of the parties. The obligating provisions concern, first of all, the implementation of the CLA and its observance (Article 240 §1 item 2 LC). The parties may provide for, *inter alia*, the mode of publication of the CLA and the dissemination of its content, the procedure for a periodical evaluation of the CLA, the mode of clarification of the content of the CLA and resolution of disputes in that respect (Article 241^1 LC). The rules and procedures for collective bargaining aimed at making amendments to the CLA can be also provided for, as can be the consequences of a breach of the CLA-contained obligations, including the stipulated penalties, the management of welfare facilities established by the CLA, etc. Certain duties are imposed on the parties, regardless of whether expressly inscribed in the CLA or not. First, it is the duty to observe the provisions of the CLA, following from the very fact that the collective agreement has been concluded. The duty consists in the parties' adherence to the CLA's obligations, the subjects bound by the CLA provisions (the employees and employers) being expected to act accordingly. Second, by virtue of an express legal provision, the parties to the CLA are supposed to adhere to the interpretation to the CLA as made by themselves (Article 241^6 LC) and to maintain social peace. The latter duty consists in a prohibition to initiate and conduct a dispute to amend the CLA before the date of a notice given to terminate it (Article 4 part 2 CDSA). The discussed part of the CLA may also include other provisions adopted by the parties. These do not have to necessarily be related to the operation of the agreement itself but may concern, in particular, mutual relations between the employer and trade unions, e.g., the provision of office space and equipment to the workplace trade union organization, the financing of training courses to the trade union activists by the employer, modes and procedures of cooperation between the employer and the workplace union organization, exchange of information and consultations.

713. The third part of a CLA includes matters not provided for by normative and contractual provisions of the CLA. The provisions may include the employer's labour welfare activities, arrangement of welfare (e.g., a canteen) and cultural facilities at the workplace, the establishment of a company welfare fund (and the amount of the latter) or welfare activities carried out in other forms (Article 4 part 1 of the Workplace Welfare Fund Act 1994). That very part of the CLA also provides for the rules of acceptance of employees to work, terms of improvement of the occupational qualifications of the staff, benefits to the ex-employees and employee families. In addition, the CLA may provide for the rights of the persons not working under the employment relationship (those employed under the contract for performance of services, home workers or agents).

---

437. A more complete overview can be found in *the Annual Reports of the General Labour Inspector*, available also at the website http:///www.bip.gov.pl/.

VII. Amendments to a CLA

714. Amendments to a CLA are made by means of additional protocols to which provisions concerning the CLAs (Article 241^9 §1 LC) are applicable accordingly. This means, *inter alia*, that the protocol whereby the amendments are introduced is made in the mode prescribed for the conclusion of the collective agreement and is also subject to registration. An amendment to the CLA, after the additional protocol has come into effect, exerts the same impact on the content of the concluded employment relationships as the entry into force of the CLA does.

VIII. Suspension of Application of a CLA

715. Parties to the company CLA may also conclude an agreement on the suspension of its application, in whole or in part, for a time not longer than three years. On similar conditions the parties capable of concluding a workplace-level CLA may suspend the application of a supra-workplace CLA to the staff of the work establishment. The agreement on suspension is subject to registration (Article 241^{27} LC). The agreement may be concluded considering the financial standing of the employer. They should be, thus, counted among the agreements aimed at assisting the company to cope with the financial difficulties faced by it.

IX. Termination of a CLA; Completion of a CLA Application

A. Termination

716. A CLA is terminated upon a joint statement of the parties to the CLA, upon the lapse of the notice period or with the expiry of the period for which the CLA was concluded. The notice period for the termination of a CLA is three calendar months unless the parties have provided otherwise in the CLA.

B. Completion of a CLA Application

717. Upon the deletion of a terminated CLA from the register, terms and conditions of employment following from the CLA are applicable until the expiry of the period of notice to terminate the terms and conditions by the employer (Article 241(7) in conjunction with Article 241^{11} $§5^5$ LC). The current provision, which entered into effect at the end of 2002, departing from the principle traditionally adhered to in Polish legislation, means that the terminated collective agreement stays applicable until the conclusion of a new one.[438]

---

438. Departure from the principle results from the judgment of the Constitutional Tribunal of 18 Nov. 2002, K 37/01, given at the request of the *Polska Konfederacja Pracodawców Prywatnych* (Polish Confederation of Private Employers. The Tribunal found the principle incompatible with Art. 59 part 2 of the Constitution of the Republic of Poland, Art. 4 of ILO Convention 98/1949, Art. 6 part

718. The employer may also derogate from the provisions of a CLA, in whole or in part, if the employers' organization(s) or all trade union organizations being parties to a workplace-level or supra-workplace CLA have been dissolved (Article 241^{19} §2 and Article 241^{29} §3 LC). Where a work establishment covered by a CLA has been transferred to another employer, the new employer may derogate from the application of the current CLA within a period of one year from the date of the take-over of the work establishment (Article 241^{8} LC). In neither of the above-indicated situations does the derogation itself from a CLA release the employer automatically from the application of current terms and conditions of contracts of employment to the employees. In order to attain such an effect, the employer has to give individual notices to terminate the terms and conditions of employment to each of the employees.

§3. Other Nominate Normative Collective Accords

I. General Remarks

719. As already mentioned, besides CLAs also other collective accords can be concluded. If these are based on statutory law, provisions of such accords concerning rights and duties of parties to the employment relationship are recognized by the LC as labour law provisions (Article 9 LC). The fact means that, similarly to the CLAs, the accords shape the content of the employment relationships automatically, directly and following the principle of the employee's privilege, a breach of their provisions being equivalent to a breach of substantive law.[439] The accords of the kind are referred to as nominate normative collective accords, not being CLAs.

720. The agreements in question are less formalized than CLAs and need not be registered. A majority of them are, by their very nature, concluded only at the workplace level.[440] A priority to sign such accords is given to the trade union organization, but in some specified cases, there being no trade union, the accords can be also concluded by the ad hoc representatives. The requirements concerning the composition of the trade union side are less complex and easier to meet than the requirements concerning the conclusion of a CLA. Only exceptionally does the law set up increased requirements concerning the cooperation of trade union organizations or their representativeness. The subject matter of the accords is usually limited to the regulation of a specific case or situation indicated in law.

721. It should be noted in passing that almost all the matters provided for by the accords can be regulated by a CLA. The reason for the category of the accords to

2 of the European Social Charter of 1961 and Art. 20 of the Constitution. In the opinion of the Tribunal, it challenged the economic freedom and the dialogue and cooperation of social partners; the latter did not have equal bargaining positions as the trade union side did not bear any risk of a change of the situation caused by the CLA expiry.

439. Cf., for instance, the Supreme Court judgment of 19 Oct. 2010, II PK 96/10.

440. A cross-workplace pension agreement being the only exclusion.

be distinguished in law is to make it easier for the parties to the collective bargaining to provide for terms and conditions of work in special situations in which the application of a formalized CLA would prove difficult, if not impossible.

722. In case of a majority of the collective accords, their legal nature as the 'nominate normative collective accords' does not give rise to doubts. They are undoubtedly based on a piece of legislation clearly indicating the parties to such accords, the subject matter of the arrangements and, occasionally, also a special procedure for their conclusion. Only the qualification of two types of accords (ones of great practical importance, though) stirs discussion and disputes. These are the so-called social packages and the accords ending a collective dispute.

II. Types of Nominate Normative Accords

723. A few categories of the now discussed accords can be distinguished. The first of those are the crisis-driven accords. The category includes the accords concluded to reduce the operating costs of the work establishment at the time of financial hardships. An accord falling into this group is the agreement on the suspension of the application (for a period of up to three years) of labour law provisions (Article 9^1 LC). The suspension may not concern provisions of statutory law (the common sources of law) but only the autonomous provisions of labour law mentioned in Article 9 LC, i.e., collective accords, regulations and statutes providing for the rights and duties of the parties to the employment relationship.[441] An accord on the application of the terms and conditions of employment less favourable than those based on the staff's contracts of employment may be also concluded. The accord may concern only the employers not covered by a CLA or employing fewer than twenty workers (Article 23^{1a} LC). The same category also includes an accord providing for the rules, conditions and length of time off from work or the reduction of the working hours of employees of the enterprise in which a considerable drop in the volume of business occurred.[442]

724. Another group of the accords are the ones concerning flexibilization of the working time. The group includes the accords on the introduction of the interrupted working time (Article 139 §2 LC), extension of the working time reference period (Article 150 §3 in conjunction with Article 129 §2 LC) and the introduction of variable work schedules (Article 150 §3 in conjunction with Article 140^1 LC).

725. A separate group is formed by the accords related to the restructuring of companies, such as those stating the rules for the performance of redundancies

441. For the suspension of a CLA, *see*, §2, VIII above.
442. *See* Art. 4 of the Act of 11 Oct. 2013 on Particular Solutions Related to Protection of Jobs (*Journal of Laws* (2013), item 1291. Within the period indicated in the agreement the workers covered by the exemption from the duty to work or working time reduction receive compensation financed from the resources of the Workers' Wage Guarantee Fund.

(Article 3 ETA, 2003 and the accords concerning terms and conditions of employment of the staff in connection with transfer of the undertaking onto another person (Article 26^1 TUA).

726. Among other nominate normative accords the workplace and cross-workplace pension agreements and the agreements on terms and conditions of telework (Article 67^6 §1 LC) are well worth mentioning.

III. Issues of Difference

727. As already mentioned above, the legal qualification of social packages and the accords ending collective disputes as nominate normative agreements is a controversial issue. In both cases the problem is whether the accords are based on a statute, as required by Article 9 §1 LC to account an agreement to labour law provisions. First of all, the phrase 'based on a statute' is not quite clear. In legal writing and in the judiciary the dominating view is that based on a statute is the agreement that has, at its foundation, a specific legal provision. While, according to certain opinions, it is sufficient for a piece of legislation to name a specific type of the accord, others argue that it should follow from the legislation that the accord is allowed to provide for rights and duties of an employment relationship (terms and conditions of work) in a specified scope. In practice, when assessing specific situations, it is the former opinion that prevails. As the Supreme Court puts it, the notion of an accord being 'based on a statute' should be understood broadly, as an expressed (or lending itself to such interpretation) indication, provided by a piece of legislation, that a collective agreement may be concluded.[443]

728. Social packages are agreements concluded in connection with the privatization of state-owned enterprises, acquisition of the company by a new investor (investors) and the restructuring of companies. By the conclusion of a social agreement, social peace is sought by the employer(s) in the above-mentioned situations. In connection with the said, the main objective of the negotiations is to guarantee jobs and remuneration. Often, particularly in case of privatization-related agreements, attractive privileges are granted to the employees, such as long-term (e.g., ten-year) guarantees of employment.[444] The agreements are frequently signed by trade unions with the potential buyer of the enterprise (an investor or a group of investors) who, even in case of the acquisition of a majority or control block of shares/stock, does not necessarily have to become the employer of the employees represented by the organizations. The Supreme Court acknowledged that deemed to be a party to the privatization-related agreement may be an investor not being the employer but one who, after the purchase of the shares/stock, becomes the parent undertaking of the subsidiary being the actual employer. Meanwhile, in its recent

443. *See*, in particular, the resolution of seven judges of 23 May 2006, III PZP 2/06; judgment of 7 Dec. 2012, II PK 128/12.

444. *See* E. Maniewska, 'Przywileje pracownicze w pakietach socjalnych a Article 8 KP', *Praca i Zabezpieczenie Społeczne*, vol. 4 (2011), 35.

judgments, the Supreme Court departed from the view expressed in some of its earlier decisions in which it had recognized the normative nature of all collective accords specifying the terms and conditions of employment. As a consequence, in recent rulings a general principle has been adopted that terms and conditions should be provided for in CLAs or other nominate normative collective arrangements based on the statues in the above-described broad meaning thereof.[445]

The above-presented standpoint is also adopted as far as the accords ending the collective disputes are viewed by the judiciary (*see* below Chapter 4, §7 II).

445. *See* the rulings cited above.

Chapter 4. Collective Disputes; Strikes and Other Legal Industrial Actions

§1. Notion of Collective Dispute

I. Statutory Regulation

729. The Act of 23 May 1991 on Settlement of Collective Disputes (CDSA) provides that a collective dispute (Polish: *spór zbiorowy*) of employees with the employer(s) may concern terms and conditions of employment, remuneration or social benefits as well trade union freedoms of employees or other groups entitled to form trade unions (Article 1). The main subject matter of a collective dispute is, thus, employee interests reflected in favourable terms and conditions of employment, remuneration or social benefits. Disputes concerning the interests may not be the object of court proceedings. This has been clearly expressed in Article 262 §2 item 1 LC, exempting disputes on the establishment of new terms and conditions of work and remuneration from the jurisdiction of labour courts. Neither is it allowed to conduct a collective dispute in order to support individual employee claims if they may be resolved in the proceedings before the body relevant for settlement of such disputes (Article 4 part 1 CDSA).[446] The provision is also applicable to the situation where a breach of rights that can be pursued before the body resolving individual disputes concerns a greater number of employees. In such a situation no collective dispute is actually present but a series of individual ones.

730. It is essential to observe that according to Article 5 CDSA the concept of a collective dispute is narrowed to denote a dispute with an employer within the meaning of Article 3 LC (*see* above Part I, Chapter 1, §3, I). It is, thus, not allowed to conduct the dispute with public authorities unless they formally operate as an employer. Similarly, it is not a multi-plant company that is a party to the dispute but individual employers within the meaning of Article 3 LC, as identified within its structure. Such a notional limitation of the entity to which employee claims may be directed is criticized in the scholarly writing as moving away from the facts of life. In case of a number of disputes, it closes the door to addressing the claims to the actual employer, e.g., a public body or a company behind the formal employer. The fact that the regulation contradicts the right to strike, in particular, in the light of the decisions of the ILO Committee on Freedom of Association, is also pointed out. In practice, especially in the public or semi-public sectors, such as the education, healthcare system or mining, while disputes are started by trade unions with formal employers, negotiations with the government are demanded by the unions, and it is

446. Nevertheless, the Supreme Court has not precluded recognition for a dispute about granting a time off to an employee for performance of functions at the workplace trade union's board as a collective dispute although found it right to assert the claim for granting such a leave through the judicial system (the labour court); *see* the judgment of 5 Jun. 1996, I PRN 37/96.

with the government that the actual dispute is then carried out.[447] Acts like these are tolerated in order to avoid further exacerbation of social tensions.[448]

731. On the workers' side the scope of the right to conduct a dispute has been set out (in Article 1 CDSA) by the limits of the right to join trade unions. Consequently, the right is a collective right not only of employees but also of other working people. Article 6 of the Act expressly states that its provisions referring to employees are applicable accordingly to other persons entitled to join trade unions.

732. Conflicts which do not fall under the definition of a collective labour dispute but concern collective rights or interests of employees or employers may not qualify as collective disputes. The said include, *inter alia*, disputes going beyond the statutorily determined subject matter of such disputes (demands for changes in the company's management, objections to privatization, change of the owner of the business, restructuring actions and the like) or disputes directed against public authorities (e.g., concerning social security issues). Such disputes can be settled, depending on the matter of the dispute, e.g., through a goodwill mission (*see* below point V in §3), in tripartite bodies, by political means.

733. A collective dispute may involve a single work establishment (a company collective dispute) or a number of those (multi-workplace dispute).

II. Representation of the Parties

734. As regards a collective dispute, the CDSA provides for employee representation by trade unions in a manner different from that concerning the representation under the collective bargaining schemes. In particular, the principle of representativeness is not applicable to collective disputes and if there is more than one trade union organization operating in a work establishment, each of the organizations can represent the interests of all employees. It is true that trade union organizations can appoint a joint representation, but if they fail to do so, the dispute is conducted by

447. For instance, 5,433 collective disputes were notified in 2008 to district labour inspectorates as compared to mere 433 such disputes in the year that followed (2009). The high number of collective disputes in 2008 resulted from the teachers' trade union clashes with the government, the dispute being formally started in each and every school. *Source*: report of the General Labour Inspector for the years 2008 and 2009.

448. *See*, in particular, M. Kurzynoga, *Warunki legalności strajku* (Warsaw, Wolters Kluwer Polska, 2011), pp. 143–147 and 122–127, including the literature and examples cited there. It should be added that in certain cases the demands are addressed directly to the government, not even an appearance of observance of the statutorily prescribed procedure being created. For instance, in a dispute emerged in connection with the plan to close down four mines of *Kompania Wąglowa* (Coal Mine Company) owned by the State Treasury, mining trade unions started a collective dispute and launched strikes directed immediately against the government. The dispute ended with an agreement, signed on 17 Jan. 2015, between the trade unions, government and management boards of Kompania Wąglowa and the companies established to carry out the process of mining industry restructuring.

the organization that has started the dispute whether the organization is representative or not. Where the dispute has been launched by a number of organizations, it is conducted by each of those, separately (Article 3 CDSA).

735. In a collective dispute employees can be represented only by trade unions (Article 2 part 1 CDSA). The rule of exclusive trade union representation holds valid also where the work establishment is non-unionized. In such a situation the collective dispute can be conducted, on behalf of the employees, by the organization to which the employees turned for representation of their collective interests (Article 3 CDSA).

736. The rights and interests of employers in collective disputes can be represented by relevant employer's organizations (Article 2 part 2 CDSA). As regards a company dispute the said means that the employer may act on his/her own or use the services of the organization in which he/she is a member.

III. Notifying the Dispute

737. It is only the employee side that is entitled to start a collective dispute. Neither the employer nor the employer's' organization is entitled to do so. A collective dispute originates on the day when the party representing employees' interests notifies to the employer the demands if the employer has not accepted all the demands within the period specified in the demand, being not shorter than three days. Hence, where the employer has not met the demands within the period in question, the dispute exists not since the date of the refusal but the date in which the demands were produced. The party who initiates the dispute may warn that in case of non-acceptance of the demands, a strike will be declared (Article 7 CDSA).

738. Immediately after the dispute was initiated, the employer is obliged to notify the competent regional labour inspector that a collective dispute has occurred. It is not required to inform the inspector about further course taken by the dispute, e.g., the declaration of strike or the date and way of completion of the dispute. Where, from the notification, it seems that labour law provisions may have been broken by the employer in matters covered by the powers of the SLI, in line with the adopted practice, a control at the work establishment is ordered by that agency, parties to the dispute being informed about its results.[449] It is being claimed that the announcement on the results of the control and application of sanctions, if any, for the ascertained violations of law, contributes to wiping out some part of the disputes.[450] A preventive role of the SLI can be, thus, spoken of. As the practice of the

449. *See*, for instance, *Report of the General Labour Inspector on the operation of the State Labour Inspection in 2013* (Warsaw, 2014), pp. 29–30.

450. There is no official data showing results of this activity. It was estimated that in the range of disputes covered with inspections, it refers to 40% of all union demands and 20%–25% of disputes; K. Kloc, *Labour conflicts and strikes in Poland in the 1990s and methods of solving them*, Paper given at the ILO First Conference of Central and Eastern European Labour Mediators and Arbitrators, 14–21 Jun. 2002, Budapest, unpublished report, p. 10.

operation of the Inspection shows, in situations of conflict trade unions request the agency to carry out control whether the collective dispute has been notified or not.[451]

IV. Social Peace Clause

739. Article 4 part 2 CDSA provides for a ban on the initiation and conducting of a collective dispute over the content of a CLA or other collective accord before the date in which a notice to terminate them was given. The ban is, on the one hand, rather wide, as it goes beyond the prohibition of strike (a no-strike clause) alone but concerns a collective dispute in general. On the other hand, however, it is only the dispute on amendments to the CLA or other collective accord and only between the parties to the agreement that is banned. The ban is of statutory nature and is binding on the parties regardless of their will. As the Supreme Court – the Social Arbitration Committee – has proclaimed, even where the parties to an agreement allow for a possibility to renegotiate the latter, a party requesting such negotiations is not entitled to initiate a collective dispute to that end prior to the date of a notice to terminate or termination of the agreement.[452]

The problem whether the trade union side may commit itself not to launch a strike or not to initiate a collective dispute in cases going beyond the limitations which result from the above-discussed statutory ban remains a matter of controversy. Views concerning the issue are different although the prevailing opinion is that conclusion of such an agreement would be allowed.[453] No opinion on the issue has been voiced by the Supreme Court so far.

§2. Legal Conflicts (Interpretation of the Content of Collective Agreements)

740. Conflicts connected with the interpretation of the content of the CLA or another collective accord may be solved in two ways. The first one is based on explaining doubts by the parties to the agreement. The other one consists in settling a dispute concerning the interpretation of the agreement by a court of law.

741. The right of the parties to explain the content of the agreement is confirmed by the LC stating that in case of any doubt the content of the agreement is explained by the parties together (Article 241^6 of LC). A procedure of an interpretation and resolving a dispute that may arise from it may be defined by the parties

451. *See*, for instance, *Report of General Labour Inspector on the operation of the State Labour Inspection in 2010* (Warsaw, 2011), p. 32.
452. Decision of 26 Jan. 2006, III KAS 1/05.
453. *See*, in particular, L. Florek, *Ustawa i umowa w prawie pracy* (Warsaw, Wolters Kluwer Poland, 2010), pp. 260–262.

in an agreement. Normally, it reduces to setting up a common committee of the parties. The autonomous interpretation is not binding for courts; however, a court should aim at identifying the purpose, will and intentions of the parties to the agreement.[454]

742. In practice, an important way of resolving problems connected with the interpretation of the content of a collective agreement is court proceeding. While trying cases resulting from individual claims, based on normative provisions of the collective agreement, a court, if needed, performs appropriate interpretation of the provisions. The admissibility of settling, before the court, cases connected with the interpretation of provisions defining the mutual duties of the parties to the collective agreement, is controversial. A dominant view is that, save situations clearly indicated by the law, such cases may be resolved only by way of a collective dispute.[455] However, there is a minority opinion that obligations of parties included in a collective agreement are obligations that can be the subject matter of a lawsuit.[456]

§3. Settlement of Collective Disputes by Means of Statutory Procedures

I. Introduction

743. Collective disputes can be resolved by means of procedures stated by the law (statutory procedures) or on the basis of procedures agreed between the sides of the conflict (agreed procedures). The statutory procedures include: negotiations, mediation, arbitration and a goodwill mission.

II. Negotiations

744. Negotiations are based on direct talks and adjustments between the parties, starting immediately after a dispute has been announced. The employer is obliged to enter into negotiations. A refusal to do so may be considered an offence of impeding the start of a legal collective dispute. The negotiations end with the signing of an agreement. In the case where no agreement has reached the parties should draw up a discrepancy record indicating the position of each party (Article 7 of CDSA).

454. The resolution of seven judges of the Supreme Court of 11 Feb. 2004, III PZP 12/03; the judgment of the Supreme Court of 12 May 2004, I PK 339/02.

455. *See*, in particular, the resolution of the Supreme Court of 23 May 2001, III ZP 17/00.

456. For more, *see* Z. Hajn, *Zbiorowe prawo pracy. Zarys system* (Warsaw, Wolters Kluwer, 2013), pp. 161–163. Similar position has been expressed recently in the Supreme Court judgment of 24 Jun. 2015, I PK 250.14. The judgment has started a controversy in the judiciary that ought to be resolved by future developments in the Supreme Court standpoint in the matter.

III. Mediation

745. Mediation is started after finishing negotiations if the union's side upholds its demands. Mediation means resolving a dispute with the participation of an independent third party whose role is to make it easier for the parties to come to an agreement. The parties should, within five days, agree on a mediator. The step not having been made, each of the parties may ask the minister competent for labour issues to appoint a mediator from the list of mediators established by the minister in agreement with the union and employer organizations representative within the meaning of the CDSA. According to a settled practice, the minister does not appoint the mediator against the sides' will. The mediator should be a person that guarantees impartiality. His/her powers are only of advisory nature. The statute indicates, e.g., that the mediator may propose making detailed or additional findings concerning the subject of the dispute, propose arrangement of an expert opinion or changing the date of the start of a strike. It is, however, the parties to the dispute that make a decision on the proposals.

746. If the course of the mediation justifies the belief that it will not lead to settlement of the dispute within the fourteen-day' period from the notification of the demands to the employer, the union organization may organize a warning strike. A warning strike may be organized only once and for a time not longer than two hours (Article 12 of CDSA).

747. A mediation procedure ends with the signing of an agreement or drawing up a discrepancy record. A mediator is entitled to remuneration and refunding of transportation and accommodation costs as agreed in the contract concluded by him/her with the parties to the dispute. The minimum remuneration is fixed by the law, but a higher payment may be agreed in the contract. The costs of mediation are shared equally by the sides unless some other method of sharing is fixed. Exceptionally, the Minister of Labour may cover the costs.

IV. Arbitration

748. Where mediation has been completed, no agreement having been arrived at, the trade union organization or a joint trade union representation conducting the dispute has the right to go on strike. It can, however, submit the dispute to social arbitration instead (Article 16 CDSA). A workplace dispute is considered by the social arbitration committee at a regional court, whereas a multi-company one – by the Social Arbitration Committee of the Supreme Court. The proceedings are initiated at the request filed by the trade union side with the president of the competent court of law. The employer or organization of employers is obliged to submit themselves to arbitration. The panel of arbiters is composed of the chairperson (being a professional judge) and six members appointed by both parties (three by each). The panel should induce the parties to arrive at an agreement. The content of the agreement, concluded before the panel, should be recorded in the minutes of the meetings and confirmed by the signatures of the parties. Should an agreement be not reached, the committee, upon completion of the proceedings, issues their judgment by a majority of votes. The judgment is binding on the parties unless they have decided otherwise prior to submitting the dispute to the committee. Considering the fact, the discussed proceedings are ones of voluntary nature, despite the employer being obliged to join in.

V. Goodwill Mission

749. Parties to the dispute may also resort to a special type of statutory proceedings – a goodwill mission. This procedure is now regulated by the Social Dialogue Council Act, 2015 (CDCA). The goodwill mission scheme was established at the beginning of 2003 by an amendment to the Tripartite Commission Act, 2001, preceding the CDCA. While the main objective of the amendment was to create a statutory instrument for the settlement of disputes not actually falling within the concept of a collective labour dispute as defined in Article 1 of the Collective Disputes Settlement Act (CDSA), the goodwill mission may also serve as a means of resolving disputes within the meaning of the Act,[457] as the category includes social or economic issues giving rise to conflicts between the employers and employees which may be submitted to the mission. Authorized to initiate a goodwill mission is the *voivodeship* (regional) SDC. The council operates at a request by the trade unions, employers' organization, governmental agencies or parties to the conflict presenting to the council, in writing, the conflict-causing issue. Where the council finds it appropriate, the procedure to appoint a person for a goodwill mission is initiated, the person being selected solely from the list of mediators, as mentioned in Article 11 CDSA. The provisions merely state that the person to whom the mission has been entrusted assists the parties in conflict resolution. Decisions as to the time and forms in which the mission is to be carried out and completed are left to the person and parties to the conflict.

750. If the parties to the conflict are willing to accept the services of the person undertaking the goodwill mission they may choose not to initiate the statutory proceedings specified in the CDSA or suspend the pending negotiations/mediation in order to make use of the mission. A goodwill mission may also be carried out parallel to the procedures provided for in the Act. If, however, the dispute cannot be resolved through the mission, legal strikes may not be launched by the trade union without previous negotiations and mediation conducted following the procedure set forth by the CDSA.

457. Out of the total number of fifty-five disputes registered with the Department of Social Dialogue and Partnership of the Ministry of Labour and Social Policy in 2013, five were made subject to a goodwill mission; *see Rozwiązywanie sporów zbiorowych. Informator 2013* (Warsaw, Ministry of Labour and Social Policy, 2014), p. 35.

§4. Agreed Procedures

751. Parties to the collective bargaining (in case of a potential collective dispute), or parties to a collective dispute after the latter has emerged, may set forth, by means of an agreement, procedures of dispute resolution of their own.

If, however, in such a case the dispute cannot be resolved using the agreed procedure, the trade union may not go on strike legally without the required statutory proceedings having been carried out. This is because the legality of a strike is conditional, by Article 17 part 2 CDSA, upon exhausting the opportunities to resolve the dispute by means of negotiations and mediation carried out in the mode prescribed by law. The only departure from the rule has been provided by Article 241^3 §2 LC mentioned above.[458] As per Article 241^3 §2 LC, if an agreement has been concluded determining the mode of resolution of matters of dispute concerning collective bargaining, provisions on collective dispute resolution are not applicable to its parties. The parties may agree, though, that the said provisions will be applied to a specific extent. It is, thus, allowed to the parties to set up rules, establish bodies and a dispute resolution procedure of their own or make use of the provisions of the Collective Disputes Settlement Act instead. Parties to the collective dispute may depart from the application of the amicable solutions provided by the statutory law and replace them with agreed procedures also in the case of disputes not related to collective bargaining.

§5. Strike

I. The Right to Strike

752. The right to strike has been set forth in the Constitution in a manner different from that concerning other trade union freedoms. Whereas the freedom to associate and the right to collective bargaining have been – in principle – modelled as boundless categories, the right to strike is subject to certain limitations. It should be noted, however, that even international law allows the states to limit the right to strike by means of statutory law. In particular, Article 8 of the International Covenant on Economic, Social and Cultural Rights of 1966 obliges its signatories to ensure workers' right to strike subject to execution of the right in conformity with the legislation of a specific country.[459]

753. As the Constitution of the Republic of Poland provides, trade unions are entitled to organize workers' strikes or other forms of protest subject to limitations

458. In scholarly writings it has been proposed to expressly recognize the priority of the agreed procedures and not to make the legality of a strike conditional upon the exhausting of the statutory procedure if the parties have established a procedure of their own. *See*, for instance, Ł. Pisarczyk, 'Pokojowe (ireniczne) metody rozwiązywania sporów zbiorowych', in Baran (ed.) *System prawa pracy. Tom V. Zbiorowe prawo pracy* (Warsaw, Wolters Kluwer, 2014), p. 611.

459. *See* L. Florek, 'Zakres ograniczenia wolności związkowych', *Państwo i Prawo* vol. 12 (2000), 7; for an extensive presentation of opinions of the scholars and judiciary *see* M. Kurzynoga, *Warunki legalności strajku* (Warsaw, Wolters Kluwer Polska, 2011), pp. 24–37.

specified by statute. The scope of the right may only be subject to such statutory limitations as are permissible in accordance with international agreements to which the Republic of Poland is a party. However, for the protection of public interest, statutes may limit or forbid the conduct of strikes by specified categories of employees or in specific fields (Article 59 part 3 and 4 of the Constitution of the Republic of Poland). Any limitation upon the exercise of the right to strike, similar to the limitations concerning the use of other constitutional freedoms and rights, may be imposed, according to Article 31 part of the Constitution, only by statute and only when necessary for the protection of the state or public order or to protect the natural environment, health or public morals or the freedoms and rights of other persons. Such limitations shall not violate the essence of the right to strike, either. In addition, as per Article 233 part 1 and 3 of the Constitution, the right to strike may be limited by statute in times of martial law and states of emergency and natural disasters. It should be added that the Supreme Court has found the right to strike to be one of the fundamental human rights and trade union freedoms. In view of the said, doubts regarding the interpretation of legal regulations concerning strike should – in accordance with the *in dubio pro libertate* principle – be resolved for the sake of, and not against, the freedom of strike.[460]

754. A twofold role is played by the strike-related legislation. First, it limits the freedom to organize strikes in order to protect public interest, the interests of third parties and the employer. Second, it is supposed to protect the participants and organizers of a legal strike or other action of protest against repression.

755. The right to strike is a collective employee right, yet the strike can only be organized by trade unions. An employee solely has the right to participate in it.[461] Participation in a strike is voluntary (Article 18 CDSA). However, the fact that the right to strike is, in its very essence, the right of employees, has a fundamental meaning. A conclusion was drawn from it by the Supreme Court that without the decision of the authorized employees the trade union is not allowed to organize a strike.[462]

756. A kind of a financial guarantee of the right to strike is the trade unions' right to establish and use strike funds. The funds are not liable to seizure (Article 24 CDSA) and, consequently, claims of neither the employer nor persons affected by

460. Judgment of 7 Feb. 2007, I PK 209/06.

461. The opinion prevailing among legal scholars is one supportive to the regulation. It is also being indicated, referring to the conclusions of the European Committee of Social Rights of the Council of Europe, that the ease of trade union formation in Poland makes it possible to state that the reservations regarding the trade union's right to organize a strike do not violate Art. 6 part 4 of the European Social Charter 1961 and Art. 6 part 4 of the Revised European Social Charter 1996 (not ratified by Poland). Moreover, Poland has not included Art. 6 part 4 of the European Social Charter 1961 in the list of provisions it is bound with; *see* the statement of the President of the Republic of Poland to the act of the Charter ratification (*Journal of Laws* (1999), No. 8, item 67, as amended).

462. Judgment of 17 Feb. 2005, II PK 217/04.

the strike can be satisfied from the resources pooled in the fund. The latter is earmarked to finance the measures related to organization of the strike and other actions of protest, including *inter alia*, payment of strike fees.[463]

II. Legal Definition

757. According to Article 17 CDSA a strike is a collective work stoppage by employees for the purpose of settling a dispute concerning interests referred to in Article 1, i.e., those that can be a matter of a collective dispute. On that basis it is acknowledged that a strike is a collective action, consists in work stoppage and its objective is to resolve a collective dispute.

758. The collective nature of a strike is manifested in the simultaneous behaviour of a group of employees aiming at the achievement of a common objective. Provisions of the law do not specify any minimum expected number of participants of the strike. As the Supreme Court has put it, the statutory requirement for a 'collective' work stoppage should be viewed merely as a term expressing opposition to instances of individual behaviour of the employees. It is, thus, not only the simultaneous and agreed work stoppage of the entire staff or the greater part of it that qualifies as a strike but also the work stoppage by 6 employees of a cement factory staff of 1,070 people expressing in such a manner their solidarity protest of clearly specified objectives.[464]

759. The notion of 'work stoppage' is, nonetheless, disputable in itself. Some authors believe that it should mean complete refraining from doing the job. Others claim that qualified as a strike can be also forms of collective action consisting in reduced pace of the work (the go-slow) if the latter is, actually, just pretended.[465] The 'work stoppage' notion has not been, so far, put to interpretation by the Supreme Court.

760. A strike may not have other objectives than the resolution of a collective labour dispute, i.e., a dispute over terms and conditions of work, remuneration or social benefits as well as trade union rights and freedoms.

---

463. In legal writings opinions are voiced, however, that – a clear prohibition lacking – the resources of the fund can be also destined to other statutory objectives of a trade union (e.g., A. M. Świątkowski, M. Wujczyk, 'Polskie regulacje z zakresu rozwiązywania sporów zbiorowych w świetle standardów europejskich na przykładzie prawa do strajku', in: Wypych-Żywicka, Tomaszewska, Stelina (eds.), *Zbiorowe prawo pracy w XXI wieku* (Gdańsk, Fundacja Rozwoju Uniwersytetu Gdańskiego, 2010), p. 288). The view raises doubts, though, as it could lead to the trade union keeping all its financial resources in the strike fund, thus, evading financial liability.
464. Judgment of 27 Nov. 1997, I PKN 393/97/.
465. More broadly, M. Kurzynoga, *Warunki legalności strajku* (Warsaw, Wolters Kluwer Polska, 2011), pp. 53–64.

761. In principle, a strike can be organized to protect the strikers' own interests. A solidarity (sympathy) strike is allowed only to a limited extent. It may be undertaken for the protection of rights and interests of the employees who do not have the right to strike by a trade union operating at another work establishment. The action cannot exceed one half of a working day. The provisions on primary strike apply to this kind of industrial action accordingly (Article 22 CDSA). Support strikes, organized to back up another one, are not allowed by law.[466]

III. Illegal Strike

762. The notion of an illegal strike is one of practical importance. The issue whether the strike was legal or not proves essential when it comes to claiming damages caused by the action, application of sanctions to its participants, organizers or leaders of the strike. Also, maintenance of the rights the employee has as a participant of a strike depends on the latter's legality.

The notion of an illegal strike appears in Article 35 paragraph 3 TUA which provides that the liability for leading an illegal strike is determined by the CDSA. In the light of the latter, an illegal strike is 'one organized contrary to the provisions of this Act' (Article 26 paragraph 2). It is, thus, provisions of law and not of the trade union statute or resolutions that set up a criterion for the assessment of strike legality. Behaviour inconsistent only with the statute of the trade union is, thus not considered to be sufficient grounds for finding a strike illegal. The notion of an illegal strike covers both a strike organized with a minor breach of the law in force and an action violating the fundamental provisions of the law on strikes. The degree to which the strike is illegal (provisions of the law are violated) has an impact on the employee's liability for the organization of and leading a strike action or participation in it.[467] Yet another conclusion following from Article 26 CDSA is that the essence of the illegality of a strike lies in the possibility to attribute unlawful actions to the strike organizer.

763. No specific procedure of making a binding declaration that the strike (planned or being already under way) is legal or illegal has been established by law. Most often, the issue is considered by courts of law, *ex post*, when handling claims of the employees with whom the employment relationships were terminated on the allegation that they organized an illegal strike or participated in it. More seldomly, the ascertainment is made as a prejudicial question in cases concerning the liability for damages of persons having organized the strike or led it. Sporadically, attempts to declare a strike illegal are also made through the filing of a declaratory action.[468]

---

466. In scholarly writings the limitations are viewed as too far-going. It is suggested, in particular, that a sympathy support strike should be allowed in groups of enterprises. More broadly, M. Kurzynoga, *Warunki legalności strajku* (Warsaw, Wolters Kluwer Poland, 2011), pp. 131–138.

467. Supreme Court judgment of 7 Feb. 2007, I PK 209/06.

468. Proposals to establish a special procedure for finding a strike legal are made in scholarly writing. *See*, more broadly, M. Kurzynoga, 'Prawo pracodawcy do wystąpienia z powództwem o ustalenie nielegalności strajku i wnioskiem o zabepieczenie roszczenia w drodze zakazu zorganizowania strajku', *Praca i Zabezpieczenie Społeczne*, vol. 5 (2014), 16.

IV. Procedural Requirements

764. The legality of a strike is conditional upon, first of all, observance of the legal procedure of collective dispute preceding the start of the action. Elements of the procedure include the above-described notification of the dispute, making an attempt to amicably resolve it by means of negotiations and, in case of the latter failing, mediation and appropriate completion of those stages of the dispute by signing an agreement or a discrepancy record.

765. At least five days prior to the start of the strike the trade union organization (or a trade union body leading a multi-workplace dispute) should proclaim it. The said means that the employer and its staff (employers and their staff) should be notified about a definite decision on the organization of the strike on a specified date (Article 20 part 3 CDSA). A warning about the strike, should the employee demands be not met by the employer, may already be included in the notification of the dispute. The action may not, however, start earlier than after fourteen days from the notification of the dispute or before a later date of the strike, fixed at the mediator's request, in accordance with Article 13 part 3 CDSA.

766. A strike in the work establishment may be declared by the trade union organization after winning the approval of the staff expressed in a referendum, provided that at least 50% of the workers employed in the establishment participated in the voting and a majority of them approved the strike. A multi-workplace strike shall be declared by the trade union body indicated in the by-laws after approval by a majority of the voting employees in each establishment in which the strike is to take place was given, provided that in each of the establishments at least 50% of employees participated in the voting (Article 20 CDSA).

767. The mode of holding a referendum is an internal matter of trade unions. The law does not require secret ballot voting. A referendum may not, however, be organized in a way prohibiting the free exercise of will by the employees, e.g., by putting pressure on those voting or falsification of the voting results. A free expression of will by the employees is an essential condition of the legality of the strike, compliance with the condition being amenable to judicial review. A situation in which the employer poses obstacles for the organization of the referendum and exerts pressure on the employees justifies repetition of the voting. And rewarding, by the employer, those not approving the strike means a violation of the right to strike.[469]

469. *See* the Supreme Court judgment of 5 Jul. 2012, I PK 58/12 and the rulings cited in reasons for the judgment.

V. Limitations of the Right to Strike

768. The right to strike is limited, first of all, by the subjective and objective boundaries of a collective dispute. In addition, Article 17 sets up certain rules providing for more specific limitations the right to strike is subject to. First, the only purpose of a strike can be the settling of a dispute (the principle of purpose). Second, a strike is the last resort and may not be declared until all possibilities for settlement of the dispute by means of negotiations and mediation, carried out in accordance with the rules of law, have been exhausted (the ultimate reason /*ultima ratio*/ principle). Without observance of the procedures the strike may only be declared if illegal acts of the employer prevented the application of the procedures or if the employer has terminated the employment contract with the trade union representative responsible for leading the dispute. The ultimate reason principle also implies that during the strike demands not mentioned in the notification of the dispute and not submitted to negotiations and mediation may not be raised; neither can be raised demands in case of which the negotiations or mediation ended with the signing of an agreement. Third, the organizer of the strike should ensure that demands are commensurate with the losses the strike entails (the principle of commensurability). The principle is applicable not only to the losses sustained by third parties but also those suffered by the employer.[470] It is also recognized by the judiciary that the threat to life and health of participants of a hunger strike, should such a method be employed, is a breach of the commensurability principle.[471]

769. More detailed limitations of the right to strike have been established by Article 19 CDSA and provisions contained in other pieces of legislation. The CDSA prohibits any work stoppage, caused by a strike, which affects work-stands, facilities and installations where the interruption of work poses a threat to human lives or health or to the security of the State (Article 19 part 1 CDSA). Article 19 parts 2 and 3 of the said Act provides that prohibited is the organization of strike at the Agency of Internal Security, the Intelligence Agency, Military Counterintelligence Service, Military Intelligence Service, Central Anti-Corruption Bureau, State Protection Service, in units of the Police and Armed Forces of the Republic of Poland, Prison Service, Frontier Guard, National Tax Administration in which the officers of the Customs and Tax Service perform their duties as well as units of the Fire Brigades. In addition, also persons employed in public authorities, governmental and regional administration, courts and public prosecutors offices do not have the right to strike. In legal writings the limitations imposed by Article 19 part 2 and 3 are considered too far-going as they lead, in fact, to a ban on strike in the entire public service.[472] Attempts to determine the scope of the limitations by referring solely to

---

470. For instance, in its judgment of 17 Feb. 2005 II PK 217/04 the Supreme Court stated that a strike, entailing irreparable losses, which was caused by delays in distribution of working shoes and clothing, could be found as contrary to the principle of commensurability of demands.

471. According to the Supreme Court, the threat to human life and health resulting from a hunger strike is – in principle –always non-commensurable with the financial benefits from the potential winning of such a protest; *see*, the judgment of 27 Nov. 1997, I PKN 393/97.

472. For example, A. M. Świątkowski, M. Wujczyk, 'Polskie regulacje z zakresu rozwiązywania sporów zbiorowych w świetle standardów europejskich na przykładzie prawa do strajku', in

Article 19 CDSA may be misleading, though, as the legislation concerning individual groups of employees covered by Article 19 parts 2 and 3 CDSA imposes the ban on strike on narrower groups of employees and officers.[473] The problem of the relation between the provisions in question has not been, hitherto, clarified in legal writing, nor judicature.

770. Assuming that expressed in Article 19 CDSA is the legislator's concern for the provision of what is termed as essential services, it is hard to refrain from commenting that hardly has the issue been regulated properly. In particular, while imposing broad limitations on various types of work and services (aimed at securing uninterrupted operation of those), the Act does not attempt at making the ban precise. No powers in that respect have been granted, in any case, to employers and trade unions.

VI. Protection of Employers' Interests

771. The organizers of strikes are obliged to cooperate with the head of the work establishment to ensure the protection of the establishment's assets and the continued operation of the structures, facilities and installations, the immobilization of which could constitute a threat to human life or health or to the resumption of normal activities of the establishment. The manager of the establishment must not be hampered in the performance of duties and exercising of rights in relation to employees who do not take part in the strike (Article 21 CDSA). The law does not forbid the employment of workers to replace those being on strike. They cannot, however, be replaced with temporary workers.[474]

VII. Legal Situation of Participants, Organizers and Persons Leading the Strike

772. Participation in a strike organized in compliance with law does not constitute a breach of employee's duties and may not result in the employee being held liable. For the time of the strike the employee's duty to do work is, however, suspended, as is the employer's duty to pay the remuneration for work.[475] Other rights following from the employment relationship and the right to social performances

Wypych-Żywicka, Tomaszewska, Stelina (eds.), *Zbiorowe prawo pracy w XXI wieku* (Gdańsk, Fundacja Rozwoju Uniwersytetu Gdańskiego, 2010), pp. 281–284; M. Kurzynoga, *Warunki legalności strajku* (Warsaw, Wolters Kluwer Poland, 2011), pp. 86–90 and the literature cited therein.

473. For example, the Act of 16 Sep. 1982 on Employees of Governmental Offices (consolidated text: *Journal of Laws* (2013), item 269, as amended, extends the ban only on public officials, and not all employees of the offices; the Act of 27 Aug. 2009 on Customs Service (consolidated text: *Journal of Laws* (2013), item 1404, as amended) refers the prohibition to the customs officers alone and not to other persons working for the customs offices. The issue has been provided similarly in other specific pieces of legislation.

474. Article 8 part 2 of the Temporary Workers Employment Act 2003.

475. This is why the employee receiving remuneration in advance must account for the necessity to return it; *see* the judgment of the Supreme Court of 8 Dec. 1994; I PZP 49/94.

are retained by the employee, just as retained are non-proprietary rights, such as the right to demand that the certificate of employment be issued to the employee, or assistance in receipt of social security benefits be rendered to him/her. The time of work stoppage due to strike is reckoned towards the period of employment with the work establishment (Article 23 CDSA).

773. In principle, participation in an illegal strike is a breach of employee duties, the fact justifying the application of disciplinary measures towards the employee, including termination of employment relationship. However, according to the well-established opinion of the Supreme Court, the difference between the legal strike and one departing from the model provided for in the Act is not always clearly marked. The liability for participation in an illegal strike is, thus, contingent upon finding that the employee was aware of participation in an illegal act. Also, the liability of the employees organizing the action is conditional upon proving that they committed a culpable breach of employee duties. It is nevertheless assumed that they should display increased diligence when assessing the conformity of the strike with the law.[476]

774. Relatively little has been done so far to examine the issues of liability for damages related to illegal strikes. The reason is employers seldom deciding to seek the damages. The CDSA does not provide for liability of participants of the illegal strike for the damages caused by them in connection with the strike. Their liability for damages is, thus, assessed under provisions of the LC (Articles 114–122 LC).[477] The CDSA does provide for the strike organizers' liability for damages. As far as the matter is concerned, Article 26 part 3 of the Act states that for the damages caused by a strike or other protest acts organized contrary to the provisions of law the organizer is held liable in accordance with the principles set out in the Civil Code. The compensation can be claimed by the employer or any other person affected by the strike. Deemed to be the organizer can be both a trade union organization and individuals organizing the strike, e.g., members of the strike committee. The liability of the organizations or person may be joint and several. It is a fault-based liability in tort, emerging regardless of the degree of fault and weight of the breach of the law. As the opinions expressed in legal writings have it, the liability is too severe and may prejudice the right to strike. A view is also expressed that where it is an employee that is the organizer of a strike, the liability borne by the person should be based on the milder rules set out in the LC. The Supreme Court has stated, however, that an employee being a member of the body of a trade union organizing a strike should bear liability based on provisions of the Civil Code if he/she obviously violated the law when implementing the body's resolution or if he/she undertook to implement an obviously unlawful resolution of the body.[478] Clarification of the divergences definitely needs time.

---

476. *See*, for instance, the Supreme Court judgments: of 18 Mar. 1992, I PRN 11/92; 27 Nov. 1997, I PKN 393/97; 17 Feb. 2005, II PK 217/04; 7 Feb. 2007, I PK 209/06, I.
477. *See* Supreme Court judgment of 24 Sep. 2013, III PK 90/12.
478. *Ibid.*

775. Leading a strike or other acs of protest organized contrary to provisions of law is a misdemeanour liable to punishment of a fine or restriction of freedom (Article 26 part 2 CDSA). Criminal cases based on such allegations are rare.[479]

§6. Protest Actions Other Than Strikes

776. In the light of Article 59 part 3 of the Constitution of the Republic of Poland a trade union has the right to organize not only workers' strikes but also other forms of protest subject to limitations specified by statute. The limitations are set forth in Article 25 part 1 CDSA. As the provision provides, in order to defend the employee rights and interests which can be the subject matter of a collective dispute, after the attempts to resolve the dispute through negotiations have been exhausted, the application of forms of protest other than a strike is authorized. These must not endanger human lives or health, though, nor involve a work stoppage and the legal order must be respected when exercising them.

777. Compliance with the legal order is of key importance for the admissibility of the above-said other actions of protest. As the common opinion expressed in legal writing has it, the legal order in question should be understood broadly and include all general and individual norms effective in a specific country, the observance and protection of which can be enforced through courts of law or other law-enforcing bodies, duties stemming from the employment relationship not being excluded. Considered illegal will be any action violating the legal order in the above-presented meaning, whereas an illegal strike is only a law-breaking action.

778. The discussed right can be also exercised by people not having the right to strike, including those employed at state authorities, agencies of central and local/regional government, courts of law and public prosecutors' offices, as well as by police officers and officers of similar services. Specific regulations provide, however, that the actions organized by them are authorized, provided that they do not disturb the regular operation of the offices, the fact meaning that they may not, in practical terms, go beyond the expression of the persons' views and demands. Not entitled to actions of protest are officers of militarized services who do not have the right to form trade unions (e.g., officers of the Armed Forces of the Republic of Poland, Agency of Internal Security, Intelligence Agency, Central Anti-Corruption Bureau).

779. Qualifying specific actions to other forms of the actions of protest within the meaning of Article 25 part 1 CDSA is, however, not without controversy in legal

479. *See*, for instance, the situation described in the reasons to the judgment of 17 Feb. 2005, II PK 217/04. Issues of the liability are discussed more broadly by L. Pawlak, *Przestępstwa i wykroczenia przeciwko indywidualnym i zbiorowym prawom pracowników. Wykorzystanie metody karnej dla ochrony dóbr indywidualnego i zbiorowego prawa pracy* (Warsaw, Oficyna Prawa Polskiego, 2010), pp. 258–260.

writing.[480] Despite the rather frequent application of such protests in practice, in reality there are no judicial decisions that would clarify the emerging doubts.

780. There is no doubt that actions of that type include demonstration, rallies and marches and protest meetings, held in compliance with the administrative regulations concerning public meetings. Counted among the actions are also: peaceful picketing, leaflet dissemination and badge-wearing by protesters. On the other hand, blockades of public roads and railway lines, border crossings, occupation of public buildings and facilities are deemed to disturb the legal order.[481]

781. Doubts keep lingering about the compliance of actions infringing the employer's property with the legal order (flags or posters placed around the work establishment, signs on the employer-owned vehicles or occupation of the establishment premises). Also controversial is the nature of actions leading to work stoppage (such as coordinated taking sick leave and vacation leave on demand) or of nature similar to work stoppage (e.g., the go-slow strike or the so-called work to rule).[482]

782. The actions in question may be organized instead of a strike but can also precede or accompany the latter; seeking approval of the employees for the organization of those (by means of a referendum) is not required.

783. Participation in a legal action of protest may not be the base of employee liability. As regards labour law-based civil and criminal liability of the participant, organizers and leaders of an illegal action are analogous to that concerning an illegal strike.

§7. Lockout

784. Polish law does not provide for the right to lockout. There is no official data concerning lockouts. It can be claimed that they almost do not occur in practice. Neither there exist any published judicial decisions concerning the issue. Given, however, the poor knowledge about lockout among the public, events of such nature may not even be recognized and qualified as such.[483]

480. For a broader discussion, *see*, e.g. B. Cudowski, 'Pozastrajkowe środki prowadzenia sporów zbiorowych', *Monitor Prawa Pracy*, vol. 4 (2009).

481. Cf. W. Kulesza, *Demonstracja. Blokada. Strajk (Granice wolności zgromadzeń i strajku w polskim prawie karnym na tle prawa niemieckiego)* (Łódź, Wydawnictwo Uniwersytetu Łódzkiego, 1991), pp. 115–143.

482. More broadly discussed by Z. Hajn, *Zbiorowe prawo pracy. Zarys system (*Warsaw, Wolters Kluwer, 2013), pp. 197–198.

483. For example, in 2008, the governor of the Mazowieckie Voivodeship (Province) deleted two wards of the Voivodeship Specialist Hospital in Radom from the register of healthcare centres since they stopped operation without the governor's consent and did not admit new patients. The reason for the decision was the medical doctors' refusal to accept the opt-out clauses and work more than forty-eight hours a week. The decision resulted in an agreement signed with the manager, under which agreement the doctors consented to signing the clauses in question. *See* Z.

785. The view prevailing among legal scholars is that lockouts have foundations in international law[484] and the rule of equal treatment of social partners, which facts considered its application by employers should not be banned. Given lack of legal clarity it is, however, doubtful whether the lockout scheme could, in fact, be exercised. Especially difficult to assess are legal consequences of a lockout in the light of the employer's duty to pay remuneration to the employee who is ready for work, yet cannot do it for reasons attributable to the employer. These reasons considered, it is suggested that clear provisions concerning the proclamation of lockout and the status of the employees affected by it should be enacted. Admitting defensive lockouts is, in particular, postulated.

§8. Completion of a Collective Dispute

I. Ways of Completion of a Collective Dispute

786. A collective dispute is completed by an agreement between the parties or an arbitration decision binding on them. A dispute can also be completed as a result of the trade union side having renounced their demands. Viewed as having the same effect is the actual stoppage of the dispute when trade union demands have become obsolete.

II. Agreement Ending a Collective Dispute

787. An agreement to complete a collective dispute may be concluded at any time during the dispute. Depending on the subject matter it can concern terms and conditions of employment or other issues, e.g., the rights of the trade union organization. In the latter case the agreement is only of an obligating nature. As opposed to it, the agreements on terms and conditions of employment have, according to the view dominating in legal writing and judicial decisions, the nature of a nominate normative agreement.[485]

Dąbrowska, I. Dudzik, 'Protestujący lekarze zostali bez pracy' (Protest-Holding Doctors Lost Their Jobs), *Dziennik Gazeta Prawna* (21 Mar. 2008), 1.

484. To justify the view, the following provisions are usually indicated to: Art. 3 of ILO Convention 87/1948, §7 of ILO Recommendation 92/1951 concerning Voluntary Conciliation and Arbitration Recommendation, Art. 153 part 5 of the Treaty on the Functioning of the European Union and Art. 6 part 4 of the European Social Charter 1961, not included by Poland, however, in the list of legal provisions binding on it.

485. *See* the recent Supreme Court judgment of 8 Jul. 2014, I PK 312/13. The standpoint is, however, contested by part of the legal scholars supporting the view that existence of a separate category of agreements ending a collective dispute, based on a statute within the meaning of Art. 9 part 1 LC, cannot be talked of. They bear such a nature only if concluded in the mode and in the form of an agreement being a labour law source (e.g., in the shape of an agreement providing for the rules of conducting mass redundancies). In other cases they are agreements requiring that the dispute-ending arrangements should be entered in a CLA, workplace regulations or contracts of employment (*see* M. J. Zieliński, 'Glosa do wyroku Sądu Najwyższego z 8 lipca 2014 (I PK

III. The Arbitration Award

788. The award of a social arbitration committee ends a collective dispute since it has a binding nature. As it was pointed out above, the award bears such a nature if the parties, prior to submitting the dispute to arbitration, have agreed so. Where the dispute was submitted to arbitration on the understanding that the award would not be binding, the dispute may be continued.

789. The prevailing opinion expressed in legal writing is that the arbitral awards are not labour law provisions within the meaning of Article 9 LC. The award should, thus, be implemented through the conclusion of or amendment to a CLA or other collective accords or via the issue of company regulations. It is also acknowledged that where a binding accord has not been implemented by the employer, the trade union side is authorized to organize a strike or other action of protest with no need to follow the normally required procedure of a collective dispute.

312.2013) dotyczącego charakteru normatywnego tzw. porozumień strajkowych i postrajkowych', *Praca i Zabezpieczenie Społeczne*, 12 (2014), 35 and the views quoted therein.

Chapter 5. Participation of Employees in Workplace Management

§1. Legal Basis

790. Unlike the right to collective bargaining and strike, which the Constitution of Poland counts among the 'freedoms and rights of the human and citizen' (Chapter II), the right of employees to participate in workplace management has been omitted from the Constitution. The participation in management was, however, included, by an Act of 1996 amending the LC, into fundamental principles of labour law. According to Article 18^2 LC, employees participate in the management of the workplace to the extent and on principles provided for in separate regulations. As seen above, the content of the provision points to the specific nature of the rule in question. The participation, unlike the right of trade unions to collective bargaining, is not based on a presumption of the right of employee representatives to act in that respect but has to be derived, in each and every case, from the authorization following from provisions of law. The pattern followed by Polish law is, thus, exactly the same as that adopted by the law of the EU and international law, limiting the right of employees to participate in workplace management to instances indicated in law.[486]

791. The rights of employees to participate in workplace management may be also based on the employer's consent expressed unilaterally or (the solution having a greater weight in practice) in a collective agreement.[487] Collective accords also play an essential role in determining the scope and way of implementation of employee participation rights. A good example is the agreements of employee councils with employers on the rules for information and consultation and agreements governing the establishment and operation of employee representatives in Community-scale undertakings. The agreements do not, however, alter the general rule that the scope of employee participation in management is determined by law or the employer's consent.

---

486. *See*, in particular, Art. 27 of the Charter of Fundamental Rights of the European Union and Arts 21 and 22 of the European Social Charter (revised).
487. For instance, in the accord of 19 Jul. 2007, concluded with trade unions operating in ENERGA SA Group, the employers of the Group undertook to seek agreement with trade unions on all restructuring processes essential from the staff's point of view. When resolving a dispute concerning the obligation, the Social Arbitration Committee at the Supreme Court stated, among others, that restructuring is, in principle, a matter of corporate management, yet the shareholders can 'share' whatever lies in their competences. Consequently, once they undertook to seek an agreement on restructuring-related issues with their partner of collective bargaining, they should meet the obligation with due diligence and do whatever is possible to actually arrive at an agreement (Judgment of 21 Oct. 2008. III KAS 2/08).

792. According to Article 18^3 LC employers and governmental agencies are expected to create conditions for the employees to exercise their rights of participation in workplace management. The rule serves mostly as guidance for the interpretation of detailed provisions specifying employers' obligations in the discussed field of collective labour relations, especially those concerning facilitation of activities of employee representatives.

793. Participation of employees in workplace management has a long history in Poland and can be traced back to pre-war times. Regulating that sphere of collective labour relations was, however, started only after World War II.[488] Few pieces of law enacted before 1989, the year ending the period of the communist regime, have remained in force to date, however.[489] A legacy of that period is the substantial powers of trade unions in workplace management, taken over, from earlier pieces of legislation, by the Trade Union Act of 1991.

794. The provisions enacted since the beginning of the 1990s gradually, and parallel to privatization of the economy, deviated from the previous model of employee participation existing in state-owned enterprises, based on the staff powers of co-determination exercised through a referendum or via employee representatives (workers' councils) in many fields of enterprise operations, towards participation based mostly on the right to information and consultation. Also, the model of information and consultation itself has been changed, to a considerable extent, due to the need to align Polish law with the EU standards. It is true that the previous regulations established relatively wide employer obligations concerning information, but the duties were ones of responsive nature; they were met in reaction to the requests made by employee representatives. In principle, neither were determined procedures for meeting the duties nor sanctions for a failure to fulfil them.[490] As opposed to such a scheme, under the information and consultation standards imposed by EU directives, the management of undertakings and establishments is supposed to provide information specified by law to employee representatives following a prescribed procedure and in due time. Particularly important in that respect is the fact that the employer's duty to provide information has been designed not only as an obligation to do so at the request by employees' representatives but also, and in particular, as a legal duty to provide the information without such a request 'in the situation of anticipated changes or contemplated actions'. This is essential since it is the employer, as the person or entity running the enterprise and taking initiative in employment relationships, that has information about the issues, the very existence of which may be completely unknown to the employees and their representatives. Also important is the weight attached by the Community law to the relevant protection of those interests of employers which are related to the confidentiality of information. The above-described standards of information and consultation have

488. *See* the Decree of 6 Feb. 1945 on Establishment of Works Councils.
489. The most important of those is the Act of 1983 on Social Labour Inspection.
490. The regulations have been described by M. Smusz-Kulesza, *Zbiorowe prawo do informacji* (Warsaw, Wolters Kluwer, 2012), pp. 54–61.

been introduced to Polish law following the patterns set up in the directives concerning collective redundancies, transfer of undertaking onto a new employer, safety and health of workers, informing and consulting employees, as well as directives concerning participation in (transnational) Community-scale undertakings.

795. It is believed that, unlike in the case of collective bargaining with its inherent conflict of interest and collective dispute, the employee participation in management is based on the recognition of common interests whereby labour and capital are united in the work establishment. The thought was expressed, *inter alia*, by the Constitutional Tribunal stating that the procedure of informing employees and consulting with them specified matters concerning the employer, as provided for in the Act of 7 April 2006 on Informing and Consulting Employees, is a manifestation of employee participation being an essential component of cooperation between the 'labour and capital' and constructing of the social order.[491]

§2. Scope of Participation

796. Employee participation in management within the meaning of Article 18(2) LC concerns managerial decisions made both in business- and labour-related matters. The former category includes decisions regarding, e.g., the restructuring, reduction or suspension of operations, change in the business profile, transfer of the undertaking or work establishment. Covered by the latter category are decisions on personal and social matters or issues of occupational safety and health, such as dismissals and promotions, recreation, canteens, loans granted for social and housing purposes. Participation of employees' representatives in management concerns not only those employer's decisions which affect the staff as a whole but also decisions in individual matters, e.g., acceptance for work or termination of an employment relationship.

797. Article 18^2 LC provides generally for participation in workplace management. The participation refers, thus, both to decisions of the employer and decisions of the management of the undertaking or a group of undertakings to which the work establishment is a member, if they affect the latter. Certain pieces of legislation go beyond the limits of that – otherwise broad – concept and allow the employees to have a say in the management of larger organizational structures (the said undertakings or groups of those) to which the work establishment belongs. This holds true, in particular, as regards transnational undertakings or groups of those, operating in more than one EU Member State.

491. Judgment of 1 Jul. 2008, K 23/07.

§3. EMPLOYEE REPRESENTATION IN MANAGEMENT OF NATIONAL WORK ESTABLISHMENTS

I. Introductory Remarks

798. The representation of employees in managing work establishments and undertakings operating in Poland is multi-channelled in nature. In the first place, the functioning of trade unions has to be stressed, with their structures, based at work establishments, playing the main role in that respect. The role of employee councils is also seen by the law as important, the bodies having been established especially to perform the functions determined in Directive 2002/14 EC. In the companies emerged from the commercialization and privatization of state-owned enterprises the employees are entitled to elect part of the composition of the entities' bodies. In all work establishments the employees have the right to information and consultation on matters of occupational safety and health, which the functions – in larger of work establishments – are performed via their representatives or special OSH committees.

799. All the above-indicated representations may operate side by side, the scope of their responsibilities not always being separable. Considering that, the employer may be obliged to cooperate, on the same matters, with a few employee representations, the case being, in particular, the cooperation with the trade union organization(s) and the employee council.

II. Work Establishment Trade Union Organization

800. Work establishment trade union organizations cooperate with the employers in making essential managerial decisions concerning both individual and collective matters. The TUA offers to the organization a unique responsibility, not conferred onto any other employee representation, to control the observance of labour law provisions at work establishment, the OSH-related provisions in particular. In order to perform the function effectively, the trade union organization may appoint social labour inspection at the work establishment, guide its activities and cooperate with the SLI (Article 26 TUA) (*see* §3, V below).

801. As stated above, a characteristic trait of Poland's legislation is that the work establishment trade union organization is vested in the right to represent the employee in the course of individual personal decisions being made by the employer, as regards both members of the organization and non-union employees if they requested the organization to do so. In accordance with Article 23^2 LC, the employer is obliged to cooperate with the trade union organization representing the employee in individual matters specified by law. Among other things, the employer has to:

– seek the opinion of the trade union organization prior to giving a notice to terminate or terminating an employment relationship concluded for an indefinite

period without notice; prior to giving an employee a notice to change his or her terms and conditions of employment or pay; prior to making a decision regarding the objection raised by an employee against the penalty for the breach of work order or determining the amount of compensation from the employee for a damage done to the employer in certain cases mentioned in law;
- seek, in cases mentioned in law, consent of the organization for giving a notice to terminate or termination without notice of an employment relationship with an employee enjoying particular protection or for granting to an employee a benefit from the company welfare fund.

802. The rights to influence decisions of the employer regarding matters of collective importance refer, *inter alia*, to:

- the requirement that work rules, that regulate, among others, rules for stay on the work establishment premises both during work and upon its completion, supplying of employees in materials and tools and well as working clothes and shoes, means of individual protection and personal hygiene should be provided for in the workplace rules, are made by the employer in agreement with the trade union (Article 104^1 LC);
- the requirement that the establishment of a company welfare fund, the level of the fund and distribution of its resources, rules for and conditions of use of the services and benefits financed from the fund should be provided for in a CLA or pay rules created in agreement between the two aforementioned parties (Articles 4 and 8 of the relevant Act and Article 27 TUA);
- the requirement that an agreement has to be reached if the development of the vacation leave schedule is to be abandoned at the workplace;
- execution of social supervision over the operations of the workers' savings and loan association and cooperative savings and credit union (Article 39 TUA);
- consultation on the intention to carry out collective redundancies and conclusion of an agreement specifying the rules for those (Articles 2 and 3 ETA);
- the obtaining of information on the contemplated transfer of the work establishment onto another employer and negotiations on the agreement related thereto (Article 26^1 TUA);
- agreement on the introduction of telework at the work establishment and terms and conditions of doing work of that type (Article 67^6 LC);
- reaching an agreement on the employment of temporary workers (Article 23 of Temporary Workers Employment Act 2003).

803. The role of trade unions in workplace management is further enhanced by the influence which the work establishment union organization has on the composition of other types of staff representation. This concerns, in particular:

- election of employee representatives for OSH-related consultations and to sit on the occupational safety and health committee;
- arranging election of social labour inspectors;

– appointment of the work establishment environmental committees and social environmental inspectors;[492]
– appointment of employee representatives in Community-scale undertakings or groups of undertakings, in the European company, European cooperative society and the company resulting from a cross-border merger.

804. The weak point of the scheme under which trade union organizations are vested in the above-discussed responsibilities regarding participation in work establishment management lies in the fact that a majority of work establishments in Poland are non-unionized ones.[493] Given the said, ever more often opinions are voiced by legal scholars that powers of the kind should be granted to some kind of a non-union body. The situation is not helped by the fact that certain union rights are conferred onto ad hoc employee representatives at non-unionized work establishment (*see* Part II, Chapter 2, §4).

III. Employee Councils

A. General Remarks

805. The employee councils have been established by the Informing and Consulting Employees Act of 2006,[494] implementing Directive 2002/14/EC on informing and consulting employees in the European Community.

806. Employee councils are established at the employers carrying out economic activity and employing at least fifty employees. The employer is obligated to advise the staff that such a level of employment has been reached. An employee council is a non-union body. The councils are established both in the undertakings in which trade unions operate and in those non-unionized. Trade unions do not exert any institutionalized influence on the election of employee councils and their composition.

B. Election and Powers of Members of the Employee Council

807. Election of members of the employee council is organized by the employer at the application, in writing, of a group of at least 10% of employees. Candidates to the council are proposed by at least 10 employees, and where the employer has more than 100 employees the proposed candidate must be backed by at least 20 employees. The number of members of the council is 3, 5 or 7 persons depending

492. Article 45 part 2 of the Act of 3 Oct. 2008 on Disclosure of Information on Natural Environment and Its Protection, Participation of the Society in Environmental Protection and Environmental Impact Assessments, *Journal of Laws* (2008) No. 199, item 1227, as amended.
493. In 2014, as little as 39% of the inquired employees declared that trade unions were operating in their work establishments; *see Związki zawodowe i prawa pracownicze* (Warsaw, Centrum Badania Opinii Społecznej, 2014), p. 4.
494. Act of 7 Apr. 2006, *Journal of Laws* (2006), No 79, item 550, as amended.

on the numbers of the staff (50, 251 and 501 respectively). The term of office of members of the employee council lasts four years.

808. Members of the council enjoy particular protection against the notice to terminate or termination of their employment relationship as well as a unilateral change of conditions and terms of work and pay to their detriment. They are also entitled to paid time off if their council-related tasks cannot be performed outside of their working hours. Costs related to the election and operation of the employee council is borne by the employer.

C. Rules of Council Operation

809. In principle, rules for the operation of the employee council should be set forth by the parties in an agreement concluded between them. Only where such an agreement has not been signed, and also in matters not covered by it, provisions of the Act are applicable.

In the agreement, the employee council and the employer should set principles of cooperation between them; in particular, the rules for and mode of disclosure of information and conducting consultations, the way of settling matters of dispute, the financing of the costs of the operations of the council and obtaining expert opinions, the number of council members, etc. The terms of informing and consulting, determined in the agreement, should be at least equal to those specified in the Act and take into account the interests of the employer and employees (Article 5 of Informing and Consulting Employees Act 2006).

Considering the inaccurate determination of the scope and matter of information and consultations in the Act it is vital that the issues should be specified in the agreement as, in principle, the Act only sets the general framework for the employer's duties related to information and consultation.

D. Powers of the Employee Council in the Field of Information and Consultation

1. Types of Power

810. Powers of the employee council concern mostly the obtaining of information from the employer about the employer's activities and the standing of the undertaking and consultations held with the employer on the latter's decisions in the fields specified in the Act. The council may also opine on certain issues and conclude agreements with the employer.

2. Information

811. The information disclosed to the employee council by the employer concerns:

(1) the employer's activity and the standing of his/her business as well as changes anticipated in that respect;
(2) the situation, structure and probable development of employment and on any anticipatory measures envisaged to maintain the level of employment;
(3) decisions likely to lead to substantial changes in work organization or in bases of employment.

812. The employer is obliged to provide the information on anticipated changes or intended actions without a request from the council. In other situations the disclosure is done at a written application by the employee council. The information should be provided within the time limit and in the format and scope enabling members of the council to get themselves acquainted with the matter and prepare for the consultation.

813. It should not be expected that the employer will inform the council about all the issues that fall within the scope of the above-mentioned fields. Generally speaking, it is reasonable to consider that the information will concern decisions and activities in the discussed areas entailing changes which require the employees to adapt to the new situation, in particular, when the changes may pose a threat to employment (recital 8 of Directive 2002/14/EC)

3. Opining

814. The council may express its opinion on any issues covered by the duty to provide information. Each member of the council may attach to the opinion his or her dissenting view.

4. Consultation

815. On matters mentioned at (2) and (3) under 'Information' above, the employer is obliged to consult with the council. The consultation should be conducted at a relevant level of management, at the time, form and scope enabling the employer to take up actions in the issues covered by the consultation and to arrive at an agreement between the employee council and management. It is, therefore, clear that, at the request of the council, the employer should enter into consultation in order to conclude an accord on the matters which the consultation concerned. The consultation should be conducted in good faith and with mutual respect for the legitimate interests of both parties.

E. Confidential Information

816. The employee council and the experts whose assistance is used by the council are obligated not to disclose the information obtained in connection with the function performed by them being a business secret or a secret qualified as such under separate pieces of legislation. In particularly justified cases the employer is allowed not to disclose to the employee council the information which, if disclosed, could seriously disturb the operation of the undertaking or establishment or cause considerable harm to it. The employee council may approach the district 'court-business' court asking for a release from the duty to keep information confidential or for an order to be given to disclose information or to conduct consultation.

F. Sanctions for Violation of Duties

817. Violation of certain provisions of law concerning, e.g., the establishment of the council and failure of the employer to meet his duties regarding providing information and consulting is considered, by law, a petty offence liable to the penalties of a fine or restriction of personal liberty. Also, the disclosure of confidential information provided by the employer, by members of the council of experts cooperating with them, is a petty offence.

IV. Employee Representatives Sitting on Company Bodies

818. Participation through employee representatives sitting on company bodies concerns, in Poland, companies formed as a result of commercialization and privatization of state-owned enterprises and commercialization of municipal undertakings.[495] The Act of 30 June 1996 on Commercialization and Privatization[496] grants to the employees the right to elect two-fifths of the composition of the supervisory board in the companies where the State Treasury remains the sole shareholder. In addition, in the companies in which the State Treasury holds not less than half of the shares and which annually employ, on average, over 500 employees, also the right to appoint one member of the management board. The rights are retained by the staff even after privatization, i.e., after the State Treasury has sold more than half of the shares of the company emerged as a result of commercialization. However, in such a situation the participation of employee representatives in the supervisory board is reduced to roughly one-third of its composition (depending on the number of members of the supervisory board).

819. Representatives of the staff sitting on the supervisory board have the same rights and duties as representatives of the shareholders do.

820. The Act does not provide for any particular mechanisms whereby the representatives are tied with the staff, save for the fact that they are elected by employees and can be removed by them. Employee representatives in supervisory and

495. For more, *see*, J. Wratny, 'Problematyka prawna i funkcje reprezentacji pracowników w radach nadzorczych spółek', in: Sobczyk (ed.), *Stosunki zatrudnienia w dwudziestoleciu społecznej gospodarki rynkowej. Księga pamiątkowa z okazji 40-lecia pracy naukowej Profesor Barbary Wagner* (Warsaw, Wolters Kluwer, 2010).

496. *Journal of Laws* (2015), item 747.

management boards are elected in a secret ballot, under a direct and common election scheme. A representative can be removed in a voting held at an application made, in writing, by at least 15% of the general number of company employees.

821. The company is not allowed to give a notice to terminate employment relationship to an employee of the company being a member of its supervisory board during his or her term of office and within a year after its completion. During the same period terms and conditions of work and pay may not be changed by the company to the detriment of the employee.

822. The law also allows the employees to elect roughly one-third of the Supervisory Board in single-shareholder companies formed under transformation of municipal enterprises. They lose the right, however, if just a single share has been disposed of by the municipality.

V. Social Labour Inspection

823. Social labour inspection is a representation of the workplace staff established to cooperate with the employer in matters of occupational safety and health, control of provisions and the actual situation in that respect and supervision over the observance of labour law. The operation of the inspection is provided for in the Act of 24 June 1983 on Social Labour Inspection.[497] The Act continues, in general, the model of the institution existing in Poland since 1950.[498]

824. The inspection is guided by trade unions and it is only a trade union member that may be, as a rule, a social labour inspector. Election of the inspectors is held by trade unions following rules adopted by themselves. The links between the social labour inspection and trade unions result in the non-existence of the inspection in non-unionized work establishments.

825. The main task of the social labour inspection is to exercise control of the condition of buildings, machinery, technical and sanitary facilities and technological processes for occupational safety and health, as well as control of the observance of labour law regarding OSH, parenthood-related rights of employees, employment of juveniles and the handicapped, vacation leaves and working time, benefits on account of accidents at work and occupational diseases. The inspection is also concerned about the observance of environmental protection provisions.

826. The inspection has considerable control and supervisory powers. The social labour inspector has the right to enter, at any time, the premises and facilities of the work establishment to meet the tasks specified in the Act. He or she may also

497. *Journal of Laws* (1983), No. 35, item 163, as amended.

498. For a broader discussion of the structure and operations of the social labour inspection *see* W. Sanetra (ed.) *Społeczna inspekcja pracy w systemie organów ochrony nad warunkami pracy* (Wrocław, 1985).

demand disclosure of information and documents on matters falling within the scope of the inspector's powers by the management of the work establishment and its staff. Where threats have been identified by the inspector he or she has the right to intervene in the appropriate manner, including the right to instruct that operation of machinery should be stopped or the conducted work interrupted.

827. Costs related to the operation of the social labour inspector are borne by the employer. The inspectors are protected against a notice to terminate and termination of the employment relationship and change of the conditions and terms of work and pay to their detriment. The activities of social labour inspectors should be carried out mostly outside of their working hours. But where their tasks should be performed during working hours or where they have to participate in meetings and training courses, their right to remuneration is retained. In the situation of a considerable number of duties, at the application by work establishment trade union organizations, the head of the work establishment may fix a lump-sum monthly fee payable to the social labour inspector.

VI. Information and Consultation on Matters of Occupational Safety and Health

A. *Concept of Protection of Employee Life and Health*

828. While it is the traditional name of 'occupational safety and health' that is used by the LC, current regulation of the issues is based on the assumption of protection of the broadly termed employee health, not just protection against dangers in the working environment. The protection is grounded on information, dialogue and cooperation between employees and employers in that respect. The assumption was put into practice by, in particular, amendments to the LC having entered in force in 2004 and 2009, which conferred on the employees broad powers as regards obtaining of information and consultation on employers' decisions in the area in question.

B. *Information on Matters of OSH*

829. The employer is obliged to provide employees with information on threats to health and life occurring at the work establishment and rules of conduct in such cases, actions taken to eliminate or reduce the threats and the employees appointed to provide first aid and to take measures concerning fire protection and evacuation of the staff (Articles 207^1, 208 and 209^2 §1 LC). According to Article 226 LC the employees should be informed about occupational hazards related to the work done by them and rules of protection against the hazards. The way in which the employees should be informed about the occupational hazards is determined by the work rules (Article 104^1 §1 item 8 LC). In principle, information in the above-mentioned scope should be provided immediately to the employees. Only in cases mentioned in law may the employer confine himself to delivering it to employees' representatives (e.g., Article 208 §1 item 4 LC).

C. Consultation on OSH Matters

830. Any employer, regardless of the number of the staff, is expected to consult all actions related to occupational safety and health with the employees or their representatives. This concern, in particular, matters directly indicated in law, such as changes in the work organization and equipment of work-stands, introduction of new technological processes, chemical substances and preparations, if they may pose a threat to the life and health of the employees. Employees or their representatives may also present to the employer proposals concerning the elimination or reduction of occupational hazards and, at their reasoned request, concerning a threat to employee life, that health inspectors of the SLI carry out checks and apply measures provided for in the legislation on the SLI.

831. In practice, the representatives are elected at major work establishments by work establishment trade union organizations or – such organizations lacking – by the employees, in the mode adopted at the work establishment. The employer provides appropriate conditions for the consultation, being, in particular, obliged to hold it during the working hours. For the time off related to participation in consultation, the employees and their representatives retain the right to remuneration. In addition, they may not bear any negative consequences of their participation in the consultation or work with the OSH committee.

D. OSH Committee

832. Any employer with more than 250 employees has the obligation to establish an OSH committee as a body operating in an advisory and opinion-giving capacity. The committee consists of equal numbers of representatives of the employer and the employees, including a social labour inspector. The OSH committee is chaired by the employer or a person authorized by the latter. Its tasks include reviews of working conditions, periodical assessments of measures adopted by the employer to prevent accidents at work and occupational diseases, making proposals concerning the improvement of working conditions and cooperation with the employer as regards the employer's meeting of his duties in the OSH field. Where a committee like the said is established, consultation may be conducted at its forum.

§4. Employee Representation in Management of Union-scale Undertakings

I. Introductory Remarks

833. The aim of the laws providing for the participation of employees in the management of Union-scale undertakings is making it possible to employees employed in various states of the EU in which a Union-scale undertaking (company, cooperative society) or a group of undertakings operates, to have access to information from the top (central) governing bodies making decisions of importance for the employees and to consult the decisions at the entity's central level.

834. The matters are provided for by the following pieces of legislation:

(1) The Act of 5 April 2002 on European Works Councils.[499]
(2) The Act of 4 March 2005 on European Economic Interest Grouping and European Company.[500]
(3) The Act of 22 July 2006 on European Cooperative Society.[501]
(4) The Act of 25 April 2008 on Employee Participation in the Company Emerged from Cross-Border Merger of Companies.[502]

835. The legislation is without prejudice to employee representations at the national level. Consequently, the systems of employee participation at the national and the Community level complement each other.

836. Of particular importance is the Act on European Works Councils. The solutions adopted in it can be applied in any type of transnational undertakings meeting the conditions set in the Act. As opposed to it, the laws on the European Company and European Cooperative Society pertain only to undertakings operating under Council regulations concerning the entities in question. As a result, the provisions on the Works Councils are, in a sense, more general than the specific Acts concerning employee representations in the European Companies and Cooperative Societies. Hence, if in the course of the procedure of establishment of an employee representation at a European Company or a Cooperative Society, the parties eventually decide not to create it, then to the undertakings and groups of undertakings having the status of such companies or cooperative societies the provisions on the European Works Councils are applicable (Article 1 paragraphs 4 and 5 of European

499. Consolidated text: *Journal of Laws* (2012), item 1146. The Act, which entered in force on 1 May 2004, transposes the European Works Councils Directive 2009/38/EC.
500. *Journal of Laws* (2005), No. 62, item. 551, as amended. The Act transposes the European Company Directive 2001/86/EC.
501. *Journal of Laws* (2006), No. 149, item 1077, as amended. The Act transposes the European Cooperative Society Directive 2003/72/EC.
502. *Journal of Laws* (2008), No. 86, item 525. The Act transposes the cross-border mergers of limited liability companies Directive 2005/56/EC.

Works Councils 2002). Meanwhile, to the company emerged as a result of cross-border merger of companies the Act on the European Works Councils is fully applicable since the Act on Employee Participation in the Company Emerged from Cross-Border Merger of Companies does not provide for the employees' rights to information and consultation; it only provides for employee participation in the company supervisory board.

II. European Works Councils

A. *Scope of Application of the Act*

837. The European Works Councils Act sets forth the rules for informing and consulting employees in Community-scale undertakings and groups of undertakings, the central management of which is located in Poland (Article 1 paragraph 2). A Community-scale undertaking or group of undertakings is one with at least 1,000 employees within the Member States and at least 150 employees in each, or at least two, Member States (Article 2 items 2 and 3). The Act concerns informing and consulting only in matters concerning the entire Community-scale undertaking or a group of undertakings or at least two undertakings or work establishments situated in two various Member States.

B. *Determining the Way of Exercising the Right to Information and Consultation*

838. The way of exercising the right to information and consultation is determined in negotiations between the central management and representatives of employees that form a so-called special negotiating body. Polish members of the body are appointed by trade union organizations representative at the work establishment level, and if no such organizations exist at the work establishment, they are elected directly by the employees (Articles 8 and 9). The special negotiating body may decide not to undertake negotiations or complete them with no agreement having been concluded, which means waiver of the rights granted by the statute. The waiver is not final, though, since the employees may file a new application for the appointment of a special negotiating body.

839. Where an agreement has been reached, the parties thereto may decide that the informing and consulting scheme will take the shape of a European works council, its composition, powers and rules of operation being determined at the same time (Article 19). The agreement should also determine the flow of information between the European works council and the employee representatives at the national level. Should the issue be not provided for by the parties, the duty to convey the essential decisions to the relevant management of undertakings and work establishments in Member states in order to pass them on to the employees rests with the central management (Article 19a).

840. In the agreement concerning the establishment of a European works council the special negotiating body and central management may not provide for the above-mentioned issues and decide that the council will operate following the standard rules set in the Act (Article 20).

841. The parties may also not to establish the council and decide that the employee rights concerning information and consultation will be exercised in a different mode and determine the mode in the agreement (Article 18).

C. Standard Rules

842. If the central management and European works council in the agreement concluded between them so decide, the council operates on the standards rules set forth in the statute. The council is established on the general rules also in the case where the central management does not take up negotiations within six months of the date of the application filed by the employees on the issue or where the agreement has not been concluded within three years of the start of the negotiations (Article 20).

843. As per the standard rules the European works council is composed of not fewer than three and not more than thirty members. Polish members of a European works council are appointed or elected in the same way as members of the special negotiating body are (Article 23).

844. The council is entitled to obtain information and conduct consultation concerning the entire Community-scale undertaking or group of undertakings or at least two work establishments or two undertakings situated in various Member States (Article 28 part 1). Covered by the information and consultation are to be, in particular, the following issues: the structure of the Community-scale undertaking or group of undertakings; its business and financial standing and prospective development of operations, including production, sales and investments; employment and possible developments in the field; introduction of essential organizational changes; introduction of new working methods or new technological processes; a change of the location of the undertaking or work establishment or an essential part of the undertaking or work establishment and shift of production to another work establishment or undertaking, merger and division of work undertakings and work establishments; limitation in size or stoppage of the operation of an undertaking or work establishment or an essential part thereof; collective redundancies (Article 29). Should there arise any extraordinary circumstances essentially affecting situation of the employees, e.g.,collective redundancies, change of location of the undertaking or plant, the central management is obliged to inform about it the presiding body of the council, and where such a body has not been appointed – the council itself (Article 30).

D. Confidential Information

845. In order to protect interests of the employer, the Act does not allow representatives of the employees to disclose the information, being a business secret. Besides that, the central management has the right not to disclose information if such a disclosure could seriously disturb the operation of the companies or expose them to a serious harm. Disputes related to the issues are resolved by business courts (Article 36).

E. Protection of and Facilitation for Employee Representatives

846. Employee representatives are protected against a notice to terminate or termination of the employment relationship as well as against change of conditions and terms of work and pay to their detriment. They also enjoy the right to time off with pay. Costs of the operation of a special negotiating body and European works council is borne by the central management, which also provides them with office space and office service. They can also make use of services of experts financed in accordance with the rules specified in the Act (Articles 15, 33 and 34).

III. Employee Participation in Management of European Company and European Cooperative Society as well as a Company Emerged as a Result of Cross-border Mergers of Companies

847. The Act on the European Economic Interest Grouping and European Company as well as the Act on the European Cooperative Society, when mentioning the employee participation in management, refer to it as the 'involvement of employees'. The said 'involvement of employees' means any mechanism, including information, consultation and participation, through which employees' representatives may exercise influence on the decisions to be taken within an undertaking. The employee participation in management should at least correspond with the level enjoyed by the employees in the entities from which the European company or cooperative society has been formed.

848. The discussed legal provisions confer on the employees not only the right to information and consultation but also to participation. The latter is understood as the influence of employees' representatives on the composition of the supervisory board or the administrative board of the company or cooperative society (e.g., through election of part of members of the bodies) and having a say in their operation. Otherwise, the regulation of employee participation in managing European companies and cooperative societies is similar to the regulations concerning European works councils. This holds true, in particular, as far as the following matters are concerned: negotiating the rules of involvement of the employees by a special negotiating team, appointment of employees' representatives and their powers, standard competences of employees' representative bodies regarding information and consultation as well as protection of employees' interests.

849. The Act on Employee Participation in the Company Emerged from Cross-Border Merger of Companies provides only for matters related to participation of employees' representatives in the company supervisory board. The rights to information and consultation of the employees of such a company are exercised under the Act on European Works Councils.[503]

IV. Employee Share Ownership

850. Employee participation in workplace management may also consist in equity participation or the employee share ownership, providing a title to participation in management which is different from that based on the fact of employment in that the employees' rights are derived from their participation in equity (through holding company shares or interests).[504] Participation of that kind was mandatorily introduced in privatized state-owned and municipal enterprises.[505] In particular, the employees are entitled to acquire, free of charge, 15% of the company shares held by the State Treasury. Thanks to such a solution they can voice their interests at the general meeting of shareholders. The Act also enables them to exercise their voting rights at the general meeting through a representative elected from among themselves. Preferential purchasing of shares by employees may be also introduced using collective accords and internal regulations of companies and holdings, including resolutions of company bodies.[506]

503. *See* recital 12 to Directive 2005/56/EC.

504. For a broader discussion of the legal regulation of the participation and its different forms, *see*, M. Leski, 'Akcjonariat pracowniczy w Polsce', *Praca i Zabezpieczenie Społeczne*, vol. 8 (2012), 7.

505. Chapters IV and V of the Act of 30 June, 1996 on Commercialization and Privatization and Art. 12 of the Act of 20 December, 1996 on Municipal Management (consolidated text: *Journal of Laws* (2011), No. 45, item 236.

506. *See*, for instance, Arts 345, 362, 448 of the Code of Commercial Companies.

Selected Bibliography

Legislation

Dziennik Ustaw Rzeczypospolitej Polskiej – Official journal of law where the universally binding law of the Republic of Poland, i.e., the Constitution, statutes, ratified international agreements, and governmental regulations are published. Used abbreviations are: Dziennik Ustaw, Dz.U.

Dziennik Urzędowy Rzeczypospolitej Polskiej 'Monitor Polski' – Official journal of law where the internally binding legal acts laid down by the Parliament, the President as well as by the Government of the Republic of Poland are published. Used abbreviations are: Monitor Polski, M. P.

Kodeks pracy – Labour Code. For English version see A. Jamroży (translation), N. Faulkner (language editor), *The Labour Code. Kodeks pracy. Bilingual edition,* 2nd edn (Warsaw, C.H. Beck, 2014).

Case law

Orzecznictwo Trybunału Konstytucyjnego. Zbiór Urzędowy - Official journal of the Constitutional Tribunal. Used abbreviation: OTK.

Orzecznictwo Sądu Najwyższego. Izba Pracy, Ubezpieczeń Społecznych i Spraw Publicznych – Official journal of the Supreme Court's Labour, Social Security and Public Affairs Chamber judgements. Used abbreviations are: OSNP, OSNPUSiSP.

Orzecznictwo Sędów Polskich – Monthly presenting chosen judgments of Polish courts with gloses (Warsaw, Wolters Kluwer). Used abbreviation: OSP.

Iwulski J., Sanetra W., *Kodeks pracy. Komentarz* (Warsaw: LexisNexis), 2014 – commentary concerned on presenting the Supreme Court judgments.

Information: The cases quoted in this monograph can be found by case reference symbols:

- for the Supreme Court at: www.sn.pl/orzecznictwo/SitePages/Baza_orzeczen.aspx;
- for administrative courts at: http://orzeczenia.nsa.gov.pl/cbo/query;
- for the Constitutional Tribunal at: http://otk.trybunal.gov.pl/orzeczenia/otk.htm.

Selected Bibliography

JOURNALS IN LABOUR LAW

Praca i Zabezpieczenie Społeczne (Warsaw, Polskie Wydawnictwo Naukowe).
Monitor Prawa Pracy (Warsaw, C.H.Beck Sp. z o.o.)
Służba Pracownicza (Warsaw, Ministerstwo Rodziny, Pracy i Polityki Społecznej).

TEXTBOOKS

Baran K.W. (ed.), *Prawo pracy i ubezpieczeń społecznych* (Warsaw, Wolters Kluwer, 2015).
Florek L., *Prawo pracy* (Warsaw, C.H. Beck, 2017).
Kubot Z., Kuczyński T., Masternak Z., Szurgacz H, *Prawo pracy. Zarys wykładu* (Warsaw, Difin, 2017).
Liszcz T., *Prawo pracy* (Warsaw, Lexis Nexis, 2016).
Stelina J. (ed.), *Prawo pracy* (Warsaw, C.H. Beck, 2016).

BOOKS FOR GENERAL INTRODUCTION TO LABOUR LAW

Baran K.W. (ed.), *Zarys systemu prawa pracy. Tom I. Część ogólna prawa pracy* (Warsaw, Wolters Kluwer Sp. z o.o., 2010).
Baran K.W. (ed.), *Zarys systemu prawa pracy. Tom V. Zbiorowe prawo pracy* (Warsaw, Wolters Kluwer, 2014).
Goździewicz G. (ed.), *Aktuelle Probleme des Kollektivarbeitsrechts in Polen und in Deutschland* (Toruń, Dom Organizatora 2012).
Goździewicz G. (ed.), *Zarys systemu prawa pracy. Tom II. Indywidualne prawo pracy* (Warsaw, Wolters Kluwer Polska S.A., 2017).
Hajn Z., *Zbiorowe prawo pracy. Zarys systemu* (Warsaw, Wolters Kluwer Polska S.A., 2013).
Mitrus L., *Wpływ regulacji wspólnotowych na polskie prawo pracy* (Kraków, Zakamycze, 2006).
Pisarczyk Ł., Stelina J. (eds.), *Collective Labour Law* (Warsaw, Wydawnictwa Uniwersytetu Warszawskiego, 2015).
Seweryński M., *Polish Labour Law from Communism to Democracy* (Warsaw, Dom Wydawniczy ABC, 1999).

WEBSITE INFORMATION

Constitutional Tribunal: http://trybunal.gov.pl/en/.
Central Statistical Office: http://stat.gov.pl/en/.
Ministry of Family, Labour and Social Policy: http://www.mpips.gov.pl/en/.
Public Opinion Research Center: http://www.cbos.pl/EN/home/home.php.
Senate: http://www.senat.gov.pl/.

Seym: http://www.sejm.gov.pl/.
State Labour Inspection: http://www.pip.gov.pl/.
Supreme Administrative Court: http://www.nsa.gov.pl/en.php.
Supreme Court: http://www.sn.pl/en/SitePages/Main.aspx.

Selected Bibliography

Index

The numbers here refer to paragraph numbers.

Ad hoc employee representatives, 117, **687–689**
Administrative law, 17, 43, 44, 474
Annual leave, 26, 27, 37, 39, 56, 176, **268–271**, 508, 511

Change of employment contract, 197, **343-350**, 443
Children, 7, 62, 103, 179, 218, 236, 249, 260, 313, 328, 335, 349, **399–414**, 425–428, 438, 511, 552
Civil law, 14, 30, 35, **45, 48**, 53, 86, 97–98, 99, 108, 122, **153**, 155, 157, 222, 228, 337, 390, 428, 454, 456, 483, 494, 506, 508, 528, 547, 551, 622, 643
CLA. *See* Collective labour agreements (CLA)
Collective accords, 77-78, 692, **719-728**
Collective bargaining, 44, 62, 117, 593, 595, 603, 605, 638, 655, 657, 685, 686, 690, **691–728**, 734, 751, 752, 790, 795
Collective disputes. *See also* Legal conflicts; Lock-out; Strike
  agreed procedures, 743, 751
  notion, 729–739
  statutory procedures, 743–750
Collective labour agreements (CLA), 15, 17, 20, 71, **73–76**, 86–88, 117, 125, 147, 157, 165, 175, 191, 240, 244, 250, 256, 284, 484, 593, 603, 605, 616, 645, 649, 653–655, 679, 685, 691–695, **696–722**, 723, 739, 740, 789, 802
Collective labour law, 44, 97, 115–119, **591–594**
Collective redundancies, 33, 71, 77, 219, **351–370**, 663, 794, 802, 844
Court of labour. *See* Settlement of labour disputes
Covenants of non-competition, 481-495
Custom, 34, **84**, 183, 272, 484, 541, 577

Disabled workers, 58, 63, 137, 240, 149, 260, **429–435**, 479, 552, 616,
Discrimination. *See* Equality of employees and prohibition of discrimination

Employee
  belongings, 233
  dignity and other personal rights of, 61, 64, **104–105**, 133, 212, 221, 222, 225, 446
  evaluation, 195, 198, 219
  good, 232
  notion, 30, 154
  Employee privilege principle, **86**, 113-114, 150, 350, 719
Employee councils, 791, 798, 799, **805–817**
Employee representatives in company bodies, 818–822
Employee share ownership, 850
Employer
  notion, 155
  representation of, 156
  risk 152
Employers' organizations
  competences, 686
  notion, 673–675
  representation of employers, 683
  representativeness, 684–685
  structures, 676–681
Employment agency, 545, 553, 556, **564–567**
Employment certificate, 371
Employment contract. *See also* Change of, termination of
  atypical, 373–398
  conclusion, 172–174
  content, 175
  for definite period, 180, **184–187**, 381, 414
  for indefinite period, 180, 183
  preliminary contract, 182
  for trial period, 188–190
  for vocational training, 181, 420–422

information related to, 176-179, 204, 208-210
Employment relationship
basis of, 14
characteristics of, 151–152
contents of, 149–150, 208, 347, 350, 719
documentation, 220
not based on contract 465–478
versus civil law contracts, 153
Equal treatment and prohibition of discrimination, 61, 106, **120–148**, 212, 376, 396, 415, 523, 575, 602, 624, 709, 787
European Union Law, 29, 36-38, 59, **93-96**, 121, 130, 374, 427, 436, 437, 442, 567, 585, 658, 790European Works Councils, 37, 71, 328, **834–846**, 848, 849

Foreigners, 44, 58, 92, 545–547-549, **570-590**
Freedom to choose occupation, 62, 101-103

General agreements, 79–80
Geography, 1
Government, 3, 4, **49–58**

Information related to employment contract, *see* Employment contract
Instructions of employer, 195–198, 213, 223, 257
International Labour Law, 38, **89-92**, 108, 116, 123, 135, 400, 565, 569, 603, 622, 671, 678, 689, 730
Inventions, 496–505
Jobseekers, 547, 549, 553, 564, 602

Labour code. *See* Sources of labour law
Labour law. *See also* Sources of labour law
history, 11–42
notion, 43-44
versus other branches of law, 45–48
principles of, 97–119
Labour market, 41, 50, 71, 122, 136, 137, 380, 429, 442, **543–590**
Leave and exemptions from work, 227, 286
Legal conflicts, 740–742
Liability of employee, 30, 31, 48, 71, 98, 209, **444-459**, 801
Liability of employer, 460-466
Limitation of claims, 506-513
Lock-out, 784–785

Mobbing, 105, 133, 212, **222–230**, 460, 523
Most favourable provision principle, 88, 705

Overtime work, 13, 16, 86, 196, 237, 239, **247–253**, 267, 377, 402, 419, 433, 438, 439, 709

Participation of employees in management. *See* also Employee councils; Employee representatives in company bodies; Employee share ownership; European Works Councils; Safety and health at work; Social labour inspection; Workplace trade union organization
legal basis, 790–795
national work establishments, 798–832
scope of, 796–797
union-scale undertakings, 833–850
Part-time work, 7, 106, 181, 210, 212, 252, 291, **376-378**, 411, 582
Political system, 2-6
Posted workers, **436-443**, 580
Protest actions other than strike, 776–783

Qualifications of employee, 124, 125, 128, 132, 142, 171, 197, 211, **215-216**, 219, 291, 293, 294, 312, 325, 348, 371, 414, 421, 422, 430, 439, 471, 552, 555, 558, 559, 564, 566, 582, 584, 585, 713

Remuneration, 9, 53, 62, 63, 76, 81, 100, 107–108, **282-298**,
Rest (right to), 109, 234
Right of association, 13, 116, **595-603**
Rules of social coexistence, 84, 85, 183, 205, 221, 323, 332, 540

Safety and health at work, 110, 201, 213, **828-832**
Settlement of individual labour disputes, 514-542
Social dialogue council, 41, 51, 53, 54, 80, 115, 288, 289, **608–615**, 654, 655, 680, 697
Social labour inspection, 328, 363, 662, 800, 803, **823–827**, 832
Social partner's dialogue, 51, 61, 115, **604–617**
Social peace clause, 739
Social security law, 45-47, 284

Sources of labour law *see also* European Union Law, International Labour Law
autonomous, 15, 34, **73–82**
character of norms, 86
constitution, 61–68, 99–100
notion, 59-60
ordinary legislation, 69–72
relationships between, 87–88
versus court decisions, 83
versus custom, 84
State Labour Inspection, 13, 16, **57-58**, 153, 440, 586, 662, 738, 800, 830
Strike, 20, 22, 24, 32, 62, 100, 118, 383, 442, 475, 595, 601, 603, 730, 737-739, 745, 746, 748, 750, 751, **752-775**, 789

Telework, 124, 181, 191, 375, 391–397, 558, 688, 726, 802
Temporary work, 39, 71, 181, 375, **379–390**, 437, 438, 663, 726, 802
Termination of employment contract, 27, **301-371**
Trade union freedoms, 595-603
Trade unions
competences, 657–672
facilities, 666–672
notion, 621–630
representation of employees, 646–652
representativeness, 653–656
structures, 631–642
Transfer of work establishment, **160–171**, 210, 316

Unemployed person, 8, 33, 58, 545, 547, 549, **550-554**, 556-562, 568-569, 581Unemployment benefit, 13, 47, 369, 543, 547, 557, **568-569**

Welfare, social and cultural needs of employees, 111, 218
Work establishment. *See also* Transfer of work establishment
interest, 202–203notion of, 157
order, 199–200
part of, 159
versus employer, 158
Working time, 13, 16, 36, 37, 39, 41, 58, 109, 142, 175, 176, 199, 210, 211, **234–281**, 389, 401, 402, 404, 389, 401, 422, 424, 426, 437, 608, 688, 694, 724, 825
Workplace trade union organization, 10, 392, 632, 635, **638–641**, 646, 655, 662, 665, 667, 668, 671, 672, 690, 694, 701, 707, 712

Young employees, 236, 410, **416-424**

Index

Made in the USA
Monee, IL
18 October 2026

66041394R10188